بسم الله الرحمن الرحيم

كِتَـٰبٌ أَنزَلۡنَـٰهُ إِلَيۡكَ مُبَـٰرَكٌ
لِّيَدَّبَّرُوٓاْ ءَايَـٰتِهِۦ
وَلِيَتَذَكَّرَ أُوْلُواْ ٱلۡأَلۡبَـٰبِ

A blessed Book which We have revealed to you [O Muḥammad]
so that people may ponder over its messages,
and so that those endowed with insight may take heed.

(Sūrah Ṣād, 38:29)

Pondering Over The Qur'ān

VOLUME TWO

Published by
Islamic Book Trust
607 Mutiara Majestic
Jalan Othman
46000 Petaling Jaya
Selangor, Malaysia
www.ibtbooks.com

Islamic Book Trust is affiliated with The Other Press.

Perpustakaan Negara Malaysia Cataloguing-in-Publication Data

Islahi, Amin Ahsan, 1904-1997
Tadabbur-e-Qur'ān : Pondering over the Qur'ān. Volume Two :
Tafsīr of Sūrah Āli 'Imrān / Amin Ahsan Islahi ; Translation
Mohammad Saleem Kayani.
Includes index
ISBN 978-967-0526-19-5
1. Qur'an--Hermeneutics. 2. Qur'an--Criticism, interpretation, etc.
I. Mohammad Saleem Kayani. II. Title.
297.1226

Printed in Malaysia

Amīn Aḥsan Iṣlāḥī

Tadabbur-e-Qur'ān

Pondering Over The Qur'ān

VOLUME TWO

Tafsīr of Sūrah Āli 'Imrān

Translation

Mohammad Saleem Kayani

IBT

Islamic Book Trust

Kuala Lumpur

Transliteration Table

Hamzah	ء	’
bā’	ب	b
tā’	ت	t
thā’	ث	th
jīm	ج	j
ḥā’	ح	ḥ
khā’	خ	kh
dāl	د	d
dhāl	ذ	dh
rā’	ر	r
zāy	ز	z
sīn	س	s
shīn	ش	sh
ṣād	ص	ṣ
ḍad	ض	ḍ
ṭā’	ط	ṭ
ẓā’	ظ	ẓ
‘ayn	ع	‘
ghayn	غ	gh
fā’	ف	f
qāf	ق	q
kāf	ك	k
lām	ل	l
mīm	م	m
nūn	ن	n
hā’	هـ	h
wāw	و	w
yā’	ي	y

Vowels

Short:	a; u; i
Long:	ā; ū; ī; iy
Diphthongs:	aw; ay

Contents

بِسْمِ ٱللَّهِ ٱلرَّحْمَٰنِ ٱلرَّحِيمِ

TAFSĪR OF SŪRAH ĀLI 'IMRĀN

1. The sūrah's theme in relation to the previous sūrah

This sūrah is closely related to the previous sūrah, al-Baqarah in several ways:

i. They both have a common theme, affirming and attesting to the truth of the Prophet of Islam to all humankind in general and to the People of the Book in particular.

ii. Both elucidate the basic principles of the *dīn* (true religion) in detail.

iii. The name of both the sūrahs is the same: they are both named as Alif Lām Mīm.

iv. In form, the two sūrahs appear to be like two large branches stemming from a common root. The Prophet, peace be upon him, likened them to the sun and the moon and said that on the Day of Judgement the two will appear as two clouds. Such similarity in description and their proximity point to a deeper affinity between the two sūrahs.

v. The two are like a pair. What is said briefly in one is discussed in detail in the other. The one fills any gap left in the other. Thus the two sūrahs together fully and most beautifully encapsulate and portray a most noble ideal.

2. Distinguishing features of Sūrah al-Baqarah and Sūrah Āli 'Imrān

Notwithstanding their similarity, the two sūrahs have distinct characteristics that set them apart.

Reflect on Sūrah al-Baqarah and you realise that it must have been revealed at a time when the People of the Book had clearly realised that the new dispensation, Islam, as it steadily grew from strength to strength, was indeed the true religion. However, because of jealousy and stubbornness, they refused to accept it. This placed them in a difficult predicament. Driven by emotion they were determined to fight the new religion but were yet not clear how precisely they should confront it. Consequently, they hurled at Islam whatever objections they could think of and which they found convenient. Some among them maintained that no prophets or messengers from Allah could arise from any people outside the descendants of Israel, as they alone were the people specially chosen for this purpose. Others said that the Torah was more than enough for guidance and in its presence no new Divine guidance was needed. In their frenzy, they even cast aspersions against the angel Gabriel saying that he had always been their enemy. Some others tried to form a united Jewish-Christian front against Islam. They said that Judaism and Christianity were the only two legitimate sources of guidance and so whoever wanted guidance should turn to one of these religions. There was no other – third – way to guidance. Yet another group resorted to duplicity and deception. They tried to convince the Muslims that they too were believers and that faith was not the monopoly of Muslims only. Like the Muslims, they too, they said, believed in God, the life hereafter and in their own prophets; so what difference did it make if they did not believe in Muḥammad, peace be upon him, who claims that he is also a prophet from God.

These were the prevalent conditions when this sūrah was revealed. The sūrah addresses all the objections and questions raised by the People of the Book. At the same time, it draws their attention to their scriptures that contained strong evidence validating the position of Prophet Muḥammad, peace be upon him, as the final messenger of God. Thirdly, it also explains how, with the advent of the unlettered Prophet, the true religion was revived and perfected. Thus this sūrah is an invitation to embrace belief, an affirmation of the position of the Prophet, and also a call for jihad to liberate the *qiblah.* The ensuing battle of Badr is thus closely associated with it.

As against this, when we look at Sūrah Āli 'Imrān we realise it must have been revealed at a time when the signs of truth and the dominance of Islam over the horizon were increasingly obvious and it was no longer possible for the People of the Book to oppose it openly. This situation divided them into two groups. One group accepted Islam but only formally; their hearts remained untouched by their verbal professions. The second group did not accept Islam, but they tried to reach an understanding and a compromise with the Muslims. For this compromise, they asserted that every religion is true for its own followers. Let the Muslims follow their religion and leave them to follow their own Jewish or Christian dispensations. Thus they all could follow their respective religions and still co-exist peacefully.[1]

Thus, though the attitude of these two groups towards Islam changed, it was not the result of any change of heart, but of considerations of expediency.

1. In the beginning of Sūrah al-Baqarah, there is a reference to this group, which had not yet fully come into the open (see Sūrah al-Baqarah, verses 8-16). This group stood for a view similar to that propagated under the name of the unity of all religions.

The first group aligned itself with the Muslims and Islam in the hope of sharing in the future successes of the Muslims, while the other sought peace with them in order to protect themselves against possible harm.

In the meanwhile, when the battle of Uḥud took place, the Muslims suffered a temporary setback due to the imprudence of a group among them. One effect of this on the above-mentioned two groups of the People of the Book was that they changed their policy toward Islam once again. Those who had joined the Muslims in the hope of material gains, finding that in this path they could also suffer loss, reverted to their former state of *kufr* and refused to be part of what they now regarded as a losing deal. The second group, on seeing that the rising tide of Islam could be checked and defeated, concluded that perhaps their policy of peaceful co-existence was a mistake. Why not, instead, join forces with others and jointly get rid of the Islamic threat once and for all. So they too openly declared their opposition to Islam.

These two groups were now openly hostile to Islam and Muslims. They tried hard to implant various doubts and suspicions in the minds and hearts of the Muslims in order to cause dissension among them, destroy their unity such as they themselves were afflicted with, and thus effectively neutralise their power. Under these circumstances, it was therefore necessary to explain clearly the basic truth that Allah did not send down many religions for humans to follow but had revealed only one true religion – Islam – for their guidance. There is no room in this religion for any division or option to accept a part and reject the rest. Rather, it must be accepted or rejected as a whole. This religion invites human beings to obey Allah and abide by His commandments under all circumstances and conditions, favourable or unfavourable, harsh and difficult, or easy and smooth. Whether one is threatened with persecution, trials and tribulations at every step of the way, one must stand firm and follow the true path. For, truth is unique in that sometimes it is hidden just as a kernel is within a pod, but it never vanishes. Under such conditions, only those can remain steadfast whose knowledge and faith are strong and firm, while those who are ignorant of truth flounder and fall by the wayside.

The battle of Uḥud was just another test for these groups. Whereas the battle of Badr was a criterion that clearly distinguished the truth from falsehood, the battle of Uḥud was, in a way, an allegorical sign containing a profound wisdom within, but whose exterior proved a trial for the weaker people. It clearly sorted out the sincere and true believers from the seditious who still sought trouble.

It was under these conditions that this sūrah was revealed. As such, we find in it a commentary on all weaknesses and errors that came to the surface during this period, on the part of both the Muslims and the People of the Book. It explains the error of scepticism and vacillation on the part of the People of the Book, and also describes the dire consequences of disagreement and disobedience on the part of the hypocrites and weak Muslims. Alerting the Muslims to the conspiracies against them by their enemies, it effectively removes the frustration and dismay felt by the Muslims after the defeat in the battle of Uḥud. Considered from this aspect, we find that if Sūrah al-Baqarah is the sūrah of the battle of Badr, this – Sūrah Āli 'Imrān – is the sūrah of the battle of Uḥud. Furthermore, you will also realise that whereas in Sūrah al-Baqarah *īmān* or faith is explained, in this sūrah the true significance of Islam is explained. In other words, Sūrah al-Baqarah is an invitation to believe in Allah and His messenger, while this sūrah is a call to enter the fold of Islam and submit to Allah.

In brief, in Sūrah al-Baqarah the aspect of faith is pre-eminent while in this sūrah the focus is on the aspect of Islam or submission. The practice of the Prophet, peace be upon him, also supports this conclusion. Thus the traditions say that he would sometimes recite a verse dealing with *īmān* in one *rak'ah* from Sūrah al-Baqarah and a verse of Islam from Sūrah Āli 'Imrān in the second *rak'ah* of prayer. This was, we may say, a subtle hint to the respective themes and subjects of the two sūrahs. Sūrah al-Baqarah concludes with a verse that is the most comprehensive verse of *īmān*: "The Messenger has believed in what has been revealed to him from his Sovereign Sustainer, and the believers (also) have believed. All of them believe in Allah, His angels, His books, and His messengers." The verse ends with an emphasis on total submission and obedience to Allah, in order to show that Islam is the essential consequence of *īmān*. The presence of sound belief or *īmān* must always lead to Islam or obedience to Allah in practice. The concluding verse of Sūrah al-Baqarah amply illustrates its coherence and relationship with Sūrah Āli 'Imrān.

The second distinguishing feature of the two is that Sūrah al-Baqarah is mostly addressed to the Jews as they occupied the position of the real People of the Book, with the Christians being no more than a sub-sect of theirs. That is why, in Sūrah al-Baqarah when the Qur'ān addresses the Christians it is only in a cursory manner. In Sūrah Āli 'Imrān, however, the Qur'ān addresses the Christians directly and for the most part the focus is on them. The introduction to the sūrah is of a comprehensive nature and appropriate for both the Jews and the Christians, and as it progresses it steadily moves toward open repudiation of the Christian position.

The third distinguishing aspect is that whereas in Sūrah al-Baqarah the argument is mostly based on natural phenomena that is equally relevant to the disbelievers as well as to the People of the Book, in Sūrah Āli 'Imrān the argument is for the most part built around Divine attributes and the specific beliefs and principles accepted by the People of the Book.

The fourth distinguishing feature is that although both these sūrahs contain a strong reprimand for the People of the Book, the style and nature of the reprimand varies in the two. In Sūrah al-Baqarah, there is a direct reprimand while in Sūrah Āli 'Imrān it is indirect. In the first place, the message is addressed to the Prophet to warn the People of the Book. This in a way suggests that after their failure in discharging their trust faithfully, they no longer deserved to be directly addressed by Allah. From now onwards, only the Prophet and his companions deserve this honour.

3. The Sequence of the two sūrahs

Considering the respective themes, the historical background and distinguishing features of the two surāhs as outlined above, it is quite obvious that notwithstanding their similarity in subject matter, their mutual relationship is such that their received sequential arrangement is the most appropriate. The reasons for placing Sūrah al-Baqarah before Sūrah Āli 'Imrān are amply clear in that:

Īmān (the main theme of Sūrah al-Baqarah) is the basis of Islam, as is knowledge of action.

Chronologically, the Jews precede the Christians, and it was necessary therefore that the argument against them should first be fully established.

Compared to the argument based on Divine attributes, the arguments from nature are clearer, historically older and far more comprehensive. That is why in the Qur'ān the argument based on nature precedes other arguments.

Similarly, Prophets Adam and Ibrāhīm, peace be on them both, are two of the earliest prophets and as such it was quite natural that a covenant with them is cited as a basic argument. Thus in Sūrah al-Baqarah there is a reference to a covenant with them followed by covenants with other prophets mentioned in later sūrahs.

Viewed from this angle, it is clear that the idea that the sūrahs of the Qur'ān are arranged according to their length is not correct. In our view, they are arranged in accordance with their subject matter, message, and theme. When there are two sūrahs with a similar message and significance, it is quite possible that the longer of the two is placed before the shorter one. This is, however, no more than a mere supposition, because even in such cases one feels that there must have been some subtle wisdom behind their arrangement, placing one before the other, even though we are not able to fully grasp that wisdom.

4. INTER-RELATIONSHIP OF THE TWO SŪRAHS – IN SUBJECT MATTER

What has been said above relates to the theme of the sūrah, its external structure and its relationship with the previous sūrah. Now we would like to say a few words about its internal structure and the mutual relationship between its various parts.

Looking closely, we find that this sūrah is divided into two major sections. In the first, it affirms obedience to Allah and points out the errors of the People of the Book. In its second half it warns the Muslims of the nefarious designs and conspiracies against them from the People of the Book that they are engaged in or will resort to in the days ahead in order to deflect them off the right course. At the same time, the Muslims are admonished to hold fast to the rope of Allah and to abide by His guidance, to strive hard in His cause, to be steadfast in the path of truth and to avoid dissension and disagreement in their ranks. Only in this way can they truly follow the path of Islam. If they disobey and violate these commandments, they will face dire consequences similar to those suffered by the followers of Prophet Moses, peace be upon him, who were punished for their disobedience to their prophet and who were condemned to wander for forty years in the wilderness.

In other words, the first section is a preamble, and the second contains its real message. Studied in the light of these remarks, it should not be difficult to understand the internal coherence and mutual relationship among the verses of the sūrah and grasp the real purpose of the preamble. Regarding the coherence of various verses with one another and their meaning and message, we will discuss these when we study the various parts and sections, as we have done in Sūrah al-Baqarah. With these brief words, in the name of Allah and seeking His guidance, let us begin the tafsīr of Sūrah Āli 'Imrān. And indeed there is no power or strength except with the help of Allah.[2]

2. This introductory discussion is mostly based on the writings of Imām Fārahī, may Allah bless his soul.

Tafsīr of

Sūrah Āli ʻImrān

Sūrah 3

Āli ‘Imrān (The Family of ‘Imrān)

Revealed at Madīnah, 200 verses.

Verses 1-6: thematic continuity

بِسۡمِ ٱللَّهِ ٱلرَّحۡمَٰنِ ٱلرَّحِيمِ

In the name of Allah, the most Gracious, the ever Merciful.

الٓمٓ ١

This is Alif Lām Mīm.(1)

ٱللَّهُ لَآ إِلَٰهَ إِلَّا هُوَ ٱلۡحَيُّ ٱلۡقَيُّومُ ٢

Allah is the only God! There is no god but He, the Living, the Self-Subsisting and All-Sustaining.(2)

نَزَّلَ عَلَيۡكَ ٱلۡكِتَٰبَ بِٱلۡحَقِّ مُصَدِّقٗا لِّمَا
بَيۡنَ يَدَيۡهِ وَأَنزَلَ ٱلتَّوۡرَىٰةَ وَٱلۡإِنجِيلَ ٣

It is He Who has sent down to you in truth, the Scripture, confirming what went before it; and He sent down the Torah (the Law) and the Injīl (Gospel). (3)

مِن قَبۡلُ هُدٗى لِّلنَّاسِ وَأَنزَلَ ٱلۡفُرۡقَانَۗ إِنَّ
ٱلَّذِينَ كَفَرُواْ بِـَٔايَٰتِ ٱللَّهِ لَهُمۡ عَذَابٞ
شَدِيدٞۗ وَٱللَّهُ عَزِيزٞ ذُو ٱنتِقَامٍ ٤

Before this, as a guide to humankind, and then He sent down the Criterion (of judgment between right and wrong). Then those who reject faith in the signs of Allah will suffer the severest penalty, and Allah is Exalted in Might, Possessor of the means of retribution. (4)

إِنَّ ٱللَّهَ لَا يَخۡفَىٰ عَلَيۡهِ شَيۡءٞ فِي ٱلۡأَرۡضِ وَلَا
فِي ٱلسَّمَآءِ ٥

Verily, from Allah nothing is hidden on earth or in the heavens. (5)

هُوَ ٱلَّذِى يُصَوِّرُكُمْ فِى ٱلْأَرْحَامِ كَيْفَ يَشَآءُ ۚ لَآ إِلَٰهَ إِلَّا هُوَ ٱلْعَزِيزُ ٱلْحَكِيمُ ﴿٦﴾

He it is Who shapes you in the wombs as He pleases. There is no god but He, the Exalted in Might, the most Wise. (6)

Word study and explanation

الٓمٓ ﴿١﴾

Alif Lām Mīm. (1)

For an explanation of these *ḥurūf muqaṭṭaʿāt* (disjointed letters), please refer to Sūrah al-Baqarah where we have discussed these letters and have also given the viewpoint of Imām Farāhī concerning them.

ٱللَّهُ لَآ إِلَٰهَ إِلَّا هُوَ ٱلْحَىُّ ٱلْقَيُّومُ ﴿٢﴾

Allah is the only God! There is no god but He, the Living, the Self-Subsisting and All-Sustaining. (2)

All the beautiful names of Allah used in this verse have been explained before in the tafsīr of sūrahs al-Fātiḥah and al-Baqarah. Please refer to these sūrahs for detail.

Al-Ḥayy and *al-Qayyūm*

As mentioned above, most of the argument in this sūrah is based on the Divine attributes of Allah. Of all the Divine attributes, only two – *Al-Ḥayy* and *al-Qayyūm* – are mentioned here. *Al-Ḥayy* means that Allah is eternal, living, while *Al-Qayyūm* means He is self-subsistent and all-sustaining. Both of these attributes we have discussed in our comments on verse 255 – *āyatu-l kursī* – of Sūrah al-Baqarah.

The reference to these two attributes in the present context, as shown by the later verses, is meant to affirm and stress the need for Divine scripture. In other words, since there is no god except Allah and He is the living God, this inevitably means that He sees all that we do or say; that He responds to our supplications to Him as and when He in His wisdom deems appropriate, and that He shall reward or punish us depending on how good or bad is our performance in earthly life. Furthermore, by implication, this also means that human beings must conform in life to the way He, their Creator and Sovereign

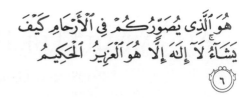

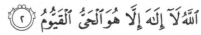

Sustainer, has chosen and prescribed for them. His faithful servants should thus be eager to find out more about what He likes for them and what He does not, and then to abide by His will and guidance, and surrender to and obey Him so as to achieve success and the good eternal life that He has promised them.

The People of the Book were well aware of phrases such as "God, your Sustainer" and "the Living God." These phrases are frequently used in their scriptures. Whenever Allah's might, knowledge and His glory and majesty are mentioned, the words "the living God" are used. Even the Christians, who according to their belief worship a crucified deity, were well aware of the phrase "the Living God". This is a clear contradiction in their stance: the concept of a living God was well known among them, yet they believe that He was crucified.

Likewise, the Divine attribute of *Qayyūm* is frequently used in the earlier scriptures. Allah is *Qayyūm* means that whatever exists in the heavens and on earth and in between them is sustained and maintained only by Him. This is one of those basic attributes of Allah, which, both in the light of reason and the teachings of the Prophets, is an integral part of belief. Christians also claim to believe in all these ancient scriptures and yet they also believe in the Divinity of Jesus. They admit that Jesus felt hunger and thirst and needed food and water like the rest of us. Without these things he could not even maintain his own existence. But when asked how could he then be God, who according to their own scriptures must possess the attribute of being *Qayyūm*, (self-subsistent and all-sustaining) they can offer no satisfactory answer. Also, if their attention is drawn to the statements found in their gospels that say Jesus wept when faced with hardships and difficulties, that he was distressed and that he cried for help on the cross, then how could he be considered as the one who maintains and sustains the heavens and earth? Their only response to questions such as these is sheer bigotry and intransigence or evasion.

The reference here to the Divine attribute of Allah being *Qayyūm* clearly implies that being a self-subsistent and all-sustaining God, He has to provide guidance for us. In other words, Allah alone is our Creator and the Giver of life. As mentioned in the verse of the throne, He is also the only Sustainer, Nurturer and Caretaker of His creatures. Accordingly, He has provided us with all kinds of resources and means in this life. So how could it be possible that Allah, Who provided us with material means and resources for our physical life, would fail to provide us with guidance for our collective life to ensure its continued stable existence, and the fulfilment of the real purpose of our creation? This is the real basis of justice or *qisṭ* and the reason for the revelation of the Divine law and commandments. In the absence of this Divine law and guidance, human nature could hardly realise its true potential that is latent within it.

Verses 1-6

Allah is *Qayyūm* – that is, He is self-subsisting and all-sustaining. This implies that He watches over His servants and whenever they misuse their freedom and try to subvert His just order, He would raise others of His servants who would strive to the best of their abilities to protect it and re-establish it. The history of the world bears witness that before the advent of Prophet Muḥammad, the final Prophet, peace be upon him, Allah raised numerous prophets and messengers to establish humankind on truth and justice and guide them to His straight path. After the perfection of religion through the final Prophet and securing the Divine scripture against all kinds of interference, He ensured that in every age and period there would be a group, however small, in the Muslim community, to uphold truth and justice and invite others to establish them. The Prophet, peace be upon him, has also referred to this in various aḥādīth. In this sūrah also there are some very subtle references to it, which will be discussed at their appropriate places.

نَزَّلَ عَلَيْكَ ٱلْكِتَٰبَ بِٱلْحَقِّ مُصَدِّقًا لِّمَا بَيْنَ يَدَيْهِ وَأَنزَلَ ٱلتَّوْرَىٰةَ وَٱلْإِنجِيلَ ﴿٣﴾

It is He Who has sent down to you in truth, the Scripture, confirming what went before it; and He sent down the Torah (the Law) and the Injīl (Gospel). (3)

مِن قَبْلُ هُدًى لِّلنَّاسِ وَأَنزَلَ ٱلْفُرْقَانَ ۗ إِنَّ ٱلَّذِينَ كَفَرُوا۟ بِـَٔايَٰتِ ٱللَّهِ لَهُمْ عَذَابٌ شَدِيدٌ ۗ وَٱللَّهُ
عَزِيزٌ ذُو ٱنتِقَامٍ ﴿٤﴾

Before this, as a guide to humankind, and then He sent down the Criterion (of judgment between right and wrong). Then those who reject faith in the signs of Allah will suffer the severest penalty, and Allah is Exalted in Might, Possessor of the means of retribution. (4)

For a detailed explanation of the word *ḥaqq*, please refer to our comments in the beginning of the tafsīr of Sūrah al-Baqarah.[1] Here, *ḥaqq* means a conclusive word or decision concerning an issue or a difference of opinion. At various places, the Qur'ān mentions that the Jews and the Christians caused differences concerning the scripture that was given to them and as a result they lost the truth. It is to explain and elucidate this message that Allah revealed the Qur'ān so as to guide human beings to truth, to settle their differences and controversies and to help them follow the true religion.

---

1. See also comments on verses 71, 147, 176, 180 and 188 of Sūrah al-Baqarah – *Pondering over the Qur'ān*, volume I. (Translator)

Confirming what went before it

This phrase has also been fully discussed in the previous sūrah.[2] One famous interpretation of this phrase is that the Qur'ān basically affirms all the sound teachings of the earlier scriptures; it rejects only what was interpolated by others into them. This similarity and uniformity of its teachings with those of the previous scriptures is a clear proof that they are all from the same Divine source and have come from one and the same origin of light and guidance. Another meaning of it is that the Qur'ān and its bearer are both mentioned in the prophecies found about them in the earlier scriptures. These prophecies were finally fulfilled with the advent of Prophet Muḥammad, peace be upon him, and the revelation of the Qur'ān. This is a most important proof of the truth of the Qur'ān while at the same time it also confirms the veracity of the prophecies of the earlier scriptures about it and its bearer, Prophet Muḥammad, peace be upon him. With his advent, these prophecies finally found their fulfilment. As such, those claiming to believe in the earlier scriptures should have been the first to welcome the revelation of the Qur'ān as it clearly attests the Divine origin of their scriptures. Instead, out of sheer intransigence, they rejected it and failed to respond to its message.

And He sent down the Torah (the Law) and the Injīl (Gospel) before this, as a guide to humankind, and then He sent down the Criterion (of judgment between right and wrong).

This is further elaboration of the above piece and explains the need for the revelation of the Qur'ān. In other words, as the Living, Self-subsisting and all Sustaining God, Allah has sent down this scripture to us as a criterion between truth and falsehood, and to guide and help us follow the path of justice and truth. Before this, He revealed the Torah and the Injīl for the guidance of people, but their followers distorted their teachings by perverting and changing their texts. This led to differences and controversies that made it almost impossible to sort out truth from falsehood. This situation required that Allah should send down the Qur'ān as a criterion to distinguish between right and wrong, and truth and falsehood. The Qur'ān was revealed to settle the conflicts and controversies created by the followers of earlier scriptures around truth and the true message of Allah. This is a Divine criterion for determining truth and falsehood and therefore anyone who rejects it will suffer a most grievous punishment for obstructing the just order of life that Allah wants to be established by the revelation of the Qur'ān. Justice and a just order are

2. Please refer to the tafsīr of Sūrah al-Baqarah, (*Pondering over the Qur'ān,* volume I) comments on verses 41, 62, 89, 91 and 101 (Translator).

necessary for the well-being and welfare of God's creatures and servants – in this life as well as in the hereafter. If the enemies of justice go unpunished, it would mean that Allah is no longer interested in the continued existence of this world and that He has given it over to the forces of destruction. But as we read in verse 18 of this sūrah, He is the One Who "stands firm on justice – *qā'iman bi-l qisṭ.*" This means that as the Maintainer of equity and justice Allah must take the enemies of justice to task and punish them appropriately. He is Mighty and All-Powerful, not helpless or weak, and cannot be overcome by anyone. He is also the Lord of Retribution, which means with respect to justice, that He is extremely sensitive and concerned; in this matter He is not neutral, or merely a spectator silently observing the subversion of His system of justice and equity. It is the manifestation of these attributes of Allah in history that first gave respite to the nations who proved unjust, but then they were all destroyed for their transgression and violation of the laws of justice and equity. And whenever there was any attempt to remove or distort His revealed laws and commandments, He refreshed and refurbished them. The words "Allah is Lord of Retribution" refer to the Divine law prescribed by Him to protect and maintain justice and equity in the life of this world and the universe.

Establishment of justice is a necessary corollary of the Divine attributes.

إِنَّ ٱللَّهَ لَا يَخۡفَىٰ عَلَيۡهِ شَيۡءٞ فِي ٱلۡأَرۡضِ وَلَا فِي ٱلسَّمَآءِ ﴿٥﴾

Verily, from Allah nothing is hidden on earth or in the heavens. (5)

هُوَ ٱلَّذِي يُصَوِّرُكُمۡ فِي ٱلۡأَرۡحَامِ كَيۡفَ يَشَآءُۚ لَآ إِلَٰهَ إِلَّا هُوَ ٱلۡعَزِيزُ ٱلۡحَكِيمُ ﴿٦﴾

He it is Who shapes you in the wombs as He pleases. There is no god but He, the Exalted in Might, the Wise. (6)

The punishment mentioned above for the enemies of the Divine scripture – in fact, the enemies of justice – is reinforced in these two verses by taking the argument a step further. Allah is well aware of whatever happens in the world. Nothing small or great, in the heavens or on earth, is hidden from Him, for His knowledge is all-comprehensive. No one should therefore be under any delusion that they can escape His justice or evade it. He is the creator of all, He fashions them in their mothers' wombs as He wills, and He knows all His creation in a manner that none else can: "Should He not know – He Who created?" (The Qur'ān, 67:14).

He is the one and the only God; He is Mighty (*ʿAzīz*) and Wise (*Ḥakīm*). In other words, He has created this world and placed the human being on earth for a higher purpose, for a higher wisdom. The notion that He is neutral in matters of good and evil, justice and injustice, is false. Such a notion robs life and existence of any real significance, meaning and higher goal. It reduces it to a meaningless play and a cruel joke on the part of its Creator Who would then have created it merely to entertain and amuse Himself. Good and evil, obedience and disobedience, fidelity and treachery would then be all the same to Him. The verse, however, emphasises that the Creator of this life and universe is All-Wise and Mighty and to say that He will not discriminate between good and evil is a slander against Him. He has created this world for a higher wisdom and a nobler purpose and He is pleased with those who mould their lives in conformity with this higher goal and displeased with those who deviate from this sublime path. He is mighty: He will take account of the performance of all human beings in their worldly life. He will reward the good and punish the evil and the disobedient – those who deny the truth and the guidance that He has revealed to proclaim the truth and restore justice with all its manifestations and implications in this world.

Verses 7-17: thematic continuity

After explaining the need for the revelation of the Qur'ān, the following verses deal with its rejecters and their own ostensible reasons for this rejection. The real reason for their refusal to believe, however, lies in their perversity and their seditious disposition. That is why instead of focussing on the core teachings of the Qur'ān, they only search for what they could exploit and use in planting doubts and suspicions in people's minds about the Qur'ān and its teachings. In the process, they devise various excuses for their own deviance and try as far as possible to mislead others. They leave aside the clear, basic teachings – *muḥkamāt* – and focus only on the *mutashābihāt* or the allegorical verses in the Qur'ān. These latter verses contain parables and allegories that deal with the life hereafter and could be relatively easily manipulated and misinterpreted by sophistry to justify their own negative stance and the seduction of others.

As against these, the people who are mature in thought and well grounded in knowledge are then mentioned. They are the ones who appreciate the Qur'ānic message and abide by and benefit from it. They appreciate and believe in what is allegorical in the Qur'ān just as they follow and abide by its unambiguous and clear commandments. Instead of using the allegorical parts of it to find fault and cast aspersions, they believe in them all, turn them into a means of enhancing their knowledge, and benefit from them. If they fail to understand or comprehend a certain part, they do not insist on knowing the unknowable and unravelling its mysteries or use it as a means of causing dissension. Rather, they refer such matters to Allah and focus their attention on the core and clear teachings of Allah's Book. This attitude of theirs is a logical consequence of their sincerity of belief and maturity of understanding. Moreover, they firmly believe in the life hereafter and constantly pray to Allah for protection and security against the whisperings of devilish elements, to keep them firm on the straight path and protect them from straying off it.

After referring to the causes of error that destroyed earlier peoples and to some of their recent successes, the Muslims are categorically warned that if they should fail to learn the appropriate lesson from all these events they would also face a gruesome end like others before them.

Some of the psychological barriers – such as their preoccupation with worldly pleasures – that prevented them from responding to the Qur'ānic message are highlighted. The transitory nature of worldly life and its pleasures, because of which they turn their backs to the Qur'ān, are explained. This world and its pleasures are no more than a mirage and an illusion. Instead of chasing these fleeting delights and fantasies, they are invited to strive for enduring blessings and to win the pleasure of Allah by following the path of patience, truth and obedience, by spending in His cause and seeking His forgiveness. In the light of these preliminary remarks, let us now study the following verses:

He it is Who has sent down to you the Book: in it are substantive verses (clear and lucid): they are the core of the Book. Others are allegorical. Those in whose hearts is perversity go after the allegorical verses, seeking discord and searching for their hidden meanings, but no one except Allah knows their real meanings. And those who are firmly grounded in knowledge say: "We believe in it; all this is from our Sustainer." But only the people of understanding take heed. (7)

هُوَ ٱلَّذِىٓ أَنزَلَ عَلَيْكَ ٱلْكِتَٰبَ مِنْهُ
ءَايَٰتٌ مُّحْكَمَٰتٌ هُنَّ أُمُّ ٱلْكِتَٰبِ وَأُخَرُ
مُتَشَٰبِهَٰتٌ فَأَمَّا ٱلَّذِينَ فِى قُلُوبِهِمْ زَيْغٌ
فَيَتَّبِعُونَ مَا تَشَٰبَهَ مِنْهُ ٱبْتِغَآءَ ٱلْفِتْنَةِ
وَٱبْتِغَآءَ تَأْوِيلِهِۦ وَمَا يَعْلَمُ تَأْوِيلَهُۥٓ إِلَّا
ٱللَّهُ وَٱلرَّٰسِخُونَ فِى ٱلْعِلْمِ يَقُولُونَ ءَامَنَّا
بِهِۦ كُلٌّ مِّنْ عِندِ رَبِّنَا وَمَا يَذَّكَّرُ إِلَّآ أُو۟لُوا۟
ٱلْأَلْبَٰبِ ﴿٧﴾

"Our Sustainer! Let not our hearts deviate now after You have guided us and bestow upon us mercy from Your presence. Indeed, You are the true Giver of bounties without measure. (8)

رَبَّنَا لَا تُزِغْ قُلُوبَنَا بَعْدَ إِذْ هَدَيْتَنَا وَهَبْ لَنَا
مِن لَّدُنكَ رَحْمَةً ۚ إِنَّكَ أَنتَ ٱلْوَهَّابُ ﴿٨﴾

"Our Sustainer! You will indeed gather humankind together for a day about which there is no doubt. Indeed, Allah does not fail to fulfil His promise." (9)

رَبَّنَآ إِنَّكَ جَامِعُ ٱلنَّاسِ لِيَوْمٍ لَّا رَيْبَ
فِيهِ ۚ إِنَّ ٱللَّهَ لَا يُخْلِفُ ٱلْمِيعَادَ ﴿٩﴾

Those who reject faith, neither their possessions nor their children will in the least avail them against Allah; and it is they who shall be the fuel of the fire. (10)

إِنَّ ٱلَّذِينَ كَفَرُوا۟ لَن تُغْنِىَ عَنْهُمْ
أَمْوَٰلُهُمْ وَلَآ أَوْلَٰدُهُم مِّنَ ٱللَّهِ شَيْـًٔا ۖ
وَأُو۟لَٰٓئِكَ هُمْ وَقُودُ ٱلنَّارِ ﴿١٠﴾

As was the case with the people of Pharaoh, and those before them: they denied Our signs, and so Allah called them to account for their sins. For Allah is severe in punishment. (11)

كَدَأْبِ ءَالِ فِرْعَوْنَ وَٱلَّذِينَ مِن قَبْلِهِمْ ۚ
كَذَّبُوا۟ بِـَٔايَٰتِنَا فَأَخَذَهُمُ ٱللَّهُ بِذُنُوبِهِمْ ۗ وَٱللَّهُ
شَدِيدُ ٱلْعِقَابِ ﴿١١﴾

Say to those who reject faith: "You shall be overcome and gathered together to hell. What an evil resting place!" (12)

قُل لِّلَّذِينَ كَفَرُوا۟ سَتُغْلَبُونَ
وَتُحْشَرُونَ إِلَىٰ جَهَنَّمَ ۚ وَبِئْسَ
ٱلْمِهَادُ ﴿١٢﴾

There has already been for you a sign in the two hosts that met in battle: one was fighting in Allah's cause and the other denying Him. With their own eyes, they saw the others as twice their own number. And Allah strengthens with His aid whom He pleases. In this, there is indeed a lesson for all who have eyes to see. (13)

قَدْ كَانَ لَكُمْ ءَايَةٌ فِى فِئَتَيْنِ ٱلْتَقَتَا ۖ
فِئَةٌ تُقَٰتِلُ فِى سَبِيلِ ٱللَّهِ وَأُخْرَىٰ
كَافِرَةٌ يَرَوْنَهُم مِّثْلَيْهِمْ رَأْىَ
ٱلْعَيْنِ ۚ وَٱللَّهُ يُؤَيِّدُ بِنَصْرِهِۦ مَن يَشَآءُ ۗ
إِنَّ فِى ذَٰلِكَ لَعِبْرَةً لِّأُو۟لِى
ٱلْأَبْصَٰرِ ﴿١٣﴾

Alluring to human beings is the enjoyment of the love of things they covet: women and children; heaped-up treasures of gold and silver; horses of high pedigree (for blood and excellence); and cattle and cultivable lands. These are the possessions of this world's life; but with Allah is the fairest resort (to return to). (14)

زُيِّنَ لِلنَّاسِ حُبُّ ٱلشَّهَوَٰتِ مِنَ
ٱلنِّسَآءِ وَٱلْبَنِينَ وَٱلْقَنَٰطِيرِ ٱلْمُقَنطَرَةِ
مِنَ ٱلذَّهَبِ وَٱلْفِضَّةِ وَٱلْخَيْلِ
ٱلْمُسَوَّمَةِ وَٱلْأَنْعَٰمِ وَٱلْحَرْثِ ۗ ذَٰلِكَ
مَتَٰعُ ٱلْحَيَوٰةِ ٱلدُّنْيَا ۖ وَٱللَّهُ عِندَهُۥ
حُسْنُ ٱلْمَـَٔابِ ﴿١٤﴾

Say: Shall I tell you of something far better than those (worldly pleasures)? For the righteous there are Gardens with their Sustainer, with rivers flowing beneath; therein to dwell forever; and spouses pure, and Allah's goodly acceptance. And in Allah's sight are (all) His servants. (15)

۞ قُلْ أَؤُنَبِّئُكُم بِخَيْرٍ مِّن ذَٰلِكُمْ ۚ
لِلَّذِينَ ٱتَّقَوْا۟ عِندَ رَبِّهِمْ جَنَّٰتٌ تَجْرِى
مِن تَحْتِهَا ٱلْأَنْهَٰرُ خَٰلِدِينَ فِيهَا
وَأَزْوَٰجٌ مُّطَهَّرَةٌ وَرِضْوَٰنٌ مِّنَ
ٱللَّهِ ۗ وَٱللَّهُ بَصِيرٌۢ بِٱلْعِبَادِ ﴿١٥﴾

Those who say: "Our Sustainer! We believe: forgive us then our sins, and save us from the agony of the fire." (16)

ٱلَّذِينَ يَقُولُونَ رَبَّنَآ إِنَّنَآ ءَامَنَّا
فَٱغْفِرْ لَنَا ذُنُوبَنَا وَقِنَا عَذَابَ ٱلنَّارِ
﴿١٦﴾

They are the steadfast, the truthful, the humble; they spend in the cause of Allah, and seek forgiveness in the small hours of the morning (17)

ٱلصَّٰبِرِينَ وَٱلصَّٰدِقِينَ وَٱلْقَٰنِتِينَ
وَٱلْمُنفِقِينَ وَٱلْمُسْتَغْفِرِينَ
بِٱلْأَسْحَارِ ﴿١٧﴾

WORD STUDY AND EXPLANATION

هُوَ ٱلَّذِىٓ أَنزَلَ عَلَيْكَ ٱلْكِتَٰبَ مِنْهُ ءَايَٰتٌ مُّحْكَمَٰتٌ هُنَّ أُمُّ ٱلْكِتَٰبِ وَأُخَرُ مُتَشَٰبِهَٰتٌ ۖ
فَأَمَّا ٱلَّذِينَ فِى قُلُوبِهِمْ زَيْغٌ فَيَتَّبِعُونَ مَا تَشَٰبَهَ مِنْهُ ٱبْتِغَآءَ ٱلْفِتْنَةِ وَٱبْتِغَآءَ تَأْوِيلِهِۦ ۗ وَمَا
يَعْلَمُ تَأْوِيلَهُۥٓ إِلَّا ٱللَّهُ ۗ وَٱلرَّٰسِخُونَ فِى ٱلْعِلْمِ يَقُولُونَ ءَامَنَّا بِهِۦ كُلٌّ مِّنْ عِندِ رَبِّنَا ۗ وَمَا يَذَّكَّرُ
إِلَّآ أُو۟لُوا۟ ٱلْأَلْبَٰبِ ﴿٧﴾

He it is Who has sent down to you the Book: in it are substantive verses (clear and lucid): they are the core of the Book. Others are allegorical verses. Those in whose hearts is perversity go after the allegorical verses, seeking discord and searching for their hidden meanings, but no one except Allah knows their real meanings. And those who are firmly grounded in knowledge say: "We believe in it; all this is from our Sustainer." But only the people of understanding take heed. (7)

The words "*He it is Who has sent down to you the Book*" refer to Allah, the Living, the Self-Subsisting and All-Sustaining God, mentioned above, draw our attention to several points.

Firstly, the verse points to the great blessing bestowed upon humankind in the form of this Book. This blessing is a clear manifestation of Allah's attributes of being the Living, Self-subsisting and all-Sustaining God. He has revealed this Book to bestow the gift of eternal life upon His servants, human beings, and to guide them to the straight path. It is only proper and fair for His servants to appreciate this great blessing upon them, believe in it and embrace its message so as to win the gift of an enduring existence and eternal bliss.

Secondly, in the verse there is also an element of admonition and warning for those who reject and deny this Book, for He Who has revealed this Book is the Mighty, Self-subsisting and all-Sustaining God. Considering His wisdom and might and the fact that all depend on Him while He depends on none, it is inevitable that He should call to account those who stand in the way of His commandment to establish truth and justice or actively try to subvert their establishment.

Thirdly, the verse sheds light on the distinctive characteristic of this Book. It is the revealed word of Allah, the Mighty and All-Wise. As such, it is also mighty and full of wisdom. This is stressed at several places in the Qur'ān. In other words, this Book is not revealed for disputation and controversy.[3] Rather, it is a book of guidance so that everyone may benefit from its inexhaustible treasures of wisdom according to his or her respective capacity, because no one can ever hope to fathom all its mysteries. Whatever is beyond the reach of our understanding, we should refer it to Allah and pray for help and guidance instead of using such verses to stoke up controversy and doubts.

Certain words used in this verse are part of Qur'ānic terminology, and unless these are fully explained it is difficult to grasp the message of this verse. We will therefore begin by explaining these terms.

3. See Sūrah Fuṣṣilat, 41:41: "Those who reject the Message when it comes to them and surely it is a Book Sublime..." And also Sūrah Yūnus, 10:1: " Alif Lām Rā. These are the verses of the Wise Book."

Āyāt muḥkamāt

The term refers to such verses of the Qūr'an that deal with the manifest truths of life and nature and the universally accepted norms of good and evil, virtue and vice that all humans, all right-minded and sensible people, accept. All these are truths that are endorsed by reason, provided one's mind is free of prejudice and is not influenced by perverse sophistry and emotion. These basic truths or *muḥkamāt* form the foundations of all true religion. All Prophets and revealed religions, without any exception throughout history, have upheld and preached these very truths. Being firmly ingrained in human nature, these basic truths are deep-rooted and raging storms of doubt and scepticism fail to shake their hold. It is for this reason that the Qur'ān describes them as *muḥkamāt* or basic and fundamental truths.

Ummu-l kitāb

Āyāt muḥkamāt are defined as the *ummu-l kitāb* which means that for the rest of the teachings of the book, these *āyāt muḥkamāt* serve as a reference point. They form the conclusive basis for any discussion on all issues: in fact everything depends on and flows from them. In cases of conflict and controversy, they serve as the criterion for judgement and decision. These *muḥkamāt* verses alone qualify to be taken as containing the main principles from which further subsidiary rules are derived, and trusted, as the main principles are.

What is meant by *mutashābihāt*?

Mutashābihāt are those verses that are allegorical and deal with a world beyond the reach of our senses, observation and perception. The basic truth enshrined in these verses is quite obvious and clear and human reason can easily understand their necessary message. However, since these verses speak about an unseen world, the Qur'ān presents them in the form of a parable or an allegory. The seekers of true knowledge can benefit from these according to their capacity without trying in vain to determine their precise form, nature and meaning. They should better leave these matters to Allah and repose their trust in Him. These relate to questions about Allah's attributes and His acts, or they concern the blessings and punishment in the life hereafter. Of these, we can easily grasp whatever is necessary for our guidance. This adds to our knowledge and faith. However, if we try to go beyond this limit in an effort to determine their precise nature and form, we risk exposing ourselves to unnecessary temptation, fraught with spiritual and moral hazards. Consequently, in trying to answer one doubt, one may end up with numerous new barbs of doubt and suspicion. In the search for what is essentially unattainable, one may lose whatever is already gained and is in one's possession. Some people may reject an obvious fact simply because its final form and nature is not yet crystal clear. Referring to this, the Qur'ān says, "Nay, but they are bent on rejecting everything the wisdom whereof they do not comprehend, and before its inner meaning has become clear to them" (Sūrah Yūnus, 10:39).

Some examples of *mutashābihāt*

We give below some examples of these *mutashābihāt* or allegorical verses from the Qur'ān. In Sūrah al-Muddaththir, the chastisement of hell is portrayed in these words:

> *Soon will I cast him into hell-fire! And what will explain to you what hell-fire is? It spares not, nor does it leave alone – scorching the bodies of humans! Over it are nineteen (angels).* (74:26-30).

The punishment mentioned in the above verse is real and anyone believing in accountability and the law of reward and punishment cannot deny it. However, as its details are related to a world unseen, we cannot fully grasp its true form and nature. In matters like these, a sensible approach would be to take whatever is comprehensible and refrain from delving into what is beyond our range of perception and knowledge in this worldly life and what will essentially remain incomprehensible to us. This should be the normal attitude. However, those with a certain perversity in their hearts tend to be obsessed with unravelling the hidden meaning of the allegorical statements and parables, exposing themselves and others to temptation and doubts. Thus, for instance, in the case of the above verse, mischievous people have ignored its real message, focused instead on the word "nineteen" and occupied themselves solely with the nature and meaning of the figure nineteen and its possible significance. Commenting on such an attitude, the Qur'ān says:

> *And We have set none but angels as wardens of the hell-fire; and We have fixed their number only as a trial for unbelievers – in order that the People of the Book may arrive at certainty, and the believers may increase in faith – and that no doubts may be left for the People of the Book and the believers, and that those in whose hearts is a disease and the unbelievers may say, "What does Allah intend by this symbol?" Thus*

does Allah leave to stray whom He wills, and guide whom He wills; and none can know the forces of your Sovereign Sustainer, except He. And this is nothing but a warning to human beings. (Sūrah al-Mudaththir, 74:31)

Similarly, in Sūrah al-Baqarah, in an allegorical description of heavenly blessings, we read that when the people of Paradise receive these gifts they will exclaim with joy that these gifts were similar to the ones they were previously told about in the Qur'ān: "Why, this is what we were given before," for they are given things similar (to what they were given in worldly life)" (Sūrah al-Baqarah, 2:25). This description of the heavenly gifts in the form of an allegory is an example of *mutashābihāt.* This is beneficial to the believers as it gives them a glimpse of the heavenly blessings in this life, thanks to these allegorical descriptions in the Qur'ān. At the same time, these allegories and parables present yet another stumbling block, a trial and a temptation for those with twisted minds and warped thinking, increasing their error and deviance. The Qur'ān says:

Allah disdains not to use the similitude of things, the lowest as well as the highest. Those who believe know that it is the truth from their Sustainer; but those who reject faith say: "What does Allah mean by this similitude?" By it He causes many to stray, and many He leads to the right path, but He causes not to stray, except those who forsake (the path). (Sūrah al-Baqarah, 2:26).

From this discussion, it is clear that the *āyāt mutashābihāt* are those verses of the Qur'ān in which either some blessings or punishments of the life hereafter are described in the form of a parable or some attributes and acts of Allah that are presented allegorically: for instance, the breathing of Allah into Adam of His spirit or causing Jesus to be born without a father. Such verses, as mentioned above, increase the believers in knowledge and faith while mischievous people target them with their convoluted arguments, and engage in hair-splitting and wrangling over them.

Ta'wīl: its meaning

The term *ta'wīl* has been used in this verse in a specific sense. It refers to the nature and form of something mentioned previously, for instance, as in the verse: "He said: 'O my father! This is the fulfilment of my vision (*hādhā ta'wīlu ru'yāya*)! Allah has made it come true!" (Sūrah Yūsuf, 12:100).

Some important points about this verse

Here we would like to draw attention to a few points that are worth bearing in mind. These will, Allah willing, answer most of the questions pertaining to this verse.

Firstly, the style in which this verse is couched is not exhaustive or exclusive; it does not represent all the categories of the Qur'ānic verses. Therefore it should not be assumed that the verses of the Qur'ān are only of two kinds: basic or *muḥkamāt* and allegorical or *mutashābihāt*. Here, only these two contrasting kinds are mentioned in order to bring out the difference in attitude and preferences between the mischievous people and true seekers of guidance. The perverse-minded are interested solely in the allegorical verses to find material to cause mischief and create doubts in minds. On the other hand, the primary focus of those who seek truth and guidance is on the *muḥkamāt* or the clear and unambiguous verses. Regarding the *mutashābihāt*, they derive benefit from whatever part they can comprehend. What they cannot, they leave it alone and do not unnecessarily expend their efforts in trying to unravel their hidden meanings. Because of their firm grasp of the *muḥkamāt* or the clear and basic part of Qur'ānic teachings, they remain firmly rooted in their faith. And they fully accept the allegorical verses that they understand are, by their very nature, beyond human perception in this life. So they place their faith in their Sustainer and move on.

There are many other kinds of verses in the Qur'ān apart from these two categories but, as the purpose here is not a description of all these kinds, they are left out at this place. Some of these are, for instance, the stories, and the parables, or the allusions and suggestions of the Qur'ān. These, however, are neither of the degree and status of the *ummu-l kitāb* or the foundation of the Book nor would it be correct to categorise them as *mutashābihāt* or allegorical, searching for and reflecting on whose interpretation and meaning is discouraged and forbidden.

Secondly, it must always be borne in mind that the question whether certain Qur'ānic verses are basic (*muḥkamāt*) or allegorical (*mutashābihāt*) is determined not by their wording but by their meaning. The Qur'ān in its entirety is in plain and clear Arabic. Whatever differences there are about the interpretation of Qur'ānic words, these are usually traceable to three reasons. It was either due to a lack of proper consideration, contemplation and research, or to some unreasonable bias in favour of a deviant dogma, or to ignorance of the Arabic language. Obviously, wherever some problem is caused by such factors, it should be resolved by considering it in the light of the generally accepted norms and rules of the Arabic language. Consideration of such matters is not something that is prohibited.

Thirdly, both these kinds of verses – *mutashābihāt* and *muḥkamāt* – in the Qur'ān are quite distinct and known. They are not indistinguishable as some scholastics have wrongly asserted nor is the connection between the words and their meaning in any way doubtful and suspect. Those who hold such a view are utterly wrong. The first of these assertions is absolutely baseless while the second is extremely vague and causes one to lose all hope and faith in the Qur'ān, notwithstanding the fact that Allah has revealed it as 'a light (*nūr*)' and 'a clear proof (*burhān*)'. Whatever we need to know about matters belonging to the unseen world, Allah has given us knowledge about them that should suffice for our needs in this worldly life. And the part that is kept hidden from us concerns only its true meaning and interpretation.

Fourthly, the Qur'ān has used the terms *muḥkam* and *mutashābih* here in a special sense. At some other places also, the Qur'ān uses these words but only in their literal sense. For instance, it uses the term *muḥkam* with regard to a statement that is comprehensive, clear and concise. The word *mufaṣṣal* or detailed is the opposite of *muḥkam* in this sense. For instance, consider the verse: "(This is) a Book, whose verses are made compact – (*muḥkamāt*), and then further explained in detail from Allah, the all-Wise and all-Aware (Sūrah Hūd, 11:1). As a rule, Allah in the beginning revealed His messages and teachings in short, concise and compact sentences. These are easy to understand and easy to repeat, while their teachings are easy to grasp and absorb. Later, they were elaborated through further revelation or through the sunnah or example of His Prophet, peace be upon him. Similarly, the word *mutashābih* in its general sense means something that is similar and resembles another, the two being mutually in perfect harmony and in accord with each other. In this sense the whole of the Qur'ān is *mutashābihah*: "Allah has revealed the best of all teachings in the form of *kitāban mutashābihan mat͟hānī* – a book fully consistent within itself and with its sūrahs arranged in pairs' (Sūrah az-Zumar, 39: 23).

Fifthly, human life and the natural world, very much like the Qur'ān, also contain two sets of ayahs or signs: *muḥkamāt* and *mutashābihāt*. The attitude of the people of knowledge, and of those with perverse minds to these two categories of signs – *muḥkamāt* and *mutashābihāt* – as mentioned above sets them apart. Those who are well grounded in knowledge and wisdom gain further certainty and conviction through the *muḥkamāt*. Instead of getting entangled in a web of doubt and suspicion by grappling unnecessarily with what is allegorical and unclear (*mutashābihāt*), they refer them to Allah's care and wisdom, frankly admitting the insufficiency and limited nature of their imperfect knowledge. But those in whose hearts there is any perversity focus on the *mutashābihāt* and consequently go astray and also mislead others. (This issue is discussed in detail in our comments on Sūrah al-Kahf). The incident of the battle of Uḥud, as pointed out in the preliminary remarks, was also a sort of an allegorical event. The revelation of this glorious verse after the battle was meant to unveil a most momentous truth of this life. The battle of Badr was a day of distinction between truth and falsehood that brought comfort to believers and convinced them of the truth of the promises of their Sovereign Sustainer. The battle was also a clear and unambiguous sign for the disbelievers that firmly proved the argument against them. The battle of Uḥud, on the other hand, was an allegorical sign (*ayāh mutashābihāh*). It seemed initially that the disbelievers had won the battle and they therefore thought that success or defeat in a battle depended solely on material resources and the strategy of war; and that God is not concerned with such matters nor had this anything to do with the question of truth and falsehood. This was clearly an erroneous view and a serious misunderstanding that had to be rectified. So when the time was ripe, Allah dispelled their misunderstanding in this sūrah with the revelation of this glorious verse on the subject.

Meaning and significance of the word *zayg͟h*

The real meaning of *zayg͟h* is to incline downwards or to deviate. It carries simultaneously two senses: decline and collapse or downfall. An upright structure that is bent or crooked is likely to fall down. This is a diametrically opposite condition to that described in the verse by the words "those who are firmly grounded in knowledge".

A common malady of the People of the Book

Such convoluted or deviant thinking has been a common characteristic of most errant people, but the People of the Book seem to have been especially prone to it. Jewish history shows how the descendants of Israel succumbed to this disease at the very beginning of their history even when a Prophet was present among them and consequently incurring the wrath of Allah:

> *And remember, Moses said to his people: "O my people! Why do you hurt me, though you know that I am the messenger of Allah (sent) to you?" So when they were crooked, Allah made their hearts crooked, and Allah does not guide the treacherous.* (Sūrah aṣ-Ṣaff, 61:5)

Difference between the Jews and the Christians

It was the Jews whose philosophical hair-splitting about "the word of God" and other similar terms that turned these terms into an irresolvable mystery. Such hair-splitting misled the Christians into believing that Jesus was the son of God. The Christian error grew worse as they blindly followed the idolatrous people, gradually drifting so far away that they lost contact with truth and succumbed to manifest error. Referring to this aspect, the Qur'ān says: "They do blaspheme who say: "God is Christ the son of Mary." (Sūrah al-Mā'idah, 5:73).

The only difference in their respective errors was one of nature. In the case of the Jews, it was reflected in their practical behaviour whereas the Christian error was manifest in their beliefs and creed. Because of this difference, their respective attitudes towards the message of truth were markedly different. The Jews opposed the Qur'ān while knowing that it was a true revelation. The Christians were previously misled on account of their over-indulgence in the allegorical part of the Torah and the Injīl. Similarly, in the case of the Qur'ān they were interested solely in its *mutashābihāt* or allegorical verses. These were the targets of their hair-splitting arguments. They used these to create new controversies, cast doubts and implant suspicions in minds. They thus misled themselves and others. Regarding the basic teachings or *muḥkamāt* of the Qur'ān, they never paid any serious attention to them nor allowed anyone else under their influence to do so. In short, so far as their convoluted thinking and fascination with the allegorical teachings or *mutashābihāt* were concerned, there was little difference between the Jews and the Christians. They were afflicted with a similar malady. Their taste and inclinations were, however, somewhat different: the Jews were interested in causing controversy and trouble; the Christians were concerned more with unravelling the hidden meaning behind the allegorical descriptions. As these diseases are fairly universal and found in almost all errant groups, the Qur'ān mentions them in general terms without specifically mentioning the Jews or the Christians. But those who are familiar with the Qur'ānic approach and style know that the clear hint is to them. For instance, they are previously referred to in Sūrah al-Fātiḥah without specifically naming them. Instead, the general terms *maghḍūbi 'alayhim* and *aḍ-ḍāllin* are used there. While these two general terms may refer to all errant groups, yet they are specifically directed at the Jews and the Christians.

How the pursuit of *mutashābihāt* led to error

The Christians are an example of people who succumbed to error as a result of their excessive fascination with the allegorical part of the revelation. For instance, both the Qur'ān and the Injīl agree that Jesus is "Allah's word". The meaning of this is quite clear: it symbolises Allah's command and decree. As Jesus was born through a supernatural process, Allah described him as His word, namely, he was born as a result of Allah's commandment, "Be!" This is meant to stress that the crucial factor in bringing anything into existence is only the commandment of Allah and that all the apparent causes are no more than its outward manifestation. The Qur'ān has explained this point very clearly and eloquently and it is easy for anyone with a fair and open mind to grasp it. The Qur'ān declares in quite unequivocal terms:

إِنَّ مَثَلَ عِيسَىٰ عِندَ ٱللَّهِ كَمَثَلِ ءَادَمَ خَلَقَهُۥ مِن تُرَابٍ ثُمَّ قَالَ لَهُۥ كُن فَيَكُونُ ٥٩

The similitude of Jesus before Allah is as that of Adam: He created him (Adam) from dust, then said to him: "Be", and he was. (Sūrah Āli 'Imrān, 3:59).

In other words, it was by the word or command "*Kun!*" or "Be!" that Allah made Adam a living being, endowed him with intelligence and the capacity to reason and articulate his ideas. At another place, the Qur'ān has described this phenomenon as the "breathing of the spirit" into Adam. The case of the conception of Jesus, peace be upon him, is described in the Qur'ān as similar to that of Adam[4]

Christians ended up by distorting this rather obvious fact. This happened when they came into contact with idolatrous nations and engaged with them in religious dialogue. The idolaters asserted that as the Christians worshipped a crucified god, they (the idolaters) were far better and superior to them for they worshipped heavenly gods. To counter this objection, the Christians tried to recast their creed into a mould similar to that of their adversaries. Thus, they claimed that Jesus was the Son of God and not a created being like others. In order to embellish their new creed, they borrowed some ideas from the Greeks, Magians, and the Jewish scholastics who emerged during the latter period of Jewish history. These not only believed in the existence of intermediaries between God and humans but also held that they had an independent existence of their own. They described these intermediaries as the word of God. The Christians adopted an identical belief concerning the

4. See the Qur'ān, 32:9, 15:29 and 38:72 (for Adam) and 21:91, 66:12 (for Jesus). (Translator)

person of Jesus. This continued for some time but then gradually this one error led to further deviant views and beliefs, until they finally declared Jesus as equal or comparable to God; that he was of the same essence and that he was co-eternal with Him. In order to lend further support to this creed, certain statements were interpolated in the beginning of the gospel of John.

In the light of the above details, at the end of the sentence *wa mā ya'lamu ta'wīlahu illā Allāh* (but no one knows its real meaning except Allah), there is clearly a pause or *waqf* as the majority of the *ahl as-sunnah* scholars hold. A similar position is reported from Ibn 'Abbās, 'Ā'ishah, 'Alī, Ḥasan, Mālik ibn Anas, al-Kisā'ī and al-Farrā'. Shi'ahs and some scholastics, however, hold that there is *waṣl* or continuity and therefore this sentence must be read in conjunction with the previous clause. Thus they hold that besides Allah, those who are firmly grounded in knowledge – *ar-rāsi<u>kh</u>ūna fi-l 'ilm* – also know the hidden meaning of the *mutashābihāt* verses, since they believe that their imams have knowledge of everything. Others who hold this view do so because they take the word *ta'wīl* in the sense of 'meaning', although this is not supported by the context of the verse as explained above[5].

After the above explanation of this verse and its parts, its correct interpretation should be quite clear. However, in view of its importance, we would like to clarify the essence of its message further.

The verse teaches us that Allah – the mighty and wise, the living, the self-subsisting and all-sustaining God – Who previously revealed the Torah and the Injīl, has also revealed this Qur'ān, as both of these previously revealed books were corrupted and their teachings changed or distorted. This was the natural consequence of His wisdom and the fact that He alone is the all-sustaining and self-sustaining God. Therefore He has revealed the Qur'ān to guide human beings to the right path and to make clear and distinct the good from evil. Those who resist its message and light should bear in mind that Allah will not allow the truth to be vanquished by falsehood, but will surely punish all its enemies.

The verse then explains that the real reason why the People of the Book are opposed to the Qur'ān – the criterion between truth and falsehood – is not because of any flaw or deficiency in it. Rather, the real reason is the perversity of their hearts. Because of this perversity, they are not interested in the Qur'ān's core message – the *muḥkamāt* – that constitute the basis and essence of its teachings, wisdom and philosophy. Instead, they are interested only in

5. Most of this discussion is based on Ustā<u>dh</u> Farāhi's work. I have only added some explanatory remarks to elaborate some points. Therefore what is correct, its credit must go to Ustā<u>dh</u> Farāhi and whatever is weak, I alone am responsible for it.

its allegorical part or *mutashābihāt*, the part that deals with matters beyond the reach of human perception and are couched in parables or allegories.

Because of their convoluted thinking and crookedness, they concentrate on the allegorical statements, and in order to fan flames of controversy and trouble, they try to find the hidden meaning of the allegorical statements while none except Allah knows or understands their true meaning, form or nature.

Whatever knowledge of these matters is necessary for us has been clearly explained by Allah. We should thus be content with whatever has been given to us. With regard to the true form and nature of the allegorical, we can only know and understand them fully in the life hereafter. That is precisely the attitude of those who are well-grounded in knowledge. Such people appreciate and believe in both the *muḥkamāt* and *mutashābihāt* as equally valuable gifts from their Sovereign Sustainer. They are fully aware of the fact that the real purpose of the Divine verses is to remind and admonish people. As sensible and rational people, they try to benefit from these signs as much as they possibly can rather than waste their talents, energy and time in futile pursuits. Only those who are sensible and who use their faculties of understanding and reasoning honestly and properly benefit from Allah's signs and messages. This is in accordance with Divine law.

رَبَّنَا لَا تُزِغْ قُلُوبَنَا بَعْدَ إِذْ هَدَيْتَنَا وَهَبْ لَنَا مِن لَّدُنكَ رَحْمَةً ۚ إِنَّكَ أَنتَ الْوَهَّابُ ﴿٨﴾
رَبَّنَا إِنَّكَ جَامِعُ النَّاسِ لِيَوْمٍ لَّا رَيْبَ فِيهِ ۚ إِنَّ اللَّهَ لَا يُخْلِفُ الْمِيعَادَ ﴿٩﴾

"Our Sustainer! Let not our hearts deviate after You have guided us; and bestow upon us mercy from Your presence. You are the true Giver of bounties without measure. (8)
"Our Sustainer! You will gather humankind together for a day about which there is no doubt: for Allah never fails to fulfil His promise." (9)

This is the supplication of those who are described as well-grounded in knowledge. It shows that in the matter of their religion, they are neither indifferent nor so careless and reckless as to invite doubts and suspicions and so wreck their faith and belief. Instead they constantly pray to their Sovereign Sustainer for protection and to keep them firm and steady in the path of truth. They beseech their most bounteous and gracious Creator to strengthen their faith and reinforce them with His special help and support when they are confronted with trials and hardships in the pursuit of truth.

The second verse describes the conviction in the life hereafter of these people who are firmly grounded in knowledge. The verse clearly shows that it is this certainty of belief that really safeguards both the human heart and reason. In the absence of such certain belief, nothing can check the human mind and thought processes from straying off into blind alleys. People without such a firm belief see life as having little or no real value and are ever ready to sacrifice it at the altar of every passing whim. On the other hand, those who firmly believe in the life hereafter are extremely cautious and ever vigilant. This caution and vigilance helps them follow the straight path firmly and steadily.

إِنَّ ٱلَّذِينَ كَفَرُوا۟ لَن تُغْنِىَ عَنْهُمْ أَمْوَٰلُهُمْ وَلَآ أَوْلَٰدُهُم مِّنَ ٱللَّهِ شَيْـًٔا ۖ وَأُو۟لَٰٓئِكَ
هُمْ وَقُودُ ٱلنَّارِ ﴿١٠﴾

كَدَأْبِ ءَالِ فِرْعَوْنَ وَٱلَّذِينَ مِن قَبْلِهِمْ ۚ كَذَّبُوا۟ بِـَٔايَٰتِنَا فَأَخَذَهُمُ ٱللَّهُ بِذُنُوبِهِمْ ۗ وَٱللَّهُ شَدِيدُ
ٱلْعِقَابِ ﴿١١﴾

Those who reject faith, neither their possessions nor their children will in the least avail them against Allah; and it is they who shall be the fuel of the fire. (10) *As was the case with the people of Pharaoh, and those before them: they denied Our signs, and so Allah called them to account for their sins. For Allah is severe in punishment.* (11)

The real obstacle in the path of truth

The words "those who reject faith" as mentioned in verse 4 above refer to the deniers of the Qur'ān. They are warned that their love of wealth and children – because of which they reject the most obvious truth, will not save them from the punishment of Allah. They should not therefore be blinded by their love for these transitory pleasures, nor should they forget their obligations to Allah. Their first and foremost duty is to their Sovereign Sustainer whose punishment is also most severe.

Wealth and children are mentioned here as the real impediment to the acceptance of truth. In verse 14 below, these impediments to the path of truth are explained in detail. One's fascination with these possessions has always been a great hurdle in the acceptance of truth. Few among human beings, however, would be ready to admit this. Instead, most offer false excuses to conceal their moral weakness and real motives. Their real weakness, we are told, is their fascination with wealth and children and this prevents them from responding to the message of truth. To cover this weakness, they pick some of the allegorical statements of the Qur'ān and use them to concoct spurious objections to show that they have some genuine and valid reasons for not accepting an obvious truth.

Efforts to cover up the real disease

This attitude of those who reject the message of truth, we are further informed, is similar to that of the people of Pharaoh and other nations who previously rejected the messengers of Allah. They deliberately, and purely out of love for worldly pleasures, rejected the message of truth while alleging that the prophet or the messenger sent to them was merely a soothsayer or a sorcerer and that their miracles and signs were nothing but subterfuge and chicanery. The result was that they were ultimately overtaken by Divine punishment for their sins and insolence.

"Allah is severe in punishment" – *shadīdu-l ʻiqāb* – implies two truths. One, whatever punishment humans receive from Allah is in consequence to their misdeeds and is a just response to their actions. Two, like the physical laws, the moral laws of Allah concerning consequences of actions are also impartial and immutable. They take effect at their proper time and place, surely and inexorably, and none can escape them nor in any way help others.

A warning to the rejecters of the Qur'ān

قُل لِّلَّذِينَ كَفَرُوا۟ سَتُغْلَبُونَ وَتُحْشَرُونَ إِلَىٰ جَهَنَّمَ ۚ وَبِئْسَ ٱلْمِهَادُ ﴿١٢﴾

Say to those who reject faith: "You shall be overcome and gathered together to hell". What an evil resting place! (12)

This is an open warning to all deniers of the Qur'ān. Whatever their evil designs against it, they are bound to fail and suffer defeat at the hands of the bearers of the Qur'ān. Their material resources, equipment and numbers that they are so proud of, will not in the least benefit them; they will be vanquished in this world and consigned to hell fire in the hereafter. This is a serious warning that should not be taken lightly; Hell is a most horrible and dreadful place. This warning was needed because it is difficult for one to visualise or grasp correctly the awesome nature and seriousness of what is unseen and beyond the range of the human. Or even if comprehensible to some extent, one may easily lose focus and ignore it because of forgetfulness and lethargy.

Lessons of the Battle of Badr

قَدْ كَانَ لَكُمْ ءَايَةٌ فِى فِئَتَيْنِ ٱلْتَقَتَا ۖ فِئَةٌ تُقَـٰتِلُ فِى سَبِيلِ ٱللَّهِ وَأُخْرَىٰ
كَافِرَةٌ يَرَوْنَهُم مِّثْلَيْهِمْ رَأْىَ ٱلْعَيْنِ ۚ وَٱللَّهُ يُؤَيِّدُ بِنَصْرِهِۦ مَن يَشَآءُ ۗ إِنَّ فِى

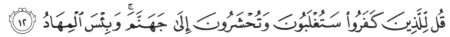

ذَٰلِكَ لَعِبْرَةً لِّأُوْلِي ٱلْأَبْصَٰرِ ﴿١٣﴾

There has already been for you a sign in the two hosts that met in battle: one was fighting in Allah's cause and the other denying Him. With their own eyes they (the latter) saw the others as twice their own number. And Allah strengthens with His aid whom He pleases. In this, there is indeed a lesson for all who have eyes to see. (13)

In support of the claim made above, a reference in this verse is made to a recent event that was still fresh in memory – the battle of Badr. This battle clearly showed that in the conflict raging between the followers of Islam and its opponents, in this case the Quraysh, the truth will finally prevail. This battle was a clear sign that those fighting to establish the word of Allah are bound to vanquish the disbelievers and the supporters of *ṭāghūt* or evil. There were over a thousand disbelievers ranged against the Muslims, who were three hundred and thirteen in all. But when the two parties actually confronted each other, the disbelievers saw the Muslim army as twice their numbers. This happened through the special help and support of Allah specially enjoyed by those who strive to make this word prevail on earth. Those with eyes could clearly see the future course of events as mirrored in this incident and how the on-going conflict between good and evil is bound to end.

The Battle of Badr as a sign for the disbelievers

In the encounter of Badr, there was a sign of the ultimate triumph of truth for all those who were aggressively fighting against the message of the Qur'ān. Of these, three groups were pre-eminent: the Jews, the Christians and the disbelieving Quraysh. The battle of Badr was a clear sign for each of these three groups.

A sign for the Jews

As mentioned in our commentary on Sūrah al-Baqarah, for the Jews the battle of Badr was a repeat of the battle between Ṭālūt (Saul) and Goliath, so far as the objectives, planning, strategy and the number of combatants involved. Like the descendants of Israel before them, the Muslims were also expelled from their homes and deprived of their *qiblah*. The Jews had lost the Ark of the Covenant to their enemies and similarly the *qiblah* of the Muslims was, at the time, in the hands of the Quraysh. The number of the Muslims accompanying the Prophet, peace be upon him, in the battle of Badr was three hundred and thirteen, and as indicated by some Jewish traditions, almost similar to the number of those who accompanied Ṭālūt in the battle against Jālūt (Goliath). And just as the Prophet, peace be upon him, tested the morale of his army before the encounter, Ṭālūt also specifically tested the resolve and discipline of his men. At Badr, Allah granted victory to the Muslims under apparently adverse and unfavourable conditions and most of the prominent leaders of the Quraysh were killed in the ensuing battle. Ṭālūt and his companions were similarly blessed with Divine help, routing the enemy; their fearsome head, Goliath, fell victim to David's slingshot.

This close similarity between the two battles was quite obvious to the Jews. They could read about the one in detail in their scriptures and the other they had seen unfolding before their own eyes. As such it was not difficult for them to appreciate that the battle of Badr was not merely a clash of arms, but an encounter between truth and falsehood and a confrontation between angels and demons. There is a suggestion found in the Qur'ān, as we shall explain in our commentary on Sūrah al-Anfāl, that the Jews were well aware of this aspect of the matter but still they failed to appreciate this clear sign of the truth of Allah's final Prophet, peace be upon him, and persisted in their hostility.

A sign for the Christians

For the Christians also, this battle represented a clear sign of the truth of Prophet of Islam. In the gospel of John, it is clearly stated that when the promised final Prophet, peace be upon him, appears he will wage jihād with the power of truth, accompanied by a host of angels[6].

This prophecy was duly fulfilled at the battlefield of Badr and the people saw the angels with their own eyes fighting alongside the believers. But even after this clear sign, the Christians remained trapped in the futile controversy about the allegorical and non-allegorical, and they too failed to recognise and welcome the messenger of truth. It was indeed a great loss and a misfortune.

A sign for the Quraysh

As for the Quraysh, this battle was a clear sign for them and an irrefutable argument of the truth of Islam and the Qur'ān, for they had explicitly asked for such a sign. Prior to the battle, they had categorically declared that the outcome of this battle would be a clear indication of truth and falsehood: whoever was victorious would be in the right and the vanquished party would be deemed in the wrong. When the warriors advanced to battle and drew near

6. See Revelation, 19:11 (Translator)

to one another, Abū Jahl cried, 'O God, destroy this morning the one who more than any of us has severed the ties of kinship'.

The Qur'ān and the Prophet, peace be upon him, had in unambiguous words foretold the victory of Islam in this battle that was fulfilled to the letter. The Prophet had even specified the places where some prominent leaders of the Quraysh were to fall on the battlefield. These prophecies were proved true. That is why the Qur'ān has described the battle of Badr as the criterion that clearly distinguished truth from falsehood and provided yet another proof of the truth of Islam while establishing a clear argument against its intractable opponents.

Use of the elliptical style in the Qur'ān

The verse defines the believers as those who "fought in the cause of Allah" but is silent about the cause the disbelievers were fighting for. This omission is in accord with a well-known style of the Arabic language that is frequently used in the Qur'ān. When two opposites are mentioned one of them is omitted, for the sake of brevity, especially as the unmentioned opposite is easily understandable from what is mentioned. Bearing this in mind, the complete sentence would read: *fi'atum mu'minatum tuqātilu fi-sabīlillāh wa ukhrā kāfirtun tuqātilu fi-sabīliṭ-ṭāghūt* (a believing party fought in the cause of Allah and another, a disbelieving party, fought in the cause of the devil). In the first part of the sentence the word *mu'minah* (believing) is dropped while in the second part the words *fi-sabīliṭ-ṭāghūt* (in the cause of the devil) are dropped, because the description of the second party as *kāfiratun* contains a strong hint that its opposing party is *mu'minah.* Similarly, a reference to the first as the one fighting in Allah's cause *(fi-sabilīllāh)* indicates that the second party was fighting in the cause of the devil *(fi-sabīliṭ-ṭāghūt).* This elliptical style is often used in the Qur'ān and those who are unaware of it may easily fail to appreciate the true force and beauty of the Qur'ān. Ellipsis represents brevity and economy of words and is the very essence of eloquence.

Who saw the other as twice their own number?

Nāfi', who is one of the seven authorities on *qirā'ah* (recitation) reads the word *yar-awnahum* in the phrase *yarawnahum mithlayhim* as *tarawnahum* which in our view is merely for the purpose of *tafsīr* or explanation of the verse. This verse is addressed to the disbelievers, telling them that they saw the Muslims as twice their actual number. According to this interpretation, it was the disbelievers who saw the Muslims confronting them as twice their number. This interpretation of Nāfi' appears to be correct as it is explicitly stated in the verse that Allah made this a sign for the disbelievers that they witnessed with their own eyes. On the other hand, if the Muslims had seen the disbelievers as twice their actual numbers, it could not have constituted a sign for the disbelievers and mentioned as a sign for them.

A question and its answer

A question may, however, arise in some minds here. In Sūrah al-Anfāl, where the battle of Badr is mentioned, it appears that both the Muslims and the disbelievers were shown to each other as less than their real strength, which apparently contradicts the above interpretation of the verse. The answer to this question is that this phenomenon of showing them more or less to each other happened in two different stages and in two different forms. Before the commencement of the battle, undoubtedly both the Muslims and their enemies saw each other as very weak and vulnerable, but when the battle actually began the situation suddenly changed. Now the disbelievers found that the position had drastically changed. After the angels joined in, the numbers of the Muslim army swelled and the disbelievers saw them as almost double their number. From the statement of the Qur'ān, it appears that the course and completion of the encounter in two stages was also a part of the Divine scheme: to strike the truth against falsehood and then help the truth by invisible forces so as to establish the argument against the enemies of truth. For this reason, in the first stage, both the Muslims and the disbelievers were shown to each other as less than their adversary so that they would not hesitate in entering the battlefield. But after the battle began, Allah helped the Muslims with hosts of angels who changed the entire battle scene and struck fear into the hearts of the disbelievers.

In the light of the following verses from Sūrah al-Anfāl, the difference between the two occasions and the underlying wisdom may be easily grasped:

> *Remember you were on the nearer side of the valley, and they on the farther side, and the caravan was on lower ground than you. Even if you had made a mutual appointment to meet, you would certainly have failed in the appointment. But (thus you met), that Allah might accomplish a matter already decreed; that those who died might die after seeing a clear sign, and those who lived might live after seeing a clear sign. And verily Allah is all-Hearing, all-Knowing. Remember in your dream Allah showed them to you as few: if He had shown them to you as many, you would surely have been discouraged, and you*

would surely have disputed in (your) decision; but Allah saved (you): for He knows well the (secrets) of hearts. And remember when you met, He showed them to you as few in your eyes, and He made you appear as contemptible in their eyes: that Allah might accomplish a matter already decreed. And to Allah do all questions go back (for decision). (Sūrah al-Anfāl, 8:42-44)

From the above detail, it is clear that the context and the timing of this verse of Sūrah Āli 'Imrān and that of the above verses of Sūrah al-Anfāl are different. In Sūrah al-Anfāl the reference is to a time prior to the beginning of the battle, and the verse under discussion refers to the situation when the battle had begun and Divine support for the Muslims in the form of angelic hosts had also appeared. Thus the two statements of the Qur'ān are in full accord with each other. We may also bear in mind that in Sūrah al-Anfāl there is a clear hint that after the battle started the disbelievers found a completely changed battle scene that greatly demoralised them. We will discuss this point at its proper place and there we shall also show that the Jews were behind the conspiracy of causing the Quraysh to attack the Muslims, but on seeing the battle scene of Badr they too were taken aback and demoralised[7]. In the words "And Allah strengthens with His aid whom He pleases", the clear reference is to the fact that Allah helps whoever He pleases: no one can withhold His hand and for Him the question of smallness or greatness of numbers is irrelevant. He can cause a small and insignificant group to overpower and vanquish a large and powerful army. There have been a great number of small and weak groups who defeated and vanquished large hosts. In His hands alone rests victory or defeat; He alone decides who wins or loses.

In this there is an *'ibrah* (a lesson) for all who have eyes to see

The word *'ibrah* means admonition or warning, literally, to move from one fact to another, to cross over from one to another, to consider or ponder. The major difference between an insightful person and an unthinking person is that while the latter is unable to see beyond his nose, for the other even a small sign, a hint and a warning opens up a whole new universe of meaning and wisdom, and if he is conscientious doors to higher wisdom will open up before him. The Qur'ān calls these people "those who have eyes to see" for they are blessed with sight as well as insight and are able to witness the whole in a part or an ocean in a drop and vice versa.

7. Please see author's comments on verse 48 of Sūrah al-Anfāl, where he shows that the Jews were behind the attack on the tiny state of Madīnah and verse 16 of Sūrah al-Hashr in a similar context (Translator).

Significance of worldly allurements

زُيِّنَ لِلنَّاسِ حُبُّ ٱلشَّهَوَٰتِ مِنَ ٱلنِّسَآءِ وَٱلْبَنِينَ وَٱلْقَنَـٰطِيرِ ٱلْمُقَنطَرَةِ مِنَ
ٱلذَّهَبِ وَٱلْفِضَّةِ وَٱلْخَيْلِ ٱلْمُسَوَّمَةِ وَٱلْأَنْعَـٰمِ وَٱلْحَرْثِ ۗ ذَٰلِكَ مَتَـٰعُ ٱلْحَيَوٰةِ
ٱلدُّنْيَا ۖ وَٱللَّهُ عِندَهُۥ حُسْنُ ٱلْمَـَٔابِ ﴿١٤﴾

Alluring to human beings is the enjoyment of the love of what they covet: women and children; heaped-up treasures of gold and silver; horses of high mark (for pedigree and excellence); and cattle and (cultivated) lands. These are the possessions of this world's life; but with Allah is the fairest resort (to return to).(14)

The word *shahawāt* (lusts) is used here in the sense of what people covet, such as spouses, wealth, property, and children and are very dear to them as they are essential for individual and collective survival, and continuity. But the verse does not refer merely to their attraction for people but emphasises their allurement that makes these things so fascinating that one looks at life and everything else in their light only. It is impossible for such people to rise above their fascination, their sole object in life. Such a fascination with any worldly pleasure or object is manifestly contrary to the will of the Creator of life and human beings. This fascination leads to and creates crookedness and imbalance in life, deflecting further away from the straight course, the natural course and Divine law or Sharīʿah. It is a sickness caused by one's lack of insight and respect for the bounds of natural law or, in other words, by the lack of *taqwā* or God-consciousness. The real culprits in all this are the human being and the devil that instigates and encourages him. When one is driven by the desire to gratify lusts, one is bound to exceed the natural bounds. The devil goads a person on, painting a deceitful picture on which his attention becomes riveted to the exclusion of all else. That is why the Qur'ān describes such a fascination with transitory worldly pleasures as being a result of devilish allurement.

Qinṭār and *muqanṭarah*

The word *qinṭār* means great wealth. Its plural *qanāṭīr* is used with the related adjective *muqanṭarah* to signify wealth accumulation on a massive scale.

Musawwamah

This is the past participle of *sawwama* and means something that is marked. As it is usually the horses of noble breed that are marked, the word gradually came to signify nobility and high quality.

Use of the word *nās* for a specific group

The phrase *li-n nās* (for people) is a general term. Here, however, it refers to a specific group. The Qur'ān also uses it in this sense at other places. In its present context, it is used for a group of people who lack understanding and are also devoid of any fear of Allah (*taqwā*) in their hearts. Consequently, all they are concerned with in life is the gratification of their physical desires, and are not willing or ready to pay any heed to higher, nobler moral values to which the Qur'ān invites them.

Grades of various allurements

It is worth bearing in mind that in its reference to worldly allurements, the Qur'ān has mentioned them in a special sequence. At the head of these is placed the family and children because they occupy the prime position in one's heart. All other things and one's attachment to them are mostly subject to one's love for family and children and are alluring on account of them. Next, gold is mentioned as the most precious compared to other forms of wealth. As to property, horses are placed at the top because for the Arabs their horses were their most precious possession, as objects of adornment and a means of pride and defence. Next come cattle or livestock, since prior to the advancement of civilisation people living in the desert mostly depended on them. Fields and gardens are mentioned last as they acquired importance after humankind entered the age of civilisation and were settled in villages and cities.

These are the possessions of this world's life

A whole universe of meaning is compressed into this short sentence. It refers to the transitory nature of this worldly life, its pleasures and enjoyments, and the stupidity of throwing away the eternal life of the hereafter and its enduring pleasures in the blind pursuit of the fleeting joys of this worldly life.

So far as context and thematic continuity is concerned, this verse in a way further elaborates verse 10 above. It explains that the real cause of the hostility and opposition of these people to the Qur'ān is their greed and fascination with material pleasures. However, they try to conceal their real motives and nefarious designs – their real disease – by forging lies and spurious objections to justify their rejection of truth.

۞ قُلْ أَؤُنَبِّئُكُم بِخَيْرٍ مِّن ذَٰلِكُمْ ۚ لِلَّذِينَ اتَّقَوْا عِندَ رَبِّهِمْ جَنَّاتٌ تَجْرِي مِن تَحْتِهَا
الْأَنْهَارُ خَالِدِينَ فِيهَا وَأَزْوَاجٌ مُّطَهَّرَةٌ وَرِضْوَانٌ مِّنَ اللَّهِ ۗ وَاللَّهُ بَصِيرٌ
بِالْعِبَادِ ﴿١٥﴾

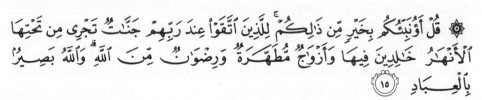

ٱلَّذِينَ يَقُولُونَ رَبَّنَآ إِنَّنَآ ءَامَنَّا فَٱغۡفِرۡ لَنَا ذُنُوبَنَا وَقِنَا عَذَابَ ٱلنَّارِ ﴿١٦﴾
ٱلصَّٰبِرِينَ وَٱلصَّٰدِقِينَ وَٱلۡقَٰنِتِينَ وَٱلۡمُنفِقِينَ وَٱلۡمُسۡتَغۡفِرِينَ بِٱلۡأَسۡحَارِ
﴿١٧﴾

Say: Shall I tell you of something far better than those (worldly pleasures)? For the righteous there are gardens with their Sustainer, with rivers flowing beneath – therein dwelling forever; and spouses pure, and Allah's goodly acceptance. And in Allah's sight are (all) His servants. (15)
Those who say: "Our Sustainer! We believe: forgive us our sins, and save us from the agony of the fire." (16)
They are the steadfast, the truthful, the humble; they spend in the cause of Allah, and seek forgiveness in the small hours of the morning (17)

An invitation to review their position

This is an invitation to people to review their position and stance, because without such a change it is not possible to truly appreciate the higher values and norms the Qur'ān stands for. The real problem with human beings is their shortsightedness and meanness of spirit. Often they are deceived into treating their transitory sojourn on earth as synonymous with total life. This distorts their outlook on life making them blind to everything except worldly pleasures that become the sole focus of their attention and efforts. The life hereafter seems too remote and beyond the range of their interest, even though that is the real life with its enduring pleasures and blessings. To win this eternal life and its pleasures, there is only one condition: that is, one must follow the path of *taqwā* or righteousness. In other words, one must abide by the rules of what is lawful and unlawful as defined by Divine law. That is the sure way to win Allah's pleasure and His blessings that are far greater and beyond what can ever be conceived of in the life of this world.

***Azwāj muṭahharah* (pure companions)**

Among the blessings, 'pure companions' are specifically mentioned. For the significance of this phrase please refer to commentary on verse 25, Sūrah al-Baqarah (*Pondering over the Qur'ān*). Here they are mentioned as a special blessing in Paradise because, as stated in verse 14 above, one's family and children are the closest and dearest to one's heart and no blessing can be complete without them.

Riḍwān

Riḍwān means Allah's pleasure and acceptance by Him, and in the Qur'ān it is generally used as a reference to the blessings of Paradise as a whole. It includes all blessings, the ones that can be described in words as well as those that are beyond the grasp of our perception and notions, even beyond the reach of our imagination or dreams.

Wallāhu baṣīrum bi-l 'ibād

The phrase is both a message of comfort and a warning. In the present context, it carries a message of comfort and assures sincere believers who are mindful of the life of the hereafter and their accountability and have chosen the path of virtue and sacrifice. Allah is well aware of all their sacrifices and efforts and He shall fully reward them. No effort or sacrifice of theirs will go unappreciated.

Alladhīna yaqūlūna ... wa qinā 'adhāban-nār (Those who say: "Our Sustainer! We believe: forgive us, then, our sins, and save us from the torment of the Fire"). This further elaborates the character of the righteous who respond to the call of the Qur'ān. They are truly and sincerely remorseful for their past lapses. They repent and enthusiastically respond to the call to faith, piety and good deeds. Imbedded in this is also an invitation to join the ranks of the believers to those who were still reluctant to respond to the truth and gave rather spurious excuses for not doing so.

Aṣ-ṣābirīn wa-ṣ ṣādiqīna ... *Ṣabr* and *ṣidq*, are two qualities that further define the salient characteristics of the believers and their essential moral attributes as the bearers of the Qur'ānic message. This verse portrays a moral character and a personality in contrast to the one described above in verse 14: "alluring to human beings is the enjoyment of love of things they covet ..."

This verse mentions five moral characteristics: *ṣabr, ṣidq, qunūt, infāq* and *istighfār*.

Ṣabr in essence means to stand firm and to pursue the truth steadfastly under all kinds of conditions and circumstances, whether easy or difficult, whether one is afflicted with poverty, disease, or distress and even when faced with bitter hostility. To pursue truth with fortitude and to confront whatever comes one's way patiently – without despairing or losing heart, without regret or complaint and refusing to surrender to falsehood come what may. A major portion of the *dīn* – the religion of Islam – is based on *ṣabr* or patience and fortitude.

In the absence of *ṣabr*, one can easily be distracted from the straight path by greed and other base emotions and succumb to evil. Anyone cherishing the desire to follow and abide by truth must, first and foremost, be patient. Inevitably, such a person is bound to encounter hurdles and hardships in this path at every turn where his patience will be his only companion and weapon. In essence, Islam has appropriately been described as half gratitude and half patience. Human experience shows that in the absence of patience one cannot even be truly grateful. The two are inseparable: one cannot exist without the other. People addressed here are invited to the most sublime goal: the truth. They are encouraged to attain its pinnacle through *ṣabr* or patience. *Ṣabr* is specially highlighted here as the most important means to scale the heights and reach the pinnacle – their goal of truth.

Ṣidq

Ṣidq in essence means being in full harmony with reality or facts. It signifies firmness and solidity or substantial nature. A spear with patently strong joints is described as *ṣadiqa-l ku'ūb,* which when tested, is actually found to be strong, firm and reliable. Some of the manifestations of *ṣidq* are harmony between heart and tongue, words and deeds, the apparent and the internal life of a person, and consistency between one's beliefs and actions. All these are various manifestations of *ṣidq* and they give human life light and beauty, and its apparent and hidden dimensions. Without these moral qualities – truth and patience, human existence loses all meaning. It is these higher values that provide humans with the incentive to soar to higher spiritual realms, and to the pinnacle of moral and spiritual excellence. This in turn further reinforces patience and endurance.

Qunūt

As to *qunūt*, its essence is humility and self-abasement before Allah, born out of the realisation of a sense of gratitude for the countless blessings of Allah and His limitless power, glory and majesty. *Qunūt* transforms any blessing received into a form or means of showing our gratitude to Him, while any misfortune or hardship encountered along the way offers yet a fresh opportunity to exercise patience. A true believer is grateful to his Sovereign Sustainer when blessed, and is patient when tried with hardship and distress. Whatever the case, he always turns to Allah and so steadily moves towards his goal. *Qunūt* initially denotes humility of mind and heart and it is essentially reflected in one's appearance, speech, gait and character. In fact one's entire life is coloured by it and the slightest change in heart and mind is directly reflected in appearance and conduct. *Qunūt* is thus the direct opposite of the proud and arrogant attitude born out of the mistaken notion that whatever Divine blessings one receives are one's by right for which no gratitude is due to anyone. It is also the opposite of the impatience and fretfulness that come from the lack of the qualities of *ṣidq* (truthfulness) and *ṣabr* (patience).

Infāq

As for *infāq*, it is obviously the opposite of spending on worldly pleasures for one's selfish gratification, as mentioned in the above verse. The overblown lust for worldly pleasures that overwhelms a person and prevents him from his obligations toward Allah and fellow human beings is described in the Qur'ān as things "made alluring to human beings". The characteristic of spending on others is a clear proof that in one's eyes the life hereafter and its enduring blessings are more important and worth striving for rather than wasting one's energies on worthless trinkets of this transitory life on earth. On the other hand, a person who avoids spending in the cause of Allah actually seems to be saying that he cares for nothing other than the worldly life and its transient pleasures. Such a person has no concept whatever in his or her mind of any life in the hereafter.

Istighfār

Istighfār means calling upon Allah and supplicating to Him in humility to cover one's lapses, sins and shortcomings. Such a lament and cry for help is the result of the humility and fear induced in a person on realising the infinite blessings of his Sustainer upon him along with the thought that He is the Lord of impeccable justice and retribution. The addition of the words "who pray for forgiveness in the early hours of the morning" shows that this is the most suitable time for the acceptance of supplications for forgiveness. This time is most secure against the hazards of showing off, and most appropriate for concentrating the mind and pondering earnestly over the messages of Allah. Both the Qur'ān and Ḥadīth have variously stressed and explained its importance. It is indeed a great bounty of our Most Generous Sustainer that He has not only directed us to make *istighfār* but has also at the same time taught us about the most suitable time for its acceptance.

Pondering over the contents of this section, we find that on the one hand it describes the salient characteristics of the bearers of the Qur'ān, while on the other it underlines the obstacles and hurdles preventing some from responding to its message. The latter have no patience to withstand temptations, the fascination with physical pleasures or the whisperings of the devil. They lack the truthfulness that can reveal the disharmony between their beliefs and actions, their words and deeds, and between their public and private life. They also have no *qunūt*, the humility that should have helped them surrender to the command of their sovereign Creator to show their gratitude. They are stiff-necked and, in their perversity, refuse to bow and recognise their true Benefactor. They are indifferent to the idea of an eternal life in the hereafter and refuse to forgo the worldly pleasures of this life and to wait for the enduring pleasures in the afterlife. They also have no perception or appreciation of God's blessings and retribution strong enough to leave their comfortable beds and to stand before their Sustainer in the early hours of morning in prayer and supplication. The subtle way these characteristics are presented here imply that only those who have wholeheartedly embraced the message of the Qur'ān and are actively striving for its cause possess all these characteristics. In fact, because of these characteristics, they are the ones fit to bear this onerous burden.

Verses 18-22: thematic continuity

The above theme is here revisited with a rather grand opening. The upshot of it is that since the beginning, Allah, His angels and all those endowed with true knowledge have testified to the fact that there is no god other than Allah, the one and only true God, Who upholds justice and is mighty and wise. The religion that He has chosen for human beings to help them abide by justice is Islam, the only true religion with Him. This is the religion revealed to us through His prophets and messengers, but on account of their rivalry the Jews and the Christians deliberately and knowingly introduced disagreements in this religion and instead of Islam set up for themselves the idols of Judaism and Christianity.

Addressing the Prophet, the revelation tells him that if the Jews and the Christians disputed the validity of the true religion, he should not be overly concerned. Instead, he should openly and clearly declare to the People of the Book and the Quraysh that those who are with him have decided to follow the religion of Islam. It is for them now to decide what course of action they would follow: the path of Islam or persistence in their error. The Prophet's responsibility was only to convey the message to them. Having conveyed the message to them, their affairs rest with Allah. He is well aware of the condition of all and He will punish the guilty for their crimes.

The people of the Book are then warned that for those who have persistently rejected the messages of Allah, wilfully killed Allah's prophets and persecuted and tortured their own pious religious reformers who called for justice and fairness, it is time that they should be called to account. They cannot escape Divine justice. All their deeds, both in this as well as the next life, will be rendered worthless without anyone being able to give them help or support. Bearing these points in mind, let us read and study the following verses:

Allah, the angels and the people of knowledge all bear witness that there is no god but He, upholding justice. There is no god other than Him. He is supreme and most wise. (18)

شَهِدَ ٱللَّهُ أَنَّهُۥ لَآ إِلَٰهَ إِلَّا هُوَ
وَٱلْمَلَٰٓئِكَةُ وَأُو۟لُوا۟ ٱلْعِلْمِ قَآئِمًۢا بِٱلْقِسْطِ ۚ لَآ
إِلَٰهَ إِلَّا هُوَ ٱلْعَزِيزُ ٱلْحَكِيمُ ﴿١٨﴾

The true religion acceptable to Allah is Islam. The People of the Book caused differences in it, after they had received knowledge, merely on account of their mutual jealousy. Those who reject the signs of Allah should bear in mind that Allah is swift in reckoning. (19)

إِنَّ ٱلدِّينَ عِندَ ٱللَّهِ ٱلْإِسْلَٰمُ ۗ وَمَا
ٱخْتَلَفَ ٱلَّذِينَ أُوتُوا۟ ٱلْكِتَٰبَ إِلَّا
مِنۢ بَعْدِ مَا جَآءَهُمُ ٱلْعِلْمُ بَغْيًۢا
بَيْنَهُمْ ۗ وَمَن يَكْفُرْ بِـَٔايَٰتِ ٱللَّهِ فَإِنَّ
ٱللَّهَ سَرِيعُ ٱلْحِسَابِ ﴿١٩﴾

If they dispute with you about this, tell them, "I and my followers have submitted ourselves to Allah," and ask the People of the Book and the unlettered Arabs, "Are you also ready to submit in Islam?" If they embrace Islam in this way they are guided aright, but if they turn away then you are only responsible for conveying the message to them. Allah sees and watches His servants. (20)

فَإِنْ حَآجُّوكَ فَقُلْ أَسْلَمْتُ وَجْهِىَ لِلَّهِ
وَمَنِ ٱتَّبَعَنِ ۗ وَقُل لِّلَّذِينَ أُوتُوا۟ ٱلْكِتَٰبَ
وَٱلْأُمِّيِّـۧنَ ءَأَسْلَمْتُمْ ۚ فَإِنْ أَسْلَمُوا۟ فَقَدِ
ٱهْتَدَوا۟ ۖ وَّإِن تَوَلَّوْا۟ فَإِنَّمَا عَلَيْكَ
ٱلْبَلَٰغُ ۗ وَٱللَّهُ بَصِيرٌۢ بِٱلْعِبَادِ ﴿٢٠﴾

Those who have been rejecting the signs of Allah, killing the prophets unjustly and putting to death those among the people who called for justice and fairness, give them the news of a painful chastisement. (21)

إِنَّ ٱلَّذِينَ يَكۡفُرُونَ بِـَٔايَٰتِ ٱللَّهِ
وَيَقۡتُلُونَ ٱلنَّبِيِّـۧنَ بِغَيۡرِ حَقّٖ
وَيَقۡتُلُونَ ٱلَّذِينَ يَأۡمُرُونَ
بِٱلۡقِسۡطِ مِنَ ٱلنَّاسِ فَبَشِّرۡهُم
بِعَذَابٍ أَلِيمٍ ٢١

They are the ones whose works in this life and in the hereafter are rendered in vain. They will have no helpers. (22)

أُوْلَٰٓئِكَ ٱلَّذِينَ حَبِطَتۡ أَعۡمَٰلُهُمۡ
فِي ٱلدُّنۡيَا وَٱلۡأٓخِرَةِ وَمَا لَهُم
مِّن نَّٰصِرِينَ ٢٢

WORD STUDY AND EXPLANATION

شَهِدَ ٱللَّهُ أَنَّهُۥ لَآ إِلَٰهَ إِلَّا هُوَ وَٱلۡمَلَٰٓئِكَةُ وَأُوْلُواْ ٱلۡعِلۡمِ قَآئِمَۢا بِٱلۡقِسۡطِۚ لَآ إِلَٰهَ إِلَّا هُوَ
ٱلۡعَزِيزُ ٱلۡحَكِيمُ ١٨

Allah, the angels and the people of knowledge all bear witness that there is no god but He, upholding justice. There is no god other than Him. He is supreme and most wise. (18)

Three aspects of testimony of *tawḥīd* (belief in the oneness of God) and *qisṭ* (Divine justice)

The testimony of angels and the people endowed with knowledge is cited here: there is only one true God, Allah, and He upholds and runs all affairs with justice. This testimony is significant on three counts.

Testimony of creation

Firstly, it is the testimony of all creation. The way its Creator has created this universe and the way He is running its affairs and looking after it, make it abundantly clear that He is one and only one, that He has no partner and that He shares power with none. The Qur'ān has referred to this testimony of the oneness of God at great length and therefore needs no further elaboration. Furthermore, from the order prevalent in the physical universe, the Qur'ān shows that in every corner of it, its Creator has placed a balance of justice. No part of it can stray off the course appointed for it in the slightest degree. This shows that the Originator and Creator of this universe loves justice, equity and order and does not like any of His creatures to deviate from this path. Of the various instances where this is referred to in the Qur'ān, we refer here to only one verse:

> *The sun and the moon follow courses (exactly) computed; and the stars and the trees – all (alike) bow in adoration. And the firmament He has raised high, and He has set up therein the balance (of justice), (All this is) in order that you may not transgress (due) balance, but establish weight with justice and fall not short in the balance.* (Sūrah ar-Raḥmān, 55:5-9)

This clearly shows that its Creator has indeed made justice and balance critical to the way the universe functions. All things in this universe, the sun and the moon, trees and stones, the heavens and the earth, faithfully follow the courses appointed for them without the least deviation or reluctance. Their every move is measured and fixed. They seem to be telling the human being that he too, in the same way, should follow the just course appointed for him by Allah and not exceed the bounds.

Testimony of history

With this universal testimony also comes the history of nations. The Qur'ān refers to history to show that this world is not a playground of blind chaotic forces but is managed and run by its Creator and Controller in accord with a just and fair system. He allows various nations to appear on the stage of history and tests them on whether they use their powers and faculties within the framework of His equitable law or follow the path of transgression and insolence. If a people exercise their powers within the prescribed limits, He lets them flourish and grow, but when they deviate from these laws and take the path of insolence, He grants them respite for a certain time. Then, if they still do not mend their ways, He destroys them and replaces them with another people. The Qur'ān has dealt with this *sunnat Allah* or Divine law in detail.

Testimony of human nature

Secondly, human nature is referred to as evidence that Allah has fashioned it in such a way that it constitutes a standing witness not only to *tawḥīd* (the affirmation of the oneness of God) but also reinforces the fact that He stands firm on justice. We have at various places in this book touched on the evidence based on this testimony and have also written specifically on this subject in our two books entitled, *Ḥaqīqat Shirk* (The True Nature of Polytheism) and *Ḥaqīqat Tawḥīd* (The Essence of *Tawḥīd*). For a detailed discussion of these subjects please refer to these two books. It is because of this innate, monotheistic disposition of human nature that the Qur'ān calls monotheism or *tawḥīd* the natural religion of human beings: "the nature as designed by Allah according to which He has created humankind." (ar-Rūm, 30:30). It is against the backdrop of this instinctive human yearning for justice that the Qur'ān poses the question: "What, shall We then treat those who submit like the guilty? What is the matter with you? How ill do you judge!" (al-Qalam, 68:35-36).

Testimony of revelation

Thirdly, revelation is presented to corroborate the evidence of creation and human nature. Throughout history Allah has sent numerous prophets and messengers to reveal to humans His will, commandments and laws, explaining what He likes and what He does not like for them. All these prophets and messengers invariably testified that Allah is one and only one, that He stands firm on justice, running all affairs in perfect justice and fairness. The evidence for this is found in the traditions and scriptures of various peoples, who unfortunately ignored all these traditions and embraced instead concepts and beliefs that were contradictory to a belief in the oneness of God and the justice on which His dominion rests. This wrong conduct of these errant nations, however, does not mean that Allah no longer possesses His sublime attributes. In fact, He is, and will always be, in possession of these Divine attributes. Consequently, as mentioned above in the introductory remarks to this segment, He revealed the Qur'ān as a criterion to make truth distinct from falsehood, and to guide human beings afresh to the straight path – the path of truth and justice, so that no one has any excuse to persist in error for lack of guidance.

From the above details, it is clear that the evidence for *tawḥīd* (the oneness of Allah) and His standing firm on justice is not based on any solitary aspect but is three-fold. The creation of the physical universe, its order and functioning and its history all corroborate and support the above evidence. This is further upheld and supported by human nature and still further corroborated by all the prophets and messengers who were raised from among humans. Without exception, they all proclaimed this essential truth: God is one, He stands firm on justice and runs His dominion in perfect justice. This is briefly stated in this verse, but is elaborated in detail in the rest of the Qur'ān.

Verses 18-22

Testimony of the angels

Along with His own testimony, Allah has also cited the testimony of the angels, who are instrumental in the enforcement of His will in the universe. It is through their agency that He sends revelation to His prophets. As the prime witnesses, they stand at the head of those bearing witness to the oneness of Allah and His justice. Their testimony, apart from being a statement of fact, is especially significant because some foolish people set them as partners with Allah and regarded them as a means of intercession with Him. Such a notion, if accepted, nullifies both the concept of *tawḥīd* and justice since it implies that through intercession evil can escape its punishment and the operation of perfect Divine justice can be subverted. This renders the notion of Allah being the guardian and upholder of perfect justice meaningless.

In order to remove this misunderstanding about the angels, the Qur'ān has cited their own confessions in this regard at several places. The angels are mentioned at one place as saying:

> *For every one of us there is a fixed place appointed, and we are indeed ranged in ranks (for service), and we are indeed those who declare His glory!* (aṣ-Ṣāffāt, 37:164-166).

For a detailed discussion about the angels, please refer to our comments on articles of faith as mentioned in Sūrah al Baqarah[8].

Testimony of the people of knowledge

Next, the testimony is mentioned of the people endowed with *al-'ilm* – a Qur'ānic term – meaning the true knowledge that is received through the prophets and messengers of Allah. This has also been discussed at another place. Throughout history, all those endowed with this knowledge have invariably believed in and testified to the oneness of Allah and that His dominion is established on justice. This is a reference to the reformers and callers to true religion who were raised in every age and who strived to cleanse Allah's religion of innovations, and who presented the Divine message in its purest form and reformed laws, customs, practices and morals in its light. These are the people who are referred to in the next verse as those "who called for justice and fairness" (*ya'murūna bi-l qisṭ*) many of whom were killed by the People of the Book.

A point of Qur'ānic wisdom worth noting here is that the people of knowledge are mentioned along with Allah and the angels, while along with

8. See comments on verse 177 of Sūrah al-Baqarah.

tawḥīd is mentioned justice and equity. This shows the importance of the people of knowledge in the sight of Allah and the pre-eminence of justice and equity in Divine law. The people of knowledge are placed in the same category with the angels while justice and equity occupy so prominent a place in the order of Divine attributes that it is appropriately placed and mentioned next to *tawḥīd* or the affirmation of the oneness of Allah.

Qā'imam bi-l qisṭ,[9] is a phrase that means that Allah is one and only one, that all authority and powers rest with Him and that He uses these in accordance with perfect justice and equity.

Qisṭ, its meaning and significance

Qisṭ carries a sense usually described by words such as justice, truth and equity, its opposite being injustice, cruelty and other similar words. In thought, action, morals and character, in the outer form and manifestations, in fact in every part of life whether apparent or hidden, there is a point that is well within the boundary of natural disposition as created by the Creator and is clearly defined by certain constraints. This may be described as the middle point or a reference point in terms of justice and equity. The slightest deviation from this point signifies a deviation from justice and equity. In various areas of life and relationships, such a deviation is described in different ways. In some cases, it is called injustice and cruelty, while in other areas it is called ugliness and deformity while the opposite of this is symmetry and harmony, or truth and justice. In other areas, we call this beauty and elegance. The intrinsic reality, however, in all these cases, is always the same: whenever something is removed from its natural position it is corrupted and flawed, and when it is placed in its natural paradigm, alongside its pair, it regains its natural harmony and poise.

The Creator of the universe is its originator and its controller and likes order instead of disorder and chaos to prevail in it. He has fashioned the physical order in such a manner that all parts are in perfect harmony with one another. If at times, for some higher reason, He allows any flaw somewhere therein to appear, His powerful hand intervenes forthwith to set it right so that the harmony and balance on which this whole universe is based is not disturbed or threatened. His love of balance is also apparent in our area of life where He has granted us limited autonomy. Whenever we misuse our will and

9. Grammatically, we take the phrase *qā'imam bi-l qisṭ* as a circumstantial phrase showing condition (*ḥāl*) with the particle and the pronoun *annahu* omitted before it, so it would read: *annahu qā'imam bi-l qisṭ*.

create corruption in some sphere of action and morals, He grants us respite but only for a certain time. His love of justice does not allow anyone a free hand to follow his or her desires and lusts and upset order in His creation. Rather, He watches over His creation and calls all those guilty of injustice and disorder to account. He sets things right by eliminating any disharmony injected by human transgression and disobedience, because He sustains justice and governs with justice.

The law of accountability that He has laid down reflects this justice in human affairs. For this purpose, He sent the prophets and through them revealed the Divine law. And if there were any distortions and innovations introduced into the Divine system, reformers were raised from among humans to revive true religion, if need be, at the risk of their own lives. So He made the rise and fall of nations subject to their moral excellence or decline. Finally, it is for the ultimate and full manifestation of this justice that He has appointed a special day when the scales of justice will be set up to measure the good and evil each individual might have done in this earthly life and to determine the reward or punishment they would receive without the least injustice to anyone.

It is noteworthy that in the above verse the essence of *tawḥīd* – affirming that there is no god but He – is repeated twice, each time accompanied by two different attributes of Allah. In the first instance it is said that there is no god except Allah and that He is established in justice, while in the second it is said that there is no god beside Him and that He is *'Azīz* (mighty) and *Ḥakīm* (wise). For the People of the Book, who are addressed here, this style implies a serious warning. They are warned that Allah, the angels and all people of knowledge bear witness that there is no god except Allah, that He is not neutral or unconcerned with what happens in this world, and that He does not give people a free rein to indulge unhampered in their desires and lusts, without holding them accountable for their misdeeds. He is a Living, Self-Subsisting and all-Sustaining God and He will definitely make His just and fair system prevail whether people like it or not, and no one will be able to frustrate His will. And why should this not be so since He is the One True God and He is both Mighty and Wise. Both His might and wisdom strongly suggest that He must indeed be so, because if He is not, it would mean that He is helpless and is not concerned whether truth prevails or not, or that He is a capricious being who has created this world as a sport for self-amusement. Such a notion cannot be taken seriously about Allah, the Creator of this life and universe, the Just, Merciful and All-powerful God!

إِنَّ ٱلدِّينَ عِندَ ٱللَّهِ ٱلْإِسْلَٰمُ ۗ وَمَا ٱخْتَلَفَ ٱلَّذِينَ أُوتُوا۟ ٱلْكِتَٰبَ إِلَّا مِنۢ بَعْدِ
مَا جَآءَهُمُ ٱلْعِلْمُ بَغْيًۢا بَيْنَهُمْ ۗ وَمَن يَكْفُرْ بِـَٔايَٰتِ ٱللَّهِ فَإِنَّ ٱللَّهَ سَرِيعُ ٱلْحِسَابِ
١٩

The real religion acceptable to Allah is Islam. The People of the Book caused differences in it, after they had received the knowledge, merely on account of their mutual jealousy. Those who reject the signs of Allah should bear in mind that Allah is swift in reckoning. (19).

Islam is the only true revealed religion

The word *al-dīn* in the text means the real religion, the one revealed by Allah for the guidance of human beings. The prefix *al* before din is similar to the one before *al-kitāb,* as discussed in the beginning of our commentary on Sūrah al-Baqarah[10].

Al-'ilm means the true knowledge as revealed by Allah to guide to the straight path and to remove disagreements. As the upholder and sustainer of justice in life and the universe, Allah has revealed the true religion, teaching humans how to live and conduct themselves in this world. This religion is called Islam. As such, it constitutes a criterion for justice and equity and it is on this very principle that our physical universe functions. This religion is in full harmony with genuine human nature. All prophets and messengers raised from among the human race invited their fellow human beings essentially to this very religion. But because of mutual hostility and jealousy, people wrangled and disagreed among themselves. Jews and the Christians are one such obvious example. They set up separate versions of religion – Judaism and Christianity. The disagreement between them, however, was not based on any ignorance on their part, but was a result of mutual disagreements, animosity and insistence on their respective innovations that they had introduced in the true religion and which lead to ever more disagreements. They set up their separate religions although their disagreements were not based on any ignorance of the truth, but clearly were the outcome of their mutual rivalry, stubbornness and jealousy. As a result of this, they lost the great blessing – the guidance to the straight path – that was given to them. Allah, the Living, Self-subsisting, all-Sustaining and Just God, Who maintains and is established in justice, could not however allow this condition to continue and allow the

10. Please see *Pondering over the Qur'ān,* volume I, Sūrah al-Baqarah, verse 2. (Translator)

human race to be plunged into darkness once again. Hence came a fresh revelation of the just and pure system of life – Islam, in its perfected form, in order to guide humanity back to the straight path, the path of success in both this life and in the one to come.

Anyone persisting in their old ways and rejecting the final message of Allah will henceforth be called to account by their Creator and Sovereign Sustainer. The respite given to people should not deceive them into thinking that the day of reckoning is far off. The Prophet John the Baptist, (Yaḥyā), peace be upon him, is reported to have said: "The axe is laid to the root of the trees; every tree that does not bear good fruit is cut down and thrown into the fire" (Luke 3: 9). So will they also be judged, and soon.

In Sūrah al-Baqarah, the appearance of religious disagreement in human society is also mentioned. Please refer to our comments on verse 213 of Sūrah al-Baqarah:

> *Humankind was one single community, and Allah sent messengers with glad tidings and warnings; and with them He sent the Book in truth, to judge between people in matters wherein they differed. But the very people to whom these were given, differed among themselves, after the clear commandments had come to them, on account of selfish jealousy. Allah by His grace guided the believers to the truth, concerning that wherein they differed. For Allah guides whom He wills to a path that is straight.*

فَإِنْ حَآجُّوكَ فَقُلْ أَسْلَمْتُ وَجْهِيَ لِلَّهِ وَمَنِ ٱتَّبَعَنِ ۗ وَقُل لِّلَّذِينَ أُوتُوا۟ ٱلْكِتَـٰبَ وَٱلْأُمِّيِّـۧنَ
ءَأَسْلَمْتُمْ ۚ فَإِنْ أَسْلَمُوا۟ فَقَدِ ٱهْتَدَوا۟ ۖ وَّإِن تَوَلَّوْا۟ فَإِنَّمَا عَلَيْكَ ٱلْبَلَـٰغُ ۗ وَٱللَّهُ بَصِيرٌۢ
بِٱلْعِبَادِ ﴿٢٠﴾

If they dispute with you about this, tell them, I and my followers have submitted ourselves to Allah, and ask the People of the Book and the unlettered Arabs, Are you likewise ready to submit (to Allah) in Islam? If they embrace Islam in this way they are guided aright, but if they turn away then you are only responsible for conveying the message to them. Allah sees and watches His servants. (20).

Aslamtu waj-hiya li-llāhi, literally, I submit my countenance to Allah, means submitting one's whole self to Allah. The countenance of a person is the noblest part of his body and its submission to Allah implies one's total submission to Him. Similarly, bowing one's head to someone is expressive of obedience and submission and shows extreme humility and surrender. In the present context, 'submitting one's face to Allah' is initially used for embracing

Islam while, at the same time, emphasizing its real essence. This was a timely warning to the self-declared custodians of religion who were so vehemently opposed to Islam. It was a warning to them that they were waging a war against Allah, His final message and those who had responded to His call.

Ummī and *ummiyyūn*

Ummī (pl. *ummīyyūn)* means one who has not received any formal education or training in reading and writing, the unlettered or illiterate. The Qur'ān uses the word *ummīyyūn* for the descendants of Ismā'īl as a title, because they had maintained their Bedouin simplicity and were unused to any formal reading or writing. As a group, this marked them out from the descendants of Israel, the bearers of the revealed book. The "unlettered ones" or *ummīyyūn* was perhaps a title used initially for the Arabs by the People of the Book. The Torah also refers to Ismā'īl's descendants as the unlettered and desert people. The use of this word, however, implied no derogatory sense.

The Qur'ān uses this term merely to distinguish them from the People of the Book and also uses the term "unlettered prophet" for the prophet Muḥammad, peace be upon him. Its use refers to the prophecies found in the Torah about the prophet of Islam. The Arabs themselves used this term and this clearly shows that they did not consider it to be derogatory. According to some aḥādīth, it appears that the prophet, peace be upon him, used this term for his people. Thus, in one ḥadīth, he is reported to have said, "We are an unlettered people." At some places in the Qur'ān where it is used to convey a derogatory meaning, it is used in its literal sense. Hence in verse 2:78, the phrase *minhum ummīyyūna lā ya'lamūna-l kitāb.* There it refers to the illiterate among the Jewish community "who do not know the scripture."

'A 'aslamtum (Are you ready to submit (to Allah) in Islam?)

This is both an invitation and a warning, and reflects an overall sense of displeasure. This means: believe if you would, we are no longer ready to waste time in useless disputation with you. We have chosen our path and we do not want to spend our time in fruitless disputation.

The Jews and the Christians who had changed and distorted the religion of Allah, Islam, and are now opposing the Prophet and his message in the name of Judaism and Christianity, are in fact trying to defend their deliberate distortion of truth. They know very well the true nature of the message that Islam has brought them. It is therefore futile to engage in any argument with them. The Prophet, peace be upon him, is therefore told to declare to them as well as to the unlettered Arabs: "I and my companions have submitted ourselves to Allah and have resolved to follow the path of Islam. If you are willing, we welcome you. Come and join us, otherwise leave us alone. We no longer want to waste our time in futile disputation with you." The verse goes on to comfort the Prophet with the advice that if they still persist in their erstwhile ways, he should leave them alone, for he is responsible only for conveying the message to them and this he had already fulfilled. Now, their affair rests with Allah. He is watching and observing all their actions and He shall recompense them fully and equitably.

إِنَّ ٱلَّذِينَ يَكْفُرُونَ بِـَٔايَٰتِ ٱللَّهِ وَيَقْتُلُونَ ٱلنَّبِيِّـۧنَ بِغَيْرِ حَقٍّ وَيَقْتُلُونَ
ٱلَّذِينَ يَأْمُرُونَ بِٱلْقِسْطِ مِنَ ٱلنَّاسِ فَبَشِّرْهُم بِعَذَابٍ أَلِيمٍ ﴿٢١﴾

Those who have been rejecting the signs of Allah, killing the prophets unjustly and have been putting to death those among the people who called for justice and fairness, give them the news of a painful chastisement. (21)

Killing the prophets without any justification

In the clause *yaqtūluna-n nabbiyyīna bi-ghayri ḥaqqin* (killing the prophets unjustly), the phrase *bi-ghayr ḥaqqln* – unjustly, shows first of all the serious nature of their crime, as killing anyone unjustly is a grievous crime, especially the killing of a prophet of Allah. Secondly, it emphasises the pivotal importance of truth, *ḥaqq*, in relation to anything else. Even the prophets are subject to *ḥaqq* or truth. Our prophet, peace be upon him, has explained this basic importance of truth in several of his aḥādīth or sayings.

Those who called for justice and fairness

"Alladhīna ya'murūna bi-l qisṭ (those among the people who called for justice and fairness). This refers to those reformers who worked for the revival of religion among common people and who tried to rectify or eliminate the distortions of the Jews and the Christians in an effort to bring justice and truth in their lives. The Jews and the Christians treated them as they had the prophets from Allah. They used all means at their disposal to subvert the efforts of these reformers.

At the end of the previous verse it was stated: "Allah sees and watches His servants". This implies that He would guide or leave people astray depending on what each one deserved. In this verse, the implications of this statement become clearer. Those who have always rejected the messages of Allah, killed His prophets and others who from time to time tried to call them to reform and mend their ways and establish truth and justice in their lives – they would not change their ways, nor would they change their attitude and behaviour. They are used to perverting the course of justice and truth deliberately since they are violently opposed to anyone who tried to call them to true religion. Their descendants are blindly following in the footsteps of their forefathers who distorted the Torah and the Injīl and killed Allah's prophets and reformers. How could the Prophet, peace be upon him, expect that they would tolerate him and the book that he has brought with him and that stands for truth and justice? How can anyone then expect them to do anything other than what their forefathers did? They have scant regard for truth or Divine guidance. The frustration of prophet Jesus, peace be upon him, as reported in the Gospel, concerning the children of the Prophets' killers that they will believe and be saved can be understood in a similar context. The Qur'ān has described this aspect of their character in its own unique style. On account of their persistent misbehaviour and insolence, they have lost the ability to see and embrace truth or to receive the good news of enduring success. Give them rather the news of a painful punishment that awaits them in the life hereafter.

أُوْلَٰٓئِكَ ٱلَّذِينَ حَبِطَتۡ أَعۡمَٰلُهُمۡ فِي ٱلدُّنۡيَا وَٱلۡأٓخِرَةِ وَمَا لَهُم مِّن نَّٰصِرِينَ ٢٢

They are the ones whose works in this life and in the hereafter are rendered in vain. They will have no helpers. (22)

Ḥabiṭa ʿamal or rendering one's work in vain means wastage of all one's efforts efforts and strivings. The ostensibly pious works of such people are, in the words of Jesus, peace be upon him, akin to "straining out a gnat while swallowing a camel"; their actions are hollow and useless and will not bring them any reward in the hereafter. As to the efforts that they were exerting against Islam and the Qur'ān, to frustrate the re-establishment of a true and just system of life, these will similarly fail and they will end up as losers both in this life and in the life to come. At the same time, it is also predicted that they would find no helper to save them from humiliation. They will fail to achieve their purpose, no matter what help and support they may receive from any group or nation. History bears witness to the truth of the Qur'ānic prediction.

Belief in Divine justice is an integral article of faith

The message of these verses for the Muslim community is clear, as explained above. Belief in Allah is strengthened by the knowledge that His dominion is firmly established on justice. This is most significant as a part of faith. It occupies a most prominent place in the scheme of Islam, so much so that justice and Islam are almost synonymous and interchangeable. In view of the importance of justice in Islamic teachings, we would like to give here some of the observations of Ustādh Farāhi on this subject for the guidance of those who would like to delve deeper into the wisdom of *dīn* or true religion, as enshrined in Islam. According to Ustādh Farāhi, this attribute is significant for the following reasons:

Four aspects of *īmān bil qisṭ* (belief in Divine justice)

Firstly, īmān, or faith, is derived from *amān* or trust. In other words, trust is its intrinsic part. This means that for a person to have faith, he must have a firm belief in the existence of Allah. This cannot be achieved unless we accept that reason is initially given to humans in order to guide rather than misguide them. Human reason is an instrument of justice placed within human beings. This in turn leads us to yet another conclusion: the Creator has created and fashioned nature on the principles of truth and justice, as He essentially loves justice and wills to establish and confirm it in all its forms. All these conclusions are rational imperatives and are rather self-evident truths. This shows that it is impossible to prove the truth of anything without accepting that their Creator is true and just, and hence all His acts can be verified and affirmed as true and just. Just as this is essential from the rational standpoint, so also it is morally essential because the moral imperatives likewise constitute an important proof for truth and justice. Briefly, this may be explained by saying that Allah has ingrained virtue in human nature and has placed in human hearts an inclination to respect and accept it. How can we then accept that Allah does not like virtue while we ourselves hold virtue so dear and desirable? How can we be sure of the validity and soundness of our love for virtue without being also sure of our Creator's love for virtue? After all, we do good deeds and acts of virtue to please Him since we believe that He likes righteousness and goodness. Similarly, we attribute the best attributes to Him since we are convinced that our choice of these attributes as the "best attributes" is sound and reflects the soundness of our nature.

Secondly, the essence of *īmān* or faith is love for Allah. We believe in a Deity Whom we adore and love, to Whom we look with hope and strive to win His pleasure. This is not possible unless we firmly believe that He is free of all traces of injustice and cruelty and that He will reward only those who obey Him and punish those who justly deserve such recompense for their misdeeds. To love an unjust and cruel master is utterly abhorrent to human nature.

Thirdly, the incentive to believe in Allah that arises out of our reflecting over His blessings and the manifestations of His grace is rooted in our sense of gratitude. But this sense of gratitude becomes active only when we accept that we owe it to Him as our true Benefactor and as a necessary consequence of His blessings upon us. That is why the Qur'ān describes *shirk*, or associating others with Allah, as injustice; while *īmān*, or belief, is described as an act of gratitude. Under this principle, the privilege of entitlement to rights is linked to the obligation of establishing justice as a necessary condition. This is an obvious truth about the Islamic Sharī'ah or law. Every Divine law is essentially based on justice and equity.

Fourthly, the first fruit of belief, or *īmān*, is obedience to Allah while the fruit of obedience is attainment of the pleasure of Allah. This relationship between actions and their effects has been established by Allah through His acts of creation and command and His arrangement and control of affairs. He has explained and guided us to this right way of obedience by various means. As we fully believe in these consequences of human actions, we obey and serve our Creator and Sustainer and place our trust in His promise. In the absence of such a faith and trust in His promise, the entire basis and fabric of our actions and our life collapses. Thereafter, we will have no option but to put our trust in hopes and beliefs like those of the Christians, for example, who pin their hopes on the false notion of intercession by Jesus whom they worship as a deity and whom they love more than they love Allah. Or, like the Jews, we would be utterly lost as they were, due to their injudicious behaviour. They refused to accept the Divine decision because of pride and transgression and are still adrift. They behaved as if in their sight Allah had instituted no specific law to distinguish the good from the evil. To safeguard ourselves against such deviance, it is essential to believe that Allah is established in justice and maintains justice and, moreover, that all His promises are true as He has told us: "The word of your Sovereign Sustainer does find its fulfilment in truth and in justice."[11]

Consideration of the above four points will clearly show that the belief in justice – *īmān bi-l qisṭ* – is an integral article of belief and on it rest some extremely important and basic creedal, moral and legal issues.

---

11. Sūrah al-An'ām, 6:119.

Verses 18-22

VERSES 23-27: THEMATIC CONTINUITY

This segment of verses begins with an expression of surprise at the condition of these deniers of the Qur'ān. Being the bearers of the Book or Scripture, they were justifiably expected to be pleased on finding afresh a part of the book that they had lost through their misfortune. They were also expected to welcome it, settle their differences in its light and follow the path of truth and justice once again. Instead, however, they adopted the usual path of aversion and rejection.

The Qur'ān gives us a clue to an important cause of their aversion. They think that they are a chosen people and wrongly believe that no matter what they do, they are immune from any Divine chastisement. And even if they are punished and consigned to hell, it will be only for a very short time, to be cleansed of their sins and then sent to Paradise. This is a pure fabrication of theirs and it has no basis in reality. But this self-delusion has made them completely heedless of the day of reckoning that is bound to come to pass when they will be called to account for their performance in this life. That day, they will find the complete record of all their deeds before them, to be judged with perfect justice without any favour or prejudice.

This is followed by a declaration that both the Jews and the Christians are being removed from the moral leadership of the human race. In their place, a new community fully capable of this trust – the Divine Sharī'ah – is being entrusted with it. Allah is the Sovereign Sustainer of this universe and it is for Him alone to give, or to take away, this honour to whomever He pleases. He alone bestows honour or afflicts with humiliation. With Him alone rests the power to cause the day to enter into night or the night into the day, or to bring the dead out of the living and the living out of the dead.

All this is couched in the form of a supplication. There is a clear hint in this supplication that it is to Allah alone that human beings should turn for help and support. It is indeed an onerous responsibility and a sacred trust from Allah and only by His grace and support can they successfully discharge this trust. To Him alone should they direct their supplications for comfort and strength to fulfil their trust successfully. Bearing this in mind, let us now study these verses.

Just consider the case of those who have been given a portion of the Book. They are invited to the Book of Allah, to judge between them, but a party among them turn back and they are the ones who turn back and decline. (23)

أَلَمۡ تَرَ إِلَى ٱلَّذِينَ أُوتُواْ نَصِيبٗا مِّنَ
ٱلۡكِتَٰبِ يُدۡعَوۡنَ إِلَىٰ كِتَٰبِ ٱللَّهِ لِيَحۡكُمَ
بَيۡنَهُمۡ ثُمَّ يَتَوَلَّىٰ فَرِيقٞ مِّنۡهُمۡ وَهُم
مُّعۡرِضُونَ ٢٣

This is because they say: "The Fire shall not touch us but for a few numbered days." Their forgeries have deceived them concerning their own religion. (24)

ذَٰلِكَ بِأَنَّهُمۡ قَالُواْ لَن تَمَسَّنَا ٱلنَّارُ
إِلَّآ أَيَّامٗا مَّعۡدُودَٰتٖۖ وَغَرَّهُمۡ فِي دِينِهِم مَّا
كَانُواْ يَفۡتَرُونَ ٢٤

But how (will they fare) when We gather them together for a day about which there is no doubt, and each soul will be fully recompensed for what it had earned, and they will not be wronged? (25)

فَكَيۡفَ إِذَا جَمَعۡنَٰهُمۡ لِيَوۡمٖ لَّا رَيۡبَ فِيهِ
وَوُفِّيَتۡ كُلُّ نَفۡسٖ مَّا كَسَبَتۡ وَهُمۡ
لَا يُظۡلَمُونَ ٢٥

Say: "O Allah! Possessor of all Dominion! You give power to whom You please, and You take away power from whom You please. You endow with honour whom You please, and You bring low whom You please. In Your hand is all good. Verily, over all things You have power. (26).

قُلِ ٱللَّهُمَّ مَٰلِكَ ٱلۡمُلۡكِ تُؤۡتِي ٱلۡمُلۡكَ
مَن تَشَآءُ وَتَنزِعُ ٱلۡمُلۡكَ مِمَّن تَشَآءُ
وَتُعِزُّ مَن تَشَآءُ وَتُذِلُّ مَن تَشَآءُۖ بِيَدِكَ
ٱلۡخَيۡرُۖ إِنَّكَ عَلَىٰ كُلِّ شَيۡءٖ قَدِيرٞ ٢٦

"You cause the night to gain on the day, and You cause the day to gain on the night; You bring the living out of the dead, and You bring the dead out of the living; and You give sustenance to whom You please, without measure." (27)

تُولِجُ ٱلَّيۡلَ فِي ٱلنَّهَارِ وَتُولِجُ ٱلنَّهَارَ فِي
ٱلَّيۡلِۖ وَتُخۡرِجُ ٱلۡحَيَّ مِنَ ٱلۡمَيِّتِ وَتُخۡرِجُ
ٱلۡمَيِّتَ مِنَ ٱلۡحَيِّۖ وَتَرۡزُقُ مَن تَشَآءُ بِغَيۡرِ
حِسَابٖ ٢٧

WORD STUDY AND EXPLANATION

أَلَمْ تَرَ إِلَى ٱلَّذِينَ أُوتُوا۟ نَصِيبًا مِّنَ ٱلْكِتَٰبِ يُدْعَوْنَ إِلَىٰ كِتَٰبِ ٱللَّهِ لِيَحْكُمَ بَيْنَهُمْ ثُمَّ يَتَوَلَّىٰ فَرِيقٌ مِّنْهُمْ وَهُم مُّعْرِضُونَ ﴿٢٣﴾

Just consider the case of those who have been given a portion of the Book. They are invited to the Book of Allah, to judge between them, but a party among them turn back and they are the ones who turn back and decline. (23)

Significance of '*a lam tara*' as the opening of the verse

The verse opens with the words '*A lam tara…*' (literally, Have you seen or considered…). The significance of this form of address as discussed in Sūrah al-Baqarah, though commonly found in the second person singular is always used for groups as well. Thus, when a group of people is so addressed it implies that each and every member of the group is directly addressed. Besides, it is also expressive of an implied sense of surprise at the behaviour, conduct and response of such people.

The relationship between the Qur'ān and the previous scriptures is as of a whole to a part

The words *naṣībam mina-l kitāb* (a portion of the Book) in the text refers to the *Tawrāh* and the *Injīl* while *kitābi-llāhi* (the Book of Allah) means the Qur'ān. Just as the relationship between the Islamic Sharī'ah and the earlier revealed religions is like that of a whole to a portion, similarly the relationship between the Qur'ān and the previous scriptures is like that of a whole to a part. The Islamic law was revealed gradually according to the gradual evolution of the human mind and human society. We, the human beings, were given the Divine law and the Book in their perfect form only when we were finally able to fully appreciate and understand them. Previously, through earlier scriptures, humans were given necessary instructions and laws according to their conditions and needs during their particular period of history. These were, however, part of the same Scripture and the Law that were in their entirety to be given to humanity at a later stage in history. Thus the teachings of the Israelite prophets are not something different from those of the Final Prophet, Muḥammad, peace be upon him. They were part of the same teachings that were relevant to their particular conditions and circumstances. The Torah and the Injīl are similarly not unrelated and separate from the

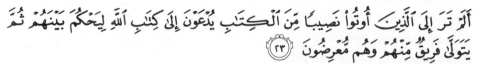

Qur'ān, the perfect Scripture revealed through Prophet Muḥammad, peace be upon him.

All revealed scriptures are different parts and chapters of one and the same Divine Book and in their original form they are all in perfect harmony with one another. Had the Torah and the Injīl been free from distortion, interpolation and corruption, one would have noticed little difference between them and the teachings of the Qur'ān except what may be found between a summary and detail or the beginning and the completion. Even today an insightful reader can easily discern the thread of uniformity running through them and come to the conclusion that they are indeed the offshoots of one and the same noble tree or the rays of the same blessed light.

In the presence of this harmony and affinity between them, their bearers should have had no difficulty in recognising the Qur'ān as the true book of Allah, but blinded by their prejudices and bias and stubborn refusal to see, they turned their backs on it. How could a people who had read the introductory chapters of a book, who were well familiar with its special style and nature, who had received its preliminary instructions and teachings, who had known about its prophecies and who were actually waiting for the arrival of the prophesied Prophet – how could such people fail to recognise the Sacred Book when it was presented to them in its full splendour? How strange it is that they not only failed to recognise it, but turned away from it and behaved as if they knew nothing about it, that it was something utterly alien to them!

Purpose of the revelation of the Qur'ān – to settle disagreements

Li yaḥkuma baynahum (to judge between them). These words describe the purpose of the Qur'ān that should have been welcomed by the People of the Book if they had any real regard for the Divine law or Sharī'ah. As mentioned above, Allah had revealed the Torah and the Injīl for their guidance, but they created a host of disagreements in them. To settle these disagreements and to clarify the truth, Allah revealed the Qur'ān. This is reiterated to emphasise that they are invited to embrace the truth not because of selfish motives on the part of the caller but, in all sincerity, for their own good. They are asked to accept the truth so that the disagreements that they had created concerning the Divine law could be settled once and for all in its light. The guidance that they had lost could then be restored to its pristine purity for their benefit and guidance.

Thumma yatawalla farīqum-minhum wa hum mu'riḍūn. The word *thumma* used in the text is expressive of surprise. And the words *farīqum-*

minhum do not mean that only a small group of the People of the Book is averse to Allah's book, because as we know they were collectively guilty of this crime. Only a few from among them, however, as is clear from other places in the Qur'ān, finally embraced Islam. As such, the real significance of the word *minhum* (among them) is the emphasis on the surprise that this group who were averse to the book of Allah was from among the People of the Book, They were expected to be the first and foremost in welcoming and believing in it. Instead of this, they were the first to reject it and oppose it.

Mindset of the Jewish community

The concluding words of the verse – *wa hum mu'riḍūn* – shed light on the true character of the People of the Book as a whole. Their aversion to truth is nothing new. They have always behaved in this manner regarding the truth. Implied in this sentence is a strong reprimand for the People of the Book and also a message of consolation and hope for the Prophet, peace be upon him. The verse tells him that if the people – whose aversion to truth has become their second nature – do not respond to your message of truth, there is indeed no blame on you nor it is because of any flaw in your message. This aversion to truth is a natural consequence of their perversion and corruption. Fresh springs of water cannot flow out of the dry and barren rocks that they have turned into.

ذَٰلِكَ بِأَنَّهُمْ قَالُوا۟ لَن تَمَسَّنَا ٱلنَّارُ إِلَّآ أَيَّامًا مَّعْدُودَٰتٍ ۖ وَغَرَّهُمْ فِى دِينِهِم مَّا كَانُوا۟ يَفْتَرُونَ ﴿٢٤﴾

This is because they say: "The Fire shall not touch us but for a few numbered days". Their forgeries have deceived them concerning their own religion. (24)

The subject of this verse has already been dealt with in Sūrah al-Baqarah where we have explained all its aspects. There it is said: "And they say: 'The fire shall not touch us but for a few numbered days'. Say: 'Have you taken a promise from Allah, so Allah will not break His promise? Or do you attribute to Allah something of which you have no knowledge?' Certainly, those who earn evil, and are encompassed by their sins, they are the companions of the fire; they will remain in it forever. (2:80-81).

An example of false Jewish desires

The above verse in Sūrah al-Baqarah occurs in the context of refuting the baseless desires of the descendants of Israel which are unsupported even by their own scriptures. These were merely the fabrications of their scholars that had, over a period of time, become part of their laws. As a reflection of the popular vain desires, their masses cherished these fabrications. Their sole trust for success and salvation rested on these false notions and desires. Of these false notions, one was the idea that, being the descendants of Israel, they were a chosen people, and no matter how evil their actions in life or how serious their sins, there will be no abiding punishment for them in the hereafter. They will not be sent to hell and if at all they are, it will be only for a short while, and after being cleansed by the fire of their sins they will be sent to Paradise. Obviously, for a people with such a belief there was no need on their part to fulfil the real obligations that their religion prescribed for them. Why should such a people bother about the revealed scripture that is the Qur'ān and pay any attention to it, especially when it sought to bring them out of this fools' paradise and face their true obligations?

The Qur'ān categorically rejects this false belief of theirs as a fabrication against Allah and a slander. Allah never gave the descendants of Israel a license or a free hand to do whatever they wished, without holding them to account for their deeds. Nor did He ever give them the undertaking that they will be sent to Paradise after a short punishment for a limited number of days. On account of believing in such superstitions and innovations, they are deluded concerning their religion. Religion for them is no more than a number of their cherished desires and dreams according to which Allah owes them a long list of rights and privileges but imposes no corresponding responsibility upon them, apart from a few rituals.

فَكَيْفَ إِذَا جَمَعْنَٰهُمْ لِيَوْمٍ لَّا رَيْبَ فِيهِ وَوُفِّيَتْ كُلُّ نَفْسٍ مَّا كَسَبَتْ وَهُمْ لَا
يُظْلَمُونَ ﴿٢٥﴾

But how (will they fare) when we gather them together for a day about which there is no doubt, and each soul will be fully recompensed for what it had earned, and they will not be wronged? (25)

This refers to their vain desires and wishful thinking about the life in the hereafter. These will not avail them when they are gathered on the Day of decision to face the consequences of their misdeeds in this worldly life. The day of decision is inevitable and bound to come to pass. Grammatically, the particle *li* in *li yawmim la rayba fīhi* in our opinion can also give the sense of 'for' because it does carry an adverbial sense of space or time. Considering the rules of Arabic grammar, a *muḍāf* after the preposition (*ḥarf jarr*) may also be supposed as omitted. We have explained the verse bearing in mind this second aspect.

Verses 23-27

One attribute of this day, as described here, is that its advent is beyond any doubt; it will definitely come to pass. And its second attribute mentioned here is that every soul that day will be paid in full for whatever it does in this life without any loss or injustice. In other words, it is now for the People of the Book to heed this message considering the dire consequences that await them when they come out of their wishful thinking and find themselves face to face with reality.

قُلِ ٱللَّهُمَّ مَٰلِكَ ٱلْمُلْكِ تُؤْتِى ٱلْمُلْكَ مَن تَشَآءُ وَتَنزِعُ ٱلْمُلْكَ مِمَّن تَشَآءُ وَتُعِزُّ مَن
تَشَآءُ وَتُذِلُّ مَن تَشَآءُ ۖ بِيَدِكَ ٱلْخَيْرُ ۖ إِنَّكَ عَلَىٰ كُلِّ شَىْءٍ قَدِيرٌ ﴿٢٦﴾

تُولِجُ ٱلَّيْلَ فِى ٱلنَّهَارِ وَتُولِجُ ٱلنَّهَارَ فِى ٱلَّيْلِ ۖ وَتُخْرِجُ ٱلْحَىَّ مِنَ ٱلْمَيِّتِ وَتُخْرِجُ ٱلْمَيِّتَ
مِنَ ٱلْحَىِّ ۖ وَتَرْزُقُ مَن تَشَآءُ بِغَيْرِ حِسَابٍ ﴿٢٧﴾

Say: "O Allah! Possessor of all Dominion! You give power to whom You please, and You take away power from whom You please. You endow with honour whom You please, and You bring low whom You please. In Your hand is all good. Verily, over all things You have power. (26)
"You cause the night to gain on the day, and You cause the day to gain on the night; You bring the living out of the dead, and You bring the dead out of the living; and You give sustenance to whom You please, without measure." (27)

Immensely good news for the Prophet and the Muslims

This is a supplication taught to the Prophet, peace be upon him, and through him to his community. Its main points may be summarised as follows:

1. There is the immensely good news implied in it for the Muslim community. It promises them that despite the jealousy, hostility and intransigence of the People of the Book, the moral and spiritual leadership is being transferred to the children of Ismāʿīl. No matter how vehement the opposition of the descendants of Israel, previously entrusted with the moral and spiritual leadership of humankind, this cannot change the decree of Allah. He alone is the Sovereign. The dominion is His, and He takes it away from whomever He wishes and bestows it upon whomever He pleases. He alone bestows honour and He alone causes whomever He wishes to go down. He alone is the Possessor of all the treasures of good and He gives out of these to whomever He likes. The notion of the descendants of Israel that all good is exclusively for them alone and that no one else, especially the children of Ismāʿīl, will have any share in it, is false. This supplication utterly rejects this

false notion of theirs. In this there is a clear hint that the Sovereign Sustainer of this universe has finally decided to take away the keys of His treasure of goodness from its dishonest and treacherous custodians to give them to those who are honest and qualified to bear this sacred trust.

2. Together with this implied glad news in this supplication, there is also a warning to the descendants of Israel that flows naturally out of the above good news for the children of Ismā'īl. The transference of moral and spiritual leadership to the children of Ismā'īl means a loss for the descendants of Israel. By using terms such as appointing and dismissal, honour and humiliation, and both life and death, the Qur'ān pronounces the judgement concerning the fate of both its adherents and its opponents.

3. It also has a serious admonition for the Muslim community. Now that this great trust is being given to them they should not, like the Jews, be deluded into thinking that it is given to them because they were entitled to it or that they deserved it because of their race or lineage. They should clearly understand that it is purely a bounty of Allah and the Muslims will continue to enjoy it so long as they discharge the obligations that go with this trust, honestly and faithfully, and continuously seek Allah's help and guidance in this regard.

From the above details, it is clear that this verse is an announcement of the removal of the Jews from the position of moral leadership while conveying good news for the Muslim community. It is couched, however, as a supplication rather than a declaration and announcement of good news. For this, there are two reasons. Firstly, at the time of the revelation of this verse, all these events were still hidden in the womb of the future and for things still hidden from view, this is clearly the most suitable style. It teaches the Muslim to pray and supplicate for these blessings. Secondly, implied in this style is the subtle hint that the Muslim community should receive this glad news not with pride or arrogance but with a deep sense of humility, modesty, and submissiveness and with a supplication from their hearts and on their lips. This is so because all power and authority rests solely with Allah. He alone has the power to give to whomever He wishes or to take away from whomever He pleases. Whatever we get, we get from Him alone and whatever we are deprived of, it is only by His command.

There are some other most eloquent examples in the Qur'ān of the use of a supplication to convey a glad tiding. For instance, a little before the hijrah of the Prophet, peace be upon him, to Madīnah, he was taught the following supplication:

Verses 23-27

Say: "O Allah! Let me enter with truth and honour, and likewise let me leave with truth and honour; and grant me from Your presence a supporting authority." And say: "Truth has (now) come, and falsehood has perished; for falsehood is bound to perish." (Sūrah Banī Israel, 17:80-81).

This supplication prefigures the imminent hijrah of the Prophet, peace be upon him, from Makkah to Madīnah. It also carries the good news for him that he will leave Makkah with honour and enter Madīnah, the abode of the hijrah, with honour. Besides, it also suggests that Allah will grant him a special escort that will lead him to security and victory with His permission. Implied in this supplication is also a subtle hint that the arrangements for his honourable entry are already in place long before his leaving Makkah, as indicated by the mention of entry in the supplication before the mention of "leaving" with truth and honour. Further consideration of the verse also shows that the hijrah is in fact a preamble to victory and the beginning of the ultimate triumph of truth. All these blessings are however, mentioned in the form of a supplication rather than that of an announcement of good news: the wisdom behind it is similar to what is mentioned above.

Testimony of nature and creation

Tūliju-l layla. The words *tūliju-l layla* (You cause the night to gain on the day) in the verse refer to the testimony from the physical universe in support of what is stated above. In other words, this means that Allah Who causes the night to enter the day and brings out the day from the night, and Who brings the living out of the dead and the dead out of the living, has the sole power to bestow authority or take it away from whomever He pleases. He gives honour or takes it away from whomever He wishes. He alone commands absolute authority, without sharing it with anyone.

A beautiful portrayal of natural phenomena is used in the description of the day entering the night and of the night entering the day. Apparently, both day and night seem to be in hot pursuit of each other, sometimes the night enters the day and sometimes the day is covered by the night, and this goes on incessantly and without any deviation from a well-defined pattern. In the Qur'ān the metaphor of night and day is used in various contexts, styles and manners. Similarly, signs of death coming out of life and life emerging from death are also manifest everywhere, in the physical world as well as in the moral and spiritual. There is also a subtle hint in this description of the moral decline (death) of the descendants of Israel and the signs of emerging new life in Arabs, the children of Ismāʿīl. The sapling planted in the fertile soil of Palestine by prophet Ibrāhīm had shrivelled and was dead, and in the words of prophet Yaḥyā, an axe was already at the root of the tree. As against this, the plant that Ibrāhīm had planted in the dry and barren land of Arabia and that had shown no signs of life so far, was beginning to bloom and blossom, and in the words of prophet Jesus, was soon to grow into a huge tree and provide shelter for a whole new world.

Two fold significance of *the words bi-ghayri ḥisāb* used in the verse

Rizq here refers to Divine bounty and blessing and not in any limited sense of subsistence. The phrase *bi-ghayri ḥisāb*, means two things. One, a sense of plenty; that is, Allah blesses whomever He wishes with His bounty and blessings without measure, as is alluded to in the verse *innamā yuwaffa-ṣ ṣābirūna ajrahum bi-ghayri ḥisāb* ("Those who patiently persevere will truly receive a reward without measure!" (Sūrah Az-Zumar, 39:10). Two, it also gives the sense of what is beyond one's imagination, as in the verse *wa yarzuq-hu min ḥaythu lā yaḥtasib* ("And He provides for him from (sources) he never could imagine)". (Sūrah aṭ-Ṭalāq, 65:3)

Verses 28-32: thematic continuity

From the above verses, it is clear that the People of the Book were now like a dilapidated house marked for demolition. The weaker Muslims and the hypocrites among them who were favourably inclined to the People of the Book, especially the Jews, are warned in the following verses that they were trying in vain to protect and safeguard a desolate house. Those looking for refuge behind its walls will perish under the debris of this ill-fated house.

The hypocrites are warned against their hypocrisy and their behaviour, hiding in their hearts the love for disbelief (*kufr*) and the disbelievers. They should not forget that nothing is hidden from Allah. He knows everything and a day will come when everyone will be confronted with whatever he or she had done openly or secretly. Allah will judge them in perfect justice, with everyone receiving his or her due reward or punishment. As Allah is most kind and compassionate to His servants, this warning is thus given to them, well before it comes to pass, to protect themselves against the dire consequences that await them on the day of judgement if they ignore this warning.

The discourse moves on to explain the true implications of belief (*īmān*) and love for Allah, saying that for those who claim to believe in and love Allah, it is not permissible for them to forge bonds of co-operation with His and His messenger's enemies. The only correct behaviour for them is to follow Allah's messenger and Allah will love them. Obedience to Allah's messenger is the only way to win the love of Allah. Those who deliberately take any course other than this are in fact disbelievers and Allah does not like disbelievers. With this in mind, let us now study the following verses.

لَّا يَتَّخِذِ ٱلْمُؤْمِنُونَ ٱلْكَٰفِرِينَ أَوْلِيَآءَ مِن
دُونِ ٱلْمُؤْمِنِينَ ۖ وَمَن يَفْعَلْ ذَٰلِكَ فَلَيْسَ
مِنَ ٱللَّهِ فِى شَىْءٍ إِلَّآ أَن تَتَّقُوا۟ مِنْهُمْ
تُقَىٰةً ۗ وَيُحَذِّرُكُمُ ٱللَّهُ نَفْسَهُۥ ۗ وَإِلَى ٱللَّهِ
ٱلْمَصِيرُ ﴿٢٨﴾

Let not the believers take unbelievers for friends and protectors in preference to believers, and whoever does so Allah has nothing to do with them unless it is to protect yourselves from them as you ought to. And Allah warns you to beware of Him. And to Allah is the final return. (28)

قُلْ إِن تُخْفُوا۟ مَا فِى صُدُورِكُمْ أَوْ
تُبْدُوهُ يَعْلَمْهُ ٱللَّهُ ۗ وَيَعْلَمُ مَا فِى ٱلسَّمَٰوَٰتِ
وَمَا فِى ٱلْأَرْضِ ۗ وَٱللَّهُ عَلَىٰ كُلِّ شَىْءٍ
قَدِيرٌ ﴿٢٩﴾

Say: "Whether you hide what is in your hearts or reveal it, Allah knows it all. He knows what is in the heavens and what is on earth. And Allah has power over all things". (29)

يَوْمَ تَجِدُ كُلُّ نَفْسٍ مَّا عَمِلَتْ مِنْ خَيْرٍ
مُّحْضَرًا وَمَا عَمِلَتْ مِن سُوٓءٍ تَوَدُّ لَوْ أَنَّ
بَيْنَهَا وَبَيْنَهُۥٓ أَمَدًۢا بَعِيدًا ۗ وَيُحَذِّرُكُمُ
ٱللَّهُ نَفْسَهُۥ ۗ وَٱللَّهُ رَءُوفٌۢ بِٱلْعِبَادِ ﴿٣٠﴾

On the day when every soul will be confronted with all the good it has done and all the evil it has done, it will wish there were a great distance between it and its evil. But Allah warns you to beware of Him. And Allah is most compassionate to His servants. (30)

قُلْ إِن كُنتُمْ تُحِبُّونَ ٱللَّهَ فَٱتَّبِعُونِى
يُحْبِبْكُمُ ٱللَّهُ وَيَغْفِرْ لَكُمْ ذُنُوبَكُمْ ۗ وَٱللَّهُ
غَفُورٌ رَّحِيمٌ ﴿٣١﴾

Say: "If you do love Allah, follow me, and Allah will love you, and forgive you your sins, for Allah is most Forgiving, most Merciful." (31)

Say: "Obey Allah and His Messenger," but if they turn away, Allah loves not the disbelievers. (32)

قُلْ أَطِيعُوا۟ ٱللَّهَ وَٱلرَّسُولَ ۖ فَإِن تَوَلَّوْا۟ فَإِنَّ ٱللَّهَ لَا يُحِبُّ ٱلْكَـٰفِرِينَ ﴿٣٢﴾

WORD STUDY AND EXPLANATION

لَّا يَتَّخِذِ ٱلْمُؤْمِنُونَ ٱلْكَـٰفِرِينَ أَوْلِيَآءَ مِن دُونِ ٱلْمُؤْمِنِينَ ۖ وَمَن يَفْعَلْ ذَٰلِكَ فَلَيْسَ مِنَ
ٱللَّهِ فِى شَىْءٍ إِلَّآ أَن تَتَّقُوا۟ مِنْهُمْ تُقَىٰةً ۗ وَيُحَذِّرُكُمُ ٱللَّهُ نَفْسَهُۥ ۗ وَإِلَى ٱللَّهِ ٱلْمَصِيرُ
﴿٢٨﴾

Let not the believers take unbelievers for friends and supporters in preference to believers, and whoever does so Allah has nothing to do with them, unless it is to save yourselves from them as you ought to. And Allah warns you to beware of Him. And to Allah is the final return. (28)

The word 'believers' is a general term and is used in the above verse specifically for those among the Muslims who were not yet single-minded in their commitment to Islam. In part, due to selfish considerations and in part for not being fully sure about the future prospects of Islam, they were inclined towards the Jews. The Jews found them easy to manipulate and used them in their plots and conspiracies against the Muslims. It is these weak Muslims who are addressed here and who are told that forging relationships of friendship and co-operation with Jews is like standing guard over a house that is marked for demolition and a contradiction of their professed belief in Islam.

The word *kāfirīn* (unbelievers) here refers to the People of the Book, especially the Jews whose disbelief is specifically mentioned in verse 21 above.

Prohibition of helping and supporting any group of disbelievers against the interests of Islam and Muslims

The word *walī (*pl. *awliyā')* means a guardian, supporter, companion, friend and a helper to whom one turns in times of need and whom one supports actively and enthusiastically. The verse says that it is not permissible for Muslims to take the disbelievers as *awliyā'*. This is, however, qualified by the words *min dūni-l mu'minīn* (in preference to believers), if such an alliance is directed against the believers. In other words, only such co-operation with the disbelievers is disallowed which is against the believers or contrary to their interests and well-being. The defence of the rights of Muslims and Islam and their interests supersede all other rights and interests. For no Muslim individual or group is it permissible to side with any group of disbelievers against the interests of Islam and Muslims or to forge any links of co-operation with them in this regard. Islam does not prohibit kind, fair, just and equitable treatment of all human beings including non-combatant disbelievers. The Muslims may enter into friendly, political and economic agreements with non-Muslim governments and entities, provided they are not "against other Muslims", *min dūni-l mu'minīn.* We will discuss this issue at some other suitable place in the following pages.

Correct meaning of the verse *illā an tattaqū minhum tuqātan* (unless it is to save yourselves from them as you ought to)

The word *tuqātan* in the text is used as an 'absolute object' (*maf'ūl muṭlaq*) as it has been in verse 102 of this sūrah. This reinforces the emphasis on the undesirability of 'friendly relations' of co-operation with disbelievers against Islam and Muslims. As stated at another place, *wa man yatawallāhum minkum fa-innahu minhum,* (and whoever among you takes them (disbelievers) for friends, they are of them (Sūrah al-Mā'idah, 5:51). One cannot have friendship with Allah and with His enemies at the same time. Those who aspire to gain the love of Allah and friendship with Him must keep away from those who are His enemies, the enemies of His *dīn* and of His faithful servants[12].This sentence marks an exception to the above rule stated as *laysa min Allāhi fi shay'in* (Allah has nothing to do with them). In other words, this rule does not apply to those who avoid befriending and co-operating with the disbelievers in opposition to Islam and Muslims – in fact, those who protect themselves from having friendship with them that would be to the detriment of Islam and Muslims. Those who have tried from this to justify *taqīyya* or dissimulation and subterfuge in dealing with others, have completely ignored all linguistic evidence, Qur'ānic usage and the context of the verse. After this interpretation of its true meaning and significance, there is hardly any need to say more on this subject to refute this wrong notion.

A specific warning to the hypocrites

The cautionary *words 'Wa yuḥadhirukumu Allāhu nafsahu* (Allah warns you to beware of Him)' contain a special warning for the hypocrites. They are warned that they should not be deluded by the compassion, generosity and

12. In this regard we would do well to bear the following verse in mind: "You will not find any people who believe in Allah and the Last Day, loving those who resist Allah and His Messenger, even though they were their fathers or their sons, or their brothers or their kindred" (Sūrah al-Mujādilah, 58:22).

grace of Allah into thinking that they will not be called to account. It is true that Allah overlooks the mischief of humans, gives them respite, and does not hasten in punishing them. This does not mean, however, that in His sight good and evil are equal and that He does not differentiate between these two, or that evil is no longer evil in His sight or that He is unable to call its perpetrators to account. Rather, the real reason why He does not call people to account immediately is that He gives them respite until the end, which is limited to their fixed term on earth. Thereafter, He will judge between them and reward or punish them according to His faultless and perfect justice. Being just is yet another of His important attributes. If it is not manifest yet, it does not mean that it will never take place. There may be apparent delay in Allah's decisions but there is no trace of injustice in them. When this attribute of Divine justice is finally and fully exhibited on the day of judgement, it will shine forth in all its splendour. He is the all-Powerful and none can frustrate or subvert His justice and He has the full control and power to enforce His decisions. It is of this Divine attribute of justice that Allah has warned His servants here and at other places in the Qur'ān. At one place, we read, "O human being! What has lured you away from Your Sustainer most generous?" (Sūrah al-Infiṭār, 82:6).

The weaker Muslims and the hypocrites admonished here are also mentioned later in this sūrah. This throws light on some of the subtle aspects of this verse:

> *O you who believe! Take not into your intimacy those outside your ranks. They will not fail to corrupt you. They only desire your ruin. Rank hatred has already appeared from their mouths. What their hearts conceal is far worse. We have made plain to you the signs, if you have wisdom. Here you are, you love them, and they love you not; you believe in the whole of the Book. When they meet you, they say, "We believe." But when they are alone, they bite off the very tips of their fingers at you in their rage. Say: "Perish in your rage! Allah knows well all the secrets of the heart." If anything that is good befalls you, it grieves them; but if some misfortune overtakes you, they rejoice at it. However, if you are constant and do right, not the least harm will their cunning do to you; for Allah encompasses all that they do.* (Sūrah Āli ʻImrān, 3:118-120).

قُلْ إِن تُخْفُوا۟ مَا فِى صُدُورِكُمْ أَوْ تُبْدُوهُ يَعْلَمْهُ ٱللَّهُ ۗ وَيَعْلَمُ مَا فِى ٱلسَّمَـٰوَٰتِ وَمَا فِى
ٱلْأَرْضِ ۗ وَٱللَّهُ عَلَىٰ كُلِّ شَىْءٍ قَدِيرٌ ﴿٢٩﴾
يَوْمَ تَجِدُ كُلُّ نَفْسٍ مَّا عَمِلَتْ مِنْ خَيْرٍ مُّحْضَرًا وَمَا عَمِلَتْ مِن سُوٓءٍ تَوَدُّ لَوْ أَنَّ بَيْنَهَا
وَبَيْنَهُۥٓ أَمَدًۢا بَعِيدًا ۗ وَيُحَذِّرُكُمُ ٱللَّهُ نَفْسَهُۥ ۗ وَٱللَّهُ رَءُوفٌۢ بِٱلْعِبَادِ ﴿٣٠﴾

Verses 28-32

Say: "Whether you hide what is in your hearts or reveal it, Allah knows it all. He knows what is in the heavens, and what is on earth. And Allah has power over all things. (29)
"On the day when every soul will be confronted with all the good it has done, and all the evil it has done, it will wish there were a great distance between it and its evil. But Allah warns you to beware of Him. And Allah is most compassionate towards His servants. (30)

The words, "what is in your hearts" refer to their hypocrisy and inclination towards the disbelievers. They are told that whether they hide or openly declare their real intentions Allah knows all. He is well aware not only of the secrets of their hearts but knows whatever is in the heavens and the earth and what goes on in them and, moreover, He has full power over them. If, however, despite all this power and knowledge, He gives them respite, it is because He has fixed a special day of judgement to judge them, a day when all people will be confronted with all the good or evil they earned during their sojourn on earth. On confronting their day of reckoning – the day that they previously regarded as remote and were least bothered about, they would wish there were a great distance between them and the evil consequences of their misdeeds.

In the text, after the words *mā 'amilat min sū'in,* the word *muḥḍaran* is omitted while in the first part of the sentence it is clearly indicated (*yawma tajidu kullu nafsin mā 'amilat min khayrin muḥḍarran*). Therefore to avoid unnecessary repetition, it has been omitted in the second part of the sentence. In *baynahā* and *baynahu,* the attached pronoun in the first word refers to the human soul and in the second to the evil consequences of its misdeeds.

Wa yu-ḥadh-dhirukum Allāhu nafsahu wa Allāhu ra'ūfum bi-l 'ibād

As discussed above, the dominant sense of the word *ra'ūf* is the repulsion of evil. As Allah is most compassionate towards His servants and wants to save them from the evil consequences of their misdeeds, He repeatedly warns them to fear Him, lest they be deluded by the respite that He gives them. Undoubtedly He is very lenient and generous in granting respite but then He is also very severe in chastisement.

قُلْ إِن كُنتُمْ تُحِبُّونَ ٱللَّهَ فَٱتَّبِعُونِى يُحْبِبْكُمُ ٱللَّهُ وَيَغْفِرْ لَكُمْ ذُنُوبَكُمْ ۗ وَٱللَّهُ غَفُورٌ رَّحِيمٌ ﴿٣١﴾
قُلْ أَطِيعُوا۟ ٱللَّهَ وَٱلرَّسُولَ ۖ فَإِن تَوَلَّوْا۟ فَإِنَّ ٱللَّهَ لَا يُحِبُّ ٱلْكَٰفِرِينَ ﴿٣٢﴾

Say: "If you do love Allah, follow me, and Allah will love you, and forgive you your sins, for Allah is most Forgiving, most Merciful." (31)

Say: "Obey Allah and His Messenger," but if they turn away, Allah loves not the unbelievers. (32)

This admonition is addressed to the weaker elements among the Muslims who were still hesitant and not fully committed. They are taught the correct attitude and approach as true Muslims. If they truly love Allah, then they should know that they cannot at the same time love the enemies of Allah, His messenger, His book and His *dīn*. The only correct course for them, as true and sincere believers, is to follow the example of Allah's messenger. This is the only way of loving Allah. Allah will in return love them and whatever weaknesses or mistakes they might have made so far, He shall forgive them all, because He is most Forgiving and Compassionate.

A clear and categorical warning is then given to them, through the messenger, to obey Allah and follow the messenger sincerely and honestly. If they turn away from this advice, they would be reckoned as a part of the disbelievers with whom they have friendships and whom Allah does not like.

In these two verses, some points are especially worth bearing in mind. Firstly, the tone of the two verses is distinctly different. In the first verse the compassion is manifest, while the second is couched in an obvious tone of warning: indeed, there is a rather threatening tone. This represents a beautiful fusion of compassion and austerity.

Secondly, the essence of *īmān* or belief is love of Allah. For this love to be true and sincere, it should be exclusively for Allah alone and not be joined with any other love that directly or indirectly contradicts it.

Thirdly, the only correct way of loving Allah is to follow His messenger. All other ways are deviant innovations and lead to error.

Fourthly, to win Allah's love and pleasure is also dependent upon following the example of His messenger. Anyone who deviates from his example in practice and yet considers himself to be the beloved of Allah or expects others to regard him as such is steeped in sheer delusion.

Fifthly, the minimum demand of the religion of Islam is that a person should obey Allah and His messenger. Anyone who intentionally avoids fulfilling this demand must be reckoned as one of the disbelievers in the religion of Allah. And Allah does not like such people.

Verses 33-44: thematic continuity

The introduction to the sūrah ends with verse 32, and a refutation of the Christian innovations – the real theme of this sūrah – begins, prefaced with some introductory remarks. To begin with, there is a reference to the provision of guidance from Allah for human beings. In this connection some names, Adam, Nūḥ, and the descendants of Ibrāhīm and of 'Imrān are mentioned, saying that they were chosen by Allah for the guidance and leadership of people in this world. The mention of the family of 'Imrān is especially significant as an introduction to prophet Jesus. Mary, the mother of Jesus, belonged to this very blessed family.

The purpose of giving this historical account of the prophets from Adam to the descendants of Ibrāhīm and the family of 'Imrān is to show to the Christians that this account, that they too admit to be true only shows that prophet Jesus and his mother were an integral link in the golden chain of guidance established by Allah for the guidance of the people of the world. It does not show that either of them were superhuman. This blessed family was indeed honoured by Allah by choosing them for the moral and spiritual guidance and leadership of the world. This honour was, however, bestowed upon them in order to invite people to Allah and to serve Him. Like some other persons whom Allah chose to guide people to the straight path, Jesus was also one of these chosen servants of Allah. If this historical account is true, where then is the justification for exalting Jesus and his mother to the status of being a part of Allah's Divinity?

Then follows an account of the early life of Maryam, how before her birth her mother made a vow concerning the child that she was carrying at the time. She was upset when, contrary to her expectations, she gave birth to a baby girl and how Allah calmed her angst. She was taken by Prophet Zakariyyā under his tutelage and the account tells of how Allah graciously accepted her into His pleasure to an extent that even a person like Zakariyyā, of exalted moral and spiritual stature, was so impressed by her that he prayed to Allah for a pious child like her. The purpose of referring to this story of Maryam is to show to the Christians that this is the story of a most pious and devoted maidservant of Allah rather than – God forbid – as they wrongly assert, that of the mother of God!

Then Zakariyyā's supplication and its acceptance is mentioned. He had reached an extremely advanced age and his wife was barren, and yet Allah gave them the glad tidings of the birth of a son, Yaḥyā (John), who was later born in fulfilment of this good news. This shows, that contrary to the normal laws of nature, this birth was a sign of the power of Allah. It does not, however, mean that whoever is born in a supernatural manner should be elevated to the status of Divinity. If Jesus is elevated to being Divine on account of his supernatural birth, then the same argument could be used in the case of Yaḥyā, as he was also born in a supra-normal manner. Let us read now the following introduction to the refutation of Christianity.

Allah did choose Adam and Noah, the family of Abraham, and the family of ʻImrān for the guidance of the people of the world. (33)

إِنَّ ٱللَّهَ ٱصۡطَفَىٰٓ ءَادَمَ وَنُوحٗا وَءَالَ
إِبۡرَٰهِيمَ وَءَالَ عِمۡرَٰنَ عَلَى ٱلۡعَٰلَمِينَ ﴿٣٣﴾

They are offspring, one of the other, and Allah hears and knows all things. (34)

ذُرِّيَّةَۢ بَعۡضُهَا مِنۢ بَعۡضٖۗ وَٱللَّهُ سَمِيعٌ عَلِيمٌ
﴿٣٤﴾

Behold! When ʻImrān's wife supplicated: "O my Sustainer! I dedicate to You the child that is in my womb for Your special service. So accept this of me. For You alone hear and know all things." (35)

إِذۡ قَالَتِ ٱمۡرَأَتُ عِمۡرَٰنَ رَبِّ إِنِّي نَذَرۡتُ
لَكَ مَا فِي بَطۡنِي مُحَرَّرٗا فَتَقَبَّلۡ مِنِّيٓۖ إِنَّكَ
أَنتَ ٱلسَّمِيعُ ٱلۡعَلِيمُ ﴿٣٥﴾

When she had given birth, she said: "O my Sustainer! Behold! I have given birth to a female child!" – and Allah knows best what she brought forth – "And the male is not like the female. I have named her Mary (Maryam), and I commend her and her offspring to Your protection from the Devil, the rejected." (36)

فَلَمَّا وَضَعَتۡهَا قَالَتۡ رَبِّ إِنِّي وَضَعۡتُهَآ أُنثَىٰ
وَٱللَّهُ أَعۡلَمُ بِمَا وَضَعَتۡ وَلَيۡسَ ٱلذَّكَرُ
كَٱلۡأُنثَىٰۖ وَإِنِّي سَمَّيۡتُهَا مَرۡيَمَ وَإِنِّيٓ أُعِيذُهَا
بِكَ وَذُرِّيَّتَهَا مِنَ ٱلشَّيۡطَٰنِ ٱلرَّجِيمِ
﴿٣٦﴾

Her Sustainer graciously accepted her, and caused her to grow in a goodly growth and placed her in the care of Zakariyyā. Whenever Zakariyyā visited her in the sanctuary, he found her supplied with sustenance. He would ask: "O Mary! Whence (comes) this to you?" She would answer: "It is from Allah, for Allah grants sustenance to whom He pleases without measure." (37)

فَتَقَبَّلَهَا رَبُّهَا بِقَبُولٍ حَسَنٖ وَأَنۢبَتَهَا
نَبَاتًا حَسَنٗا وَكَفَّلَهَا زَكَرِيَّاۖ كُلَّمَا دَخَلَ
عَلَيۡهَا زَكَرِيَّا ٱلۡمِحۡرَابَ وَجَدَ عِندَهَا رِزۡقٗاۖ
قَالَ يَٰمَرۡيَمُ أَنَّىٰ لَكِ هَٰذَاۖ قَالَتۡ هُوَ
مِنۡ عِندِ ٱللَّهِۖ إِنَّ ٱللَّهَ يَرۡزُقُ مَن يَشَآءُ بِغَيۡرِ
حِسَابٍ ﴿٣٧﴾

هُنَالِكَ دَعَا زَكَرِيَّا رَبَّهُۥ قَالَ رَبِّ هَبْ
لِى مِن لَّدُنكَ ذُرِّيَّةً طَيِّبَةً إِنَّكَ سَمِيعُ
ٱلدُّعَآءِ ﴿٣٨﴾

There Zakariyyā prayed to his Sustainer, saying: "O my Sustainer! Grant me too, out of Your grace, a goodly offspring, for You, indeed, listen to all prayer! (38)

فَنَادَتْهُ ٱلْمَلَٰٓئِكَةُ وَهُوَ قَآئِمٌ يُصَلِّى فِى
ٱلْمِحْرَابِ أَنَّ ٱللَّهَ يُبَشِّرُكَ بِيَحْيَىٰ مُصَدِّقًۢا
بِكَلِمَةٍ مِّنَ ٱللَّهِ وَسَيِّدًا وَحَصُورًا وَنَبِيًّا
مِّنَ ٱلصَّٰلِحِينَ ﴿٣٩﴾

So, while he was standing in prayer in the chamber, the angels called to him: "Allah does give you glad tidings of Yaḥyā, who shall confirm the truth of a Word from Allah, and he shall be noble, chaste, and a prophet from among the righteous." (39)

قَالَ رَبِّ أَنَّىٰ يَكُونُ لِى غُلَٰمٌ وَقَدْ
بَلَغَنِىَ ٱلْكِبَرُ وَٱمْرَأَتِى عَاقِرٌ قَالَ
كَذَٰلِكَ ٱللَّهُ يَفْعَلُ مَا يَشَآءُ ﴿٤٠﴾

He said: "O my Sustainer! How shall I have son, seeing I am very old, and my wife is barren?" "Thus it is," was the answer, "Allah does what He wills." (40)

قَالَ رَبِّ ٱجْعَل لِّىٓ ءَايَةً قَالَ ءَايَتُكَ أَلَّا
تُكَلِّمَ ٱلنَّاسَ ثَلَٰثَةَ أَيَّامٍ إِلَّا رَمْزًا
وَٱذْكُر رَّبَّكَ كَثِيرًا وَسَبِّحْ بِٱلْعَشِىِّ
وَٱلْإِبْكَٰرِ ﴿٤١﴾

He said: "O my Sustainer! Appoint a sign for me!" "Your sign," came the answer, "shall be that you shall not speak to people other than by gestures for three days. And celebrate the praises of your Sustainer unceasingly, and glorify Him in the evening and in the morning." (41)

وَإِذْ قَالَتِ ٱلْمَلَٰٓئِكَةُ يَٰمَرْيَمُ إِنَّ ٱللَّهَ
ٱصْطَفَىٰكِ وَطَهَّرَكِ وَٱصْطَفَىٰكِ عَلَىٰ
نِسَآءِ ٱلْعَٰلَمِينَ ﴿٤٢﴾

Behold! The angels said: "O Mary! Allah has chosen you and purified you, and raised you above all the women of the world. (42)

يَٰمَرْيَمُ ٱقْنُتِى لِرَبِّكِ وَٱسْجُدِى وَٱرْكَعِى
مَعَ ٱلرَّٰكِعِينَ ﴿٤٣﴾

"O Mary! Worship your Sustainer devoutly. Prostrate thyself, and bow down (in prayer) with those who bow down." (43)

ذَٰلِكَ مِنْ أَنۢبَآءِ ٱلْغَيْبِ نُوحِيهِ إِلَيْكَ ۚ
وَمَا كُنتَ لَدَيْهِمْ إِذْ يُلْقُونَ أَقْلَـٰمَهُمْ
أَيُّهُمْ يَكْفُلُ مَرْيَمَ وَمَا كُنتَ
لَدَيْهِمْ إِذْ يَخْتَصِمُونَ ﴿٤٤﴾

This is of the tidings of unseen that We reveal to you (O Prophet!). You were not with them when they cast lots with arrows to determine which of them should take care of Mary, nor were you with them when they disputed with one another. (44)

WORD STUDY AND EXPLANATION

۞ إِنَّ ٱللَّهَ ٱصْطَفَىٰٓ ءَادَمَ وَنُوحًا وَءَالَ إِبْرَٰهِيمَ وَءَالَ عِمْرَٰنَ عَلَى ٱلْعَـٰلَمِينَ ﴿٣٣﴾
ذُرِّيَّةًۢ بَعْضُهَا مِنۢ بَعْضٍ ۗ وَٱللَّهُ سَمِيعٌ عَلِيمٌ ﴿٣٤﴾

Allah did choose Adam and Noah, the family of Abraham, and the family of 'Imrān for the guidance of the people of the world. (33)
They are offspring, one of the other, and Allah hears and knows all things. (34)

Lineage of Jesus

Adam, Nūḥ and Ibrāhīm, peace be upon them all, are the main pillars of prophethood and apostleship and they represent the whole series of prophets and messengers raised from among humans. The mention of Ibrāhīm's family refers to both its branches that trace their origin to him. It includes the family of Ishāq, from among whom Jesus was the last prophet, and also the family of Ismā'īl from among whom the final prophet, Muḥammad, peace be upon him, was raised.

The mention of the family of 'Imrān after that of Ibrāhīm has a special significance. This is the family of Maryam. 'Imrān ibn Matan was the name of her father and as such he is the maternal grandfather of Jesus, peace be upon him. The purpose of mentioning this whole genealogical tree is to show that Jesus was also an offshoot of this blessed tree. His mother, his maternal grandfather and all his other antecedents are well known. They are all inter-related. How can a member of this family then be exalted to Divinity and made into the 'son' of God?

"And Allah hears and knows all things" This refers to the fact that all those chosen by Allah as His prophets or messengers were chosen in the light of His knowledge. He chose only those who were best suited for this honour, based solely on merit, and in the light of His wisdom and faultless knowledge.

This had nothing to do with the superiority of any one particular family over others as erroneously presumed by those who were proud of their unique racial superiority.

An account of early life of Maryam

إِذْ قَالَتِ ٱمْرَأَتُ عِمْرَٰنَ رَبِّ إِنِّى نَذَرْتُ لَكَ مَا فِى بَطْنِى مُحَرَّرًا فَتَقَبَّلْ مِنِّىٓ ۖ إِنَّكَ أَنتَ ٱلسَّمِيعُ ٱلْعَلِيمُ ﴿٣٥﴾

Behold! When 'Imrān's wife supplicated: "O my Sustainer! I dedicate to You the child that is in my womb for Your special service – So accept this of me For You alone hear and know all things." (35)

In the above verse, the genealogy of the family of 'Imrān is explained and the birth of Maryam is described. Her mother, the wife of 'Imrān, was pregnant with her, when she vowed that she would dedicate the newborn to the service of Allah. Among the descendants of Israel, this meant that the newborn would be dedicated for the service of the temple.

Muḥar-raran means freeing him or her, that is, when the child grows into adulthood, it will not be burdened with the task of earning a livelihood and taking care of its family, and would be wholly devoted to the service of the temple. As mentioned below, her mother expected to have a male child but when she gave birth to a female, she was somewhat hesitant, for at the time girls and women were not accepted for the service of the temple. However, Allah accepted the vow of Mary's mother and she entered the sanctuary of the temple. The purpose of mentioning the early and later life of Mary is to show that she was a most devout servant of Allah, dedicated even before she was born to serve Allah and His temple and to worship and obey Him. She faithfully fulfilled all her obligations until the very last moment of her life. How ironic and foolish it is to exalt such a saintly devout servant of Allah and present her as the mother of God!

فَلَمَّا وَضَعَتْهَا قَالَتْ رَبِّ إِنِّى وَضَعْتُهَآ أُنثَىٰ وَٱللَّهُ أَعْلَمُ بِمَا وَضَعَتْ وَلَيْسَ ٱلذَّكَرُ كَٱلْأُنثَىٰ ۖ وَإِنِّى سَمَّيْتُهَا مَرْيَمَ وَإِنِّىٓ أُعِيذُهَا بِكَ وَذُرِّيَّتَهَا مِنَ ٱلشَّيْطَٰنِ ٱلرَّجِيمِ ﴿٣٦﴾

When she was delivered, she said: "O my Sustainer! Behold! I am delivered of a female child!" – and Allah knew best what she brought forth – "And the male is not like the female. I have named her Mary, and I commend her and her offspring to Your protection from Satan, the rejected." (36)

The words "I am delivered of a female child" show that Mary's mother expected a male child and for that reason she had made the vow to dedicate it to the service of the temple. So when quite unexpectedly she gave birth to a baby girl, she felt some apprehension and said, "O my Sustainer, I am delivered of a female child" – whereas she had intended to dedicate a male child to God's service.

"And Allah knew best what she brought forth"

This is a parenthetical interjection from Allah in the statement of Mary's mother. Her saying that "I am delivered of a female child" clearly indicated a sense of inferiority concerning the newborn baby and a rather modest offering to Allah's service. At this, Allah, the most Compassionate and most Merciful, told her that the female child that Mary's mother considered a modest offering because she was a female child, was indeed a most blessed child she had given birth to and Allah was well pleased with her gift to Him.

"And the male is not like the female." These words are a part of the statement of Mary's mother and, as explained above, suggest that Mary's mother said words to the effect that "this is a female child that is inferior to the male child that I expected to dedicate to Your service. She cannot be a substitute for what I intended to offer, but pray accept this gift from me as You are most kind and gracious".

"And I commend her and her offspring to Your protection from Satan, the accursed" This prayer is a natural expression of the motherly concern of Mary's mother. Its mention here is meant to suggest that the daughter she offers to Allah's service and prays for is somehow an inferior offering compared to the offering of a male child. The contrast between the sense of inferiority on the part of the mother for a female child and how the Christians elevated her to being God's mother is quite striking. The purpose of narrating these events is to clarify the true facts and to show how simple events have been used to weave a baseless story around them.

Moral and spiritual excellence of Maryam

فَتَقَبَّلَهَا رَبُّهَا بِقَبُولٍ حَسَنٍ وَأَنۢبَتَهَا نَبَاتًا حَسَنًا وَكَفَّلَهَا زَكَرِيَّا ۖ كُلَّمَا دَخَلَ عَلَيْهَا
زَكَرِيَّا ٱلْمِحْرَابَ وَجَدَ عِندَهَا رِزْقًا ۖ قَالَ يَٰمَرْيَمُ أَنَّىٰ لَكِ هَٰذَا ۖ قَالَتْ هُوَ مِنْ عِندِ ٱللَّهِ ۖ إِنَّ
ٱللَّهَ يَرْزُقُ مَن يَشَآءُ بِغَيْرِ حِسَابٍ ﴿٣٧﴾

Verses 33-44

Her Sustainer graciously accepted her, and caused her to grow in a goodly growth and placed her in the care of Zakariyyā. Whenever Zakariyyā visited her in the sanctuary, he found her supplied with sustenance. He would ask: "O Mary! Whence (comes) this to you?" She would answer: "It is from Allah, for Allah grants sustenance to whom He pleases without measure." (37)

"Her Sustainer graciously accepted her"

Unlike the fear expressed by the mother for her female child, Allah received her most graciously and caused her rational, moral and spiritual potential to blossom to the full. An added blessing was that she was assigned to the care of Zakariyyā, her maternal uncle who was also the chief priest of the temple at the time.

Whenever Zakariyyā visited her in the sanctuary, he found her supplied with sustenance

The word *miḥrāb* (sanctuary) in the text means either the part of the temple reserved for women to worship and to retire for *i'tikāf* or a specific chamber reserved for Maryam to live in and worship. There were many such chambers and rooms in the temple for worshippers. The words "whenever Zakariyyā visited her in the sanctuary" show two facts. One, to take care of her he frequently visited her, and two, Maryam spent all her time in her sanctuary in worship and remembrance of Allah.

"He found her supplied with sustenance (*rizq*)" indicate the exceptional spiritual excellence of Maryam that even Zakariyyā, a person of extraordinary spiritual and moral gifts, was impressed by her moral and spiritual excellence and would in great astonishment ask her, "O Maryam, whence have you got all these gifts and wisdom?"

The meaning of *rizq*

The word *rizq* here means wisdom and insight. In the Qur'ān it has been used at more than one place for revelation and spiritual guidance just as it is used in the Torah and the Injīl. Prophet Jesus is also reported as having said, "Man does not live by bread alone, but by every word that comes from the mouth of God." (Matthew 4:4). In the next verse, it is mentioned that Zakariyyā was so impressed by Maryam's wisdom and knowledge that even though he had reached extreme old age and his wife was barren, he supplicated for a righteous offspring like her. Obviously a person with spiritual gifts like Zakariyyā could not be impressed merely by provisions of grapes and apples to be moved to supplicate for offspring for himself. Only the moral and spiritual sustenance could ignite his spiritual fervour so that, on seeing its manifestation, he would marvel and wished for a child with similar moral and spiritual gifts.

"O Mary! Whence (comes) this to you?"

Clearly this rhetorical question is not meant to elicit information but is expressive of surprise and appreciation for her excellence and is a natural result of finding someone gifted far beyond her or his years in the eyes of the speaker. Such an expression is a form of appreciation and here it shows the humility and generosity of Zakariyyā that he graciously appreciates the moral excellence of a rather young girl under his care. The answer of Mary, "It is from Allah," indicates her wisdom and maturity. She describes all her achievements as a bounty and gift from Allah and does not consider it a reward for her piety and worship. "Allah grants sustenance to whom He pleases without measure" is, in our view, not a part of Mary's answer. It is rather an expression of appreciation by Allah for her and His blessings beyond measure upon her. We have explained above the significance of the phrase *bi-ghayri ḥisāb*, beyond measure.

هُنَالِكَ دَعَا زَكَرِيَّا رَبَّهُۥ ۖ قَالَ رَبِّ هَبْ لِى مِن لَّدُنكَ ذُرِّيَّةً طَيِّبَةً ۖ إِنَّكَ سَمِيعُ ٱلدُّعَآءِ ٣٨

There Zakariyyā prayed to his Sustainer, saying: "O my Sustainer! Grant me too, out of Your grace, a goodly offspring, for You, indeed, listen to all prayer!" (38)

Early life of Yaḥyā, peace be on him

Hunālika indicates that Zakariyyā was so impressed by the obvious wisdom and insight of Mary that the latent desire within him for offspring was suddenly kindled. He wished that he could also be granted such a child as his heir from Allah and supplicated to Allah for a goodly offspring. The use of words *min ladunka* shows that, considering his old age and the barrenness of his wife, he apparently found the circumstances unfavourable for the fulfilment of his wish but he earnestly believed nothing was impossible for Allah and hoped He would grant the wish of an old man like him and bless his barren wife with a child. He knew that causes and effects are merely the apparent manifestations of Allah's might and grace and that this is what really matters.

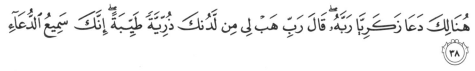

فَنَادَتْهُ ٱلْمَلَٰٓئِكَةُ وَهُوَ قَآئِمٌ يُصَلِّى فِى ٱلْمِحْرَابِ أَنَّ ٱللَّهَ يُبَشِّرُكَ بِيَحْيَىٰ مُصَدِّقًۢا بِكَلِمَةٍ مِّنَ ٱللَّهِ وَسَيِّدًا وَحَصُورًا وَنَبِيًّا مِّنَ ٱلصَّٰلِحِينَ ﴿٣٩﴾

So, while he was standing in prayer in the chamber, the angels called to him: "Allah does give you glad tidings of Yaḥyā, who shall confirm the truth of a Word from Allah, and shall be noble, chaste, and a prophet from among the righteous." (39)

The reason for using the plural form, angels (*malā'ikah*)

The word *malā'ikah* here, and especially wherever it is used in the Qur'ān in a similar context, is used in plural form. The reason for this, in our view, is that Zakariyyā heard the angel's voice but he could not recognise or locate the caller. In view of this uncertainty on his part, the Qur'ān does not mention any particular angel but mentions the tiding as coming from angels, which shows that the voice he heard was angelic, but that he did not see the speaker.

While he was standing in prayer in the chamber

He heard this voice while in his chamber standing in prayer. This reinforces the fact that it was indeed the voice of an angel. The state of prayer is most opportune in terms of proximity and closeness to angels. It also shows that the most appropriate time for supplicating to Allah is when one is in prayer and stands before Him. This gives life and warmth to human existence and establishes between us and our Creator and Sovereign a direct relationship. The repeated admonition to the Prophet, peace be upon him, in the Qur'ān to seek help in *ṣalāh* or prayer when faced with difficulties and hardships also reinforces the point that the key to all problems of life lies in prayer.

From the details concerning the prayers of the Prophet and his companions, we also find that prayer was indeed an expression of their close proximity and live personal dialogue between them and their Sustainer. They presented their worries, complaints and supplications in their prayers, standing and in a state of prostration, so that when they concluded their devotions, their prayers were never left unanswered and their requests unfulfilled. For them, prayer was an essential part of their existence, as water is to the thirsty or food is to the starving. Our prayers have lost this edge and have become mere rituals with no relationship with our real life. Strangely enough, while our *ṣalāt* or prayer is lifeless, we tend to supplicate in earnest after finishing the prayer. The real time for supplicating to Allah, though, is when a servants stands in prayer before Him.

"Allah does give you glad tidings of Yaḥyā"

Yaḥyā is mentioned in the Injīl as John the Baptist. He was born only six months before the birth of Jesus. Three characteristics of his are mentioned at the time of giving the tidings of his birth to his father.

Confirmation of a word from Allah

One is that he shall "confirm the truth of a Word from Allah". That is, he will confirm a word from Allah and give glad tidings about him. The word from Allah refers to Jesus as in verse 45 below he is explicitly mentioned in similar terms: "O Mary! Allah gives you glad tidings of a Word from Him: his name will be Christ Jesus, the son of Mary." The reason why he is mentioned as the word of Allah is because, unlike the normal rule, he was conceived by the word *'kun'* of Allah[13]. The indefinite form of the word – *kalimah* – shows that like numerous other words of Allah, Jesus Christ is also one of His words. Countless other creatures have come into being by the word 'Be' or *'Kun'* of Allah. So also was Jesus born as a result of it. This refutes one of the Christian postulates that Jesus Christ is the only word of God and that this proves his divinity.

The particle *bi* in *bi-kalimatin* shows that the confirmation of the word also carries glad tidings, meaning that Yaḥyā will also confirm the truth of Jesus Christ and also convey the glad tidings of his advent. The Gospels show that he accomplished both parts of his mission. Prophet Yaḥyā pointedly stated that he had come to pave the way for the one coming after him and to this end he even sacrificed his life. His life was a living confirmation of Jesus Christ. His birth too, like that of Jesus Christ was miraculous and contrary to ordinary natural laws. In his life of austerity, celibacy and piety also, he was almost identical to Jesus, who came after him. And the way he proclaimed the arrival of Jesus Christ was such that mountains and vales resounded with its sound.

By virtue of his natural position and being the bearer of the Divine message a Prophet is always a noble chief

Two, it is said about Prophet Yaḥyā that he would be a "*sayyid*" – meaning a noble chief. Every prophet is, by nature and with respect to his message and mission, a noble person and a leader. As a caller, he invites people to Allah; warns them and tries to wake them up; and as a guide and leader, he guides them and shows them the straight way. For this purpose, he is always well equipped with the requisite qualities and ability. His heart is filled with love

13. Please see Qur'ān 2:117, 3:47, 19:35 (Translator).

and concern for people. In his voice there is irresistible force and his style is awe-inspiring, while his bright forehead bears witness to the truth and majesty of his message. Even when he wears a garment of camel's hair, and a leather girdle round his waist and his food is locusts and wild honey[14], he inspires awe and fear in kings and rulers. In the service of truth, he reprimands and corrects the rulers as he does the ordinary folk. In the Gospels, both Yaḥyā or John and 'Īsā or Jesus are mentioned as speaking with authority. Clearly this authoritative nature of their words was a manifestation of their position as leaders. A prophet is also assigned a group of people to care for and look after, and for him it makes little difference to his position whether the people for whom he is raised do obey him or not. So long as he discharges his duty by conveying Allah's message to them, he fulfils his responsibility. And only that is expected of him.

This word – *sayyid* – also refutes the idea that Yaḥyā was only a monk and he lived far away in isolation from others. In his personal life, he was undoubtedly extremely abstemious but his entire life was otherwise devoted to the public proclamation of repentance for which he was sent and in whose cause ultimately he sacrificed his life.

The meaning of *ḥaṣūr*

Three, he is described as *ḥaṣūr,* a word that comes from *ḥaṣr* on the pattern *fa'ūl,* and literally means 'one who restrains oneself'. From here, its use was extended to a person who eschews worldly pleasures and exercises complete self-control. This self-control is an integral characteristic of the leadership mentioned above, since only the one who has self-control can be expected to control others. The lives of both prophets Yaḥyā and 'Īsā, peace be upon them both, were lives of absolute poverty and self-negation. They did not even benefit from those pleasures that would normally be described as purely this worldly. But, it seems that both of them had before them a specific mission in a specific situation. The love of this world had so deeply infected the Jews at the time that in order to change them they were presented with a completely otherworldly model of life. This was, as it were, treating a disease with its opposite, which we sometimes resort to in matters moral and spiritual just as we do in those that are purely physical and material under certain conditions. The purpose of this must have been to enable them, gradually, to adopt the middle course that was revealed later in the form of Islam, the final religion

14. "John's clothes were made of camel's hair, and he had a leather belt around his waist. His food was locusts and wild honey." (Mathew 3:4)

of Allah. However, the Christians mistook this self-denial for asceticism and then erected on it an entire system of monasticism.

The meaning of *nabīyyan min-aṣ ṣāliḥīn*

Four, it is stated that he will be a prophet of Allah. The meaning of the word prophet is clear, but this is qualified by saying that he will be from among the righteous. This is to emphasise the fact that for all his marvellous gifts and qualities, he was only one of the righteous servants of Allah. Whatever his extraordinary gifts and excellence, he was not Divine, nor did he share any part of Divinity with Allah. He was merely a righteous servant of His and totally human. There is a remarkable similarity between Yaḥyā and 'Īsā and in kinship they were closely related to each other. The birth of Yaḥyā or John, was very much similar to that of 'Īsā or Jesus. John, according to the Gospels, baptised Jesus who is reported to have said of him, "Among those born of women there has not risen anyone greater than John the Baptist." (Matthew 11:11)

قَالَ رَبِّ أَنَّىٰ يَكُونُ لِي غُلَٰمٌ وَقَدْ بَلَغَنِيَ ٱلْكِبَرُ وَٱمْرَأَتِي عَاقِرٌ ۖ قَالَ كَذَٰلِكَ ٱللَّهُ يَفْعَلُ مَا يَشَآءُ ﴿٤٠﴾

He said: "O my Sustainer! How shall I have a son, seeing that I am very old, and my wife is barren?" "Thus it is," was the answer, "Allah does what He wills." (40)

Request to confirm the good news

This question is not expressive of surprise or doubt or denial, but is rather a beautiful and eloquent way of asking for affirmation of the good news. By referring to the obstructions as he saw them in the fulfilment of the glad news, he wanted to confirm if it would indeed be fulfilled. The answer, "Thus it is" means that that is what and how Allah has willed: John would be born to an old father, who had no hope of having a child, and a barren mother. And the will of Allah is the really important factor while all other apparent causes and means are its outward manifestations. He could, if He so willed, cause springs to gush forth out of stones or make bubbling springs of water appear in the midst of a barren desert. A similar example of question and answer is also found in the story of Prophet Ibrāhīm. The two cases are identical[15].

15. Cf. Sūrah Adh-Dhāriyāt, 51:28-29.

قَالَ رَبِّ ٱجۡعَل لِّيٓ ءَايَةٗۖ قَالَ ءَايَتُكَ أَلَّا تُكَلِّمَ ٱلنَّاسَ ثَلَٰثَةَ أَيَّامٍ إِلَّا رَمۡزٗاۗ وَٱذۡكُر
رَّبَّكَ كَثِيرٗا وَسَبِّحۡ بِٱلۡعَشِيِّ وَٱلۡإِبۡكَٰرِ ٤١

He said: "O my Sustainer! Appoint a sign for me!" "Your sign," came the answer, "shall be that you shall not speak to people other than by gestures for three days. And celebrate the praises of your Sustainer unceasingly, and glorify Him in the evening and in the morning." (41)

Zakariyyā had received this glad news from an angel at an opportune time and state. Although convinced that it must have been from Allah, being a very humble, pious and cautious servant, he wanted to confirm that it was not merely a reflection of his own desire or a result of some unperceived aspect of it that the Satan might have tried to exploit. That is why he prayed to his Sustainer to appoint for him a sign that it was indeed from Him and not merely a reflection of his personal desires or a deception by Satan. Allah granted his request and told him that its sign was that for three days and nights he would not be able to speak to anyone, that he will communicate with them only by gestures and that he would be able to remember his Sustainer and celebrate His praises. So let him remember his Sustainer as much as he could and extol His greatness.

Obviously for a person to be overwhelmed by a condition for a certain period in which he is unable to utter any word about worldly affairs but is fully capable of glorifying his Sustainer and celebrating His praises cannot be the result of any satanic influence, but a clear result of Divine influence. Had it been the result of any satanic influences, its manifestation would have been quite the opposite – being at ease in talking about worldly affairs but finding it difficult to remember Allah. This was an involuntary condition experienced by Zakariyyā and it was a clear sign that the glad news of the birth of a son given to him was indeed from Allah and not the result of any satanic interference. Incidentally, the Qur'ān refutes the statement found in Luke that this condition in Zakariyyā was brought on as a punishment for not believing in the word of the angel and his alleged audacity in asking for a sign as a confirmation of the good news.

Those who are unaware of the Qur'ānic style may ask why – given that the verse says that Zakariyyā will not be able to speak to anyone except through gestures for three days – it is not explicit whether he will be able to remember and glorify his Sustainer. The answer to this question is implicit in the commandment he is given concerning glorifying Allah. In other words, he is instructed to do so because he was fully capable of it. To state it explicitly along with the commandment would have been superfluous, unnecessary and quite inappropriate for an eloquent book like the Qur'ān.

Bi-l ʻashiyyi wa-l ibkār and other such phrases as explained before, are used to cover a broad spectrum of time. For example, we use "morning and evening" or "night and day" to mean that it should be done all the time, whether morning or evening, or night and day.

وَإِذۡ قَالَتِ ٱلۡمَلَٰٓئِكَةُ يَٰمَرۡيَمُ إِنَّ ٱللَّهَ ٱصۡطَفَىٰكِ وَطَهَّرَكِ وَٱصۡطَفَىٰكِ عَلَىٰ نِسَآءِ
ٱلۡعَٰلَمِينَ ﴿٤٢﴾
يَٰمَرۡيَمُ ٱقۡنُتِي لِرَبِّكِ وَٱسۡجُدِي وَٱرۡكَعِي مَعَ ٱلرَّٰكِعِينَ ﴿٤٣﴾

Behold! The angels said: "O Mary! Allah has chosen you and purified you, and raised you above all the women of the world. (42)
"O Mary! Prostrate yourself, and bow down (in prayer) with those who bow down." (43)

What was Maryam chosen for?

Iṣṭifā', the word used in the text for choosing and selecting, in Qur'ānic terminology refers to the selection of someone by Allah for a specific purpose. Allah chose Maryam for the manifestation of one of His great signs, which was also a great trust she was going to bear. Moreover, it was also a great trial. This required that Allah would specially prepare and train her to bear this trust successfully and to cope with any hardships involved. It is this preparation and training that has been referred to here as *taṭ-hīr* for purifying her. The verse also clarifies that her *iṣṭifā'* or selection had a special significance. She was specially selected and chosen above all other women of the world. As in the present verse, when the particle *ʻalā* is used after *iṣṭifā'* it also gives a sense of preference or superiority. She was chosen out of all other women for this special purpose. It is a unique honour and she has no rival in this field.

To prepare her for this onerous burden, the heavenly voice advised her: *Uqnutī li-rabbiki* – worship your Sustainer devoutly. As explained at another place[16], the word *qunūt* means to incline towards Allah out of extreme humility and a sense of subservience. *Ṣalāh* or Prayer is the best expression of this humility and subservience.

ذَٰلِكَ مِنۡ أَنۢبَآءِ ٱلۡغَيۡبِ نُوحِيهِ إِلَيۡكَۚ وَمَا كُنتَ لَدَيۡهِمۡ إِذۡ يُلۡقُونَ أَقۡلَٰمَهُمۡ أَيُّهُمۡ
يَكۡفُلُ مَرۡيَمَ وَمَا كُنتَ لَدَيۡهِمۡ إِذۡ يَخۡتَصِمُونَ ﴿٤٤﴾

16. See page 562 of *Pondering over the Qur'ān,* volume I, Sūrah al-Baqarah, verse 238 (Translator).

This is of the tidings of the unseen that We reveal to you (O Prophet!). You were not with them when they cast lots with arrows to determine which of them should take care of Mary, nor were you with them when they disputed with one another. (44)

This verse represents an aside to the Prophet, peace be upon him, in the course of the discourse. He is told that these are the tidings of the unseen, of a world well beyond the grasp of his perception and knowledge. That is why all these details are not found in the Torah or in the Injīl. Nor was he (the Prophet, peace be upon him,) present when these events happened. How was it then possible for the Prophet, peace be upon him, to relate all these details with such accuracy in this manner that even surprised the People of the Book? Does it not clearly show that he was indeed the true messenger of Allah who was informed about all these tidings of the past through revelation? This clearly establishes a strong argument concerning his being the chosen Messenger and Prophet of Allah.

This portion of the history of the People of the Book is almost missing from the Gospels with the exception of some incoherent statements about prophet Yaḥyā (John) in Luke and some hints concerning Maryam, the mother of Jesus, sadly enough, mentioned as an ordinary woman. In fact, from some places in the Gospels, it appears that even Jesus did not respect her as a son ought to respect his mother. Whatever status the Christians might have given to Maryam as a part of their creed, the truth is that it is only the Qur'ān that has explained and given prominence to her, true exalted status among Allah's chosen servants. We shall discuss this at appropriate places in the following pages.

Nature of drawing lots in the case of Maryam

The word *aqlām* , quills, refer to the arrows used in drawing lots. Their use in gambling is forbidden in the Sharī'ah but there is no harm in using them to draw lots. In a situation where all are equal in terms of their rights, lots may be drawn to settle a matter and it is quite permissible to do so. But, was this method adopted to decide about the caretaker of Maryam only, or was it used in the case of all the others under sponsorship of the Temple? There are both the possibilities. It is quite possible that the sponsorship of all new entrants was settled in this manner. It is also possible that the case of Maryam being a girl was a sensitive one and hence it was decided by lots. The decision by lots was usually looked upon as a subtle hint from above, from the heavens. Through the use of lots, the duties at the Temple were also assigned. In Luke, we read that the day Zakariyyā received the glad tidings of a son, he was chosen for the duties assigned to him at the temple by a lot[17].

What was the dispute about?

The dispute referred to in the words *wa mā kunta ladayhim idh yakhta-ṣimūn* (nor were you with them when they disputed with one another), does not appear to be about the care of Maryam, for in such a case it would have been mentioned along with the first part rather than describing it separately. This argument, in our opinion, could have arisen among the servants of the temple about the question whether it was permissible for a girl to join the servants of the temple. At least, the history of the temple knew no such tradition. This could therefore be an issue and a cause of argument. However, it is also quite possible that this argument was the result of their eagerness to vie in deeds of goodness, as the sponsorship of a girl who was being dedicated to the service of the temple and whose Divine acceptance was obvious from the very first day, was a great blessing. None of the Temple's servants wanted to be deprived of this blessing but wanted to be a part of it.

VERSES 45-63: THEMATIC CONTINUITY

This segment opens with a statement that represents the central theme of this sūrah. As mentioned in the remarks introducing this sūrah, it is primarily addressed to the Christians and it seeks to explain the true position of Prophet Jesus, peace be upon him. The genealogy of 'Imrān's family, the birth of Maryam and her mother's vow, the supplication of Zakariyyā for a son and the birth of Yaḥyā – all these events are mentioned above as an introduction to the birth of Jesus Christ, peace be upon him.

In the present section we are told that just as an angel gave glad tidings of a son to Zakariyyā, so also Mary was given the good news of the birth of a son by an angel. He was to be born by the command 'Be' from Allah and whose name was to be Jesus Christ. And just as Zakariyyā was told that Yaḥyā would be noble, chaste, and a prophet from among the righteous, similarly Maryam was informed that Jesus would be held in honour in this world and the hereafter and that he would be among the company of those nearest to Allah. Just as Zakariyyā had expressed surprise at this glad news

17. "He was chose by lot, according to the prevalent custom of the priesthood." (Luke, 1:9)

in view of his old age and the barrenness of his wife, so also did Maryam express surprise at receiving glad tidings of the birth of a son because she was still a virgin and no man had touched her. They both received a similar answer from the angel who told them that the deciding factor in all matters was the commandment of Allah. If and when He wills a thing, He just says to it 'Be' and it is done. In this manner He will create Jesus by the word 'Be!' and teach him the book and wisdom and send him as His Messenger to the descendants of Israel.

The next three verses testify that Jesus delivered the Divine message to the descendants of Israel, affirming his apostleship and declaring his specific mission. In the next two verses, we find that the Jewish scholars and jurists rejected him. So, disappointed with them, he turned away from them and chose his disciples from among the poor who had responded to his call and believed in him. He invited them to strive actively for the cause of Allah that they had embraced. From among these poor people, his disciples, he chose some to convey the Divine message to others.

In the next four verses is mentioned the reaction to this last effort of Jesus among the leaders, rabbis and Pharisees of the Jewish community, how Allah helped and supported Jesus and his disciples and promised them further help and support in their efforts.

The next five verses represent a digression addressed to Prophet Muḥammad, peace be upon him, affirming that this was indeed the real position of Jesus Christ. So if even after this explanation, the Christians choose to continue to wrangle with you concerning this matter, then challenge them to "gather together our sons and your sons, our women and your women, ourselves and yourselves" and then "invoke the curse of Allah on those who are telling a lie". But if they try to avoid this, then know that they are the real mischief-makers. So refer their case to Allah to judge them. In the light of these remarks, let us study the following verses:

Remember when the angels said: "O Mary! Allah gives you glad tidings of a word from Him: his name will be Christ Jesus, the son of Mary, held in honour in both this world and the hereafter and of (the company of) those nearest to Allah. (45)

إِذْ قَالَتِ ٱلْمَلَٰٓئِكَةُ يَٰمَرْيَمُ إِنَّ ٱللَّهَ
يُبَشِّرُكِ بِكَلِمَةٍ مِّنْهُ ٱسْمُهُ ٱلْمَسِيحُ عِيسَى
ٱبْنُ مَرْيَمَ وَجِيهًا فِى ٱلدُّنْيَا وَٱلْءَاخِرَةِ وَمِنَ
ٱلْمُقَرَّبِينَ ٤٥

وَيُكَلِّمُ ٱلنَّاسَ فِى ٱلۡمَهۡدِ وَكَهۡلًا
وَمِنَ ٱلصَّٰلِحِينَ ﴿٤٦﴾

"He shall speak to the people in childhood and in maturity. And he shall be (of the company) of the righteous." (46)

قَالَتۡ رَبِّ أَنَّىٰ يَكُونُ لِى وَلَدٌ وَلَمۡ
يَمۡسَسۡنِى بَشَرٌ قَالَ كَذَٰلِكِ ٱللَّهُ يَخۡلُقُ
مَا يَشَآءُ إِذَا قَضَىٰٓ أَمۡرًا فَإِنَّمَا يَقُولُ لَهُۥ كُن
فَيَكُونُ ﴿٤٧﴾

She said: "O my Sustainer! How shall I have a son when no man has touched me?" He said: "Even so, Allah creates what He wills. When He has decreed a plan, He but says to it, 'Be,' and it is! (47)

وَيُعَلِّمُهُ ٱلۡكِتَٰبَ وَٱلۡحِكۡمَةَ وَٱلتَّوۡرَىٰةَ
وَٱلۡإِنجِيلَ ﴿٤٨﴾

"And Allah will teach him the Book and wisdom, the Torah and the Gospel, (48)

وَرَسُولًا إِلَىٰ بَنِىٓ إِسۡرَٰٓءِيلَ أَنِّى قَدۡ
جِئۡتُكُم بِـَٔايَةٍ مِّن رَّبِّكُمۡ أَنِّىٓ أَخۡلُقُ
لَكُم مِّنَ ٱلطِّينِ كَهَيۡـَٔةِ ٱلطَّيۡرِ
فَأَنفُخُ فِيهِ فَيَكُونُ طَيۡرَۢا بِإِذۡنِ ٱللَّهِ
وَأُبۡرِئُ ٱلۡأَكۡمَهَ وَٱلۡأَبۡرَصَ
وَأُحۡىِ ٱلۡمَوۡتَىٰ بِإِذۡنِ ٱللَّهِ وَأُنَبِّئُكُم بِمَا
تَأۡكُلُونَ وَمَا تَدَّخِرُونَ فِى بُيُوتِكُمۡ إِنَّ
فِى ذَٰلِكَ لَأٓيَةً لَّكُمۡ إِن كُنتُم مُّؤۡمِنِينَ
﴿٤٩﴾

"And (appoint him) a Messenger to the descendants of Israel. So, he invited the descendants of Israel, saying, 'I have come to you, with a sign from your Sustainer. I shall make for you out of clay the figure of a bird, and breathe into it, and it shall become a bird by Allah's leave. And I heal those born blind and the lepers, and I restore the dead to life, by Allah's leave; and I declare to you what you eat, and what you store in your houses. Surely therein is a sign for you if you would believe. (49)

وَمُصَدِّقًا لِّمَا بَيۡنَ يَدَىَّ مِنَ
ٱلتَّوۡرَىٰةِ وَلِأُحِلَّ لَكُم بَعۡضَ ٱلَّذِى
حُرِّمَ عَلَيۡكُمۡ وَجِئۡتُكُم بِـَٔايَةٍ مِّن
رَّبِّكُمۡ فَٱتَّقُواْ ٱللَّهَ وَأَطِيعُونِ ﴿٥٠﴾

"(I have come to you), to attest the Torah which was before me. And to make lawful to you part of what was (before) forbidden to you; I have come to you with a sign from your Sustainer. So fear Allah, and obey me. (50)

إِنَّ ٱللَّهَ رَبِّى وَرَبُّكُمْ فَٱعْبُدُوهُ ۗ هَٰذَا
صِرَٰطٌ مُّسْتَقِيمٌ ﴿٥١﴾

"It is Allah Who is my Sustainer and your Sustainer; so worship Him. This is the straight way.'" (51)

۞ فَلَمَّآ أَحَسَّ عِيسَىٰ مِنْهُمُ ٱلْكُفْرَ
قَالَ مَنْ أَنصَارِىٓ إِلَى ٱللَّهِ ۖ قَالَ
ٱلْحَوَارِيُّونَ نَحْنُ أَنصَارُ ٱللَّهِ ءَامَنَّا بِٱللَّهِ
وَٱشْهَدْ بِأَنَّا مُسْلِمُونَ ﴿٥٢﴾

When Jesus became aware of their unbelief, he asked: "Who will be my helpers in Allah's cause?" The disciples said: "We are Allah's helpers: We believe in Allah, and you do bear witness that we have surrendered ourselves to Him. (52)

رَبَّنَآ ءَامَنَّا بِمَآ أَنزَلْتَ وَٱتَّبَعْنَا
ٱلرَّسُولَ فَٱكْتُبْنَا مَعَ ٱلشَّٰهِدِينَ
﴿٥٣﴾

"Our Sustainer! We believe in what You have revealed, and we follow the Messenger; then write us down among those who bear witness." (53)

وَمَكَرُوا۟ وَمَكَرَ ٱللَّهُ ۖ وَٱللَّهُ خَيْرُ
ٱلْمَٰكِرِينَ ﴿٥٤﴾

And (the unbelievers) plotted and planned, and Allah too planned, and the best of planners is Allah. (54)

إِذْ قَالَ ٱللَّهُ يَٰعِيسَىٰٓ إِنِّى مُتَوَفِّيكَ
وَرَافِعُكَ إِلَىَّ وَمُطَهِّرُكَ مِنَ ٱلَّذِينَ
كَفَرُوا۟ وَجَاعِلُ ٱلَّذِينَ ٱتَّبَعُوكَ فَوْقَ
ٱلَّذِينَ كَفَرُوٓا۟ إِلَىٰ يَوْمِ ٱلْقِيَٰمَةِ ۖ ثُمَّ
إِلَىَّ مَرْجِعُكُمْ فَأَحْكُمُ بَيْنَكُمْ
فِيمَا كُنتُمْ فِيهِ تَخْتَلِفُونَ ﴿٥٥﴾

And when Allah said: "O Jesus! I will take you and raise you to Myself and clear you of those who blaspheme. I will set those who follow you above those who have rejected you, to the Day of Resurrection. Then shall you all return to me, and I will judge between you of the matters wherein you differed. (55)

فَأَمَّا ٱلَّذِينَ كَفَرُوا۟ فَأُعَذِّبُهُمْ عَذَابًا
شَدِيدًا فِى ٱلدُّنْيَا وَٱلْءَاخِرَةِ وَمَا لَهُم
مِّن نَّٰصِرِينَ ﴿٥٦﴾

"As to those who reject faith, I will punish them with terrible punishment in this world and in the hereafter, nor will they have anyone to help." (56)

وَأَمَّا ٱلَّذِينَ ءَامَنُوا۟ وَعَمِلُوا۟
ٱلصَّٰلِحَٰتِ فَيُوَفِّيهِمْ أُجُورَهُمْ ۗ وَٱللَّهُ لَا
يُحِبُّ ٱلظَّٰلِمِينَ ﴿٥٧﴾

"As to those who believe and work righteousness, Allah will grant them (in full) their reward; but Allah loves not evildoers." (57)

ذَٰلِكَ نَتْلُوهُ عَلَيْكَ مِنَ ٱلْـَٔايَـٰتِ وَٱلذِّكْرِ ٱلْحَكِيمِ ﴿٥٨﴾

"This is what we rehearse to you of Our signs and the message of wisdom." (58)

إِنَّ مَثَلَ عِيسَىٰ عِندَ ٱللَّهِ كَمَثَلِ ءَادَمَ ۖ خَلَقَهُۥ مِن تُرَابٍ ثُمَّ قَالَ لَهُۥ كُن فَيَكُونُ ﴿٥٩﴾

The similitude of Jesus before Allah is as that of Adam; He created him from dust, then said to him: "Be". And he was. (59)

ٱلْحَقُّ مِن رَّبِّكَ فَلَا تَكُن مِّنَ ٱلْمُمْتَرِينَ ﴿٦٠﴾

This is the truth from your Sustainer; so be not of those who doubt. (60)

فَمَنْ حَآجَّكَ فِيهِ مِنۢ بَعْدِ مَا جَآءَكَ مِنَ ٱلْعِلْمِ فَقُلْ تَعَالَوْا۟ نَدْعُ أَبْنَآءَنَا وَأَبْنَآءَكُمْ وَنِسَآءَنَا وَنِسَآءَكُمْ وَأَنفُسَنَا وَأَنفُسَكُمْ ثُمَّ نَبْتَهِلْ فَنَجْعَل لَّعْنَتَ ٱللَّهِ عَلَى ٱلْكَـٰذِبِينَ ﴿٦١﴾

If any one disputes in this matter with you, now after (full) knowledge has come to you, say: "Come! Let us gather together, our sons and your sons, our women and your women, ourselves and yourselves. Then let us earnestly pray, and invoke the curse of Allah on those who lie!" (61)

إِنَّ هَـٰذَا لَهُوَ ٱلْقَصَصُ ٱلْحَقُّ ۚ وَمَا مِنْ إِلَـٰهٍ إِلَّا ٱللَّهُ ۚ وَإِنَّ ٱللَّهَ لَهُوَ ٱلْعَزِيزُ ٱلْحَكِيمُ ﴿٦٢﴾

This is the true account. There is no god except Allah; and Allah is indeed the Exalted in power, the Wise. (62)

فَإِن تَوَلَّوْا۟ فَإِنَّ ٱللَّهَ عَلِيمٌۢ بِٱلْمُفْسِدِينَ ﴿٦٣﴾

But if they turn back, Allah has full knowledge of those who do mischief. (63)

Word study and explanation

إِذْ قَالَتِ ٱلْمَلَـٰٓئِكَةُ يَـٰمَرْيَمُ إِنَّ ٱللَّهَ يُبَشِّرُكِ بِكَلِمَةٍ مِّنْهُ ٱسْمُهُ ٱلْمَسِيحُ عِيسَى ٱبْنُ مَرْيَمَ وَجِيهًا فِى ٱلدُّنْيَا وَٱلْـَٔاخِرَةِ وَمِنَ ٱلْمُقَرَّبِينَ ﴿٤٥﴾

Remember when the angels said: "O Mary! Allah gives you glad tidings of a word from Him: his name will be Christ Jesus, the son of Mary, held in honour in both this world and the hereafter and of (the company of) those nearest to Allah. (45)

The repetition of *idh* (remember, when) shows that this is something separate from what Mary was initially advised in verses 42 and 43 above. Firstly, she was admonished to devote herself to worship and prayer. This was followed by the arrival of an angel to give her a glad tiding.

The meaning of the word *kalimah* and the significance of its use in an indefinite form have been fully explained above – please refer to the comments on verse 39.

Another point in the present context is worth noting. The glad tiding is delivered to Mary, a virgin and an extremely modest and pious person, informing her that she will have a son without the intervention of a man. That is why this glad tiding is given to her only of a word (*kalimah*), in very brief or vague terms. Later the mention of Jesus by name and his attributes clarifies what is meant by the word *kalimah.*

Christ (the anointed one) is the title of Jesus and as a rule it precedes the name. There has been a tradition among the descendants of Israel that his predecessor anointed the new prophet by rubbing some kind of sacred oil over his head and consecrating him as his successor. Later, when kingship was established among them the same custom was adopted to anoint kings. The prophet at the time consecrated the new king by sprinkling sacred oil over his head. This was a clear sign that the anointed one was the future king as well as the chosen one of God. From the Torah, it appears that this is how Prophet Samuel had appointed Ṭālūt and David to lead the Israelites. About Jesus, the Gospels say that he was baptised by Prophet Yaḥyā but there is no mention of anointing him by rubbing oil on his head. This is possibly due to the fact that he was born as an anointed one. From his features, as described in Bukhārī, the oil seems to be dripping from his hair. He might well have been called Christ due to this distinct characteristic. The Gospels use the words "anointed by God" for him.

The significance of the word *wajīh*

The word *wajīh* refers to nobility, as mentioned above in the case of Prophet Yaḥyā. From Luke, it appears that Jesus was twelve years old when he began teaching in the Temple. Despite his youth his speech was so full of wisdom, his description was so eloquent and forthright and his tone so sublime that the Jewish scholars, rabbis, Pharisees, the Chief Priest and the entire staff of the Temple marvelled. Who was this young man, they asked each other, who speaks with such authority, as if he has an authority from God? When he started preaching in the towns of Judea, he took them by storm. All the rabbis and the Pharisees were startled and astounded. They tried to check his popular appeal by questioning him closely on diverse subjects, but his brief and forthright answers rendered them speechless and they dared not open their mouths again. Within a short space of time his influence greatly increased, with the masses openly calling him the king of the Jews and lauding his expected kingdom. The issue became so serious that soon the Roman governor, Pilate, had to take notice of it. He too, despite his great power and Roman authority, was greatly impressed by the truth, nobility and immense popularity of Jesus Christ.

Another aspect of this nobility granted to Jesus is that though born without a father and while usually it is inconceivable to think of any nobility or honour for a child born under such conditions, being created by the word 'Be' he enjoyed unprecedented honour among the masses from the time of his birth. All his life he was surrounded by enemies but no one dared challenge his honour and dignity. A group among the Jews did speak against him but only in later times. During his life none dared speak against him or challenge him in this regard. Mary was given the good news of his nobility and honoured position along with the news of his birth so that she should not have any fear that because of his birth without a father the dignity of the child or her own position in society would in any way be affected.

A third aspect of his nobility is that this verse refutes all the false, derogatory statements found in the Gospels against Prophet Jesus, such as that the Jews (God forbid) slapped him, mocked him, abused him or spat on him. Most of these statements are, as shown below, wrong and unfounded. The enemies of Allah's Messengers do indeed try to insult them and they do have some respite from Allah in this regard, but it is limited to a fixed term. Whenever a people try to cross this threshold, Allah takes the Messenger into His own protection while his detractors are destroyed. We shall further elaborate this Divine law in the following pages.

Jesus, the son of Maryam

By describing Jesus as the son of Mary, this verse has cut the ground from under those who by flimsy arguments try to distort and pervert the most obvious and clear texts of the Qur'ān. If he was indeed the son of someone, what prevented the Qur'ān from referring him to his father instead of describing him as the son of Mary?

وَيُكَلِّمُ ٱلنَّاسَ فِى ٱلْمَهْدِ وَكَهْلًا وَمِنَ ٱلصَّٰلِحِينَ ﴿٤٦﴾

"He shall speak to the people in childhood and in maturity. And he shall be (of the company) of the righteous." (46)

Verses 45-63

Jesus speaks in the cradle

The speaking of Jesus in his cradle was a miracle from Allah to declare the chastity and innocence of Mary. The glad tidings of this miracle were conveyed to her along with the news of the child's birth. This was to assure her that Allah Who had chosen her to manifest one of His great signs, has also made arrangements so that none of her enemies could dare raise an accusing finger against her. Allah, who is extremely compassionate to His servants, could not conceivably leave her, a sincere believer and obedient servant, to become the target of accusing tongues with no one to speak in her defence and silence her accusers.

Meaning of the word *kahl*

The word *kahl* means middle age. From the existing gospels, it appears that Prophet Jesus had passed away before reaching middle age. This Qur'ānic verse, however, clearly says that Mary was also given the glad tidings of Jesus attaining to his middle age. And considering the Divine law concerning the Messengers, this seems to be the correct position. There are some hints in the Gospels that also support our assertion. For instance, in John 8:57 we read: "You are not yet fifty years old," the Jews said to him, "and you have seen Abraham!" Clearly this can be said only to a person who is in his late forties.

Mentioning his speaking in the cradle with a reference to his reaching middle age means that it was not merely childish talk but reflected maturity and wisdom because it was from Allah. At the end, by saying that "he shall be (of the company) of the righteous" it is made clear that whatever his wondrous attributes, achievements and miracles, these did not make him Divine or part of God. He was merely one of the righteous servants of Allah.

قَالَتْ رَبِّ أَنَّىٰ يَكُونُ لِي وَلَدٌ وَلَمْ يَمْسَسْنِي بَشَرٌ ۖ قَالَ كَذَٰلِكِ اللَّهُ يَخْلُقُ مَا يَشَاءُ ۚ إِذَا قَضَىٰ
أَمْرًا فَإِنَّمَا يَقُولُ لَهُ كُن فَيَكُونُ ﴿٤٧﴾

She said: "O my Sustainer! How shall I have a son when no man has touched me?" He said: "Even so: Allah creates what He wills. When He has decreed a plan, He but says to it, 'Be,' and it is!" (47)

The important parts of this verse have been explained above under verse 40. This verse, however, explains the word by which Jesus was created: "When He has decreed a plan, He but says to it, 'Be' and it is!"

وَيُعَلِّمُهُ ٱلْكِتَٰبَ وَٱلْحِكْمَةَ وَٱلتَّوْرَىٰةَ وَٱلْإِنجِيلَ ﴿٤٨﴾

And Allah will teach him the Book and wisdom, the Torah and the Gospel. (48)

Injīl is a collection of wisdom

The Torah and the Gospel (*Injīl*) are used to explain the nature of the Book and wisdom mentioned in the first part of the sentence. In other words Allah will teach him both the book and the wisdom. Prophet Jesus did not bring a separate Sharīʿah apart from that of the Torah. He was, in fact a follower of Prophet Mūsā's scripture and law. This he has repeatedly declared in the Gospels with great emphasis and clarity. He has, however, explained the true spirit of the Mosaic Law and its wisdom in a marvellously clear manner. The Gospels as such enshrine this very wisdom. The Jews had turned the Torah into a collection of lifeless commandments and rituals. This had deprived their Sharīʿah of its true spirit and made it a cumbersome burden that they carried. Jesus infused life into it by teaching them wisdom. The Jewish community of the time failed to appreciate this.

وَرَسُولًا إِلَىٰ بَنِيٓ إِسْرَٰٓءِيلَ أَنِّي قَدْ جِئْتُكُم بِـَٔايَةٍ مِّن رَّبِّكُمْ أَنِّيٓ أَخْلُقُ لَكُم مِّنَ ٱلطِّينِ كَهَيْـَٔةِ ٱلطَّيْرِ فَأَنفُخُ فِيهِ فَيَكُونُ طَيْرًۢا بِإِذْنِ ٱللَّهِ وَأُبْرِئُ ٱلْأَكْمَهَ وَٱلْأَبْرَصَ وَأُحْيِ ٱلْمَوْتَىٰ بِإِذْنِ ٱللَّهِ وَأُنَبِّئُكُم بِمَا تَأْكُلُونَ وَمَا تَدَّخِرُونَ فِي بُيُوتِكُمْ إِنَّ فِي ذَٰلِكَ لَأٓيَةً لَّكُمْ إِن كُنتُم مُّؤْمِنِينَ ﴿٤٩﴾

"And (appoint him) a messenger to the descendants of Israel. So, he invited the descendants of Israel, saying, 'I have come to you, with a sign from your Sustainer – I make for you out of clay the figure of a bird, and breathe into it, and it becomes a bird by Allah's leave. And I heal those born blind, and the lepers, and I quicken the dead, by Allah's leave; and I declare to you what you eat, and what you store in your houses. Surely therein is a sign for you if you would believe. (49)

Difference between a _nabī_ (prophet) and a _rasūl_ (messenger)

A verb is omitted before *rasūlan,* a verb such as *yabʿathu* (He will appoint or raise) and so it would read *yabʿat͟huhu rasūlan* (Allah will appoint him a messenger) making it clear that unlike Prophet Yaḥyā, Jesus was not merely a prophet, but was a prophet and a Messenger to the descendants of Israel just as Prophet Musā was sent as a Messenger to Pharaoh and his people.

Verses 45-63

There is a difference between a Prophet (*nabī*) and a Messenger (*rasūl*). The Messenger comes as a Divine judgement for the people he is sent to and their response to his message plays a crucial role in determining their fate. If their response is positive and they believe in him they are saved, but if they persist in their unbelief and try to harm the Messenger, they come to grief and are ultimately destroyed. Prophet Yaḥyā hinted at this in various statements:

> The axe is already at the root of the trees. I baptise you with water. But after me will come one who is more powerful than I. His winnowing fork is in his hand, and he will clear his threshing-floor, gathering his wheat into the barn and burning up the chaff with unquenchable fire (Matthew 3:10-12).

This clearly establishes the fact that Prophet Jesus was sent only to the descendants of Israel. He himself made this clear in no uncertain words. When he sent his disciples to propagate the message, he explicitly forbade them from approaching non-Israelites:

> Do not go among the Gentiles or enter any town of the Samaritans. Go rather to the lost sheep of Israel. (Matthew 10:5-6)

> "A Canaanite woman from that vicinity came to him, crying out, "Lord, Son of David, have mercy on me! My daughter is suffering terribly from demon-possession." He answered, "I was sent only to the lost sheep of Israel." The woman came and knelt before him. "Lord, help me!" she said. He replied, "It is not right to take the children's bread and toss it to their dogs." (Matthew 15:24-26)

The parable of the feast in the Gospels also refers to this special nature of his mission. The truths, virtues and moral values that his message embraced could be an effective argument only for the descendants of Israel. For other peoples, it was impossible to understand or appreciate them. As such, his message was by its very nature unsuitable for other nations. Thus it is a fact that other nations to whom this message was presented failed to understand it at all. All they learnt from the Gospels was that Jesus had shown very many miracles and as a result of this they exalted him as a god.

Omission of unnecessary details in the narration of stories

Innī qad ji'tukum bi āyatim mi-r rabbikum ('I have come to you, with a sign from your Sustainer'). The entire account of Jesus' life, from this glad tiding to the actual beginning of his call to the descendants of Israel as messenger, is left out here. The Qur'ān frequently uses this form of ellipsis in narrating the history of the prophets. The advantage of this method is that the reader's attention remains focused on the real theme and no irrelevant matter distracts him. The same is the case here. We are informed about the Prophet's mission and its purpose, and then he is shown as a caller addressing the descendants of Israel and explaining what he invited them to and the miracles that he showed as a proof to affirm the truth of his mission.

Difference between the descriptions of the Torah and of the Qur'ān

The miracles described here are all, with the exception of the first and the last miracle, mentioned in the Gospels. The only difference is that in the Qur'ān each of these miracles is described as subject to Allah's permission or "by the leave of Allah". In the Gospels, there is no such clarification. It may be that when Jesus was exalted to a Divine status, these words were deleted as unsuitable, considering his new status. But it is hard to conceal the truth. Despite all their efforts, the Gospels still contain shining examples of pure *tawḥīd* affirming the oneness of the one true God. One wonders how could the Christians succumb to polytheism so easily in the presence of such clear and perspicuous teachings?

Use of common noun to show universality

The use of the word *āyatin* (a sign) as an indefinite noun in the sentence *ji'tukum bi āyatin* does not denote a single sign but refers to the plurality of the signs, whatever their number, given to him. In other words, the sentence means: I have brought to you a clear warrant – irrespective of the number of the supporting arguments or signs – from your Sustainer that I have indeed been sent to you by your Sovereign Sustainer.

وَمُصَدِّقًا لِّمَا بَيْنَ يَدَيَّ مِنَ ٱلتَّوْرَىٰةِ وَلِأُحِلَّ لَكُم بَعْضَ ٱلَّذِى حُرِّمَ
عَلَيْكُمْ ۚ وَجِئْتُكُم بِـَٔايَةٍ مِّن رَّبِّكُمْ فَٱتَّقُوا۟ ٱللَّهَ وَأَطِيعُونِ ﴿٥٠﴾

"(I have come to you), to attest the Torah which was before me. And to make lawful to you part of what was (before) forbidden to you; I have come to you with a sign from your Sustainer. So fear Allah, and obey me". (50)

The meaning of *muṣaddiqan limā bayna yadayhi*

'(I have come to you), to attest the truth of the Torah which was before me).'

Muṣaddiqan, meaning attesting the truth is a circumstantial phrase that is used as a conjunctive to the preceding sentence. This signifies two things: firstly, it means that I have come to attest the truth of the Torah for which there is ample evidence found in the Gospels. Jesus Christ repeatedly and with great emphasis made it clear that he had come not to annul the Torah (literally, the law) but to affirm and establish it. He is also reported to have said that the heavens and the earth may change but not the slightest part of the Law will change until everything is fulfilled. He abided by the Mosaic Law and advised his followers to do the same. Whatever addition he made to this law was only an elucidation of the wisdom enshrined therein. As such, he unravelled the internal wisdom of the Torah to which the Jewish Pharisees and rabbis had closed their eyes. It was only during Paul's time that his followers openly rejected the Torah or the Mosaic Law.

Secondly, it means that he had come as fulfilment of the prophecies found in the Torah. The advent of Jesus affirmed all the prophecies reported from the earlier prophets and because of which the Jews had been awaiting the coming of a new prophet. So when the fame of Jesus spread, many thought that the prophet they had been waiting for had finally arrived. Some of them called him Elijah. It is reported in the Gospels that when prophet Yaḥyā, who was imprisoned by Herod, heard about him he sent some of his disciples to Jesus to ask if he was the one "we were waiting for" or should they wait for someone else. Jesus told them to go and tell him what they had seen – that the lame were healed and walked again, the dumb were beginning to speak and the blind were to see. What else were they waiting for? Jesus has referred to several prophecies about his advent reported from the earlier prophets. These are all present in the Gospels.

What forbidden things did Jesus make permissible?

(And to make lawful to you part of what was (before) forbidden to you)

Making lawful part of what was forbidden means making permissible things wrongfully declared unlawful by Jewish scholars by their false verdicts and undue excesses in religion. These invented prohibitions had, over the period of time, become entrenched traditions as part of the Sharī'ah. For instance, take the sanctity of the Sabbath which the Jewish jurists and Pharisees had so overblown, that even healing a sick person on this day was regarded by them as a sinful act and a contravention of its sanctity. There were several discussions between Jesus and the Jewish scholars on the sanctity of the Sabbath. The Gospels also tell us how Jesus and his disciples openly contravened it and when the Jewish scholars accused him of blasphemy because of this, he exposed the hollowness of their false religiosity.

إِنَّ ٱللَّهَ رَبِّى وَرَبُّكُمْ فَٱعْبُدُوهُ هَٰذَا صِرَٰطٌ مُّسْتَقِيمٌ ﴿٥١﴾

"'It is Allah Who is my Sustainer and your Sustainer. So worship Him. This is the straight way.'" (51)

Use of the word *ab* (father) for Allah

This represents the correction of the oft-repeated phrase "my father and your father" used in the Gospels. The Qur'ān corrects this mistake and explains what Jesus had stated was in fact "Allah alone is my Sustainer and your Sustainer, so worship Him and Him alone." But instead of following this clear and explicit teaching, the Christians put on it an essentially allegorical and unclear interpretation. The word *ab* in Hebrew is used both for father and sustainer or nourisher and the word *ibn* is used both for son and for *'abd* meaning a servant or a slave. Obviously, when a word is thus used in a possible dual sense, its actual sense at a specific place can be determined in the light of its context alone.

When the Christians adopted the creed of the divinity of Jesus, they used whatever material they could lay their hands on to support their creed, ignoring its context and original signification. Later, when the original *Injīl* was lost and was replaced with translations only, the meaning and interpretation of everything underwent a drastic change and distortion. However, despite all these distortions, there are still in the *Injīl* indications that clearly show that whenever Jesus uses the word *ab* for Allah, he invariably means *rabb* or Sovereign Sustainer. In fact at some places, by using other synonyms of this word, he makes his message amply clear. For instance, he is reported to have said: "Go instead to my brothers and tell them, 'I am returning to my Father and your Father, to my God and your God'" (John 20:17).

From this statement, it is quite clear that Jesus uses the word *ab* for Allah in order to emphasise Allah's providential care and compassion for His creation and definitely not to trace his lineage to Him. Moreover, Jesus also states that Allah is his God as well as the God of all.

Tawḥīd is the straight way

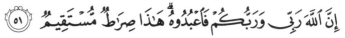

This means that the straight path to Allah is to accept Him as the Sovereign Sustainer of all, ours as well as of all others and to worship and adore Him alone. Those who have introduced crookedness in it and have consequently strayed into labyrinths of error, polytheism and unbelief – are lost. There is no crookedness in this path and it leads directly to Allah. The use of the indefinite form – *ṣirātun mustaqīmun* (straight path) – underlines the importance and pre-eminence of this natural path.

۞ فَلَمَّآ أَحَسَّ عِيسَىٰ مِنْهُمُ ٱلْكُفْرَ قَالَ مَنْ أَنصَارِىٓ إِلَى ٱللَّهِ ۖ قَالَ ٱلْحَوَارِيُّونَ
نَحْنُ أَنصَارُ ٱللَّهِ ءَامَنَّا بِٱللَّهِ وَٱشْهَدْ بِأَنَّا مُسْلِمُونَ ﴿٥٢﴾
رَبَّنَآ ءَامَنَّا بِمَآ أَنزَلْتَ وَٱتَّبَعْنَا ٱلرَّسُولَ فَٱكْتُبْنَا مَعَ ٱلشَّٰهِدِينَ ﴿٥٣﴾

When Jesus became aware of their unbelief, he asked: "Who will be my helpers in Allah's cause?" The disciples said: "We are Allah's helpers. We believe in Allah. Do bear witness that we have surrendered ourselves to Him. (52)
"Our Sustainer! We believe in what You have revealed, and we follow the Messenger. So write us down among those who bear witness." (53)

Meaning of the word *ḥawārī*

The word *ḥawārī* (disciple) seems to have been imported into Arabic from Hebrew. There is disagreement among the lexicologists about its true signification. In our opinion, it means a well-wisher, supporter and a helper. Just as the word *anṣār* is used for the first Muslims who helped and supported Prophet Muḥammad's call in its initial stage, *ḥawārīyūn* is used for the disciples of Jesus who believed in him and supported him steadfastly. He taught and trained them with great love and care. They carried his message to all the cities and towns in the land and they are mentioned in great detail in the Gospels.

Anṣār

The word *anṣār* is a plural of *nāṣir*. In our view there is not much difference in the meaning of *anṣār* and *ḥawārīyūn*. It is because of this shared meaning that in Sūrah aṣ-Ṣaff, the Qur'ān mentions the *ḥawārīyūn* of Jesus as an example for the *anṣār* of Madīnah.

This verse means that when Jesus realised that the Pharisees and the leaders of the tribe of Israel would not believe, he focussed all his attention on his poor companions who did not possess worldly wealth but were sincere believers. This has been a common practice of the prophets. In the beginning, they would try to warn and to enlist the support of the influential people in their community. However, when they realised that these arrogant and heedless people were not willing to change, they left them alone and concentrated on the destitute companions who had responded to their call.

The repeated admonition to the Prophet, peace be upon him, in the Qur'ān to leave alone the disbelievers and concentrate on the believers relates to this very phase of the Islamic movement. And it was also during this phase that Jesus invited the fishermen, who made their living by catching fish, so as to teach them how to catch people: "from now on you will catch men"[18].

A prime aspect of the character of the Prophets

This verse also throws light on the character of the prophets. They never lose hope even under the worst of circumstances nor are they discouraged by the persistent denial of their people. They continue to work ceaselessly in the cause of Allah and if the powerful and influential classes do not co-operate with them, they continue their journey in the company of the poor, weak and faithful followers who have little power or influence. The more grim a situation and the greater the apathy of their people, the greater is their will to spread light and the stronger their resolve to accomplish their mission. Allah willing, we shall discuss in detail this aspect of the prophets' character in the commentary on Sūrah Nūḥ.

"Who will be my helpers in Allah's cause?"

As pointed out above, these words show on the one hand the Prophet's zeal to convey the message, and on the other it also shows the firmness of his resolve and unshakeable faith in Allah that makes him independent of any need for others' help or company. Looked at closely, implied in this clarion call also is the message: Indeed, I have taken the path to my Sustainer. Let those who have the will and the courage, come and join me in treading this hazardous path.

This decisiveness and determination of the Prophet can infuse even the dead with life. Those who are morally alive are awakened by this call that makes them restless and all the more eager for guidance. They cover a year's journey in a few moments. It is worth noting here that in response to Prophet Jesus' call, *Man anṣārī ilā Allah,* (who will be my helpers in Allah's cause?), his disciples unhesitatingly declared, "*Naḥnū anṣārullāh* – We are Allah's helpers." In the statement of Prophet Jesus, the particle *ilā* indicates the distance that had to be traversed to reach the final destination. And that was precisely what he, as a caller to Allah, had to do: to inform them about the hardships of the path and the distance that they had to travel. The disciples in

18. Luke, 5:10

their burning fervour, as it were, seem to have reached the final goal, indeed truly befitting the intensity and depth of the state of their faith or *īmān* and of their *islām*, or obedience to Allah.

Implications of being *Anṣārūllāh* (helpers of Allah)

We may also note here that whereas the question put to them by Jesus is brief, the response of the disciples is rather detailed. They affirm their faith and make Jesus a witness to their faith. Besides affirming their faith and obedience to the Messenger, they also supplicate to Allah to record them as witnesses to the truth. This shows that the disciples were well aware of what it means to be the helpers of Allah, and its implications and consequences. One of its implications is sincere belief in Allah, willing obedience to His commandments, embracing the guidance revealed by Him through His Messenger, and bearing witness to the truth of the message by word and by deed, in life and in death. This testimony, when backed up by the sacrifice of life, is indeed the truest and the noblest testimony.

It is also noteworthy that the disciples in particular ask Jesus to witness that they are Muslims. Clearly they considered themselves to be Muslims (lit. those who submit to God) with their religion as Islam (submission to God). They had no idea of Christianity nor did they look upon themselves as Christians or Jews. This is important, considering the central theme of this sūrah that, as discussed in the introductory remarks, is Islam.

Then write us down among those who bear witness

This is their supplication: that they be counted as the bearers of, and witnesses to, truth on the Day of Judgement. It is this testimony to witness truth that is incumbent on the followers of every Prophet after him. The Prophet bears witness to truth before his community even at the risk of his life. And after him, it is the responsibility of his community that they should bear witness before others without any fear, prejudice or bias. This testimony has to be by heart, word, and deed and by sacrificing property and even life. The opposite of standing up as witnesses to truth is to hide and conceal it, the most heinous of sins in the sight of the Divine law. In the history of religion, the Jews are the prime example of such conduct because of which they incurred Divine wrath. Looked at more closely, we find an oblique reference here to this aspect of Jewish history in this supplication of Prophet Jesus' disciples.

The following verse of Sūrah aṣ-Ṣaff also deals, albeit in somewhat different words, with this subject:

O you who believe! Be the helpers of Allah, as Jesus, the son of Mary, said to the disciples, "Who will be my helpers in the cause of Allah?" The disciples answered, "We are Allah's helpers!" Then a group of the descendants of Israel believed, and a group disbelieved. So We helped those who believed against their enemies, and they prevailed (against them). (Sūrah aṣ-Ṣaff, 61:14)

Helping Allah clearly means helping and supporting Allah's Messenger and the religion that he brings to be established on earth. The fact that Allah stands in no need of help from anyone, yet helping and supporting His message is described as helping Allah. This goes to show that Allah loves the efforts in the propagation of His message ensuring the welfare and well being of His servants.

وَمَكَرُواْ وَمَكَرَ ٱللَّهُۖ وَٱللَّهُ خَيۡرُ ٱلۡمَٰكِرِينَ ٥٤

And (the unbelievers) plotted and planned, and Allah too planned, and the best of planners is Allah. (54)

Significance of the word *makr*

The word *makr* means a secret scheme to cause harm to someone. It has come to connote a negative sense as resorting to secret scheming against someone and betrays the weakness of the schemers. As it is usually the weak who fall back upon *makr* or secret schemes, its negative sense became more pronounced, and the term was taken to convey essentially a negative aspect. Wherever it is used, the assumption is that it must be in a negative sense. This is far from being true. At times, one has to resort to secret scheming to counter the schemers or to punish them. Any open action against the perpetrators of secret scheming can easily be depicted as unjust and an act of aggression. Most people who are unaware of the real facts may also be led to believe that the perpetrators were justified in their actions.

A common feature of Prophets' life

Similarly, secret scheming is necessary at times to forewarn a conspiring enemy that others are not unaware of his machinations and that these will be severely resisted. This not only shames such conspirators but also acts as a strong deterrent against any future trouble on their part. The secret planning referred to in this verse with regard to Allah is precisely of this nature and is aimed at countering the hostile conspiracies rendering them ineffective and harmless. Such counter measures often take the enemies unawares, leaving them stunned, while at the same time relieving others of trouble and harm. This is referred to in the verse by the words "*and the best of planners is Allah*". As to the question of how Allah saved Jesus Christ, peace be on him, from the conspiracies against him hatched by the Jews, we will discuss it at length in our commentary on the next sūrah – Sūrah an-Nisā'.

Jewish conspiracies against Jesus Christ

What this verse refers to is a common characteristic of the life of all Prophets. History shows that when the Prophets despaired of a positive response from the leaders of their people and turned their attention to poor people, they gained support and companions among them and their message steadily spread. The elders and leaders of the community saw this as a serious threat to their authority. To counter this threat, they resorted to conspiracies so as to eliminate the prophets and the threat to the established system posed by their revolutionary message.

Every prophet, as pointed out above, had to go through this stage during the life of his mission. Thus, for instance, the Jewish establishment, the leaders and scholars, tried to counter the threat to their religious authority from Prophet Jesus by resorting to various conspiracies against him.

They accused him and his disciples of violating the traditions of their forefathers and bringing their elders into disrepute. By this they wanted to incite the sentiments of the Jewish public against Jesus and his disciples.

They tried to trap him by asking him about various issues in order to gather sufficient material for declaring him guilty of apostasy and unbelief. The Pharisees and the Sadducees among them were prominent for their eagerness in this campaign. From Jesus's parables, they collected some material that in their eyes was sufficient for convicting him as an apostate guilty of unbelief. For this crime, he must therefore face the penalty of death, they concluded.

They also tried to turn the government of the day, the Romans, who occupied Palestine at the time, against him by putting together some "seditious" material from Jesus Christ's statements. He was questioned about the payment of tribute to the Roman authorities to show that he incited the Jewish people to refuse its payment to the Caesar. But he answered all such questions so deftly that the plotters failed to get any incriminating evidence. They also accused him of claiming to be the king of the Jews. For this, they tried to use some words and phrases from his parabolic expressions to rouse the anger of the Romans against him.

In yet another conspiracy, they bribed Judah who was one of Jesus' twelve disciples and a hypocrite, to spy on him and help them to arrest and capture him by leading them to him.

All these intrigues are mentioned in detail in the Gospels, but as the Qur'ān only refers to these in brief, we think they may well be left as brief hints only.

It is at this stage in the career of a Prophet of Allah when he leaves his own people and, after making a declaration to his enemies, makes *hijrah* to another place. This *hijrah* may take various forms as discussed later in this book.

إِذْ قَالَ ٱللَّهُ يَٰعِيسَىٰٓ إِنِّى مُتَوَفِّيكَ وَرَافِعُكَ إِلَىَّ وَمُطَهِّرُكَ مِنَ ٱلَّذِينَ كَفَرُوا۟ وَجَاعِلُ ٱلَّذِينَ ٱتَّبَعُوكَ فَوْقَ ٱلَّذِينَ كَفَرُوٓا۟ إِلَىٰ يَوْمِ ٱلْقِيَٰمَةِ ۖ ثُمَّ إِلَىَّ مَرْجِعُكُمْ فَأَحْكُمُ بَيْنَكُمْ فِيمَا كُنتُمْ فِيهِ تَخْتَلِفُونَ ﴿٥٥﴾

And when Allah said: "O Jesus! I will take you and raise you to Myself and clear you of those who blaspheme. I will set those who follow you above those who have rejected you, to the Day of Resurrection. Then shall you all return to me, and I will judge between you concerning the matters wherein you differed. (55)

Divine scheme to safeguard Jesus Christ

In this verse is described the secret plan of Allah to protect and safeguard Jesus Christ from the machinations of the Jews, frustrating all their efforts and unravelling their conspiracies against him.

Literal and metaphorical meaning of the term *tuwaffi*

The word *tuwaffi* in Arabic originally means receiving something in full, it means *al-akhdh bi-t tām-ma* – to recall something back in its entirety. Its use for death is not in its literal, but only in a metaphorical sense. Such words that may be used in their literal as well as in a metaphorical sense must be supported by contextual evidence for their correct meaning and significance.

The following contextual evidence clearly shows that at this place the word *tawaffi* is not used in the sense of causing death.

Contextual evidence that contradicts 'causing him to die'

Firstly, the Prophet Jesus Christ and his companions are here given good news and promised victory. As the stories of all of Allah's messengers show, whenever their people resolved to assassinate their prophets, Allah promised them victory and took them under His own protection. This verse also conveys the good news and a promise of victory to Jesus Christ and his disciples. How can it then be appropriate to tell him on this occasion, "I am going to cause you to die," as this was precisely what his enemies wanted, the only difference being that in one case he would have been killed by the enemies and in the other die a natural death?

Secondly, if this word at this place means causing death, then the subsequent phrase *rāfi'uka ilayya* (raise you to Myself) becomes superfluous. What is the sense of saying "I am going to cause you to die and raise you to Myself?" In the present context, obviously the words *rāfi'uka ilayya* used after *mutawaf-fīka* are meant to explain the true meaning of the term *tawaffā*. The term in fact means that I will recall you and that this recall will be in the form of raising you to Myself.

Thirdly, to take the phrase *rāfi'uka ilayya* in the present context merely in the sense of raising in ranks is also not correct. For in such a case the preposition *ilā* that follows *rāfi'uka ilayya* becomes redundant and superfluous, whereas in the Qur'ān no word or phrase is used superfluously. Had it meant to indicate the raising in rank, then according to the Arabic idiom the term *rāfi'uka* would have been enough and there was no need for using the preposition *ilā* after it. Wherever this term is used in the Qur'ān in the sense of raising someone in ranks it is always used without the addition of *ilā* to it. Thus, for instance we read:

> *Min-hum man kallama Allāhu wa rafa'a ba'ḍa-hum darajātin (To some among them Allah spoke and others He raised in degrees (of honour)* (Sūrah al-Baqarah, 2:253).

> *Wa law shi'nā la-rafa'nāhu bihā wa lākinna akhlada ilā-al arḍ (If We wished, We should have elevated him with these signs, but he was inclined to the earth* (Sūrah al-A'rāf, 7:176).

> *Wa rafa'nāhu makānan 'alīyyan. (And We raised him to a lofty station)* (Sūrah Maryam, 19:57)

If the particle *ilā* is taken into account fully – as it must indeed be – the phrase *rāfi'uka ilayya* mean "I shall raise you up to Myself with great honour and esteem."

Fourthly, at another place where the Qur'ān has mentioned this subject it has omitted the word *mutawaf-fīka*. After refuting the assertions that Prophet Jesus, peace be upon him, was killed or crucified, the Qur'ān only affirms that he was raised alive: *"Bal rafa'a-hullāhu ilay-hi"* (Nay, Allah raised him up unto Himself"). This is a clear indication that, in these words, the Qur'ān has described the manner of *tawaffi* or raising him up to Allah. Just consider the verse:

> *But they killed him not, nor crucified him, but so it was made to appear to them. And those who differ therein are full of doubts, with no (certain) knowledge, but only conjecture to follow, for, of a surety, they killed him not. Nay, Allah raised him up unto Himself; and Allah is exalted in Power, Wise.* (Sūrah an-Nisā' 4:157-158)

This was perhaps the most appropriate place to explain how Jesus Christ died. Rather, the Qur'ān here categorically refutes the claims of those who said that they had killed or crucified him. Had he met his death naturally the Qur'ān should have clearly stated that he was neither killed nor crucified but Allah caused him to die. However, the Qur'ān not only does not say this – it does not even use the word *tawaffi* at this place. Instead, it uses only the phrase *bal rafa'a-hullāhu ilay-hi* (Allah raised him up unto Himself). It requires a stretch of the imagination for any discerning person with literary sensibility to take the word *raf'a* to mean death, especially after such a categorical refutation that he was killed or crucified.

Raising up of Jesus Christ to the heaven is a kind of *hijrah*

(and clear you of those who blaspheme)

This means that Allah shall separate Jesus from this corrupt society and cause him to enter among the righteous and the faithful servants of Allah. The Divine law regarding the Prophets has always been that they stay among the people that they are sent to until there is hope that they might respond and believe. This hope ends when they resolve upon assassinating the Prophet. At this time, with the permission of Allah, the Prophet emigrates and leaves them. Just as the body undergoes a process of decomposition and decay after separation from the soul, the deniers of the Prophet invariably suffer humiliation and defeat after his departure from among them. The Prophet and his companions leave behind the evil and corrupt society and build a new, healthy and wholesome environment that further strengthens them morally and spiritually. As against this, their enemies lose all the healthy and sound elements and consequently rush headlong toward their disaster. Ustādh Farāhī has discussed all the effects and consequences of the believers' *hijrah*, (migration) in his commentary on Sūrah al-Kāfirūn. The raising up of Jesus Christ to the heaven is a kind of *hijrah* and just as all the messengers received glad tidings of victory and success in its wake, he also received glad tidings of success and victory after this *hijrah,* as is stated in the following words:

> *I will set those who follow you above those who have rejected you, to the Day of Resurrection: Then shall you all return to me, and I will judge between you of the matters wherein you differed.*

Dominance of Jesus' followers over the Jews

This is the glad tidings for Jesus Christ that his followers will always be dominant over his deniers. It is a historical fact that ever since this glad tidings, the followers of Jesus Christ have always enjoyed dominance over the Jews. Even today when apparently there exists a separate Jewish state, this is still true. The present Jewish state was established with the support and blessings of the Christians and exists only by their continued support and backing.

A question and its answer

One may however ask, can these Christians be really described as true followers of Jesus Christ when in practice they follow their own innovations contradicting the teachings of Jesus? The answer to this question is that the words "*those who follow you*" apply not only to his true followers but also include all his professed followers. Consider for instance the following points:

One, the Qur'ān uses the words *ahl al-kitāb* – people of the book – and *al-ladhīna ūtū-l kitāb* in two different senses. At some places these are used for them as a group irrespective of their actual beliefs and deeds, while at other places they refer to only the true People of the Book. In our view, the phrase *alladhīna attabaʿūka* (those who follow you) carries a wider meaning and refers to all followers of Jesus Christ, the true believers as well as those who merely profess belief in him.

Two, in this verse "*those who follow you*" are placed opposite to *those who have rejected you,* which clearly shows that the contrast here is between the outright rejecters of Jesus Christ and those who professed to follow him rather than between his sincere followers and the heretics.

Three, the occasion here is that of conveying good news to him. This has a much wider connotation. If the words *those who follow you* referred only to his sincere followers, it would have greatly restricted the area of good news. Just as when Allah gave Prophet Ibrāhīm the good news of providing sustenance to his children, it was not restricted merely to the believers among them but also applied to the non-believers among his offspring. Similarly, here the words *those who follow you* cover genuine followers of Jesus Christ as well as those who professed belief in him.

Messengers as final judgement to a nation

As mentioned above, the Messengers from among the Prophets come as final judgement to a nation. Through them, the question of truth and falsehood is settled among a people. In the controversy that follows, the Messenger and his companions emerge as victorious irrespective of whether this victory is achieved in the lifetime of the Messenger or by his followers after him. The Qur'ān tells us that Jesus Christ was sent not merely as a Prophet but a Messenger to the descendants of Israel. As such, inevitably the Messenger and his followers were bound to prevail as promised in this verse as well as at another place: "Allah has decreed: 'It is I and My Messengers who must prevail'" (Sūrah al-Mujādilah, 58:21). It is this Divine judgement that is frequently mentioned in the gospels. In view of this distinctive characteristic of the Messengers, Allah does not allow their enemies to kill them. There is no proof that any of the Messengers were ever killed at the hands of their enemies. This clearly goes against the Christian assertions that Jesus Christ was crucified. We will discuss this in detail in Sūrah al-Mā'idah.

فَأَمَّا ٱلَّذِينَ كَفَرُوا۟ فَأُعَذِّبُهُمْ عَذَابًا شَدِيدًا فِى ٱلدُّنْيَا وَٱلْءَاخِرَةِ وَمَا لَهُم مِّن
نَّٰصِرِينَ ﴿٥٦﴾
وَأَمَّا ٱلَّذِينَ ءَامَنُوا۟ وَعَمِلُوا۟ ٱلصَّٰلِحَٰتِ فَيُوَفِّيهِمْ أُجُورَهُمْ ۗ وَٱللَّهُ لَا يُحِبُّ
ٱلظَّٰلِمِينَ ﴿٥٧﴾

"As to those who reject faith, I will punish them with terrible punishment in this world and in the hereafter, nor will they have anyone to help." (56)
"As to those who believe and work righteousness, Allah will give them (in full) their reward; and Allah loves not evildoers." (57)

Such a Divine judgement is a necessary consequence of the advent of a Messenger to a people. It holds the threat of punishment both in this world and in the life hereafter. The horrible disasters experienced by the Jews in this world were a result of the rejection of truth by them. The words "and Allah loves not evildoers" clearly contain a hint that if those who profess belief in Jesus Christ relapsed into *shirk* (polytheism) and heresy they would not escape their punishment in the hereafter, because Allah likes not those who, after having believed, relapse into polytheism and heresy and thus wrong their own selves.

ذَٰلِكَ نَتۡلُوهُ عَلَيۡكَ مِنَ ٱلۡأٓيَٰتِ وَٱلذِّكۡرِ ٱلۡحَكِيمِ ﴿٥٨﴾

"This is what we rehearse to you of Our signs and the message of wisdom." (58)

This and the next five verses represent a digression that is addressed to the Prophet, peace be upon him. In between the discourse, the Prophet is comforted regarding his opponents (especially the behaviour of the Christians) and given certain important instructions. In other words, the purpose of this historical narrative is to present the true picture about Jesus Christ. This is the true account about him and, unlike the Christian version, is not a fabrication and distortion of his life and mission. These are the messages of Allah and a reminder full of wisdom. The Christians have woven a mythology around his person that can lead only to further error and misguidance. Allah has explained the truth and clarified his true position so as to open further avenues for you to appreciate truth, follow guidance, and benefit from Divine wisdom and admonition. A similar digression is found later in verse 108: "These are the signs of Allah: We rehearse them to you in truth: And Allah means no injustice to any of His creatures." This further helps explain some terms used in the present verse. This means that Allah has once again manifested the truth so that people would have no excuse for persisting in their errant ways. If they still persist, they would be held accountable for it.

إِنَّ مَثَلَ عِيسَىٰ عِندَ ٱللَّهِ كَمَثَلِ ءَادَمَۖ خَلَقَهُۥ مِن تُرَابٖ ثُمَّ قَالَ لَهُۥ كُن فَيَكُونُ ﴿٥٩﴾
ٱلۡحَقُّ مِن رَّبِّكَ فَلَا تَكُن مِّنَ ٱلۡمُمۡتَرِينَ ﴿٦٠﴾

The similitude of Jesus before Allah is as that of Adam; He created him from dust, then said to him: "Be". And he was. (59)
This is the truth from your Sustainer; so be not of those who doubt. (60)

This is the conclusive verse on this subject and it means that just as Allah created Adam from dust saying 'Be' and it was done, so did He create Jesus by His word 'Be'. In this regard Adam enjoys a clear precedence over Jesus as he was created without a father and a mother, but still the Christians do not exalt him as a god. Why should they then exalt Jesus Christ to be a god?

Use of the word *ibn* (son) for others

In fact there was no reason for confusing the matter on account of his birth just as there was no justification for error due to the use of the word 'ibn' (son) for Jesus, especially as this word has been used in the Torah and in the Gospels for Adam (Luke 3:38), for angels (Genesis 6:2, 4), for Jacob (Deuteronomy, 14:1), and also for the Christians (John, 1:11-12). If the mere use of this word were a sufficient reason to exalt some one as a god, why restrict it to Jesus only, because a whole host of 'gods' can be marshalled in the light of this logic and considering the use of the word in the Torah and the Gospels.

Here the discourse reaches its conclusion and the discussion ends with the words *al-ḥaqqu mir rabbika* (this is the truth from your Sustainer). In our opinion, the subject or *mubtada'* in this sentence is omitted (*maḥdhūf*). The purpose as explained previously, is to focus the attention of the reader on the predicate or *khabr*. In other words, this is the real position of Jesus and is clearly stated here. The rest is merely a web of fictitious stories concocted by the Christians. The words *fa-la takun mina-l mumtarīn* (so be not of those who doubt) though apparently addressed to the Prophet, peace be upon him, is as usual addressed to the Muslim community and any implied displeasure in these words is directed at the Prophet's enemies. The Qur'ān no longer consider them worthy of being addressed directly, the answer to their question is supplied indirectly through the believers.

فَمَنْ حَآجَّكَ فِيهِ مِنۢ بَعْدِ مَا جَآءَكَ مِنَ ٱلْعِلْمِ فَقُلْ تَعَالَوْا۟ نَدْعُ أَبْنَآءَنَا وَأَبْنَآءَكُمْ
وَنِسَآءَنَا وَنِسَآءَكُمْ وَأَنفُسَنَا وَأَنفُسَكُمْ ثُمَّ نَبْتَهِلْ فَنَجْعَل لَّعْنَتَ ٱللَّهِ عَلَى
ٱلْكَٰذِبِينَ ٦١

If any one disputes in this matter with you, now after (full) knowledge has come to you, say: "Come! Let us gather together, our sons and your sons, our women and your women, ourselves and yourselves: Then let us earnestly pray, and invoke the curse of Allah on those who lie!" (61)

Al-'Ilm (the knowledge)

As discussed in comments at another place[19] the term *al-'lim* refers to the true knowledge that is received through revelation from Allah, with the word *ẓann* (conjecture) being its opposite.

Omission of certain words in the verse

Certain words in the above verse are omitted, as is usually the case in Arabic. After inserting these omitted words the whole sentence would read: '*Nad'ū naḥnū abnā-a nā wa antum abnā-a kum wa naḥnu anfusanā wa antum anfusakum thum-ma nabtahil naḥnu wa antum.* In the translation, we have taken this into consideration.

19. See comments on verses 120 and 145 of Sūrah al-Baqarah (*Pondering over the Qur'ān*)

Purpose and use of *mubāhalah*

The word *ibtihāl* means a supplication and beseeching Allah with humility. It also carries a sense of abandonment and its use for mutual cursing is quite well known.

In matters where a difference of opinion is based on some rational or logical premise, the disagreement can be resolved through reasoning and argument. In a situation, however, when, after all arguments and a thorough discussion, the opponent stubbornly persists out of arrogance and a wrong sense of prestige in his demonstrably wrong stand, even if the truth is clear as the shining sun overhead, as a last resort *mubāhalah* may be the only way to settle the argument on such occasions. It is a proven historical fact that the Christians did not dare to accept this challenge of the Qur'ān which conclusively proved that they themselves did not consider their view of Jesus as correct but were apparently stuck with it and continued to voice their belief in it merely on account of their group prejudices. On the other hand, challenging them thus to mutual cursing on the part of the Prophet, peace be upon him, was a manifest proof that he was fully convinced of the truth and validity of his position.

The inclusion of one's family and all the near ones immensely increases the seriousness of the challenge. No person would knowingly dare curse his own wife, sons and other near and dear ones.

إِنَّ هَٰذَا لَهُوَ ٱلْقَصَصُ ٱلْحَقُّ ۚ وَمَا مِنْ إِلَٰهٍ إِلَّا ٱللَّهُ ۚ وَإِنَّ ٱللَّهَ لَهُوَ ٱلْعَزِيزُ ٱلْحَكِيمُ ﴿٦٢﴾
فَإِن تَوَلَّوْا۟ فَإِنَّ ٱللَّهَ عَلِيمٌۢ بِٱلْمُفْسِدِينَ ﴿٦٣﴾

This is the true account: There is no god except Allah; and Allah is indeed the Exalted in Power, the Wise. (62)
But if they turn back, Allah has full knowledge of those who do mischief. (63)

These verses speak about the real and true status of Jesus Christ. Whatever status or position he has in the sight of Allah, it is only as His Prophet and a Messenger: he has no share in Divinity. Allah alone is the true God and He is *'Azīz* (Mighty) and *Ḥakīm* (All-Wise). All His works are based on wisdom and are for the benefit of His creation. Both these Divine attributes categorically refute any kind or form of polytheism.

Shirk represents corruption on earth

In the second verse, the message is that *mubāhalah* was the last and the only way of settling this dispute. If they do not agree to it, then it clearly means that they are not willing to follow the truth. In other words, they persist in their rejection of truth, the necessary consequence of which is discord and corruption on earth.

Shirk, taking gods other than Allah, is the root cause of all corruption and discord. Had there been more than one god in the heavens and earth the entire system and order of the physical universe would have been shattered. Similarly, if in religion it were accepted that there are others who share authority with Allah, the One True God, the entire system of justice in this life would be completely destroyed.

Verses 64-71: thematic continuity

Tawḥīd is a universal reality

After explaining the true position and status of Jesus, both the Christians and the Jews are addressed in this section and invited to respond to the call of *tawḥīd*, the belief in One God, and Islam.

The section begins by stating that all true believers share the belief in One God. The message of the oneness of God brought by Prophet Muḥammad, is none other than the one brought by other earlier prophets and scriptures. Therefore, if Jews and Christians refuse to respond to this message of *tawḥīd,* they not only reject the Qur'ān but also their own prophets and scriptures that enshrine a similar message.

Prophet Ibrāhīm was a true Muslim

In this regard, referring to Prophet Ibrāhīm, peace be upon him, the Qur'ān pointedly asks them why have they dragged in his name, in support of their innovations. It asserts that Ibrāhīm was neither a Jew nor a Christian, but an upright Muslim who had submitted himself to the will of his Sustainer. Both the Torah and the Gospels were revealed long after his time. Both Judaism and Christianity are your innovations, they are told, so why do you bring him in support of your claims? The only people who are truly related to Ibrāhīm are those who follow the community of Islam – the people who are committed to Allah and have surrendered their wills to Him. They alone follow in the footsteps of Prophet Ibrāhīm who are the followers of Prophet Muḥammad, peace be upon him, rather than those who are dead set against the Divine message brought by the Prophet of Islam. This message invites them to the true religion of Ibrāhīm, which is Islam: complete and unconditional surrender to the will of God.

An admonition to the Muslims

The Muslims are thereafter warned to beware of the machinations of the People of the Book against them. All their efforts are focused on causing the Muslims to stray off the straight path. At the same time, the People of the Book are warned. They are asked what sort of vocation it is that they have chosen for themselves when they have the Torah and read the scriptures. Yet, they knowingly deny and oppose the truth, and mislead others and prevent them from embracing the truth. Bearing these brief remarks in mind, let us now read the following verses.

Say: "O People of the Book! Come to common terms as between us and you: that we worship none but Allah; that we associate no partners with Him; that we do not set up, from among ourselves, lords and patrons other than Allah." If then they turn back, say: "Bear witness that we are Muslims (committed to serve and obey Allah)." (64)

قُلْ يَٰٓأَهْلَ ٱلْكِتَٰبِ تَعَالَوْا۟ إِلَىٰ كَلِمَةٍ
سَوَآءٍۭ بَيْنَنَا وَبَيْنَكُمْ أَلَّا نَعْبُدَ إِلَّا
ٱللَّهَ وَلَا نُشْرِكَ بِهِۦ شَيْـًٔا وَلَا يَتَّخِذَ
بَعْضُنَا بَعْضًا أَرْبَابًا مِّن دُونِ ٱللَّهِ ۚ
فَإِن تَوَلَّوْا۟ فَقُولُوا۟ ٱشْهَدُوا۟ بِأَنَّا
مُسْلِمُونَ ﴿٦٤﴾

O People of the Book! Why do you dispute about Ibrāhīm, when the Torah and the Gospel were not revealed till after him? Do you not understand this? (65)

يَٰٓأَهْلَ ٱلْكِتَٰبِ لِمَ تُحَآجُّونَ فِىٓ
إِبْرَٰهِيمَ وَمَآ أُنزِلَتِ ٱلتَّوْرَىٰةُ وَٱلْإِنجِيلُ
إِلَّا مِنۢ بَعْدِهِۦٓ ۚ أَفَلَا تَعْقِلُونَ ﴿٦٥﴾

You are the ones who disputed in matters of which you had some knowledge! But why do you dispute in matters of which you have no knowledge? It is Allah Who knows, and you who know not! (66)

هَٰٓأَنتُمْ هَٰٓؤُلَآءِ حَٰجَجْتُمْ فِيمَا لَكُم
بِهِۦ عِلْمٌ فَلِمَ تُحَآجُّونَ فِيمَا لَيْسَ لَكُم
بِهِۦ عِلْمٌ ۚ وَٱللَّهُ يَعْلَمُ وَأَنتُمْ لَا تَعْلَمُونَ
﴿٦٦﴾

Ibrāhīm was not a Jew nor a Christian; but he was a Muslim single-mindedly devoted to Allah's service, and he was not of those who joined partners with Allah. (67)

مَا كَانَ إِبْرَٰهِيمُ يَهُودِيًّا وَلَا نَصْرَانِيًّا
وَلَٰكِن كَانَ حَنِيفًا مُّسْلِمًا وَمَا كَانَ مِنَ
ٱلْمُشْرِكِينَ ﴿٦٧﴾

Without doubt, the people closest to Ibrāhīm, are those who followed him, and this Prophet and those who believe in him. And Allah is the friend of believers. (68)

إِنَّ أَوْلَى ٱلنَّاسِ بِإِبْرَٰهِيمَ لَلَّذِينَ ٱتَّبَعُوهُ
وَهَٰذَا ٱلنَّبِيُّ وَٱلَّذِينَ ءَامَنُوا۟ ۗ وَٱللَّهُ وَلِيُّ
ٱلْمُؤْمِنِينَ ﴿٦٨﴾

A section of the People of the Book would love to lead you astray, but they only lead themselves astray, but they do not perceive! (69)

وَدَّت طَّآئِفَةٌ مِّنْ أَهْلِ ٱلْكِتَٰبِ لَوْ
يُضِلُّونَكُمْ وَمَا يُضِلُّونَ إِلَّآ أَنفُسَهُمْ
وَمَا يَشْعُرُونَ ﴿٦٩﴾

People of the Book! Why do you reject the signs of Allah to which you yourselves bear witness? (70)

يَٰٓأَهْلَ ٱلْكِتَٰبِ لِمَ تَكْفُرُونَ بِـَٔايَٰتِ
ٱللَّهِ وَأَنتُمْ تَشْهَدُونَ ﴿٧٠﴾

People of the Book! Why do you confound the truth with falsehood, and conceal the truth, deliberately? (71)

يَٰٓأَهْلَ ٱلْكِتَٰبِ لِمَ تَلْبِسُونَ ٱلْحَقَّ
بِٱلْبَٰطِلِ وَتَكْتُمُونَ ٱلْحَقَّ وَأَنتُمْ تَعْلَمُونَ
﴿٧١﴾

WORD STUDY AND EXPLANATION

قُلْ يَٰٓأَهْلَ ٱلْكِتَٰبِ تَعَالَوْا۟ إِلَىٰ كَلِمَةٍ سَوَآءٍ بَيْنَنَا وَبَيْنَكُمْ أَلَّا نَعْبُدَ إِلَّا ٱللَّهَ وَلَا
نُشْرِكَ بِهِۦ شَيْـًٔا وَلَا يَتَّخِذَ بَعْضُنَا بَعْضًا أَرْبَابًا مِّن دُونِ ٱللَّهِ ۚ فَإِن تَوَلَّوْا۟ فَقُولُوا۟
ٱشْهَدُوا۟ بِأَنَّا مُسْلِمُونَ ﴿٦٤﴾

Say: "O People of the Book! Come to common terms as between us and you: that we worship none but Allah; that we associate no partners with Him; that we do not set up, from among ourselves, lords and patrons other than Allah." If then they turn back, say: "Bear witness that we are Muslims." (64)

The words "People of the Book" include both the Jews and the Christians, but since this sūrah is specially addressed to the Christians, they are the main focus of attention.

Kalimatin sawā'in

The term *sawā'* means middle; hence *sawā'a-r r'as* is the middle part of the head, and the middle of the road is described as *sawā'aṭ ṭarīq*. A thing that is located in the middle of two groups is equally shared, known and familiar to them. The Qur'ān asserts that the concept of *tawḥīd* (belief in the oneness of Allah) is known and acceptable common ground between the Muslims and the People of the Book. Taking this belief as the common ground, the Qur'ān calls upon them to consider whether, in the light of this shared creed, it is Judaism and Christianity or Islam, that is its truest representation.

Wisdom and beautiful preaching

This style of discussion is perfectly in accord with what the Qur'ān commends in the verse: "Invite (all) to the way of your Sustainer with wisdom and beautiful preaching; and argue with them in ways that are best and most gracious." (an-Naḥl, 16:125)

A special aspect of this wise approach is to search for common ground with others where possible and to initiate discussion from shared premises, while avoiding over-emphasising the differences and distinctive features of contending parties. Being the bearers of revealed scriptures, the People of the Book were well aware of the teachings on *tawḥīd*; in fact, they claimed to be its sole standard bearers. In their scriptures, teachings about *tawḥīd* were mentioned and clearly explained.

The People of the Book lapsed into polytheistic beliefs and practices not because there was any support for them in their religion, but as a clear violation of the teachings of their prophets and scriptures. This was through their own false innovations and misinterpretation of allegorical statements resting on erroneous arguments. The Qur'ān invites them to join the Muslims in worshipping none except Allah, the One True God, in Whom they both believed and not to take anyone other than Him as their Lord or ascribe any rivals to Him. Pointedly, it asks them why, contrary to this accepted common belief – the oneness of God, have they set up associates for Allah in worship, installing their rabbis, jurists and mystics as Lords and patrons other than Allah.

With this starting point, the discussion gradually expands and covers the essential requisites of this belief while repudiating their innovations that clearly contradict their claim to believe in the oneness of God,

The fact that *tawḥīd* or belief in the oneness of God is common between Muslims and the People of the Book needs no explanation. Anyone who is knowledgeable about the teachings of the Torah and the Gospels (Injīl) knows this. As to the Torah, we find that in it the oneness of God is explained and categorically asserted so many times that to quote all those references would unnecessarily prolong the discussion.

Evidence of *tawḥīd* in the *Injīl*

We will instead quote some references from the Gospels on this point because it is the Christians who had the greatest difficulty in appreciating the oneness of God. As suggested above, the verse is in fact addressed to them.

> Jesus answered, "It is written: 'Worship the Lord your God and serve him only.'" (Luke 4:8)
>
> "The most important one," answered Jesus, "is this: 'Hear, O Israel, the Lord our God, the Lord is one. Love the Lord your God with all your heart and with all your soul and with all your mind and with all your strength.'" (Mark 12:29-30).
>
> Now this is eternal life: that they may know you, the only true God, and Jesus Christ, whom You have sent. (John 17:3)
>
> "Why do you ask me about what is good?" Jesus replied. "There is only One who is good. If you want to enter life, obey the commandments." (Matthew 19:17).

The word translated as "good" in the above quote should, in our view, have been translated as "pure". Similarly, the sentence "There is only One who is good" is not a correct translation. It should instead read, "There is only One who is pure." In different versions of the Gospel this verse is translated differently. Consider, for instance this translation from the King James' version: "And he said unto him, Why callest thou me good? There is none good but one, that is, God."

In the presence of these clear teachings about *tawḥīd* or belief in the oneness of God, the Qur'ān asks the People of the Book to take a critical look at their beliefs and purge whatever contradicts belief in the oneness of God as a result of their innovations and blind pursuit of allegorical statements. At the end, the Muslims are advised to declare that even if the People of the Book are averse to the teachings of their own prophets and scriptures, they (the Muslims) believe in all the teachings of the prophets and unconditionally surrender themselves to the One True God, the Sovereign Sustainer of all. This represents the very essence of Islam, which literally means submission and commitment to the service of Allah.

The words of the verse "we do not set up, from among ourselves, Lords and Patrons other than Allah" are further elucidated at another place in the

Qur'ān where it refers to the direct violation of this clear commandment by the People of the Book taking "their priests and their monks as their lords". When some of them insisted to the Prophet, peace be upon him, that they did not take their priests and monks as their Lords, he asked them whether it was not true that whatever their priests declared lawful they took it as lawful and whatever they forbade them they took it as forbidden. When the questioner replied in the affirmative, the Prophet, peace be upon him, told him that is what is meant by 'taking them as your Lords'. When someone is obeyed in this manner and is recognised as vested with authority to declare what is lawful and what is not, it is tantamount to worshipping him, even though no rituals of bowing and prostration are observed.

At the end of the verse, it is made clear that if these People of the Book are reluctant to recognise this common teaching on *tawḥīd*, then tell them clearly to bear witness that we are Muslims. The words "to bear witness" are indicative of a declaration of immunity, meaning: be warned and bear witness that we have conveyed this message to you; it is up to you to accept or reject it; you alone will be accountable before God on the day of reckoning. We have done our duty.

The concluding words *that we are Muslims* emphasise the fact that it is this spirit of *tawḥīd* that is manifest in surrender and submission as symbolised by Islam, the real purpose of life and its cherished goal. A person alien to this essence of *tawḥīd*, must also be alien to Islam, and one who is alien to Islam is essentially alien to Allah.

يَٰٓأَهْلَ ٱلْكِتَٰبِ لِمَ تُحَآجُّونَ فِىٓ إِبْرَٰهِيمَ وَمَآ أُنزِلَتِ ٱلتَّوْرَىٰةُ وَٱلْإِنجِيلُ إِلَّا
مِنۢ بَعْدِهِۦٓ ۚ أَفَلَا تَعْقِلُونَ ﴿٦٥﴾
هَٰٓأَنتُمْ هَٰٓؤُلَآءِ حَٰجَجْتُمْ فِيمَا لَكُم بِهِۦ عِلْمٌ فَلِمَ تُحَآجُّونَ فِيمَا لَيْسَ لَكُم بِهِۦ عِلْمٌ ۚ
وَٱللَّهُ يَعْلَمُ وَأَنتُمْ لَا تَعْلَمُونَ ﴿٦٦﴾
مَا كَانَ إِبْرَٰهِيمُ يَهُودِيًّا وَلَا نَصْرَانِيًّا وَلَٰكِن كَانَ حَنِيفًا مُّسْلِمًا وَمَا كَانَ مِنَ ٱلْمُشْرِكِينَ
﴿٦٧﴾
إِنَّ أَوْلَى ٱلنَّاسِ بِإِبْرَٰهِيمَ لَلَّذِينَ ٱتَّبَعُوهُ وَهَٰذَا ٱلنَّبِىُّ وَٱلَّذِينَ ءَامَنُوا۟ ۗ وَٱللَّهُ وَلِىُّ
ٱلْمُؤْمِنِينَ ﴿٦٨﴾

O People of the Book! Why do you dispute about Ibrāhīm, when the Torah and the Gospel were not revealed till after him? Do you not understand this? (65)

You are the ones who disputed in matters of which you had some knowledge. But why do you dispute in matters of which you have no knowledge? It is Allah Who knows, and you who know not! (66)
Ibrāhīm was not a Jew nor a Christian; but he was a Muslim single-mindedly devoted to Allah's service, and he was not of those who joined gods with Allah. (67)
Without doubt, the people closest to Ibrāhīm are those who followed him, and this Prophet and those who believe in him. And Allah is the friend of the believers. (68)

The meaning of these verses is fairly clear. There is no linguistic or grammatical difficulty involved. The subject they deal with has also been described at length in our commentary on Sūrah al-Baqarah.

The Religion of Prophet Ibrāhīm

Prophet Ibrāhīm, peace be upon him, was the undisputed spiritual leader of both the Banī Israel and the Banī Ismā'īl. The Jews, the Christians and the polytheists, all tried to use his name to support their position. The Jews claimed that Ibrāhīm followed their way; the Christians said he was a follower of their way, while the polytheists asserted that he was one of them. Each of these three groups claimed superiority over others in this respect but when Islam arrived on the scene, they unanimously declared that the new religion contradicted the Abrahamic religion. They used it as a common weapon against the new arrival. They said that they were the true custodians of Abrahamic religion and prophet Muḥammad, peace be upon him, was trying to deflect them from their forefathers' way and religion.

The Qur'ān refutes this false propaganda saying that both the Torah and *Injīl* were revealed many centuries after prophet Ibrāhīm. How could he then be a follower of either Judaism or Christianity? To make any such claim there must at least be some basis. There existed no basis for what they alleged about Prophet Ibrāhīm. They had raised questions about matters of which they had some knowledge and could justify their stance in the light thereof, but their claim about Prophet Ibrāhīm was utterly baseless. Why, the Qur'ān asks, did they interfere in matters about which they know nothing? In their opposition and enmity to truth, are they unable to grasp even this simple truth?

The Qur'ān says that Prophet Ibrāhīm was neither a Jew nor a Christian, but was a Muslim, which means someone solely and wholeheartedly, devoted to Allah. The word *ḥanīf* as explained in our commentary on Sūrah al-Baqarah, means one who is single-minded. In other words, he followed the straight path of *tawḥīd.* He did not follow the deviant polytheistic alleyways; he was a true Muslim. That is, he single-mindedly obeyed and served his true Sustainer. One implication of this is that both Judaism and Christianity represent deflections from the path of *tawḥīd*; they are deviant byways and instead of leading to, they take one further away from, the straight path.

The Qur'ān further makes clear that just as Ibrāhīm has nothing to do with Judaism or the Christianity, so he also has nothing to do with the polytheists of Arabia. This represents an aside in the general context as it refutes the claims of the polytheist descendants of Ismā'īl who are not addressed directly in this sūrah. As explained above, the sūrah primarily addresses the People of the Book, especially the Christians. Anything said in refutation of the polytheists is therefore of a subsidiary nature, as is the present statement. This statement is important because, like the Jews and the Christians, the polytheists of Quraysh also asserted that they had inherited their religion from Ibrāhīm, using his name to justify their polytheistic practices. They were far more boisterous in their claim, asserting that they were the true inheritors of the Abrahamic tradition.

Furthermore, we are told that the true inheritors of Ibrāhīm are those who followed his way. This inheritance is not based on family or racial connections, but is conditional upon faith and obedience. Therefore, the people who are closer to Ibrāhīm is this Prophet (Muḥammad, peace be upon him) and his companions who believe in him, rather than the Jews, the Christians and the polytheists who have distorted and changed the religion of Ibrāhīm beyond recognition. Allah is the guardian of the true believers, we are told, and He will help them and make them prevail over their enemies, as the followers of the true religion brought and taught by Ibrāhīm.

وَدَّت طَّآئِفَةٌ مِّنْ أَهْلِ ٱلْكِتَٰبِ لَوْ يُضِلُّونَكُمْ وَمَا يُضِلُّونَ إِلَّآ أَنفُسَهُمْ وَمَا
يَشْعُرُونَ ﴿٦٩﴾
يَٰٓأَهْلَ ٱلْكِتَٰبِ لِمَ تَكْفُرُونَ بِـَٔايَٰتِ ٱللَّهِ وَأَنتُمْ تَشْهَدُونَ ﴿٧٠﴾
يَٰٓأَهْلَ ٱلْكِتَٰبِ لِمَ تَلْبِسُونَ ٱلْحَقَّ بِٱلْبَٰطِلِ وَتَكْتُمُونَ ٱلْحَقَّ وَأَنتُمْ تَعْلَمُونَ ﴿٧١﴾

A section of the People of the Book would love to lead you astray, but they only lead themselves astray, but they do not perceive! (69)

People of the Book! Why do you reject the signs of Allah to which you yourselves bear witness? (70)

People of the Book! Why do you confound truth with falsehood, and conceal the truth, deliberately? (71)

Admonition to the People of the Book

The first verse is addressed to the Muslims, warning them that the Jews and the Christians know very well that Prophet Ibrāhīm has nothing at all to do with the innovations of Judaism and Christianity. However, they persist in repeating these false assertions so as to cause you to forsake the true religion. They cannot harm anyone but themselves, depriving themselves of the Divine blessings and sinking deeper in their error. A person who, in order to prove that his erroneous ways are in fact ways of guidance, deliberately sets out to misguide others and prevents them from following the right path, is himself the first victim of his own machinations. First and foremost, he misguides his own self, but obsessed with hostility to others, he fails to realise the dire consequences of his actions.

The next two verses are addressed to the People of the Book. The repetition of the words 'O People of the Book' here is indicative of both sorrow and reproach: alas, you were the bearers of the Book, but instead of guidance you chose error; and rather than openly declaring the truth you deliberately chose to conceal it from others as if this was your real mission rather than the propagation of truth.

Why do you reject the signs of Allah to which you yourselves bear witness?

Addressed to the People of the Book, this sentence may refer to two things: one, the signs of Allah that you are rejecting you know well in your hearts that they are indeed the signs of Allah. Two, the truth that you so vehemently reject in your hostile obsession, is none other than the one about which a covenant has already been taken from you, that you will support and affirm it and bear witness to its truth before others. You were yourselves witnesses to it and to the covenant that was taken from you in this regard. You indeed promised to abide by this covenant.

As to the first truth, it is self-obvious and needs no proof. A precedent for the second meaning is found in this sūrah itself in the following verse:

> *Behold! Allah took the covenant of the prophets, saying: "I give you a Book and Wisdom; then when comes a messenger to you, confirming what is with you. Do you believe in him and render him help?" Allah said: "Do you agree, and take this my Covenant as binding on you?" They said: "We agree." He said: "Then bear witness, and I am among the witnesses with you."* (Āli 'Imrān 3:81).

A detailed explanation of this verse in given in the following pages.

Verses 64-71

The significance of the prohibition of mixing up falsehood with truth is also explained in the commentary on Sūrah al-Baqarah. The entire Torah was utterly distorted, making it difficult to distinguish between truth and falsehood. In this context, these words refer in particular to the distortions that they had inserted to conceal the connection of Prophets Ibrāhīm and Ismā'īl, their construction of the Ka'bah, the house of worship of Allah, and the prophecies found in their scriptures about Prophet Muḥammad, peace be upon him. The purpose of these distortions was to confuse and hide the prophecies of the earlier prophets about the last prophet or to block them out completely. From the words of the Qur'ān 'to which you yourselves bear witness', it appears that the Jewish scholars at the time of the revelation were aware of these distortions. As the wording of the verse and the context show, the verse discusses the role of the Jewish scholars rather than the ordinary Jews.

Verses 72-76: thematic continuity

Some Jewish conspiracies

In this section, some conspiracies and schemes of the People of the Book, especially of the Jews, are mentioned that were aimed at turning the Muslims away from their religion. The deep-rooted sense of anger and jealousy that the descendants of Israel had against the descendants of Ishmael, the Arabs, is also pointed out. Because of this, they were not ready to accept the descendants of Ishmael as the bearers of a Divine scripture and Divine law like themselves, as witnesses before Allah for their crimes and sins. Thus, in their obsession and hostility, they had, as it were, installed themselves as the sole custodians of Allah's bounty. They acted as if they had the authority to decide whom Allah should or should not bless with grace and mercy.

This hostility and jealousy against the descendants of Ishmael had left a deep impact on the collective national character of the descendants of Israel. With regard to the Ishmaelites, they felt under no obligation to observe any rules or follow any moral or legal formalities; they were infidels and to cheat or usurp their property placed in their care was quite legitimate for the Israelites. There was no harm in grabbing it. The Qur'ān refers to these practices in order to warn the Muslims about the people whose anger and rancour against them was so extreme that they should not look for any advice from them that would be really beneficial and useful. The descendants of Israel could not bear to speak the truth, as they knew it, lest it should favour the Muslims. They would not hesitate to get even a penny from you. How could they then pay back the millions that they had grabbed? Would they bear witness to the truth that was entrusted to them and testify to the truth of the Prophet of Islam, peace be upon him? In the light of these few remarks, let us now study the following verses:

وَقَالَت طَّآئِفَةٌ مِّنْ أَهْلِ ٱلْكِتَٰبِ ءَامِنُوا۟
بِٱلَّذِىٓ أُنزِلَ عَلَى ٱلَّذِينَ ءَامَنُوا۟ وَجْهَ
ٱلنَّهَارِ وَٱكْفُرُوٓا۟ ءَاخِرَهُۥ لَعَلَّهُمْ يَرْجِعُونَ
﴿٧٢﴾

A section of the People of the Book say: "Believe in the morning what is revealed to the believers, but reject it at the end of the day, so that they might go back on their faith. (72)

وَلَا تُؤْمِنُوٓا۟ إِلَّا لِمَن تَبِعَ دِينَكُمْ قُلْ إِنَّ
ٱلْهُدَىٰ هُدَى ٱللَّهِ أَن يُؤْتَىٰٓ أَحَدٌ مِّثْلَ
مَآ أُوتِيتُمْ أَوْ يُحَآجُّوكُمْ عِندَ رَبِّكُمْ ۗ قُلْ إِنَّ
ٱلْفَضْلَ بِيَدِ ٱللَّهِ يُؤْتِيهِ مَن يَشَآءُ ۗ وَٱللَّهُ
وَٰسِعٌ عَلِيمٌ ﴿٧٣﴾

"And believe no one unless he follows your religion." Tell them: "True Guidance is the guidance of Allah" – lest a revelation be sent to someone (else) like that which was sent to you, or that those (receiving such revelation) should engage you in argument before your Sustainer". Say to them: "All bounties are in the hand of Allah: He grants them to whom He pleases. And Allah is possessor of vast bounty, all-Knowing." (73)

يَخْتَصُّ بِرَحْمَتِهِۦ مَن يَشَآءُ ۗ وَٱللَّهُ ذُو
ٱلْفَضْلِ ٱلْعَظِيمِ ﴿٧٤﴾

For His mercy He specially chooses whom He pleases; for Allah is limitless in His exceeding bounty. (74)

۞ وَمِنْ أَهْلِ ٱلْكِتَٰبِ مَنْ إِن تَأْمَنْهُ
بِقِنطَارٍ يُؤَدِّهِۦٓ إِلَيْكَ وَمِنْهُم مَّنْ إِن
تَأْمَنْهُ بِدِينَارٍ لَّا يُؤَدِّهِۦٓ إِلَيْكَ إِلَّا مَا
دُمْتَ عَلَيْهِ قَآئِمًا ۗ ذَٰلِكَ بِأَنَّهُمْ قَالُوا۟ لَيْسَ
عَلَيْنَا فِى ٱلْأُمِّيِّۦنَ سَبِيلٌ وَيَقُولُونَ عَلَى
ٱللَّهِ ٱلْكَذِبَ وَهُمْ يَعْلَمُونَ ﴿٧٥﴾

Among the People of the Book are some who, if entrusted with a hoard of gold, will (readily) pay it back; others, who, if entrusted with a single silver coin, will not repay it unless you constantly stand demanding, because they say, "There is no blame on us in respect of these unlettered people." They utter a lie against Allah, and they know it. (75)

On the contrary, those who fulfil their pledge with Him and fear Him, verily Allah loves all those who fear Him (and act aright). (76)

بَلَىٰ مَنْ أَوْفَىٰ بِعَهْدِهِۦ وَٱتَّقَىٰ فَإِنَّ ٱللَّهَ
يُحِبُّ ٱلْمُتَّقِينَ ﴿٧٦﴾

WORD STUDY AND EXPLANATION

وَقَالَت طَّآئِفَةٌ مِّنْ أَهْلِ ٱلْكِتَٰبِ ءَامِنُوا۟ بِٱلَّذِىٓ أُنزِلَ عَلَى ٱلَّذِينَ ءَامَنُوا۟ وَجْهَ ٱلنَّهَارِ
وَٱكْفُرُوٓا۟ ءَاخِرَهُۥ لَعَلَّهُمْ يَرْجِعُونَ ﴿٧٢﴾

A section of the People of the Book say: "Believe in the morning what is revealed to the believers, but reject it at the end of the day, so that they might go back on their faith. (72)

It is worth noting that while describing the above conspiracy by the People of the Book, the Qur'ān makes it clear that only a group among them was involved in it, which shows that even in the case of enemies, it does not in the least exceed the limits of truth and justice. If a crime is committed by a group of opponents, it holds only that group alone responsible for it. It does not hold the entire nation accountable for what only a few from among them might have committed. This approach is sound not only in consideration of justice and fairness, but it is also extremely beneficial and effective with respect to the propagation of the message of truth. Some very inspiring examples of this may be witnessed in the following pages.

A specific hypocritical scheme

The mischief mentioned here reveals the hypocritical approach and attitude of this group. They claimed that they were friends and well-wishers while, through their secret machinations, they sought to undermine Muslims and Islam. For this, they prepared certain individuals from among them who would openly profess faith in Islam and join the Muslim community and then after some time leave the fold of Islam allegedly because of certain flaws in Islam and Islamic teachings. They might have thought that, in this manner, they would achieve several goals.

Firstly, they would be able to shake the belief of many new Muslims in Islam; these would start thinking that perhaps there is really some flaw in Islamic teaching because of which such educated people are first attracted to it but are later disillusioned and leave.

Secondly, they believed that in this way they would also be able to protect their own masses from falling under the spell of Islam. They would see how some very educated persons from among them, initially attracted to Islam, were later repelled on close contact. They believed this might diminish the apparent attraction of Islam in the eyes of the rest of the tribe of Israel.

Another important aspect of this conspiracy worth bearing in mind is that whenever the Jews targeted any community, this is the first weapon they used against it: they tried to subvert it from within. The manner in which Paul successfully tried to corrupt and distort Christianity from within is a most tragic episode in the annals of religion. Similarly, working under the guise of friendship in Islamic institutions the controversies inspired by both Jewish and Christian scholars – to subvert and distort Islamic teachings – are also no longer secret. We would have pointed out some of these but because this would unduly prolong the discussion, we confine ourselves to these few remarks.

وَلَا تُؤْمِنُوٓا۟ إِلَّا لِمَن تَبِعَ دِينَكُمْ قُلْ إِنَّ ٱلْهُدَىٰ هُدَى ٱللَّهِ أَن يُؤْتَىٰٓ أَحَدٌ مِّثْلَ مَآ أُوتِيتُمْ
أَوْ يُحَآجُّوكُمْ عِندَ رَبِّكُمْ ۗ قُلْ إِنَّ ٱلْفَضْلَ بِيَدِ ٱللَّهِ يُؤْتِيهِ مَن يَشَآءُ ۗ وَٱللَّهُ وَٰسِعٌ عَلِيمٌ ﴿٧٣﴾
يَخْتَصُّ بِرَحْمَتِهِۦ مَن يَشَآءُ ۗ وَٱللَّهُ ذُو ٱلْفَضْلِ ٱلْعَظِيمِ ﴿٧٤﴾

"And believe no one unless he follows your religion." Tell them: "True guidance is the guidance of Allah" – lest a revelation be sent to someone (else) like that which was sent to you, or that those (receiving such revelation) should engage you in argument before your Sustainer." Say to them: "All bounties are in the hand of Allah: He grants them to whom He pleases. And Allah is possessor of vast bounty, all-Knowing." (73)
For His mercy He specially chooses whom He pleases; for Allah is limitless in His exceeding bounty. (74)

Some difficulties of style

Earlier scholars experienced great disagreement in interpreting this verse as there are certain difficulties concerning the style in which it is couched. We shall therefore first explain these descriptive styles and then offer our interpretation of the verse.

The first point to understand in this regard is the position of the words: 'Tell them: "True guidance is the guidance of Allah"' within the sentence. This piece is not a part of the discourse but represents a parenthetical insertion meant as a forthright repudiation of a false assertion of the people addressed here. In other words, the sentence would read as *wa lā tu'minū illā li man tabi'a dīnakum* ("And believe no one unless he follows your religion"). This was the advice they gave to their agents whom they sent to work on the Muslims. They could even declare their faith in Islam if necessary to win the confidence of Muslims, but they must not, they were emphatically told, obey anyone from outside their own circle; they must not obey outsiders, as it was not permissible for them. This false notion was the root cause of all their errors, and the Qur'ān corrects them by saying that they are biased and prejudiced and are blind followers of their sectarian teachings and innovations. So tell them that the real guidance is the guidance of Allah that they should follow, irrespective of whether it reaches them through an Israelite or an Ishmaelite prophet. The only way to success and salvation lies in following the guidance of Allah rather than Judaism or Christianity. This has been elaborated on at great length in Sūrah al-Baqarah and further references are found in the subsequent sūrahs.

The second point worth bearing in mind in order to understand this verse is that sometimes before the conjunctive *'an'*, words such as *makhāfah* or some other word similar in meaning is omitted. There are plenty of examples of these in Arabic and also in the Qur'ān. Ustādh Farāhī has collected these examples in his book *Asālīb al-Qur'ān*. We have also been pointing them out in the present book.

An apprehension of the Jewish community

Bearing this Qur'ānic style in mind, when we look at the verse in isolation from the aforementioned parenthetical clause, it would read as *an-y yu'ta aḥadun mithla mā ūtītum aw yuḥājjūkum 'inda rabbikum* (lest a revelation be sent to someone (else) like that which was sent to you, or that those (receiving such revelation) should engage you in argument before your Sustainer'). Along with the words *wa lā tu'minū illā l-man tabi'a dīnakum* (and believe no-one unless he follows your religion), it gives us their mental picture and explains their hidden motive behind admonishing their followers not to accept, under any circumstances, the claim of a non-Israeli Prophet as the true prophet from God. They were afraid lest the descendants of Ishmael should be elevated to moral and spiritual leadership. They were also apprehensive that if they spoke favourably about Islam or its prophet, the Muslims would use it against them before their Sustainer to show that they deliberately and wilfully denied the truth. The Qur'ān also refers to their fear at another place where the Jews ordered their people not to divulge before the Muslims any hint or suggestion found in the Torah about the final prophet and about the final revelation from God that the Muslims could use against them on the day of judgement. For instance, we read:

> *Behold! When they meet with those who believe, they say: "We believe," but when they meet each other in private, they say: "Shall you tell them what Allah has disclosed to you, so that they might use it in argument against you before your Sustainer?" Do you not understand? Do they not know that Allah knows what they conceal and what they reveal?* (Sūrah al-Baqarah, 2:66-67)

In the light of the explanation of the two Qur'ānic styles, the meaning of the verse should be quite obvious. Addressing the scholars and leaders of the Jewish community of the time, the Qur'ān asks them why are they encouraging prejudices among their people, teaching them that it is impermissible for them to affirm the truth of any non-Israelite prophet. This is a foolish attitude and only betrays their narrow-mindedness. The Qur'ān admonishes them like everyone else: your goal should be to search for Allah's guidance, irrespective of whether it is received through someone from among the descendants of Israel or those of Ishmael. Your present attitude is not based on love and commitment to truth but is the result your fear and jealousy, lest anyone else be granted the position of leadership, which has so far been your exclusive privilege.

The word *aḥad,* meaning anyone, in the present context refers only to the descendants of Ishmael from among whom the unlettered Prophet was raised. As this is a reference to a secret in the hearts of the descendants of Israel, the Qur'ān has referred to it in indirect terms. The words *aw yuḥājjūkum* as mentioned above, refer to a fear in their hearts that if someone from among them accidentally said something favouring Islam and its Prophet, the Muslims could use it against them on the day of judgement.

Commenting on this, the Qur'ān tells them that their religious leadership that they are trying to save does not lie in their power. Honour and precedence is for Allah alone to grant to whomever He wills and to take away from whom He wishes. It was He alone who had bestowed this honour upon you and it is He who has now decided to bestow it upon someone else. You cannot frustrate Him or reverse His decision. His commandment will definitely be enforced. The words *Allāhu wāsi'un 'alīm* show that Allah does not distribute His bounty and grace by tiny human scales in such a way that there should be no room for others after bestowing it upon some. Divine bounty and grace

Verses 72-76

is vast and beyond measure. Allah's every decision is based on His faultless knowledge. He knows those who deserve and those who do not deserve His grace and bounty.

In the verses "He grants them to whom He pleases. And Allah is the Possessor of vast bounty, All-Knowing", there is a reference to two facts. One, the advent of Prophet Muḥammad, the seal of the Prophets, is a tremendous blessing and an infinite bounty for humankind. Two, Allah has been especially most gracious to the descendants of Ishmael by choosing them for this great universal blessing. Implied in this are two noteworthy points: one, that the descendants of Ishmael must appreciate this great favour to them and be grateful to Him; and two, that despite the anger and jealousy of the Israelites, Allah has conferred this great blessing on the unlettered Arabs. He chooses whomever He wishes for His mercy and none can interfere with His decision based on His wisdom.

۞ وَمِنْ أَهْلِ ٱلْكِتَٰبِ مَنْ إِن تَأْمَنْهُ بِقِنطَارٍ يُؤَدِّهِۦٓ إِلَيْكَ وَمِنْهُم مَّنْ إِن تَأْمَنْهُ بِدِينَارٍ
لَّا يُؤَدِّهِۦٓ إِلَيْكَ إِلَّا مَا دُمْتَ عَلَيْهِ قَآئِمًا ۗ ذَٰلِكَ بِأَنَّهُمْ قَالُوا۟ لَيْسَ عَلَيْنَا فِى ٱلْأُمِّيِّۦنَ سَبِيلٌ
وَيَقُولُونَ عَلَى ٱللَّهِ ٱلْكَذِبَ وَهُمْ يَعْلَمُونَ ﴿٧٥﴾

Among the People of the Book are some who, if entrusted with a hoard of gold, will (readily) pay it back; others, who, if entrusted with a single silver coin, will not repay it unless you constantly stand demanding, because, they say, "There is no blame on us in respect of these unlettered people." They utter a lie against Allah, and they know it. (75)

The word *ummiyyīn*, unlettered people, refers to the descendants of Ismā'īl. It has been discussed in our commentary on Sūrah al-Baqarah[20]. The word *sabīl* at this place means a blame and accountability.

A forged Jewish claim

The Qur'ān has here portrayed the mind and attitude of the descendants of Israel concerning the unlettered Arabs. They found nothing wrong in violating their trust and usurping their property. In fact, they believed this was their religious prerogative. They believed that the prohibition of usurping others' property, dishonesty and usury mentioned in the Torah did not apply when dealing with non-Israelites, including the Arabs, the descendants of Ishmael. With such false and spurious religious judgements (*fatāwā*), their religious

20. See comments on verse 78 of Sūrah al-Baqarah (*Pondering over the Qur'ān*)

leaders had made permissible for them all kinds of dishonest dealings with others. They believed there was nothing wrong if they cheated, violated their promises or defrauded the non-Israelites of their wealth and property through usury. If any Arab placed with the Jewish usurers and moneylenders anything in pledge or as a trust, only the lucky few would get back their property from them. They justified their conduct by religious verdicts issued by their rabbis saying that there was no sin in grabbing the property of the infidels.

The Qur'ān has referred to this particular aspect of their moral depravity. It tells the Muslims that they should not be deluded by their being the People of the Book and entertain hopes of any moral support from them. These people are dishonest to the trust placed in them by people and would not return even paltry sums of money to their real owners. They had all kinds of pseudo-religious excuses to justify their misdemeanours. They would never support the truth and bear witness to the truth of the Prophet Muḥammad, peace be upon him, and the final revelation from Allah clearly mentioned and prophesied in their scriptures, and which they were admonished to bear witness to and support. They would never be able to stand up and bear witness to the truth that they were charged with as a sacred trust.

It is worth noting, however, that in portraying the overall moral picture of the Jewish people, the Qur'ān remains within the recognised bounds of fairness and justice. It praises those among them who were good, honest and upright. In fact, it begins by first mentioning them so as to further encourage them and exhort them along this path. These were the people who later embraced Islam.

They utter a lie against Allah, and they know it

This is a repudiation of their forgeries and pseudo-religious pronouncements described above. They said there was no blame on them in mistreating or being dishonest in dealing with the unlettered folks because moral and religious prohibitions did not apply to them. This was a blatant lie against Allah and His law and they were well aware of it, but they had devised various tricks to gratify their desires and greed for worldly goods and pleasures. Later, these pseudo-religious verdicts found their way into the Torah. Today, anyone reading the Torah gets the impression that even in general moral matters, mutual dealings and human rights, there is one law for the descendants of Israel and quite a different set of rules for the non-Israelites, described in the Torah as aliens and gentiles.

Verses 72-76

بَلَىٰ مَنْ أَوْفَىٰ بِعَهْدِهِۦ وَٱتَّقَىٰ فَإِنَّ ٱللَّهَ يُحِبُّ ٱلْمُتَّقِينَ ﴿٧٦﴾

Nay, but those who fulfil their pledge with Him and fear Him, verily Allah loves all those who fear Him (and act aright). (76)

A comment on the Jewish claims

In this verse and in all other similar verses, the main clause (*jawāb al-sharṭ*) is omitted. If this is taken into consideration, the sentence would read: "Indeed, those who fulfil their pledge with Allah, fear Him and act aright, they are the righteous, and Allah loves the righteous." This is a comment on the above-mentioned assertions of the Jewish people.

In other words, the Qur'ān rejects the validity of the Jewish claim that they enjoy a special status and position with Allah and therefore they are superior to others and have no moral obligations towards the unlettered Arabs. A person's station with Allah rests on the fulfilment of one's covenant with Allah and abiding by it under all circumstances. Such are the people who are truly righteous in the sight of Allah and the ones whom He loves. Others who challenge His authority and violate their covenant with Him and yet claim to be righteous and favourites of Allah, are living in a fool's paradise.

The phrase *awfā bi-'ahdihi* is generally translated as "They fulfil their pledges". But I believe the pronoun *hi* in *bi 'ahdihi* refers to Allah and it is supported by the Qur'ānic usage. See, for example, the next verse. Ibn Jarīr has also given a similar interpretation of this verse.

Verses 77-80: Thematic Continuity

In these verses, the People of the Book are reprimanded for their violation – or rather the bartering away – of their aforementioned covenant for error. Allah blessed them with His word and message, and sent to them His messengers and prophets to teach them and to purify and prepare them. Moreover, He honoured them with His special grace and attention, but they violated their most solemn covenant with Allah in exchange for the transitory pleasures of this world and wilfully ignored and turned their backs on His boundless grace and mercy. There is therefore no portion for them in the life hereafter.

Their distortion of the Scripture that Allah had given them to guide them is also mentioned. They distorted and changed the Scripture and interpolated words into it, giving the impression that these words were also from Allah.

The People of the Book, especially the Christians, are then invited to consider how, as the bearers of the Scripture and wisdom from Allah, they could justify their false attributions to Jesus Christ. Bearing these remarks in mind, let us study these verses:

As for those who sell Allah's covenant and their oaths for a paltry price, they shall have no share in the hereafter. Allah will not speak to them nor look at them on the resurrection day, nor will He purify them. For them awaits a painful chastisement. (77)

إِنَّ ٱلَّذِينَ يَشْتَرُونَ بِعَهْدِ ٱللَّهِ وَأَيْمَٰنِهِمْ
ثَمَنًا قَلِيلًا أُو۟لَٰٓئِكَ لَا خَلَٰقَ لَهُمْ فِى
ٱلْءَاخِرَةِ وَلَا يُكَلِّمُهُمُ ٱللَّهُ وَلَا يَنظُرُ
إِلَيْهِمْ يَوْمَ ٱلْقِيَٰمَةِ وَلَا يُزَكِّيهِمْ
وَلَهُمْ عَذَابٌ أَلِيمٌ ﴿٧٧﴾

There is among them a section who twist their tongues with the scripture, that you may think it part of the Book, when in fact it is not part of the Book; and they say, "It is from Allah," when in fact it is not from Allah. They speak falsehood against Allah, and they know it! (78)

وَإِنَّ مِنْهُمْ لَفَرِيقًا يَلْوُۥنَ أَلْسِنَتَهُم
بِٱلْكِتَٰبِ لِتَحْسَبُوهُ مِنَ ٱلْكِتَٰبِ
وَمَا هُوَ مِنَ ٱلْكِتَٰبِ وَيَقُولُونَ
هُوَ مِنْ عِندِ ٱللَّهِ وَمَا هُوَ مِنْ عِندِ ٱللَّهِ
وَيَقُولُونَ عَلَى ٱللَّهِ ٱلْكَذِبَ وَهُمْ يَعْلَمُونَ
﴿٧٨﴾

It does not behove a man, to whom is given the Scripture, and Wisdom, and Prophethood, that he should then say to people: "Be my worshippers rather than Allah's." On the contrary (he would say), "Be solely devoted to Allah because you teach the Book and also because you study it earnestly." (79)

مَا كَانَ لِبَشَرٍ أَن يُؤْتِيَهُ ٱللَّهُ ٱلْكِتَٰبَ
وَٱلْحُكْمَ وَٱلنُّبُوَّةَ ثُمَّ يَقُولَ لِلنَّاسِ
كُونُوا۟ عِبَادًا لِّى مِن دُونِ ٱللَّهِ وَلَٰكِن
كُونُوا۟ رَبَّٰنِيِّۦنَ بِمَا كُنتُمْ تُعَلِّمُونَ
ٱلْكِتَٰبَ وَبِمَا كُنتُمْ تَدْرُسُونَ ﴿٧٩﴾

Nor would he bid you to take angels and prophets as lords and patrons. Would he bid you to disbelieve after you have surrendered yourselves to Allah? (80)

وَلَا يَأْمُرَكُمْ أَن تَتَّخِذُوا۟ ٱلْمَلَٰٓئِكَةَ
وَٱلنَّبِيِّۦنَ أَرْبَابًا ۗ أَيَأْمُرُكُم بِٱلْكُفْرِ بَعْدَ إِذْ
أَنتُم مُّسْلِمُونَ ﴿٨٠﴾

Verses 77-80

WORD STUDY AND EXPLANATION

إِنَّ ٱلَّذِينَ يَشۡتَرُونَ بِعَهۡدِ ٱللَّهِ وَأَيۡمَٰنِهِمۡ ثَمَنٗا قَلِيلًا أُوْلَٰٓئِكَ لَا خَلَٰقَ لَهُمۡ فِي ٱلۡأٓخِرَةِ
وَلَا يُكَلِّمُهُمُ ٱللَّهُ وَلَا يَنظُرُ إِلَيۡهِمۡ يَوۡمَ ٱلۡقِيَٰمَةِ وَلَا يُزَكِّيهِمۡ وَلَهُمۡ عَذَابٌ
أَلِيمٞ ٧٧

As for those who sell Allah's covenant and their oaths for a paltry price, they shall have no share in the hereafter. Allah will not speak to them nor look at them on the day of resurrection, nor will He purify them. For them awaits a painful chastisement. (77)

The real meaning of the word *ishtarā*

The significance of the word *ishtarā* has been discussed previously in Sūrah al-Baqarah[21]. In a barter system as practised in the past, a commodity was exchanged for another. In such a transaction, a commodity could be the price as well as the commodity purchased. As such, the word *ishtarā* does not signify the act of purchasing as we understand it, but simply exchanging one thing for another. From this, it gradually came to be used in the sense of giving preference to one thing over another.

'Ahd Allāh or Allah's covenant

This phrase refers to the Book and the Sharī'ah because these two represent a covenant between Allah and His servants. Implied in this general sense is also the specific allusion to the covenant taken from the People of the Book about the final revelation and the final Prophet which they had not only forgotten but had tried their best to erase all its traces from their scriptures.

Aymān (pl. of *yamīn*)

The word *aymān* (pl. of *yamīn*) in *aymāni-him* refers to the covenants and contracts on which social and cultural life is based. They encourage confidence, trust and goodwill in social life and mutual dealings. The Jews had failed to live up to the noble teachings of their Prophets and, as stated earlier, had devised various excuses and legal tricks to justify their dishonest dealings and mistreatment of others. They believed they had no moral obligations to non-Jews, nor were they accountable for any treaties or contracts with them.

---

21. See comments on verses 16, 86 and 90 of Sūrah al-Baqarah (*Pondering over the Qur'ān*) (Translator).

Allah will neither speak to them nor look at them on the resurrection day

The negation of speaking and looking implies the negation of their real import as is generally understood by all who are familiar with this fairly common style in Arabic. Examples of it are not difficult to find in almost any language.

This means that Allah will not speak to or look at the people who are ready to sell their covenant with Allah for the trifles of this world; they will have no share in the blessings of the hereafter. They have proved to be dishonest in the discharge of their trust from Allah. Allah will not speak to them; neither look at them favourably nor purify them. For these wretched people, there is nothing in the life hereafter except a most painful torment.

Expression of intense disgust and dismay

Those who are familiar with linguistic nuances can easily see the intensity of disgust and dismay in these words. The People of the Book, some from among the Jewish community whose machinations are described above, had brought this upon themselves. They were the people specially honoured by speaking directly to them via their prophet. They were oppressed and humiliated by Pharaoh and his people and Allah was kind to them and rescued them from this oppression and installed them as the leaders and guides for others. A special scripture was revealed to purify them and to teach and guide them. Allah raised many prophets and messengers from among them but they failed to appreciate the honour they were given and they turned their backs on Allah's book. How then could they expect Allah to speak to them or look at them or cleanse and purify them? They have barred all doors of hope for themselves.

The negation of *tazkiyah* (purification) in this verse may mean two things. Firstly, as ordained by Allah, the life hereafter is not the place to attain purification. Rather the true place for the human being to achieve spiritual purification is his worldly sojourn. Those who let this opportunity slip away will not be able to attain purification in the life hereafter. Secondly, the nature of the sins of these people is not such that they could be purified after receiving some minor punishment in the hereafter. Their sins are so serious that they would remain in hell forever.

وَإِنَّ مِنْهُمْ لَفَرِيقًا يَلْوُۥنَ أَلْسِنَتَهُم بِٱلْكِتَـٰبِ لِتَحْسَبُوهُ مِنَ ٱلْكِتَـٰبِ وَمَا هُوَ
مِنَ ٱلْكِتَـٰبِ وَيَقُولُونَ هُوَ مِنْ عِندِ ٱللَّهِ وَمَا هُوَ مِنْ عِندِ ٱللَّهِ وَيَقُولُونَ عَلَى ٱللَّهِ
ٱلْكَذِبَ وَهُمْ يَعْلَمُونَ ﴿٧٨﴾

There is among them a section who twist their tongues with the scripture, that you may think it part of the Scripture, when in fact it is not part of the Scripture.

Verses 77-80

And they say, "It is from Allah," when in fact it is not from Allah. They speak falsehood against Allah, and they know it! (78)

Lawā and *yalwī*

Lawā and *yalwī* means to turn, bend, and twist or to bend up, down, back and over. And *yalwūna alsinatahum bi-l kitāb* means that while uttering some words of the Divine Book, they contort their tongues so that the words are distorted.

An evasive trick to evade their obligations to Allah

This was one of the ways that the People of the Book used in order to ignore their obligations towards their covenant with Allah. In the commentary on Sūrah al-Baqarah, while discussing their distortions of the Divine scripture, we have mentioned that one way of doing so was that they deliberately changed and distorted words and sentences in such a manner that their real meaning was lost. Both the Jews and the Christians have been guilty of this kind of distortion. We have mentioned the word *Marwah* that is mentioned in the Torah as the place where Prophet Ibrāhīm (peace be upon him) was commanded to sacrifice his son[22]. Among many other distortions that they introduced in the Ibrāhīmic sacrifice, they also tried to distort and change the word Marwah to Moriah (Gen. 22:2), moia, moiho and so forth[23]. All this was done in order to prove that the real place of sacrifice was not Marwah, one of the two famous hillocks in Makkah but rather a place near Jerusalem sounding somewhat similar. Thus they wanted to sever all the links of Prophet Ibrāhīm with his place of sacrifice, migration and the Ka'bah, the House of Allah, as well as with the prophecies found in the Torah regarding the last Prophet and the children of Ishmael, the Arabs. Another example is the word *Bacca* in the Psalms[24], which they changed and distorted in order to hide its relationship with Bacca or Makkah, the city of Islam.

In their audacity and intransigence, they passed off their forgeries as the word of God and part of His book. They attributed these lies to Allah knowingly and shamelessly.

مَا كَانَ لِبَشَرٍ أَن يُؤْتِيَهُ ٱللَّهُ ٱلْكِتَٰبَ وَٱلْحُكْمَ وَٱلنُّبُوَّةَ ثُمَّ يَقُولَ لِلنَّاسِ كُونُوا۟

22. See comments on verses 75 and 125 of Sūrah al-Baqarah (*Pondering over the Qur'ān*) (Translator).
23. Genesis, 22:2, also 2 Chronicles, 3:1. (Translator).
24. Psalms, 84:6 (Translator).

عِبَادًا لِّي مِن دُونِ ٱللَّهِ وَلَٰكِن كُونُوا۟ رَبَّٰنِيِّـۧنَ بِمَا كُنتُمْ تُعَلِّمُونَ ٱلْكِتَٰبَ وَبِمَا كُنتُمْ
تَدْرُسُونَ ﴿٧٩﴾
وَلَا يَأْمُرَكُمْ أَن تَتَّخِذُوا۟ ٱلْمَلَٰٓئِكَةَ وَٱلنَّبِيِّـۧنَ أَرْبَابًا ۗ أَيَأْمُرُكُم بِٱلْكُفْرِ بَعْدَ إِذْ أَنتُم مُّسْلِمُونَ
﴿٨٠﴾

It does not behove a man, to whom is given the Book, and Wisdom, and Prophethood, that he should then say to people, "Be my worshippers rather than Allah's". On the contrary (he would say), "Be solely devoted to Allah because you teach the scripture and also because you study it earnestly." (79)
Nor would he bid you to take angels and prophets as lords and patrons. Would he bid you to disbelieve after you have surrendered yourselves to Allah? (80)

Meaning of the word *ḥukm*

The word *ḥukm* means a decision and a judgement. In the Qur'ān it has been used in three different senses:

At some places, the Qur'ān uses it purely in the sense of decision, as for instance in verses *wa kunnā li-ḥukmihim shāhidīn,* 'We did witness their decision' (Sūrah al-Anbiyā', 21;78),

A'faḥukma-l jāhiliyyati yabghūna? Wa man aḥsanu min Allāhi ḥukman, 'Do they then seek a judgment of (the days of) Ignorance? But who, for a people whose faith is assured, can give better judgment than Allah?' (Sūrah al-Mā'idah, 5:50)

At other places, the term *ḥukm* is used in the sense of the power to judge and insight. For instance, we read *wa Lūṭan ātaynāhu ḥukman wa ʿilman,* (And to Lūṭ, too, We gave the power to judge and knowledge') (Sūrah al-Anbiyā 21:74).

And *wa ātaynāhu-l ḥukma ṣabīyyan wa ḥanān minl ladunnā wa zakātan,* (and We gave him judgement while still a child, as well as by Our grace, compassion and purity). (Sūrah Maryam, 19:12).

And in some other verses, the word *ḥukm* is used in the sense of command and commandment, as in the verses *fa-l ḥukmu li-llāhi-il ʿalīyyi-l kabīr,* (the Command is with Allah, the Most High, the Most Great!) (Sūrah Ghafir, 40:12). In *wa lahu-l ḥukmu wa ilayhi turjaʿūn,* (the Command belongs to Him, and to Him you shall (all) be brought back.) (Sūrah al-Qaṣaṣ, 28:70).

Considering the context of the present verse, we find the word *ḥukm* has been used in its second and third meanings.

Rabbānī

The word *rabbānī* means a worshipper of Allah, a godly person. It seems to have been imported into Arabic from Hebrew. The word *ribbi* is frequently used in both the Torah and the Injīl, somewhat different in form in either case, but there seems to be little difference in its essential signification.

This verse is especially addressed to the Christians, the real audience of this sūrah. So far the discussion has been based on tradition. This verse appeals to human reason to just consider how could someone blessed by Allah with His book and wisdom as an honoured messenger to humans, possibly turn around and instead invite them to serve and adore him, in place of Allah? In other words, this means that all your innovations are not only contrary to the teachings of Jesus Christ, your own tradition, history and the accepted beliefs of all the prophets, but they are also abhorrent in the eyes of reason and pure human nature.

Whenever Allah blesses a servant and raises him as His messenger, and grants him Scripture and wisdom, the purpose is to free people from slavery to others by inviting them to serve and worship Allah alone. A true Prophet would never ask people to serve him instead, as if they were his servants and not Allah's. Otherwise, this would mean that the prophet who has been sent as a guide to the straight path and to shepherd his flock to Allah has been engaged in misguiding them and seducing them away from the straight path. There can hardly be anything more monstrous than such an allegation about a messenger of Allah.

Thereafter, they are reminded that being the reader and teacher of a Divine scripture, the Prophet, who is the bearer of the Divine Book and wisdom, can only invite them to worship Allah and to serve and adore Him alone. A Prophet of Allah who comes to invite people to Allah cannot ask them instead to serve and worship him. He cannot invite them to take the angels and the prophets as their lords and patrons besides Allah. This is because a call to belief in Allah is not compatible with any invitation to unbelief and rejection of Allah. How can you believe that the Prophet who invites you to faith and Islam – to believe in and to surrender yourselves to Allah – can ever ask you to commit unbelief after you respond to his call? The last part of the verse has a somewhat broader implication and brings in, alongside the Christians, the Quraysh who had taken to worshipping idols of the angels and the Prophets.

VERSES 81-91: THEMATIC CONTINUITY

This section begins with a mention of a comprehensive covenant that was taken from the People of the Book concerning the Prophets, especially the final Prophet Muḥammad, peace be upon him, that they would support and respond to his call. They collectively made and confirmed this covenant but now, as detailed above, they are trying to wriggle out of their obligations.

It is strange indeed that they refuse to believe in the final Prophet, in clear violation of their covenant. Are they looking for a religion other than that of Allah? Islam is the religion of Allah, and also the religion of the entire universe, because everything in this universe is, by its nature, subject to the laws of Allah and obeys Him alone.

Citing the all-inclusive belief of the Muslim community, the prophet is admonished to leave the People of the Book alone if they continue to persist in their prejudiced attitude. The Prophet is also advised to declare openly declare that as Muslims we believe in all the Prophets without in any way discriminating among them. We worship and obey Allah alone. The section ends with a warning of the dire consequences for the followers of the earlier scripture. How could Allah bless with guidance those who reverted to unbelief after having recognised and believed in the final Prophet? And thus they brought upon themselves the condemnation of Allah, the angels and of the whole of the human race.

And remember when Allah took from you a covenant about the Prophets, saying: "I give you a book and wisdom. So when there comes to you a Messenger, confirming the (prophecies) that are with you, you shall believe in him and render him help." He asked, "Do you agree to this, and accept the obligation I lay upon you in this respect? They said: "We agree." He said: "Then bear witness, and I am with you among the witnesses." (81)

وَإِذْ أَخَذَ ٱللَّهُ مِيثَٰقَ ٱلنَّبِيِّۧنَ لَمَآ
ءَاتَيْتُكُم مِّن كِتَٰبٍ وَحِكْمَةٍ ثُمَّ
جَآءَكُمْ رَسُولٌ مُّصَدِّقٌ لِّمَا مَعَكُمْ
لَتُؤْمِنُنَّ بِهِۦ وَلَتَنصُرُنَّهُۥ قَالَ ءَأَقْرَرْتُمْ
وَأَخَذْتُمْ عَلَىٰ ذَٰلِكُمْ إِصْرِى قَالُوٓا۟ أَقْرَرْنَا
قَالَ فَٱشْهَدُوا۟ وَأَنَا۠ مَعَكُم مِّنَ ٱلشَّٰهِدِينَ
٨١

فَمَن تَوَلَّىٰ بَعْدَ ذَٰلِكَ فَأُو۟لَٰٓئِكَ هُمُ
ٱلْفَٰسِقُونَ ﴿٨٢﴾

Whoever turns away after this covenant, they are surely transgressors. (82)

أَفَغَيْرَ دِينِ ٱللَّهِ يَبْغُونَ وَلَهُۥٓ أَسْلَمَ
مَن فِى ٱلسَّمَٰوَٰتِ وَٱلْأَرْضِ طَوْعًا
وَكَرْهًا وَإِلَيْهِ يُرْجَعُونَ ﴿٨٣﴾

Do they seek for other than the religion of Allah, while all creatures in the heavens and on earth willingly or unwillingly obey Him alone, and to Him shall they all be returned? (83)

قُلْ ءَامَنَّا بِٱللَّهِ وَمَآ أُنزِلَ عَلَيْنَا
وَمَآ أُنزِلَ عَلَىٰٓ إِبْرَٰهِيمَ وَإِسْمَٰعِيلَ
وَإِسْحَٰقَ وَيَعْقُوبَ وَٱلْأَسْبَاطِ وَمَآ
أُوتِىَ مُوسَىٰ وَعِيسَىٰ وَٱلنَّبِيُّونَ مِن
رَّبِّهِمْ لَا نُفَرِّقُ بَيْنَ أَحَدٍ مِّنْهُمْ وَنَحْنُ
لَهُۥ مُسْلِمُونَ ﴿٨٤﴾

Say: "We believe in Allah, and in what has been revealed to us and what was revealed to Ibrāhīm, Ismā'īl, Isḥāq, Ya'qūb, and the Tribes, and in what has been given to Mūsā, 'Īsā, and the Prophets, from their Sustainer: We make no distinction between any of them and to Him alone we submit." (84)

وَمَن يَبْتَغِ غَيْرَ ٱلْإِسْلَٰمِ دِينًا فَلَن يُقْبَلَ
مِنْهُ وَهُوَ فِى ٱلْءَاخِرَةِ مِنَ ٱلْخَٰسِرِينَ
﴿٨٥﴾

And whoever seeks a religion other than Islam (submission to Allah), it shall not be accepted from him, and in the hereafter He shall be among the losers. (85)

كَيْفَ يَهْدِى ٱللَّهُ قَوْمًا كَفَرُوا۟
بَعْدَ إِيمَٰنِهِمْ وَشَهِدُوٓا۟ أَنَّ ٱلرَّسُولَ حَقٌّ
وَجَآءَهُمُ ٱلْبَيِّنَٰتُ وَٱللَّهُ لَا يَهْدِى
ٱلْقَوْمَ ٱلظَّٰلِمِينَ ﴿٨٦﴾

How shall Allah guide those who disbelieved after having believed while they know that the Messenger is true and that the clear signs had come to them? Allah guides not the wrongdoers. (86)

أُو۟لَٰٓئِكَ جَزَآؤُهُمْ أَنَّ عَلَيْهِمْ لَعْنَةَ
ٱللَّهِ وَٱلْمَلَٰٓئِكَةِ وَٱلنَّاسِ أَجْمَعِينَ ﴿٨٧﴾

Of such, their recompense is that Allah's curse is on them and that of the angels, and of all people. (87)

خَٰلِدِينَ فِيهَا لَا يُخَفَّفُ عَنْهُمُ ٱلْعَذَابُ
وَلَا هُمْ يُنظَرُونَ ﴿٨٨﴾

They will be under it forever. Their punishment will not be lightened, nor will they be granted reprieve. (88)

إِلَّا ٱلَّذِينَ تَابُوا۟ مِنۢ بَعْدِ ذَٰلِكَ
وَأَصْلَحُوا۟ فَإِنَّ ٱللَّهَ غَفُورٌ رَّحِيمٌ ﴿٨٩﴾

Except for those who repent after that, and put things right, for surely Allah is most Forgiving, ever Merciful. (89)

إِنَّ ٱلَّذِينَ كَفَرُوا۟ بَعْدَ إِيمَٰنِهِمْ ثُمَّ
ٱزْدَادُوا۟ كُفْرًا لَّن تُقْبَلَ تَوْبَتُهُمْ
وَأُو۟لَٰٓئِكَ هُمُ ٱلضَّآلُّونَ ﴿٩٠﴾

But those who disbelieve after having believed, and then increase in their unbelief – their repentance shall not be accepted. They are the ones utterly astray. (90)

إِنَّ ٱلَّذِينَ كَفَرُوا۟ وَمَاتُوا۟ وَهُمْ كُفَّارٌ فَلَن
يُقْبَلَ مِنْ أَحَدِهِم مِّلْءُ ٱلْأَرْضِ
ذَهَبًا وَلَوِ ٱفْتَدَىٰ بِهِۦٓ أُو۟لَٰٓئِكَ لَهُمْ
عَذَابٌ أَلِيمٌ وَمَا لَهُم مِّن نَّٰصِرِينَ ﴿٩١﴾

As to those who disbelieve, and die while they are disbelievers, there shall not be accepted from any of them even the earth full of gold, though they should offer it in ransom. For them there shall be a painful punishment, and they shall have no helpers. (91)

EXPLANATION AND WORD STUDY

وَإِذْ أَخَذَ ٱللَّهُ مِيثَٰقَ ٱلنَّبِيِّۦنَ لَمَآ ءَاتَيْتُكُم مِّن كِتَٰبٍ وَحِكْمَةٍ ثُمَّ جَآءَكُمْ
رَسُولٌ مُّصَدِّقٌ لِّمَا مَعَكُمْ لَتُؤْمِنُنَّ بِهِۦ وَلَتَنصُرُنَّهُۥ ۚ قَالَ ءَأَقْرَرْتُمْ وَأَخَذْتُمْ عَلَىٰ ذَٰلِكُمْ
إِصْرِى ۖ قَالُوٓا۟ أَقْرَرْنَا ۚ قَالَ فَٱشْهَدُوا۟ وَأَنَا۠ مَعَكُم مِّنَ ٱلشَّٰهِدِينَ ﴿٨١﴾
فَمَن تَوَلَّىٰ بَعْدَ ذَٰلِكَ فَأُو۟لَٰٓئِكَ هُمُ ٱلْفَٰسِقُونَ ﴿٨٢﴾

And remember when Allah took from you a covenant about the Prophets, saying: "I give you a scripture and wisdom; so when there comes to you a messenger, confirming the (prophecies) that are with you, You shall believe in him and render him help." He asked, "Do you agree to this, and accept the obligation I lay upon you in this respect? They said: "We agree." He said: "Then bear witness, and I am with you among the witnesses." (81)
Whoever turns away after this covenant, they are surely transgressors. (82)

The covenant of Israel concerning the Prophets

The phrase *mithāq an-nabīyyīn* refers to the covenant taken from the descendants of Israel about the Prophets. This covenant was meant to remind them that as the people entrusted with the Divine scripture and wisdom, they must respond to and believe in all the Prophets, especially the final Prophet whom they should help and support. This covenant is mentioned in the Qur'ān at various places.

> *And Allah did indeed take a covenant from the descendants of Israel, and We raised twelve leaders among them. And Allah said: "I am with you: if you establish prayer, give zakāh, believe in my messengers, honour and assist them, and loan to Allah a beautiful loan. I will wipe out from you your sins, and admit you to gardens with rivers flowing underneath; but if any of you, after this, disbelieve, he has truly strayed away from the right path."* (Sūrah al-Mā'idah 5:12)

The covenant regarding the unlettered Prophet

In this verse, the generic term *rusul* (Messengers) is used, but in another place the unlettered Prophet is specifically mentioned:

> *That (mercy) I shall ordain for those who do right, and give zakāh, and those who believe in Our signs; Those who follow the Messenger, the unlettered Prophet, whom they find mentioned in their scriptures (the Torah and the Injīl), who commands them what is just and forbids them what is evil; he allows them as lawful what is good (and pure) and prohibits them from what is bad (and impure); He releases them from their heavy burdens and from the yokes that have been upon them. So those who believe in him, honour him, help him, and follow the light that is sent down with him, it is they who will prosper.* (Sūrah al-A'rāf, 7:156-157)

These verses clearly show that a covenant was taken from both the Jews and the Christians to believe in the unlettered Prophet and to help and support him, but they neglected their covenant and failed to live up to it. Some traces of this covenant can still be seen in the Torah and the Gospel but they are covered under layers of distortions and are barely discernible.

"a Messenger, confirming the (prophecies) that are with you"

These words refer to the unlettered Prophet, peace be upon him. A special aspect of "confirming the (prophecies) that are with you" is that with the advent of the Prophet of Islam, his character and achievements, the prophecies in their scriptures were finally fulfilled. And for a Prophet with these characteristics and attributes, they had been waiting. With the fulfilment of these prophecies, they were the ones primarily honoured. The Arabic word *taṣdīq* (confirmation) is used in precisely this sense, as is shown by its use by a Ḥamāsī poet[25] in the following couplet:

> May my life and property be sacrificed for those valiant champions who, by their performance, proved the truth of my opinion about them!

Had the Jews and the Christians considered this aspect, they would have found that the advent of the Prophet Muḥammad confirmed their position and verified the truth of their scriptures. But they rejected the Prophet who confirmed them – the Prophet for whom they had waited for so long to witness his truth. When he finally came, they rejected him outright.

He asked, "Do you agree to this, and accept the obligation I lay upon you in this respect?"

The covenant, its form and historical perspective

This question has a special significance against the background of Israelite history. As a rule, whenever Prophet Mūsā received any instructions from Allah he would not merely recite these to his companions individually, but would gather the whole community or at least their chiefs in the tabernacle. With the ark placed in front of them, he would first admonish them and then recite to them the commandments of their Sustainer and take from them a covenant to obey. He would ask all of them to bear witness to this event while invoking Allah as a witness to the entire proceedings. At the same time, he would also warn them of the dire consequences of disobedience to their Sustainer's commandments in this life as well as in the life to come. Thus every Divine commandment of prohibition or permission became a covenant between the descendants of Israel and Allah. How ironic it is that while the Law was so zealously guarded, its bearers ended up violating its every single commandment. Only when, in the light of this, we consider the words "whoso turns away after this ..." can we truly appreciate the significance of "after this", *ba'da dhālika*. Who could be in a worse position than those guilty of breaking their word after having ratified their covenant with their Sustainer? The term *fāsiq* used here is not in its generic sense of merely being disobedient, but it is used in the sense contained in the Qur'ānic statement about the Devil, Iblīs: *fa-fasaqa 'an amri rabbihi* – he broke the command of his Sustainer. (Sūrah al-Kahf, 18:50).

25. Ḥamāsī, a poet mentioned in *ḥamāsah* (exhortation), the famous anthology of classical Arabic poetry, compiled by the ninth century poet Abū Tammām. (Translator).

أَفَغَيْرَ دِينِ ٱللَّهِ يَبْغُونَ وَلَهُۥٓ أَسْلَمَ مَن فِى ٱلسَّمَٰوَٰتِ وَٱلْأَرْضِ طَوْعًا وَكَرْهًا وَإِلَيْهِ يُرْجَعُونَ ﴿٨٣﴾

Do they seek for other than the religion of Allah, while all creatures in the heavens and on earth willingly or unwillingly obey Him alone, and to Him shall they all be returned. (83)

Islam is the religion of the entire creation

Here, there is an expression of surprise at the way the People of the Book avoided and ignored the message of Islam. They are asked what is the purpose of their flight from the truth. Do they seek a religion other than that of Allah? Islam is the only eternal religion of Allah since the beginning. This is the religion that was given to all Prophets and Messengers and indeed this is the religion of the entire universe: the sun, the moon, clouds, winds, heavens and earth, all follow this religion. No one can, in the slightest degree, disobey this universal law. Islam means submission to Allah and His command. No one can, in the slightest degree, deviate from His command or refuse to obey His laws. Some among His creatures, like humans, are given a limited autonomy in a particular sphere. They are, however, also subservient to His universal laws and can function only by His leave. None can escape the inevitable physical laws of life and death.

The verdict of both reason and nature is that human beings should willingly obey their Creator and Sustainer in the area where they enjoy a limited autonomy as they are otherwise subject to His physical laws in the rest of their existence. This conscious and willing obedience in their moral and spiritual life would bring harmony with the universe in which they live and all its elements. By thus surrendering their God-given freedom in favour of obedience to the Divine law, humans can achieve similarity with the prophets and angels. This is what Islam means by the hue (*ṣibghah*) of Allah. This is the religion of Allah, the religion that Adam and Noah followed and also the religion of the community of Abraham, their common ancestor. And it is this same religion that the last Prophet, Muḥammad, peace be upon him, has brought them. Why should, then, the People of the Book, being the bearers of the Book, turn their backs on this universal religion and seek for any other religion?

Wa ilayhi yurja'ūn (and to Him shall they all be returned). That is, there is no escape from submitting to Divine law, the way ahead leads only to Him. Those who die and apparently are released from the constraints of this law, in reality are not. They continue to be subject to it: for all human beings will finally be returned to Allah in submission, to be judged for their performance in their earthly sojourn.

قُلْ ءَامَنَّا بِٱللَّهِ وَمَآ أُنزِلَ عَلَيْنَا وَمَآ أُنزِلَ عَلَىٰٓ إِبْرَٰهِيمَ وَإِسْمَٰعِيلَ وَإِسْحَٰقَ
وَيَعْقُوبَ وَٱلْأَسْبَاطِ وَمَآ أُوتِىَ مُوسَىٰ وَعِيسَىٰ وَٱلنَّبِيُّونَ مِن رَّبِّهِمْ لَا نُفَرِّقُ
بَيْنَ أَحَدٍ مِّنْهُمْ وَنَحْنُ لَهُۥ مُسْلِمُونَ ٨٤

Say: "We believe in Allah, and in what has been revealed to us and what was revealed to Ibrāhīm, Ismā'īl, Isḥāq, Ya'qūb, and the Tribes, and in (the Scriptures) given to Mūsā, 'Īsā, and the prophets, from their Sustainer: We make no distinction between any of them and to Him alone we submit." (84)

All-comprehensive declaration of the Islamic creed

This verse is identical to verse 136 of Sūrah al-Baqarah. Please refer to it for its detailed discussion. This is a proclamation made through the Prophet concerning the comprehensive creed of Islam. Considered in its present context, it means that if the People of the Book desire some religion other than Islam, leave them alone and let the devil cause them to wander in the wilderness. Why should the Prophet waste his time and energy on such heedless people? Therefore, the Prophet is asked to declare openly that he and his followers believe in Allah and His religion – the religion of all the prophets, without discriminating between any of them by believing in some and rejecting the others. The Prophet and those who follow him believe in all the prophets and messengers of Allah; they are obedient to Him and repose their trust and affairs to His care.

وَمَن يَبْتَغِ غَيْرَ ٱلْإِسْلَٰمِ دِينًا فَلَن يُقْبَلَ مِنْهُ وَهُوَ فِى ٱلْءَاخِرَةِ مِنَ ٱلْخَٰسِرِينَ ٨٥

And whoever seeks a religion other than Islam (submission to Allah), it shall not be accepted from him, and in the hereafter he shall be among the losers. (85)

This is an open declaration that follows the potent arguments affirming the truth of Islam. Now, those who seek a religion other than Islam or persist in their old religious dispositions whether Judaism or Christianity or any other, it shall not be accepted from them. All such people shall be losers in the life hereafter.

كَيْفَ يَهْدِى ٱللَّهُ قَوْمًا كَفَرُوا۟ بَعْدَ إِيمَٰنِهِمْ وَشَهِدُوٓا۟ أَنَّ ٱلرَّسُولَ حَقٌّ وَجَآءَهُمُ
ٱلْبَيِّنَٰتُ ۚ وَٱللَّهُ لَا يَهْدِى ٱلْقَوْمَ ٱلظَّٰلِمِينَ ٨٦
أُو۟لَٰٓئِكَ جَزَآؤُهُمْ أَنَّ عَلَيْهِمْ لَعْنَةَ ٱللَّهِ وَٱلْمَلَٰٓئِكَةِ وَٱلنَّاسِ أَجْمَعِينَ ٨٧
خَٰلِدِينَ فِيهَا لَا يُخَفَّفُ عَنْهُمُ ٱلْعَذَابُ وَلَا هُمْ يُنظَرُونَ ٨٨

إِلَّا ٱلَّذِينَ تَابُوا۟ مِنۢ بَعۡدِ ذَٰلِكَ وَأَصۡلَحُوا۟ فَإِنَّ ٱللَّهَ غَفُورٌ رَّحِيمٌ ﴿٨٩﴾

How shall Allah guide those who disbelieve after having believed while they know that the Messenger is true and that the clear signs had come to them? Allah guides not the wrongdoers. (86)
Of such, the reward is that Allah's curse is on them and that of the angels, and of all people. (87)
They will be under it forever. Their punishment will not be lightened, nor will they be granted reprieve. (88)
Except for those that repent after that, and put things right, for surely Allah is Most Forgiving, Ever Merciful. (89)

A special meaning of the word *hidāyah*

As discussed in our commentary on Sūrah al-Baqarah, in the Arabic language as well as in the Qur'ān, the word *hidāyah* (guidance) is used in several senses and is received in three stages, the final of which is guidance to the hereafter[26]. This is the stage where a servant is guided to his objective and his efforts bear fruit. The Qur'ān uses it in this sense at several places and I am inclined to believe that it is in this sense that it is used here as well. Ustādh Farāhī takes it to mean guidance in its generic sense. The guidance, from which the descendants of Israel are barred, according to him, refers to them as a group; it does not negate guidance to them as individuals. In other words, how can a people guilty of such serious crimes find guidance to Islam!

The term *shahidū* (literally, they testified) here means the testimony of the heart. In their hearts, the People of the Book knew that this messenger was authentic as the signs of his truth were so obvious, and they were convinced of his truth, but still stubbornly persisted in denying him out of sheer intransigence, prejudice and jealousy.

This elaborates the above verse and explains the reason why Allah shall neither guide such people, nor shall they prosper in the life hereafter. They disbelieved after having believed. The Messenger came to them with clear arguments and signs and they rejected him and called him a liar although in their heart of hearts they were convinced of his truth. Still they continued to utter lies about the Prophet and his message. By this behaviour, they did tremendous wrong to their own selves, to their nature, to their understanding and reason, and to their souls. According to Divine law as laid down by Allah, no person who wilfully turns a blind eye to His signs and deliberately chooses error over guidance, will escape the consequences. Their punishment is that

26. See *Pondering over the Qur'ān*, Vol. I, and the comments on verse 2 (Translator).

they will receive the condemnation of Allah, His angels and all humans. The use of *ajmaʿīn* (meaning 'all') with *an-nās* (people) indicates that they shall be cursed and condemned by all, the good as well as the evil, on Judgement Day. The reason for the good condemning them is easy to understand and quite obvious. The evil ones will also condemn them because they were misguided and misled by them. The Qur'ān says that on Judgement Day, the misguided leaders and their followers whom they misled will curse each other. The followers will say that their leaders misled them; otherwise they would have followed the guidance. The leaders, on the other hand, will say that if they misguided them it was because they themselves were astray, and that their followers were blameworthy for blindly following their errant leadership rather than the guidance from Allah.

In the phrase *khālidīna fī-hā,* the pronoun *hā* (it) refers to hell. The condemnation symbolises, as it were, the punishment in store for them. There are many examples of this linguistic style that we shall take up in the commentary on Sūrah al-Ḥadīd. About this punishment, we are further told that at no stage will it be lightened nor will the blameworthy have any respite. All doors of hope will be closed for them thereafter. However, those who heed these warnings, mend their ways and openly declare what they had been hiding from others will be saved from punishment. They will find Allah most forgiving and most merciful.

إِنَّ ٱلَّذِينَ كَفَرُوا۟ بَعْدَ إِيمَـٰنِهِمْ ثُمَّ ٱزْدَادُوا۟ كُفْرًا لَّن تُقْبَلَ تَوْبَتُهُمْ وَأُو۟لَـٰٓئِكَ هُمُ
ٱلضَّآلُّونَ ﴿٩٠﴾
إِنَّ ٱلَّذِينَ كَفَرُوا۟ وَمَاتُوا۟ وَهُمْ كُفَّارٌ فَلَن يُقْبَلَ مِنْ أَحَدِهِم مِّلْءُ ٱلْأَرْضِ ذَهَبًا
وَلَوِ ٱفْتَدَىٰ بِهِۦٓ ۗ أُو۟لَـٰٓئِكَ لَهُمْ عَذَابٌ أَلِيمٌ وَمَا لَهُم مِّن نَّـٰصِرِينَ ﴿٩١﴾

But those who disbelieve after having believed, and then increase in their unbelief – their repentance shall not be accepted. They are the ones utterly astray. (90)
As to those who disbelieve, and die while they are disbelievers, there shall not be accepted from any of them even the earth full of gold, though they should offer it in ransom. For them, there shall be a painful punishment, and they shall have no helpers. (91)

The people whose repentance is unacceptable

These verses refer to the people whose repentance shall not be accepted. They are the ones who were guilty of all the above-mentioned crimes: they believed and then went back and disbelieved, and then went on adding layers upon layers of disbelief. When their final moment came, they professed repentance verbally, without making amends for their crimes, nor openly confessing their concealment of the truth before the Prophet and the believers. Also, they did not spend in the cause of Allah and in support of the Prophet in order to wipe off their sins. They died, in the words of the Qur'ān, falsely hoping that "Allah shall forgive us – *sa-yughfiru lanā*". The Qur'ān clearly warns all such people who thus delude themselves that their verbal repentance is no real repentance, nor will Allah accept it from them.

Similar is the case of those people who recognised the truth and believed in it and then reverted to *kufr* or unbelief and died in this state. Such people, even if they were to offer the earth full of gold in ransom to save themselves from the chastisement, it shall not be accepted from them. The style used here is meant to emphasise the impossibility of their salvation in the hereafter, for surely no one will possess anything in the hereafter to be able to offer it to any one else, nor is the life hereafter a place for wheeling and dealing. The conclusion – *Wa mā la-hum min nāṣirīn* – and they shall have no helpers – lays bare the false hopes of those who expected to be saved by the intercession of their forefathers on their behalf. They shall have none there to help them. For further details on this subject, please refer to *Pondering over the Qur'ān*, volume 1, the commentary on the following verses of Sūrah al Baqarah:

> *Those who conceal the clear evidence We have sent down, and the guidance, after We have made them clear for the People in the Book, it is these who are cursed by Allah and by those who curse. Except those who repent and make amends and openly declare (the truth), their repentance I shall accept, for I alone am the Acceptor of Repentance, Ever Merciful. Those who deny the truth, and die as deniers of the truth, on them shall be Allah's curse, and the curse of angels, and of all people. They will dwell in hell forever: Their punishment will not be lightened, nor will they be given any respite.* (Sūrah al-Baqarah, 2:159-162).

Verses 92-99: Thematic Continuity

Bearing in mind what has been said in the previous section, it should not be difficult to understand what is described in the following pages. Verse 63 above speaks about the claim of the Jews and the Christians that they are the true followers of Prophet Ibrāhīm and shows that their claim is groundless. In fact it is Prophet Muḥammad, peace be upon him, and his followers, who are the genuine followers of the community of Ibrāhīm, while the Jews and the Christians are engaged in conspiracies against them in order to conceal the real facts while seeking to deceive and mislead people. They were not ready for any sacrifices nor did they suffer any material loss, and yet considered themselves as the foremost, nay, the only, faithful servants of Allah for observing certain rituals of questionable validity.

The Qur'ān repudiates their assertion, which is based on misconceptions. They are told that the real goal of obedience to Allah cannot be attained merely by the ostentatious observance of certain rituals to impress others. The most important act in this respect is rather to spend in the cause of Allah what one cherishes most. Unless a person is ready to sacrifice his most cherished desires and possessions, he remains unfit to fulfil the demands of his covenant with Allah.

An answer to the Jewish accusation against Muslims

This is an answer to the Jewish claim that they and not the Muslims were the true followers of the community of Prophet Ibrāhīm. They said that there are certain things that are permissible in Islam whereas they were, they asserted, prohibited in Ibrāhīmic law. Thus, for instance, they claimed that the camel was forbidden in the Sharī'ah of Prophet Ibrāhīm; but was not only permissible to the Muslims, but it was also their most cherished possession, and that they regarded its sacrifice in the name of Allah as a most desirable act of devotion. As pointed out above, the purpose of all this hostile propaganda was to convince the people that Prophet Muḥammad, peace be upon him, and his companions represented a way that contradicted the path of Prophet Ibrāhīm and his community. The Qur'ān repudiates their assertion saying that the Torah itself bears witness that the prohibition of the camel was a part of the Mosaic Law rather than of the Ibrāhīmic Sharī'ah.

The Jews are then once more invited to follow the true community of Prophet Ibrāhīm. They are referred to the prophecies of the Torah concerning the Ka'bah as the first house of worship, its centrality and its being the source of blessings and guidance for all mankind. They had tried their best to conceal all evidence connecting Prophet Ibrāhīm to Ka'bah. The Qur'ān refers to some signs that clearly show that Prophet Ibrāhīm had indeed chosen this place as his dwelling place. He called it the land of peace, and made it the centre of pilgrimage and *'umrah*. This is the place where the descendants of Ibrāhīm had lived for hundreds of years and which is closely associated with his name and traditions.

Verses 92-99

The last two verses admonish the People of the Book. It was sad that they were trying to prevent people from following the straight path and misleading them instead of guiding them aright. Guiding people aright was the purpose for which they were originally raised as a community. Bearing these points in mind, let us now study the next segment of verses.

لَن تَنَالُوا۟ ٱلْبِرَّ حَتَّىٰ تُنفِقُوا۟ مِمَّا تُحِبُّونَ ۚ
وَمَا تُنفِقُوا۟ مِن شَىْءٍ فَإِنَّ ٱللَّهَ بِهِۦ عَلِيمٌ
﴿٩٢﴾

By no means can you be truly faithful to Allah unless you give (freely) of that which you love. And whatever you give, surely Allah knows it well. (92)

۞ كُلُّ ٱلطَّعَامِ كَانَ حِلًّا لِّبَنِىٓ إِسْرَٰٓءِيلَ
إِلَّا مَا حَرَّمَ إِسْرَٰٓءِيلُ عَلَىٰ نَفْسِهِۦ مِن
قَبْلِ أَن تُنَزَّلَ ٱلتَّوْرَىٰةُ ۗ قُلْ فَأْتُوا۟ بِٱلتَّوْرَىٰةِ
فَٱتْلُوهَآ إِن كُنتُمْ صَٰدِقِينَ ﴿٩٣﴾

All food was lawful to the descendants of Israel, except what Israel made unlawful for himself, before the Torah was revealed. Say: "Bring the Torah and study it, if you are truthful." (93)

فَمَنِ ٱفْتَرَىٰ عَلَى ٱللَّهِ ٱلْكَذِبَ مِنۢ بَعْدِ
ذَٰلِكَ فَأُو۟لَٰٓئِكَ هُمُ ٱلظَّٰلِمُونَ ﴿٩٤﴾

If any, after this, invent a lie and attribute it to Allah, they are indeed unjust wrongdoers. (94)

قُلْ صَدَقَ ٱللَّهُ ۗ فَٱتَّبِعُوا۟ مِلَّةَ إِبْرَٰهِيمَ
حَنِيفًا وَمَا كَانَ مِنَ ٱلْمُشْرِكِينَ ﴿٩٥﴾

Say: "Allah speaks the Truth: follow the religion of Ibrāhīm, who was single-mindedly devoted to Allah, and he was not of the polytheists." (95)

إِنَّ أَوَّلَ بَيْتٍ وُضِعَ لِلنَّاسِ لَلَّذِى بِبَكَّةَ
مُبَارَكًا وَهُدًى لِّلْعَٰلَمِينَ ﴿٩٦﴾

The first House (of worship) appointed for people was that at Bakkah: full of blessing and of guidance for all the people of the world. (96)

فِيهِ ءَايَٰتٌۢ بَيِّنَٰتٌ مَّقَامُ إِبْرَٰهِيمَ ۖ وَمَن
دَخَلَهُۥ كَانَ ءَامِنًا ۗ وَلِلَّهِ عَلَى ٱلنَّاسِ حِجُّ
ٱلْبَيْتِ مَنِ ٱسْتَطَاعَ إِلَيْهِ سَبِيلًا ۚ وَمَن
كَفَرَ فَإِنَّ ٱللَّهَ غَنِىٌّ عَنِ ٱلْعَٰلَمِينَ ﴿٩٧﴾

In it are manifest signs, (for example), the Station of Ibrāhīm. Whoever enters it attains security; and pilgrimage to this house is a duty people owe to Allah, those who can afford the journey; but if any deny faith, Allah stands not in need of any of His creatures. (97)

قُلْ يَٰٓأَهْلَ ٱلْكِتَٰبِ لِمَ تَكْفُرُونَ بِـَٔايَٰتِ
ٱللَّهِ وَٱللَّهُ شَهِيدٌ عَلَىٰ مَا تَعْمَلُونَ ﴿٩٨﴾

Say: "O People of the Book! Why do you reject the signs of Allah, when Allah is Himself witness to all that you do?" (98)

قُلْ يَٰٓأَهْلَ ٱلْكِتَٰبِ لِمَ تَصُدُّونَ عَن
سَبِيلِ ٱللَّهِ مَنْ ءَامَنَ تَبْغُونَهَا عِوَجًا
وَأَنتُمْ شُهَدَآءُ ۗ وَمَا ٱللَّهُ بِغَٰفِلٍ عَمَّا
تَعْمَلُونَ ﴿٩٩﴾

Say: "O People of the Book! Why do you obstruct those who believe from the path of Allah, seeking to make it crooked, while you are made witnesses? And Allah is not unmindful of all that you do." (99)

EXPLANATION AND WORD STUDY

لَن تَنَالُوا۟ ٱلْبِرَّ حَتَّىٰ تُنفِقُوا۟ مِمَّا تُحِبُّونَ ۚ وَمَا تُنفِقُوا۟ مِن شَىْءٍ فَإِنَّ ٱللَّهَ بِهِۦ عَلِيمٌ ﴿٩٢﴾

By no means can you be truly faithful to Allah unless you give (freely) of that which you love. And whatever you give, surely Allah knows it well. (92)

An essential requisite of fidelity to Allah

For a detailed analysis and meaning of the word *birr* please refer to our commentary on Sūrah al-Baqarah[27]. The word essentially carries a sense of fulfilment of one's promises, being faithful, and meeting one's obligations to others, whether it is to Allah or His servants. The descendants of Israel were utterly remiss in all these areas. They observed certain religious rituals and considered them as sufficient to meet their obligations to Allah. They looked upon themselves as the most faithful to Allah and hence the most favoured of all nations in His eyes, enjoying a status that no other people enjoyed before, nor could in the future. They presumed that they alone were the sole heirs of the spiritual legacy of all the prophets, including Prophet Ibrāhīm. They found it hard to believe that any other group could rival them in this field. The Qur'ān demolishes this false notion saying that true fidelity to Allah cannot be attained by vacuous claims or mere observance of ostentatious rituals; it demands sacrifice and serious effort. Unless one is ready and willing to spend and sacrifice in the cause of Allah out of one's most cherished wealth, one

27. See *Pondering over the Qur'ān*, Vol. I, and the comments on verses 44, 177 and 224 (Translator).

cannot attain the status of being the most faithful to Him. In the absence of these qualities, any claim to fealty to Him remains hollow, false and baseless.

This criterion for judging the fidelity and commitment of the Israelites to Allah and His cause was enough to expose the hollowness of their claims. Ostensibly, they performed more or less all the religious rituals, but to make any financial sacrifice, especially to spend their cherished wealth, was almost impossible for them. With this, all their claims of love evaporated into thin air, even though they were well aware that their forefather Ibrāhīm, whom they claimed to follow and regarded themselves as the sole heirs to his spiritual legacy, had attained closeness to Allah not by mere verbal professions but by a readiness to sacrifice his son at His command. At various places, the Qur'ān has hinted at their formal observance of religious rituals. Thus, for instance, we read:

> *Fidelity to Allah is not that you turn your faces towards the East and the West. Rather, (true) fidelity is the fidelity of those who believe sincerely in Allah*[28]*, and the Last Day, and the Angels, and the Divine Scripture, and the Messengers; and who spend their wealth, despite their love for it, on near relatives, orphans, the needy, the wayfarer, and those who ask, and for the freeing of captives; those who establish prayer, and pay the zakāh; and those who fulfil the contracts which they make, and especially those who are firm and patient, in pain and adversity, and in times of war. Those are the truthful, and they are the ones who are truly righteous.* (Sūrah al-Baqarah, 2:177)

The statement 'whatever you give, surely Allah knows it well', stresses the essential consequence of His knowledge. In other words, rest assured that Allah is fully aware of whatever you spend in His cause and will fully reward you for it. If you spend one farthing, you will be rewarded from ten to seven hundred times over, besides the infinite bounty of your Sustainer that lies in store for you, to bless you with ever more.

۞ كُلُّ ٱلطَّعَامِ كَانَ حِلًّا لِّبَنِىٓ إِسْرَٰٓءِيلَ إِلَّا مَا حَرَّمَ إِسْرَٰٓءِيلُ عَلَىٰ نَفْسِهِۦ مِن

28. In the sentence "*wa lākinna-al birra man āmana billāh*" (rather, (true) fidelity is that of those who believe sincerely in Allah) one of the subjoined part, *a muḍāf*, in accordance with a general rule of Arabic grammar, is omitted. Thus the full sentence would read "wa lākinna-al birra birru man āmana billāh (rather, true fidelity is the fidelity of the one who believes in Allah). Another example of such an omission of a *muḍāf* in this verse is the phrase "*wa fi-r riqab*" (and the captives), which clearly is meant to be read as "*wa fī fakki ar-riqāb*" (and in the freeing of captives). (Also see *Pondering over the Qur'ān*, volume one, for comments on the above verse).

قَبۡلِ أَن تُنَزَّلَ ٱلتَّوۡرَىٰةُۗ قُلۡ فَأۡتُواْ بِٱلتَّوۡرَىٰةِ فَٱتۡلُوهَآ إِن كُنتُمۡ صَٰدِقِينَ ٩٣
فَمَنِ ٱفۡتَرَىٰ عَلَى ٱللَّهِ ٱلۡكَذِبَ مِنۢ بَعۡدِ ذَٰلِكَ فَأُوْلَٰٓئِكَ هُمُ ٱلظَّٰلِمُونَ ٩٤

All food was lawful for the descendants of Israel, except what Israel made unlawful for himself, before the Torah was revealed. Say: "Bring the Torah and study it, if you are truthful." (93)
If any, after this, invent a lie and attribute it to Allah, they are indeed unjust wrongdoers. (94)

This is in part in answer to a Jewish objection referred to above. They claimed that only they, rather than the Muslims, were the true followers of Prophet Ibrāhīm. To support their claim, they asserted that some of the things that the Muslims have declared permissible for themselves were prohibited in the Abrahamic law, but the Muslims not only held these things permissible but regarded offering and sacrificing them in the name of Allah as a means of attaining piety and a sign of fidelity and commitment to the Divine cause, whereas all these were originally prohibited in Abrahamic law. Most probably, this meant the slaughter and sacrifice of camels since the camel was the most cherished wealth of the Arabs. In Jewish law, as mentioned in the book of Leviticus, they were forbidden[29].

The Qur'ān refutes their false notion, saying that all things good and wholesome were also originally permissible for the descendants of Israel, including the camel. However, Israel (Jacob) had forbidden to himself certain things before the revelation of the Torah. That is why there is no mention of the camels or certain other foods regarded as forbidden by them among the forbidden foods during the time of Prophet Ibrāhīm. The inclusion of the camel among the forbidden animals is a later addition and is mentioned only in the Torah (which was revealed later).

Three categories of things made impermissible by the Jews

The good and wholesome things forbidden in the Torah, unlike those mentioned in Abrahamic law, fall under three broad categories. The first kind consists of the prohibitions that were merely the result of the juristic discussions and hair splitting of Jewish jurists. In their verdicts, they sometimes declared a thing forbidden and later their verdicts were interpolated in the Torah, thus becoming a part of its edicts. The judgements and verdicts of these

29. "There are some that only chew the cud or only have a split hoof, but you must not eat them. The camel, though it chews the cud, does not have a split hoof; it is ceremonially unclean for you." (Leviticus 11:4).

jurists were in time interpolated in the Divine book. These interpolations in the Torah are related to its history and must be discussed separately.

The second kind of prohibitions consists of the things that were made unlawful for the Israelites on account of their insolence, and their excessive quibbling and hair-splitting. They raised unnecessary questions about the legality or otherwise of things and so they narrowed down their options and sometimes even good and wholesome things were also forbidden to them.

The third kind consists of the prohibitions that they had inherited from their forefathers. For instance, Prophet Ya'qūb did not use certain things as a precautionary measure or avoided them due to some personal reason, likes or dislikes, or non-suitability. Later, his descendants attributed his avoidance of these things to Prophet Ibrāhīm and thus these found their way among the prohibitions mentioned in the Torah.

It is these prohibitions that the Qur'ān describes as *isr wa-l aghlal*[30], chains and shackles. Regarding the promised Prophet to be raised from the community of Ibrāhīm, it was clearly stated in their scriptures that when he comes he would make all good and wholesome things lawful for them and thus relieve them of these chains and shackles. We shall discuss this subject in Sūrah al-Ana'ām and therefore confine ourselves here merely to these brief hints.

The verse "If any, after this, invent a lie and attribute it to Allah, they are indeed unjust wrong-doers" means that if after this explanation, those who persist in saying that the things declared by them as unlawful were also unlawful in the community of Ibrāhīm, and that they were forbidden by Allah, then clearly they are guilty of attributing a lie to Allah. And who can be a worse wrongdoer than those who attribute lies to Allah!

قُلْ صَدَقَ ٱللَّهُ ۗ فَٱتَّبِعُوا۟ مِلَّةَ إِبْرَٰهِيمَ حَنِيفًا وَمَا كَانَ مِنَ ٱلْمُشْرِكِينَ ﴿٩٥﴾

Say: "Allah speaks the Truth: follow the religion of Ibrāhīm, who was single-mindedly devoted to Allah, and he was not of the polytheists." (95)

In other words, tell them that they are attributing a lie to Allah whereas Allah has stated the truth. They should not try to show their innovations as part of the law of Ibrīhīm. Instead, invite them: Come and join me in following the true Abrahamic path to which I invite you. Ibrāhīm single-mindedly followed the path of Islam. He never deviated from this path nor was he from among the polytheists.

30. See Sūrah al-A'rāf, 7:157.

إِنَّ أَوَّلَ بَيْتٍ وُضِعَ لِلنَّاسِ لَلَّذِي بِبَكَّةَ مُبَارَكًا وَهُدًى لِّلْعَٰلَمِينَ ﴿٩٦﴾
فِيهِ ءَايَٰتٌۢ بَيِّنَٰتٌ مَّقَامُ إِبْرَٰهِيمَ ۖ وَمَن دَخَلَهُۥ كَانَ ءَامِنًا ۗ وَلِلَّهِ عَلَى ٱلنَّاسِ حِجُّ ٱلْبَيْتِ
مَنِ ٱسْتَطَاعَ إِلَيْهِ سَبِيلًا ۚ وَمَن كَفَرَ فَإِنَّ ٱللَّهَ غَنِىٌّ عَنِ ٱلْعَٰلَمِينَ ﴿٩٧﴾

The first House (of worship) appointed for humankind was that at Bakkah: full of blessing and of guidance for all the people of the world. (96)
In it are manifest signs: (for example), the Station of Ibrāhīm. Whoever enters it attains security. And pilgrimage to this house is a duty people owe to Allah, those who can afford the journey. But if any deny faith, Allah stands not in need of any of His creatures. (97)

Bakkah, and Makkah

The word *Bakkah* means Makkah[31]. That is how it is named in the old scriptures. Literally, it means a city; as for instance is Ba'lbak, the city of Ba'l. This is yet another example of how the Israelites tried to wipe off various traces of prophecies about the final Prophet through distortions. By twisting their tongues, they changed the word *Bakkah* into '*bukā*" meaning weeping. Thus by changing the valley of *Bakkah* into 'the weeping valley'[32] they lost the most significant sign that could guide people to the final Prophet. By describing Makkah as Bakkah, the Qur'ān reminds us of its ancient name that was mentioned in the Torah and that is still found in some of the scriptures, for example see Psalms 84:4-6.

This verse refers to the signs that prove that the house of worship built by Prophet Ibrāhīm is the one at Makkah, that is described as Baytullāh, the House of Allah. Prophet Ibrāhīm designated it as the spiritual centre of the Abrahamic community. And it is in this very city where, in fulfilment of his famous supplication, "*Our Sustainer! Raise from among them a Messenger* ...", that the final Prophet Muḥammad, peace be upon him, was raised from among an unlettered people and who brought a message of universal blessing for all people, as suggested by the words of the verse "full of blessing and of guidance for all the people of the world."

The House of Allah [Hebrew: bĕth'əl = house of God], as mentioned in the Torah and built by Ibrāhīm, is indeed the one in Makkah rather than the

31. Writing about the word Makkah in his work *Mufradātu-l Qur'ān*, Ustādh Farāhī says: "There is disagreement about the meaning of this word, but there is little doubt that it is a changed form of the word Bakkah which is used in the Qur'ān. That was the name of this valley when Ismā'īl was settled here. The word means a habitation as is clearly proved by the word Ba'albak. Prophet Ibrāhīm had migrated there from Babylon and it would seem he chose a new word of his language for the new settlement."
32. Psalms 84:4-6.

one built in Jerusalem. Prophets David and Solomon built the Sacred House of worship at Jerusalem hundreds of years after Ibrāhīm. This is a clear proof that only the house built at Makkah and not the one in Jerusalem, symbolises the manifestations of the blessings of Allah upon the children of Ibrāhīm.

"In it are manifest signs ...", that is, there are clear signs that this is indeed the house that was built by Ibrāhīm. Despite the efforts of the Jews to hide these signs, there is still irrefutable evidence present in the Torah to show the truth. For further details, please refer to our comments on *qiblah*, in Sūrah al-Baqarah, where this subject is dealt with at length[33].

After a brief reference to the signs in general, three things are specifically pointed out. Firstly, the station of Ibrāhīm in it; secondly, whoever enters the sacred mosque finds sanctuary; and thirdly, it is the duty of all those who can afford it, to undertake the pilgrimage to this house. All these three have been discussed at length in the commentary on Sūrah al-Baqarah[34]. However, as these constitute an important proof of the fact that this house was indeed the one built by Ibrāhīm as the spiritual centre of his community, we would like briefly to recapitulate them here.

The station of Ibrāhīm, as we have shown in the tafsīr of Sūrah al-Baqarah, means the place chosen by Ibrāhīm to settle after leaving his country. Here also is situated the mount of Marwah where he offered the sacrifice of his only son, and it was here that he settled his offspring to serve the house of Allah and establish Prayer. And it is here that a people with strong bonds with him resided for many centuries. All these events are proven facts with incontrovertible proofs still present in the Torah. In the presence of these, no just person can dare challenge these established facts.

A sanctuary of peace

"Whoever enters it, attains security" refers to the supplication of Prophet Ibrāhīm at the time of settling his offspring in this land and praying for peace and a secure life for them. Both this land and this house are a living manifestation of the acceptance of the supplication of Prophet Ibrāhīm, peace be upon him. The Qur'ān says:

> *And remember when Ibrāhīm prayed: "O my Sustainer! Make this city one of peace and security: and preserve me and my offspring against worshipping idols.* (Sūrah Ibrāhīm, 14:35).

---

33. Please see *Pondering over the Qur'ān*, vol. I, Sūrah al-Baqarah, verses 122-162 for the discussion on *qiblah* (Translator).
34. Ibid.

It was one of the blessings of this supplication that the tradition of sacred months was firmly established in this land that strictly forbade causing harm to anyone – including animals – in the vicinity of this House.

"And pilgrimage to this House is a duty people owe to Allah.... those who can afford the journey" refers to the fact that the supplication of Ibrāhīm to make this house the popular centre for people was fulfilled in the fullest sense of the word and its signs are obvious throughout this land. This Ibrāhīmic supplication is mentioned in the Qur'ān in these words:

> *O our Sustainer! I have made some of my offspring (the children of Ismā'īl) to dwell in a valley without cultivation, by Your Sacred House; in order, O our Sustainer, that they may establish Prayer. So make the hearts of some among people to incline towards them, and feed them with fruits, so that they may give thanks.* (Sūrah Ibrāhīm, 14:37)

Pilgrimage to the House

The commandment received by Prophet Ibrāhīm to proclaim the pilgrimage to this House is still valid and continues to this day:

> *And remember when We settled Ibrāhīm beside the (Sacred) House, (saying): "Associate not anything (in worship) with Me; and sanctify My House for those who go around it, or stand up, or bow, or prostrate themselves (therein in prayer). And proclaim the Pilgrimage among people: they will come to you on foot and (mounted) on every kind of camel, lean on account of journeys through deep and distant mountain highways;* (Sūrah al-Ḥajj, 22:26-27)

The purpose of referring to all these signs, as pointed out above, is to show to the People of the Book that the only House built by Ibrāhīm that can be the true centre of his community and his message, is the House of Allah built by him in Makkah. Notwithstanding all the efforts of the People of the Book to change and distort their scriptures, there are still in these scriptures clear suggestions and hints that are more than enough to reveal the real truth. For a detailed discussion of these points, please refer to our tafsīr of Sūrah al-Baqarah[35].

but if any deny faith, Allah stands not in need of any of His creatures

In other words, if after all these signs, the People of the Book continue to persist in claiming that they alone are the community of Ibrāhīm and the

35. Ibid

centre of Ibrāhīm's community is Jerusalem, they are clearly in denial of Allah's signs. And having fully explained the truth and making it clear to people, Allah does not care whether one follows the path of belief or strays off it into the darkness of disbelief.

A ḥadīth in which the Prophet, peace be upon him, is reported to have said that anyone who is capable of performing pilgrimage but does not do so, Allah cares not whether he dies as a Jew or a Christian. The reason for this, in our opinion, is that such a careless attitude of a person to pilgrimage to the House of Allah reflects the carelessness and indifference of the Jews and the Christians regarding the House of Allah, as a consequence of which they ultimately lost their true faith.

قُلْ يَٰٓأَهْلَ ٱلْكِتَٰبِ لِمَ تَكْفُرُونَ بِـَٔايَٰتِ ٱللَّهِ وَٱللَّهُ شَهِيدٌ عَلَىٰ مَا تَعْمَلُونَ ﴿٩٨﴾
قُلْ يَٰٓأَهْلَ ٱلْكِتَٰبِ لِمَ تَصُدُّونَ عَن سَبِيلِ ٱللَّهِ مَنْ ءَامَنَ تَبْغُونَهَا عِوَجًا وَأَنتُمْ
شُهَدَآءُ ۗ وَمَا ٱللَّهُ بِغَٰفِلٍ عَمَّا تَعْمَلُونَ ﴿٩٩﴾

Say: "O People of the Book! Why do you reject the signs of Allah, when Allah is Himself witness to all that you do?"(98)
Say: "O People of the Book! Why do you obstruct those who believe, from the path of Allah, seeking to make it crooked, while you are made witnesses? And Allah is not unmindful of all that you do." (99)

This is an admonition to the People of the Book, reprimanding them for rejecting the clear signs of Allah in their scriptures regarding the community of Ibrāhīm, the House of Allah built by him, and the last prophet whose advent marks the fulfilment of the prophecies in their scriptures. The last Prophet mentioned in their scriptures has come to bless and guide them to light, so why do they still persist in their denial? They deliberately mislead and cause confusion in the minds of the people, but do they not know that rejecting the signs of Allah is an affront to Allah while He watches over them? They were blessed and guided aright, and charged to guide others and enlighten them. Instead they are now spending all their efforts to misguide and confuse people about Allah and His message. They were appointed as guides and leaders but they have turned into robbers and swindlers; and instead of proclaiming the truth they hide it from others, distorting and changing it beyond recognition. Tell them that Allah is not unmindful of what they do.

VERSES 100-109: THEMATIC CONTINUITY

A warning to the Muslims against evil designs their enemies

Up to this point, the discourse has been addressed to the People of the Book. After the conclusive argument against them, attention is now turned toward the Muslims. They are warned that if they listen to the People of the Book they would find themselves back in the same abyss of darkness from which their *īmān* (faith) and *islām* (submission to God) had rescued and brought them out.

The Muslims are reminded of the great blessing in the person of the Prophet and the book of Allah, the Qur'ān. They are directed to the path by which they can guard themselves against all the machinations of the People of the Book aimed at misleading and putting them off course. They should be truly grateful to Allah for these blessings. Simultaneously, they are guided to the social system that is necessary to keep this community on the straight path. Otherwise, they may face a fate similar to that of the People of the Book before them. In the light of these remarks, let us study the following verses:

O you who believe! If you listen to a faction among the People of the Book, they would (indeed) render you apostates after you have believed! (100)

يَٰٓأَيُّهَا ٱلَّذِينَ ءَامَنُوٓا۟ إِن تُطِيعُوا۟ فَرِيقًا
مِّنَ ٱلَّذِينَ أُوتُوا۟ ٱلْكِتَٰبَ يَرُدُّوكُم بَعْدَ
إِيمَٰنِكُمْ كَٰفِرِينَ ﴿١٠٠﴾

And how could you deny faith while the verses of Allah are recited to you, and Allah's messenger is present among you? Whoever holds firmly to Allah will be shown a way that is straight. (101)

وَكَيْفَ تَكْفُرُونَ وَأَنتُمْ تُتْلَىٰ عَلَيْكُمْ
ءَايَٰتُ ٱللَّهِ وَفِيكُمْ رَسُولُهُۥ ۗ وَمَن
يَعْتَصِم بِٱللَّهِ فَقَدْ هُدِىَ إِلَىٰ صِرَٰطٍ
مُّسْتَقِيمٍ ﴿١٠١﴾

O you who believe! Fear Allah as He should be feared, and die not except in a state of Islam. (102)

يَٰٓأَيُّهَا ٱلَّذِينَ ءَامَنُوا۟ ٱتَّقُوا۟ ٱللَّهَ حَقَّ
تُقَاتِهِۦ وَلَا تَمُوتُنَّ إِلَّا وَأَنتُم مُّسْلِمُونَ ﴿١٠٢﴾

And hold fast, all together, to the rope of Allah, and be not divided among yourselves; and remember with gratitude Allah's favour on you; for you were enemies and He joined your hearts in love, so that by His Grace, you became brethren; and you were on the brink of the pit of fire, and He saved you from it. Thus does Allah make His commandments clear to you so that you may be guided. (103)

وَٱعْتَصِمُوا۟ بِحَبْلِ ٱللَّهِ جَمِيعًا وَلَا
تَفَرَّقُوا۟ وَٱذْكُرُوا۟ نِعْمَتَ ٱللَّهِ عَلَيْكُمْ
إِذْ كُنتُمْ أَعْدَآءً فَأَلَّفَ بَيْنَ قُلُوبِكُمْ
فَأَصْبَحْتُم بِنِعْمَتِهِۦٓ إِخْوَٰنًا وَكُنتُمْ عَلَىٰ
شَفَا حُفْرَةٍ مِّنَ ٱلنَّارِ فَأَنقَذَكُم مِّنْهَا
كَذَٰلِكَ يُبَيِّنُ ٱللَّهُ لَكُمْ ءَايَٰتِهِۦ لَعَلَّكُمْ
تَهْتَدُونَ ﴿١٠٣﴾

Let there arise out of you a band of people inviting all to what is good, enjoining what is right, and forbidding what is wrong. Such are the ones who shall prosper. (104)

وَلْتَكُن مِّنكُمْ أُمَّةٌ يَدْعُونَ إِلَى ٱلْخَيْرِ
وَيَأْمُرُونَ بِٱلْمَعْرُوفِ وَيَنْهَوْنَ عَنِ ٱلْمُنكَرِ ۚ
وَأُو۟لَٰٓئِكَ هُمُ ٱلْمُفْلِحُونَ ﴿١٠٤﴾

Be not like those who are divided amongst themselves and fall into disputations after receiving clear commandments. For them awaits a dreadful punishment. (105)

وَلَا تَكُونُوا۟ كَٱلَّذِينَ تَفَرَّقُوا۟ وَٱخْتَلَفُوا۟
مِنۢ بَعْدِ مَا جَآءَهُمُ ٱلْبَيِّنَٰتُ ۚ وَأُو۟لَٰٓئِكَ لَهُمْ
عَذَابٌ عَظِيمٌ ﴿١٠٥﴾

On that day when some faces will be (lit up) white, and some faces will be (in the gloom of) black: To those whose faces will be black, (it will be said): "Did you reject faith after accepting it? Taste then the penalty for rejecting faith." (106)

يَوْمَ تَبْيَضُّ وُجُوهٌ وَتَسْوَدُّ وُجُوهٌ ۚ فَأَمَّا
ٱلَّذِينَ ٱسْوَدَّتْ وُجُوهُهُمْ أَكَفَرْتُم بَعْدَ
إِيمَٰنِكُمْ فَذُوقُوا۟ ٱلْعَذَابَ بِمَا كُنتُمْ
تَكْفُرُونَ ﴿١٠٦﴾

But those whose faces will be (lit up) white, they will be in (the light of) Allah's mercy. And therein they shall dwell (for ever). (107)

وَأَمَّا ٱلَّذِينَ ٱبْيَضَّتْ وُجُوهُهُمْ فَفِى رَحْمَةِ
ٱللَّهِ هُمْ فِيهَا خَٰلِدُونَ ﴿١٠٧﴾

تِلْكَ ءَايَـٰتُ ٱللَّهِ نَتْلُوهَا عَلَيْكَ بِٱلْحَقِّ ۗ
وَمَا ٱللَّهُ يُرِيدُ ظُلْمًا لِّلْعَـٰلَمِينَ ﴿١٠٨﴾

These are the verses of Allah that We rehearse to you in truth. And Allah means no injustice to any of His creatures. (108)

وَلِلَّهِ مَا فِى ٱلسَّمَـٰوَٰتِ وَمَا فِى ٱلْأَرْضِ ۚ
وَإِلَى ٱللَّهِ تُرْجَعُ ٱلْأُمُورُ ﴿١٠٩﴾

To Allah belongs all that is in the heavens and on earth. And to Him do all questions go back (for decision). (109)

WORD STUDY AND EXPLANATION

يَـٰٓأَيُّهَا ٱلَّذِينَ ءَامَنُوٓا۟ إِن تُطِيعُوا۟ فَرِيقًا مِّنَ ٱلَّذِينَ أُوتُوا۟ ٱلْكِتَـٰبَ يَرُدُّوكُم بَعْدَ إِيمَـٰنِكُمْ
كَـٰفِرِينَ ﴿١٠٠﴾

O you who believe! If you listen to a faction among the People of the Book, they would (indeed) render you apostates after you have believed! (100)

The words "a faction among the People of the Book" refer to the people whose hostile activities and conspiracies are detailed above. Among the People of the Book there were some good and just people and the Qur'ān appreciates them as mentioned below. The Qur'ān has on all such occasions avoided any injustice to its opponents. At this place also, it warns the Muslims against the hostile schemes of a specific group of the People of the Book and advises them to be specially alert and vigilant, but without going beyond the limits of justice and attributing blame to all the People of the Book. This was necessary not only in the interests of justice, but was also the wisest and most judicious course for the propagation of the message of Islam.

A special aspect of the admonition directed at the Muslims in this verse is that, while dealing with the People of the Book, a good-hearted person might think that being a pious and religious people they could not entertain any ideas of deliberately misleading others. The simple fact is that they were so vehemently opposed to Islam that whoever listened to them and succumbed to their deceit and charm; they would not rest until they cause them to revert to unbelief or *kufr*.

وَكَيْفَ تَكْفُرُونَ وَأَنتُمْ تُتْلَىٰ عَلَيْكُمْ ءَايَـٰتُ ٱللَّهِ وَفِيكُمْ رَسُولُهُۥ ۗ وَمَن يَعْتَصِم بِٱللَّهِ
فَقَدْ هُدِىَ إِلَىٰ صِرَٰطٍ مُّسْتَقِيمٍ ﴿١٠١﴾

And how could you deny faith while the verses of Allah are recited to you, and Allah's messenger is present among you? Whoever holds firmly to Allah will be shown a way that is straight. (101)

Means of safety against pitfalls on the way

The word *i'tiṣām* means to hold on to, and to grasp something firmly. Thus the phrase *i'tiṣām billāh* means to abide by the Book of Allah and His commandments firmly and steadfastly, under all situations and conditions, whether favourable or unfavourable.

The verse means that for anyone to take the path of disbelief and rejection of truth is reprehensible and a sign of wretchedness, but to take this course now while Allah's messenger is among them and recites His verses to them, would be a most grievous act and a sure sign of ultimate misery and wretchedness. For this would mean that they stumbled and lost their way in broad daylight, without any genuine reason or excuse. Furthermore, the believers are told how to avoid such stumbling blocks and steadfastly pursue the straight course without succumbing to the machinations of their enemies. If they want to avoid this danger, they must strictly hold fast to Allah and His teachings, listen attentively and abide by them faithfully and sincerely under all conditions, and despite all hurdles and conspiracies.

يَٰٓأَيُّهَا ٱلَّذِينَ ءَامَنُوا۟ ٱتَّقُوا۟ ٱللَّهَ حَقَّ تُقَاتِهِۦ وَلَا تَمُوتُنَّ إِلَّا وَأَنتُم مُّسْلِمُونَ ﴿١٠٢﴾

O you who believe! Fear Allah as He should be feared, and die not except in a state of Islam. (102)

***I'tiṣām billāh* – its meaning and significance**

This explains the real significance and meaning of *i'tiṣām billāh* used in the above verse: it means to fear Allah as He alone ought to be feared. It also implies being conscious of Allah to the best of one's ability and capacity, as explained in the Qur'ān at another place: "So fear Allah as much as you can" (Sūrah at-Taghābun, 64:16). There is, however, a world of difference between fearing Allah and fearing others. That is why we are commanded to fear Allah as He ought to be feared. Firstly, because none else has any valid claim to obedience from humans as Allah alone has. Secondly, all the limits and laws stipulated by Allah and the punishment prescribed for their violation are only for the benefit of human beings in this life as well as in the life to come. Abiding by these laws does not benefit Allah. Only human beings gain and benefit from the faithful observance of these laws and commandments.

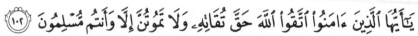

Thirdly, Allah watches over human beings and He is well aware of whatever they do, even of the secret thoughts hidden in their breasts. Fourthly, there is none who can save revolting people from the grasp of Allah and from His punishment both in this life and in the hereafter: the guilty will be consigned to an abiding torment. Unless a person is fully aware of all these aspects, it is difficult to appreciate the real significance of fearing Allah, and indeed of fulfilling one's obligations towards Him. This is the basic error of those who are scared of others and, and as a result of this fear, turn their backs on Allah and His Sharīʿah. They simply fail to realise the vast difference between the hostility of humans and the wrath of Allah.

***Wa lā tamūtunna illā wa antum Muslimūn* (and die not except in a state of Islam)**

This elucidates the subtle truth that fearing Allah is not for a temporary phase or limited to a transient period. Rather, it is a life-long commitment and this is how one ought to live and die. It is a continuous struggle that begins with birth and ends only with one's last breath on earth. If its continuity breaks even towards the very end of one's life, one could lose everything. The wording of the verse indicates that this path is far from being smooth and easy. In this path, there are many ups and downs, twists and turns. A wayfarer treading this path is bound to face hardships, trials and temptations. At every turn, his enemies lie in ambush to rob him of his faith, to conspire and plot, to distract and deflect him from his goal. Greed and sometimes fear may assail him to block his way. Only those who successfully go through all these phases, facing all these temptations and hardships with fortitude and with undiminished faith in and commitment to Allah, are the ones who are sincere in their life-long commitment until the last moment of their lives on earth. They truly feared Allah as He alone must be feared; and they are the ones who will indeed have fulfilled their commitment of *iʿtiṣām billāh* – holding fast to Allah – till the very end of their earthly sojourn.

وَٱعْتَصِمُوا۟ بِحَبْلِ ٱللَّهِ جَمِيعًا وَلَا تَفَرَّقُوا۟ ۚ وَٱذْكُرُوا۟ نِعْمَتَ ٱللَّهِ عَلَيْكُمْ إِذْ كُنتُمْ
أَعْدَآءً فَأَلَّفَ بَيْنَ قُلُوبِكُمْ فَأَصْبَحْتُم بِنِعْمَتِهِۦٓ إِخْوَٰنًا وَكُنتُمْ عَلَىٰ شَفَا حُفْرَةٍ مِّنَ ٱلنَّارِ
فَأَنقَذَكُم مِّنْهَا ۗ كَذَٰلِكَ يُبَيِّنُ ٱللَّهُ لَكُمْ ءَايَٰتِهِۦ لَعَلَّكُمْ تَهْتَدُونَ ﴿١٠٣﴾

And hold fast, all together, by the rope of Allah, and be not divided among yourselves; and remember with gratitude Allah's favour on you; for you were enemies and He joined your hearts in love, so that by His grace, you became brethren; and you were on the brink of the pit of fire, and He saved you from it. Thus does Allah make His commandments clear to you so that you may be guided. (103)

What is *ḥabl-ullāh*

Ḥabl means rope but from this primary sense it has also acquired a sense of relationship and contact and is used in this sense, for the rope binds two things together. A Ḥamāsī poet in one of his famous couplets says:

Wa lakinnī waṣaltul ḥabla minhu, muwāṣalatan bi-ḥabli abī-bayān

(But I retained my relationship, (*ḥabl*) with him, thanks to my relationship with Abū Bayān).

Later, this word was used in the sense of an agreement because, like a rope, an agreement also binds two people to each other. The Qur'ān uses it in this sense in the verse 3:112: *Illā bi-ḥablim min-Allāh wa ḥablim mina-n nās* (except when under a covenant of protection from Allah and a covenant from people). In the present verse, *ḥabl* refers to the Qur'ān because it represents a covenant between Allah and human beings, His servants. Therefore, to hold fast to Allah does not convey any physical sense but a moral commitment; it means to abide by the teachings of His book as it alone represents the link between Allah and humans. Thus the words "and hold fast, all together, by the rope of Allah" further elucidate what is referred to in verse 101 in the words *wa man ya 'tasim billāh* (and whoever holds firmly to Allah).

Of the earlier scholars, Qatādah, Saddī, 'Abdullāh ibn 'Abbās, Mujāhid and Daḥḥāk hold a similar view. On the authority of Abū Sa'īd al-Khudrī, Ibn Jarīr has also recorded a report on this subject that says Allah's messenger said: "*Kitābullāh huwa ḥablullāh-I-l mamdūd mina-s samā'i ila-l-arḍ*, (the Book of Allah is the rope of Allah that is stretched from the heavens to the earth between Allah and His servants."

I'tiṣām bi-ḥabli-llāh emphasises collective effort

In other words, it is the Book of Allah that brings servants closer to Allah, their Sustainer and Sovereign. Whoever grasps it, has, as it were, grasped the hand of Allah. Some of the earlier scholars who take *ḥablullāh* as the Divine covenant, they too hold that it means the Qur'ān, because it represents a covenant between us, the human beings, and Allah, our Sovereign Sustainer. It is in this sense that the Qur'ān and other revealed scriptures are described as symbolising a covenant or a contract between human beings and their sovereign Master, Allah. This subject will be discussed at length in the commentary on Sūrah al-Mā'idah.

The emphasis on "all together" – *jamīʻan* – along with the admonition to hold fast and the warning "and be not divided among yourselves" – *wa lā tafarraqū* – clearly indicates that this is a collective characteristic that must be reflected by the community as a whole holding fast together. This is possible only if they all hold fast to this Book, because it alone is the uniting bond between them, holding them together. They should strengthen and not weaken this common bond. It they allow it to weaken or if their attachment to it should wane, or if they should try to rely upon other "ropes" and bonds and adopt some other standards of good and evil, they will be scattered and lose their unity, like the Jews and the Christians before them.

A warning to the Muslims

Then they are reminded of the great blessing that Arabs have received in the form of this Book. Before its revelation, the hand of every Arab tribe was raised against its neighbouring tribe; there raged between them bloody wars, their gods were different and so were their interests and purposes at variance with one another. This *ḥablullāh* or the book of Allah brought them together and turned them into a single cohesive community. They were deadly enemies and it transformed them into intimate friends, loving and caring as brothers. They should appreciate this blessing and to preserve their unity they must not waver in their commitment and dedication to the book of Allah. For, if this bond between them were to weaken, the old state of ignorance in which they previously lived may yet again return, destroying their unity and harmony. They were a people who faced disaster but Allah saved them. If they are not careful and fail to appreciate this great blessing, they may again end up in the same abyss[36].

These directions given to the Muslims are extremely important and are intimately related to their future. As such, even a small deviation or misunderstanding could lead to horrific consequences. That is why these instructions are spelled out in such detail. In the presence of these, no one has any justification for going astray as is suggested by the words: "*Kadhālika yubayyinu-llāhu lakum āyātihi laʻallakum tahtadūn*, (Thus does Allah make His commandments clear to you that you may be guided)."

وَلۡتَكُن مِّنكُمۡ أُمَّةٞ يَدۡعُونَ إِلَى ٱلۡخَيۡرِ وَيَأۡمُرُونَ بِٱلۡمَعۡرُوفِ وَيَنۡهَوۡنَ عَنِ ٱلۡمُنكَرِۚ وَأُوْلَٰٓئِكَ
هُمُ ٱلۡمُفۡلِحُونَ ١٠٤

36. [Ask them:] "Would you, perchance, after having turned away [from Allah's commandment], prefer to revert to your old ways and spread corruption on earth, and [once again] cut asunder your ties of kinship?" (Qur'ān, 47:22).

Verses 100-109

وَلَا تَكُونُوا۟ كَٱلَّذِينَ تَفَرَّقُوا۟ وَٱخْتَلَفُوا۟ مِنۢ بَعْدِ مَا جَآءَهُمُ ٱلْبَيِّنَٰتُ ۚ وَأُو۟لَٰٓئِكَ لَهُمْ عَذَابٌ عَظِيمٌ ﴿١٠٥﴾

Let there arise out of you a band of people inviting all to what is good, enjoining what is right, and forbidding what is wrong. Such are the ones who shall prosper. (104)

And be not like those who are divided amongst themselves and fall into disputations after receiving clear commandments. For them awaits a dreadful punishment. (105)

Basic purpose of the establishment of the Islamic caliphate

This is the commandment to the Muslim community to establish a system that is essentially based on holding fast to Allah's rope or covenant and is a necessary prerequisite to help people to abide by its demands. For this purpose, the Muslims are instructed to appoint a group from among them to enjoin *ma'rūf* or good, or the noble conventions of society, and to forbid *munkar* or evil as defined by the Islamic Sharī'ah. The way the imperatives – enjoining and forbidding – are used concerning good and evil clearly indicates that this task is to be carried out not by mere verbal advice and admonition, but must also be enforced by law and authority. This is impossible without political power vested in such a group on behalf of the Muslim community. If the purpose were to accomplish the task of enjoining good and forbidding evil by advice and propagation of *da'wah* only, the words *yad'ūna ila-l khayr* (inviting to good) should have sufficed and there was no need to add *ya'murūna bi-l ma'rūf* (enjoining or commanding what is right). In our view, this verse proves that the establishment of the Islamic *khilāfah* or Islamic political system, is obligatory and incumbent upon Muslims. It was indeed in compliance with this Divine commandment that the first thing that the Muslims attended to was the establishment of a caliphate on the pattern of the Prophet's model of governance. The primary purpose of this institution was to monitor and stand guard so that there should be no deviation from the ideal of *i'tiṣām billāh* or holding fast to Allah. In terms of principles, it adopted three methods in order to realise this goal: inviting people to good, enjoining what is right and just and forbidding what is wrong and evil. Out of these three sprang all other departments during the rightly guided caliphate. These were used as a means of meeting all the internal and external responsibilities of the Muslim ummah.

Wa ūla'ika humu-l mufliḥūn (such are the ones who shall prosper)

These words do not specifically refer to the group charged with this task but to the Muslim community as a whole. In other words, it means that a community that maintains such measures to hold fast to Allah – *i'tiṣām billāh* – will alone prosper in this life as well as in the life to come. Next, the Muslims are warned by citing to them the example of the Jews and the Christians. Despite clear warnings, they had abandoned Allah's rope and were left groping in the dark and grasping at whatever came to their hands. Consequently, there arose among them insurmountable differences, splitting them apart into various sects. Let the Muslims take heed and avoid such dire consequences in the life of this world and the hereafter. They are warned against following in the footsteps of the Christians and the Jews, since this is not the path to success and fulfilment, but is sure to lead to disaster and a most grievous torment.

يَوْمَ تَبْيَضُّ وُجُوهٌ وَتَسْوَدُّ وُجُوهٌ ۚ فَأَمَّا الَّذِينَ اسْوَدَّتْ وُجُوهُهُمْ أَكَفَرْتُم بَعْدَ إِيمَانِكُمْ
فَذُوقُوا الْعَذَابَ بِمَا كُنتُمْ تَكْفُرُونَ ﴿١٠٦﴾
وَأَمَّا الَّذِينَ ابْيَضَّتْ وُجُوهُهُمْ فَفِي رَحْمَةِ اللَّهِ هُمْ فِيهَا خَالِدُونَ ﴿١٠٧﴾
تِلْكَ آيَاتُ اللَّهِ نَتْلُوهَا عَلَيْكَ بِالْحَقِّ ۗ وَمَا اللَّهُ يُرِيدُ ظُلْمًا لِّلْعَالَمِينَ ﴿١٠٨﴾
وَلِلَّهِ مَا فِي السَّمَاوَاتِ وَمَا فِي الْأَرْضِ ۚ وَإِلَى اللَّهِ تُرْجَعُ الْأُمُورُ ﴿١٠٩﴾

On that day, some faces will be (lit up with) white, and some faces will be (in the gloom of) black. To those whose faces will be black, (it will be said): "Did you reject faith after accepting it? Taste then the penalty for rejecting faith." (106)
But those whose faces will be (lit with) white, they will be in (the light of) Allah's mercy. And therein they shall dwell (forever). (107)
These are the verses of Allah that We rehearse to you in truth. And Allah means no injustice to any of His creatures. (108)
To Allah belongs all that is in the heavens and on earth: To Him do all questions go back (for decision). (109)

Some important admonitions

Considered in their sequential context, the following points stand out clearly from the above verses:

One, after abandoning the connection with Allah, the People of the Book were torn apart by differences and confusion that is tantamount to relapsing into *kufr* or unbelief.

Two, those who are blessed by Allah specially stretching out to them His rope to get hold of, if due to their misbehaviour they wilfully ignore it and instead shackle themselves in bondage to others, they will on the Day of Judgement face humiliation directly in proportion to the honour they were offered and which they rejected. On that day, the only people whose faces will be (lit with) light and happiness will be those who steadfastly held fast to the rope of Allah under all conditions and circumstances. They shall have rightly deserved Divine mercy and bounty.

Three, all the warnings mentioned here are true and real – *bi-l-ḥaqq*. Those who consider these warnings as empty threats and ignore them do so at their own peril and risk humiliation. Allah has warned them beforehand because He does not want to punish anyone without establishing a conclusive argument.

Four, all power and authority in the heavens and earth rests with Allah alone. All matters shall be referred to Him for final decision and His judgement is final and incontrovertible. Those who pin their hopes on others beside Him, simply delude themselves. At the dawn of truth, they will find that all along they have been merely chasing a mirage.

It is worth bearing in mind that all the above warnings are addressed specifically to the Muslims so as to avoid these pitfalls.

VERSES 110-120: THEMATIC CONTINUITY

The above-mentioned warnings clearly imply that the People of the Book have proved themselves utterly unfit for the moral and spiritual leadership that they had enjoyed so far. They are consequently going to be removed from this position and Allah will entrust it to a community who are qualified for it. Simultaneously, the Muslims are given the good news that no matter how vehemently the People of the Book oppose them, they will not be able to do any harm to them. Rather, they will be beaten back and vanquished in all such attempts; from now on, humiliation is stamped on them.

In the course of this discourse, the Qur'ān lauds those among the People of the Book who steadfastly followed the right course and were later blessed by embracing Islam. Further, it refers to the real sickness of the People of the Book that prevents them from accepting the truth. They are told that that after turning their backs on truth, their ostentatious display of religiosity will not in the least benefit them.

The Muslims are next admonished to sever all relations of friendship and goodwill with these people as their hearts are full of animosity toward them and they have lost whatever little good they had previously. Let us study the following verses in the light of these brief comments.

كُنتُمۡ خَيۡرَ أُمَّةٍ أُخۡرِجَتۡ لِلنَّاسِ تَأۡمُرُونَ
بِٱلۡمَعۡرُوفِ وَتَنۡهَوۡنَ عَنِ ٱلۡمُنكَرِ
وَتُؤۡمِنُونَ بِٱللَّهِۗ وَلَوۡ ءَامَنَ أَهۡلُ
ٱلۡكِتَٰبِ لَكَانَ خَيۡرٗا لَّهُمۚ مِّنۡهُمُ
ٱلۡمُؤۡمِنُونَ وَأَكۡثَرُهُمُ ٱلۡفَٰسِقُونَ ١١٠

You are the best community raised to guide people: you enjoin good, forbid evil and believe in Allah. If the People of the Book had believed, it would have been better for them. Some of them have believed, but most of them are disobedient. (110)

لَن يَضُرُّوكُمۡ إِلَّآ أَذٗىۖ وَإِن
يُقَٰتِلُوكُمۡ يُوَلُّوكُمُ ٱلۡأَدۡبَارَ ثُمَّ لَا يُنصَرُونَ
١١١

They cannot harm you, except (causing slight annoyance) using abusive words; if they fight you, they will turn their backs upon you, and no help shall they get. (111)

ضُرِبَتۡ عَلَيۡهِمُ ٱلذِّلَّةُ أَيۡنَ مَا ثُقِفُوٓاْ
إِلَّا بِحَبۡلٖ مِّنَ ٱللَّهِ وَحَبۡلٖ مِّنَ ٱلنَّاسِ
وَبَآءُو بِغَضَبٖ مِّنَ ٱللَّهِ وَضُرِبَتۡ
عَلَيۡهِمُ ٱلۡمَسۡكَنَةُۚ ذَٰلِكَ بِأَنَّهُمۡ
كَانُواْ يَكۡفُرُونَ بِـَٔايَٰتِ ٱللَّهِ وَيَقۡتُلُونَ
ٱلۡأَنۢبِيَآءَ بِغَيۡرِ حَقّٖۚ ذَٰلِكَ بِمَا عَصَواْ
وَّكَانُواْ يَعۡتَدُونَ ١١٢

Abasement is pitched on them wherever they are found, except when under a covenant (of protection) from Allah and a covenant with other people. They have incurred anger from Allah, and misery has been branded on them. That is because they rejected the signs of Allah, and killed the prophets in defiance of right; that is because they acted rebelliously and transgressed beyond bounds. (112)

۞ لَيۡسُواْ سَوَآءٗۗ مِّنۡ أَهۡلِ ٱلۡكِتَٰبِ أُمَّةٞ
قَآئِمَةٞ يَتۡلُونَ ءَايَٰتِ ٱللَّهِ ءَانَآءَ ٱلَّيۡلِ
وَهُمۡ يَسۡجُدُونَ ١١٣

Yet, not all of them are alike. A party of the People of the Book stand by their covenant. They recite Allah's verses in the hours of night, and they prostrate themselves in adoration. (113)

يُؤۡمِنُونَ بِٱللَّهِ وَٱلۡيَوۡمِ ٱلۡأٓخِرِ
وَيَأۡمُرُونَ بِٱلۡمَعۡرُوفِ وَيَنۡهَوۡنَ
عَنِ ٱلۡمُنكَرِ وَيُسَٰرِعُونَ فِي ٱلۡخَيۡرَٰتِ
وَأُوْلَٰٓئِكَ مِنَ ٱلصَّٰلِحِينَ ١١٤

They believe in Allah and the Last Day and enjoin the right, and forbid the wrong; and they compete in doing good deeds. They are among the righteous. (114)

وَمَا يَفْعَلُوا۟ مِنْ خَيْرٍ فَلَن يُكْفَرُوهُ ۗ
وَٱللَّهُ عَلِيمٌۢ بِٱلْمُتَّقِينَ ﴿١١٥﴾

They will not be denied the reward for any good that they do. Allah knows well the God-fearing. (115)

إِنَّ ٱلَّذِينَ كَفَرُوا۟ لَن تُغْنِىَ عَنْهُمْ
أَمْوَٰلُهُمْ وَلَآ أَوْلَٰدُهُم مِّنَ ٱللَّهِ شَيْـًٔا ۖ
وَأُو۟لَٰٓئِكَ أَصْحَٰبُ ٱلنَّارِ ۚ هُمْ فِيهَا خَٰلِدُونَ
﴿١١٦﴾

Those who reject faith, neither their possessions nor their children will avail them against Allah; these are the inmates of the Fire: they will remain there forever. (116)

مَثَلُ مَا يُنفِقُونَ فِى هَٰذِهِ ٱلْحَيَوٰةِ ٱلدُّنْيَا
كَمَثَلِ رِيحٍ فِيهَا صِرٌّ أَصَابَتْ حَرْثَ
قَوْمٍ ظَلَمُوٓا۟ أَنفُسَهُمْ فَأَهْلَكَتْهُ ۚ وَمَا
ظَلَمَهُمُ ٱللَّهُ وَلَٰكِنْ أَنفُسَهُمْ يَظْلِمُونَ
﴿١١٧﴾

The parable of what they spend in this worldly life is that of a freezing blast which smites the harvest of people who wronged themselves, and destroys it. Allah wronged them not; rather, it is they who wronged themselves. (117)

يَٰٓأَيُّهَا ٱلَّذِينَ ءَامَنُوا۟ لَا تَتَّخِذُوا۟
بِطَانَةً مِّن دُونِكُمْ لَا يَأْلُونَكُمْ خَبَالًا
وَدُّوا۟ مَا عَنِتُّمْ قَدْ بَدَتِ ٱلْبَغْضَآءُ مِنْ
أَفْوَٰهِهِمْ وَمَا تُخْفِى صُدُورُهُمْ أَكْبَرُ ۚ
قَدْ بَيَّنَّا لَكُمُ ٱلْءَايَٰتِ ۖ إِن كُنتُمْ تَعْقِلُونَ
﴿١١٨﴾

O you who believe! Take not for intimate friends any outside your ranks. They will spare no effort to harm you. They would love to see you in distress. Rank hatred has already appeared from their mouths: what their hearts conceal is far worse. We have made clear to you the signs, if you would but use reason. (118)

هَٰٓأَنتُمْ أُو۟لَآءِ تُحِبُّونَهُمْ وَلَا يُحِبُّونَكُمْ
وَتُؤْمِنُونَ بِٱلْكِتَٰبِ كُلِّهِۦ وَإِذَا لَقُوكُمْ
قَالُوٓا۟ ءَامَنَّا وَإِذَا خَلَوْا۟ عَضُّوا۟ عَلَيْكُمُ
ٱلْأَنَامِلَ مِنَ ٱلْغَيْظِ ۚ قُلْ مُوتُوا۟ بِغَيْظِكُمْ ۗ إِنَّ
ٱللَّهَ عَلِيمٌۢ بِذَاتِ ٱلصُّدُورِ ﴿١١٩﴾

Lo! You are the ones who love them, but they love you not; you believe in the Book, in the whole of it. When they meet you, they say, "We believe." But when they are alone, they bite their fingertips with rage at you. Say: "Perish in your rage; Allah knows well all the secrets of hearts." (119)

إِن تَمْسَسْكُمْ حَسَنَةٌ تَسُؤْهُمْ وَإِن
تُصِبْكُمْ سَيِّئَةٌ يَفْرَحُوا بِهَا ۖ وَإِن
تَصْبِرُوا وَتَتَّقُوا لَا يَضُرُّكُمْ
كَيْدُهُمْ شَيْئًا ۗ إِنَّ اللَّهَ بِمَا يَعْمَلُونَ
مُحِيطٌ ﴿١٢٠﴾

Whenever something good happens to you, it grieves them, while if some evil happens to you, they rejoice at it. But if you are patient and remain conscious of Allah, their cunning schemes will not in the least harm you; for Allah encompasses all that they do. (120)

WORD STUDY AND EXPLANATION

كُنتُمْ خَيْرَ أُمَّةٍ أُخْرِجَتْ لِلنَّاسِ تَأْمُرُونَ بِالْمَعْرُوفِ وَتَنْهَوْنَ عَنِ الْمُنكَرِ
وَتُؤْمِنُونَ بِاللَّهِ ۗ وَلَوْ آمَنَ أَهْلُ الْكِتَابِ لَكَانَ خَيْرًا لَّهُم ۚ مِّنْهُمُ الْمُؤْمِنُونَ
وَأَكْثَرُهُمُ الْفَاسِقُونَ ﴿١١٠﴾

You are the best community, raised to guide people; you enjoin good, forbid evil and believe in Allah. If the People of the Book had believed, it would have been better for them. Some of them have believed, but most of them are disobedient. (110)

Requisite conditions for being the best community

Kuntum khayra ummatin[37] (you are the best community) means that now you are the only community following the straight path and the true religion that was revealed by Allah but was distorted by the People of the Book through their innovations. Therefore, Allah has now chosen you for the guidance of mankind. As explained in our commentary on verse 143 of Sūrah al-Baqarah, that says "Thus have We made you a middle community, that you might be witnesses over people". Elucidating this point in our comments on verse 143 of Sūrah al-Baqarah, we wrote that this community is the best community as it follows the middle course. The subjoined phrase *–muḍāf* – before the word *li-n-nās* (for people), namely for the guidance and reformation of all people,

37. The word *kāna* in this sentence is what the grammarians call *kāna at-tam-mah* as in the sentence *kāna Allāhu 'alīman hakīman*. It is called *kāna at-tam-mah* or the complete, absolute *kāna*, because it contains the attribute in itself and does not require any other, unlike the *kāna-an-nāqiṣah*, the incomplete or defective *kāna* that requires an attribute or a complement to complete the sense. (Translator).

is omitted. Taking this into account, the sentence would read 'you are best community 'to guide, to reform and to bear witness as the bearers of Islam, the religion revealed by Allah, to all people' as stated in the above verse of Sūrah al-Baqarah: "*li-takūnū shuhadū'a 'ala-n nās* (so that you might be witnesses over all people)"[38].

Ta'murūna bi-l mā'rūf wa tanhawna 'ani-l munkar wa tu'minūna bi-llāh

(You enjoin good, forbid evil and believe in Allah).

Īmān (faith) is the fountainhead of all virtue

This provides the real reason why this is the best community. This is so because it enjoins good, forbids evil and believes in Allah. In other words, the Muslim community is the best not because of its racial superiority as the People of the Book erroneously thought about themselves. The Muslim community has been granted this special status because they enjoin good and forbid evil. This clearly means that this status and honour depends on merit, qualifications and the fulfilment of certain obligations that go with this position. As such, Allah has not assigned this designation to any specific group permanently and unconditionally.

Wa tu'minūna billāh, (and you believe in Allah)

This means that all honour and excellence in the sight of Allah rests on genuine belief in Him. One's merit and honour is valid only when they are accompanied by a belief in Allah. All honour or status depends on *īmān* or belief and is attainable in its presence only. Enjoining good and forbidding evil is genuine only when accompanied with belief in Allah. Otherwise, they are no better than the vacuous preaching and admonitions of piety to others by the Jewish scholars that the Qur'ān questions saying, "Do you command others to piety, and forget yourselves..." (Sūrah al-Baqarah: 2:40)

Fisq

The term *fisq* is used in this verse in the sense of leaving, going beyond or exceeding the bounds of faith and obedience. For a detailed explanation of this term, please refer to our comments on verses 26 and 283 of Sūrah al-Baqarah, *Pondering over the Qur'ān*, volume 1.

---

38. For a detailed explanation of this term, please refer to *Pondering over the Qur'ān*, volume 1, Sūrah al-Baqarah, verse 143 (Translator).

Proclamation of the moral leadership of the Muslim community

In its present contextual sequence, as pointed out above, this verse is a proclamation of the leadership of the Muslim community. As pointed out in our comments on the supplication at the beginning of the present Sūrah (verse 26): "*Allāhumma mālika-l mulk*...(O Allah! Sovereign of all Dominion ...)" implied in this supplication is the decision of replacing the People of the Book with the Muslim community as the moral and spiritual leaders of humankind. Thus, we find that the violations of the covenant by both the Jews and the Christians are described in great detail before announcing that it is only these believers who now deserve to be called the best community. The brief and rather terse remark about the Jews and the Christians – "it would have been better for them if they had believed in the Prophet and the Qur'ān" – evinces suppressed anger such as is hard to capture in words. The verse concludes on a sad note that as a people who have been granted a special Book from Allah to guide them, very few among them were found to respond to the call of truth and to be faithful. Most of them proved to be disobedient and treacherous, with scant regard for their covenant with their Creator.

لَن يَضُرُّوكُمْ إِلَّآ أَذًى ۖ وَإِن يُقَـٰتِلُوكُمْ يُوَلُّوكُمُ ٱلْأَدْبَارَ ثُمَّ لَا يُنصَرُونَ ﴿١١١﴾

They cannot harm you, except (causing slight annoyance) by using abusive words; if they fight you, they will turn their backs upon you, and no help shall they get. (111)

Adhā, what does it signify

The word *adhā* means pain, damage, annoyance and insult. In other words, it means that they are already broken, weakened and hardly able to do any serious damage to the Muslim community. The most they can now do is to vent their anger and frustration by raising certain objections and false accusations to slander and defame the Muslims. They dare not do anything more than that, but if they ever again tried to fight against you, they would be beaten back and thoroughly humiliated and will have none to turn to for help and support. Later on, events proved the truth of this Qur'ānic prophecy almost literally. This is also referred to in the latter part of this sūrah in these words: "...you shall certainly hear much that will grieve you, from those who received the Book before you and from those who worship many gods." (See verse 186).

ضُرِبَتْ عَلَيْهِمُ ٱلذِّلَّةُ أَيْنَ مَا ثُقِفُوٓاْ إِلَّا بِحَبْلٍ مِّنَ ٱللَّهِ وَحَبْلٍ مِّنَ ٱلنَّاسِ وَبَآءُو بِغَضَبٍ مِّنَ
ٱللَّهِ وَضُرِبَتْ عَلَيْهِمُ ٱلْمَسْكَنَةُ ذَٰلِكَ بِأَنَّهُمْ كَانُواْ يَكْفُرُونَ بِـَٔايَٰتِ ٱللَّهِ وَيَقْتُلُونَ
ٱلْأَنۢبِيَآءَ بِغَيْرِ حَقٍّ ذَٰلِكَ بِمَا عَصَواْ وَّكَانُواْ يَعْتَدُونَ ﴿١١٢﴾

Abasement is pitched on them wherever they are found, except when under a covenant (of protection) from Allah and a covenant with other people. They have incurred anger from Allah, and misery has been branded on them. That is because they rejected the signs of Allah, and killed the prophets in defiance of right; that is because they acted rebelliously and transgressed beyond bounds. (112)

A humiliating punishment

Ḍuribat 'alayhimu dh-dhillah (abasement is pitched on them), that is, just as wet plaster is plastered on a wall, abasement has been stamped on them. There is a clear hint in these words that since they chose the path of humiliation instead of honour and dignity, humiliation was pitched on them. The words, "wherever they are found", indicate the comprehensive nature of this abasement; they will live in humiliation even in their own homeland. There is hardly a place in the world where they enjoy respect and can exist on their own.

***Illā bi-ḥablim min-al-Allāh wa ḥablim mina-n nās* (except when under a covenant (of protection) from Allah and a covenant from another people)**

This means that if they are ever established in any place, it will not be on the basis of their own strength and power but solely due to the security granted to them by believers in Allah or other surrounding nations guaranteeing them safety and security. All these are, however, transitory arrangements. Thus the agreements that the Prophet, peace be upon him, had initially concluded with some of their tribes, were later cancelled due to their violations and treachery.

They were as a result either killed on account of their crimes or banished. The agreements that they had concluded with other tribes also lost their practical significance as these tribes slowly and gradually came under the protection of Islam. They were like a tree whose roots are rotten and that cannot keep standing for long with the help of artificial props. The so-called state of Israel in modern times is also no exception. It exists and survives with the help and support of countries like the United Kingdom and the United States of America; it survives by virtue of its covenant with other people referred to above in the words *wa ḥablim mina-n nās*. There is little difference in the existence or non-existence of something that depends solely on the mercy and goodwill of others.

Wa bā'ū bighaḍabim min Allāh

(And they have incurred anger from Allah').

As explained in our commentary on Sūrah al-Baqarah, this describes the real cause of the tragedy and deprivation of the descendants of Israel[39]. Where they could have returned with glory and success, due to their meanness they incurred the wrath of Allah, as a result of which abasement was pitched on them. Allah had chosen them as leaders and witnesses to truth. Had they faithfully met all their obligations, they would have had a very high position both in this life and the one to come. On account of their love for worldly riches and mean-spiritedness, however, they failed to shoulder their responsibilities and consequently brought upon themselves Divine wrath. The higher the status, the greater and harder is the fall.

Wa ḍuribat 'alayhimu-l maskanah

(and misery has been branded on them).

Maskanah here means mean-spiritedness and cowardice, which the Qur'ān has referred to at various places in some very insightful parables about the People of the Book. These show that the descendants of Israel were so overwhelmed with the love of worldly pleasures that it robbed them of any love for the hereafter and the will to sacrifice for its ultimate success. They were incapable of sacrificing even the most trivial worldly benefits for any future rewards in the hereafter, no matter how great. From the Torah, we find that even prophet Moses, peace be upon him, repeatedly reprimanded them for their cowardice and mean-heartedness, as have the prophets in the later periods. The Qur'ān refers to this at several places. The parable of the dog[40] refers to this same mean-spiritedness. Basically, it was this flaw in their collective character on account of which they incurred wrath and, consequently, were branded with abasement.

---

39. Please refer to *Pondering over the Qur'ān*, vol 1., and commentary on verses 2:61, 90.

40. Cr. The Qur'ān, 7:176: "His similitude is that of a dog: if you attack him, he lolls out his tongue, or if you leave him alone, he (still) lolls out his tongue. That is the similitude of those who reject Our signs. So relate the story; perchance they may reflect."

Verses 110-120

Dhālika bi-annahum kānū yakfurūn **(that is because they disobeyed and transgressed beyond bounds)**

In other words, they incurred Divine wrath and were marked with abasement because of their rejection of Allah's signs and their unjust killing of His prophets. Only through Allah's signs is it possible to attain to any dignity and nobility. Those who, like them, continuously reject and ignore these signs cannot escape humiliation and indignity. The Qur'ān sums it up in the parable saying, "If it had been Our will, We should have elevated him with Our signs; but he was inclined to the earth, and followed his own vain desires." (Sūrah al-A'rāf, 7:176). Similar is the case of those who killed the prophets and who killed those who enjoined justice, the very essence and cream of humanity. It is through these prophets alone and those who enjoined justice that humanity can move to higher realms of success and perfection. Those who have the audacity to kill them can only attract wrath and humiliation for themselves and their people.

Dhālika bi-mā 'aṣaw wa kānū ya'tadūn **(that is because they disobeyed and transgressed beyond bounds)**

In these words, the reason is given for their rejection of Allah's signs and the killing of His prophets. The transgression of the bounds prescribed by Allah and disobedience has been a salient feature of their behaviour underlying their rejection of the truth and the murdering of the prophets. So they incurred Divine wrath and abasement.

Taking the above explanation of the parts into consideration, the verse as a whole reinforces the proof of what is stated in the previous verse. They can cause no harm except some annoyance, as they are being punished almost everywhere and exist solely at the pleasure of others.

۞ لَيْسُوا۟ سَوَآءً ۗ مِّنْ أَهْلِ ٱلْكِتَـٰبِ أُمَّةٌ قَآئِمَةٌ يَتْلُونَ ءَايَـٰتِ ٱللَّهِ ءَانَآءَ ٱلَّيْلِ وَهُمْ
يَسْجُدُونَ ﴿١١٣﴾
يُؤْمِنُونَ بِٱللَّهِ وَٱلْيَوْمِ ٱلْـَٔاخِرِ وَيَأْمُرُونَ بِٱلْمَعْرُوفِ وَيَنْهَوْنَ عَنِ ٱلْمُنكَرِ
وَيُسَـٰرِعُونَ فِى ٱلْخَيْرَٰتِ وَأُو۟لَـٰٓئِكَ مِنَ ٱلصَّـٰلِحِينَ ﴿١١٤﴾
وَمَا يَفْعَلُوا۟ مِنْ خَيْرٍ فَلَن يُكْفَرُوهُ ۗ وَٱللَّهُ عَلِيمٌۢ بِٱلْمُتَّقِينَ ﴿١١٥﴾

Yet, not all of them are alike. A party of the People of the Book stand by their covenant; they recite Allah's verses in the hours of night, and they prostrate themselves in adoration. (113)

They believe in Allah and the Last Day; they command what is right, and forbid what is wrong; and vie with one another in good deeds. These are among the righteous. (114)
Of the good that they do, nothing will be rejected of them; for Allah knows well the God-fearing. (115)

Ummatun qā'imatun (A party of the People of the Book stand by their covenant)

Sincere believers among them

Here the Qur'ān distinguishes a group among them who remain faithful to their covenant and abide by the Divine law. *Yatlūna āyātillāhi ānā'al layli wa hum yasjūdun* (they recite Allah's verses in the hours of night, and they prostrate themselves in adoration): that is, they recite Allah's Book during the night and offer prayer and this is indicative of their being faithful to their covenant with Allah. Their eagerness to pray in the solitude of nights and recite Allah's Book shows they are very much alive and aware of their onerous obligations to Allah and His Book. The reason for alluding to prayer by saying that 'they prostrate themselves' is firstly because prostration is the most prominent characteristic of Prayer or Ṣalāh. Secondly, Prayer is the chief manifestation of the submission of the human being to Allah, his Sovereign Sustainer. Thirdly, as mentioned before, the Jews over the centuries had abandoned prostration from their ritual prayers. A mention of it here serves as a reminder to them.

This verse is about a small minority of the People of the Book as opposed to the great majority mentioned in the previous verse. All the People of the Book are not alike. There are among them some who are true to their covenant and who stand in prayer during the watches of the night and firmly believe in Allah and the life hereafter. They enjoin good, forbid evil and are ever ready to do whatever is good and beneficial to their fellow human beings. Among this group, there were some who had already declared their faith in the Prophet, peace be upon him, and others who, though had not yet embraced Islam at the time of the revelation of these verses, were true and sincere believers who eventually entered the fold of Islam. The Qur'ān reckons them among the sincere, upright and pious people and promises that they will not be deprived of the reward for whatever good they do. Besides, they will also receive the fullest reward for all their good deeds prior to formally embracing Islam. Concerning this group, at the end of this sūrah, the Qur'ān says:

And there are, certainly, among the People of the Book, those who believe in Allah, in the revelation to you, and in the revelation to them, bowing in humility to Allah. They will not sell the signs of Allah for a miserable gain! For them is a reward with their Sustainer, and Allah is swift in settling account. (Sūrah Āli 'Imrān, 3:199)

إِنَّ ٱلَّذِينَ كَفَرُوا۟ لَن تُغْنِىَ عَنْهُمْ أَمْوَٰلُهُمْ وَلَآ أَوْلَٰدُهُم مِّنَ ٱللَّهِ شَيْـًٔا ۖ وَأُو۟لَٰٓئِكَ
أَصْحَٰبُ ٱلنَّارِ ۚ هُمْ فِيهَا خَٰلِدُونَ ١١٦
مَثَلُ مَا يُنفِقُونَ فِى هَٰذِهِ ٱلْحَيَوٰةِ ٱلدُّنْيَا كَمَثَلِ رِيحٍ فِيهَا صِرٌّ أَصَابَتْ حَرْثَ قَوْمٍ
ظَلَمُوٓا۟ أَنفُسَهُمْ فَأَهْلَكَتْهُ ۚ وَمَا ظَلَمَهُمُ ٱللَّهُ وَلَٰكِنْ أَنفُسَهُمْ يَظْلِمُونَ ١١٧

Those who reject faith, neither their possessions nor their children will avail them against Allah. These are the inmates of the fire; they will remain there forever. (116)
The parable of what they spend in this worldly life is that of a freezing blast which smites the harvest of people who wronged themselves, and destroys it. Allah wronged them not; rather, it is they who wronged themselves. (117)

Kufr and *shirk* renders all good deeds in vain

Unlike the group mentioned above, these two verses are about those among the People of the Book who stubbornly persisted in their rejection of truth. They are told that their riches and children, whose love had made them forgetful of Allah, will not avail them against the reckoning of Allah, nor save them from hell-fire. Whatever they spend in this life to show off their piety will also not in the least avail them in the hereafter. Their spending is like the freezing blast that strikes and destroys the harvest of a person when he needs it most. All good works done while rejecting truth, disbelieving in Allah and associating others with Him, are null and void. *Kufr*, the rejection of truth and *shirk*, associating others with Allah, are like a freezing blast that reduces all seemingly good works to ashes and a heap of dust. However, those among them who persevered in their faith and later, after the revelation of the Qur'ān, responded to its call and embraced Islam, they will be rewarded for all their previous good deeds, but those among them who failed to abide by their covenant and did not respond to the call of Islam, will end up as losers in the life hereafter.

"Allah wronged them not, but rather they wronged themselves"

This means they are responsible for their miserable plight. Allah did not wrong them as they brought all the misery upon themselves. A tree flourishes only when its roots are healthy and firm. If the roots are destroyed then no amount of care, hard work in watering its branches and leaves can restore its beauty and vigour. For the wastage of all the effort and hard work, the person concerned is responsible rather than nature or its laws.

يَٰٓأَيُّهَا ٱلَّذِينَ ءَامَنُوا۟ لَا تَتَّخِذُوا۟ بِطَانَةً مِّن دُونِكُمْ لَا يَأْلُونَكُمْ خَبَالًا وَدُّوا۟ مَا
عَنِتُّمْ قَدْ بَدَتِ ٱلْبَغْضَآءُ مِنْ أَفْوَٰهِهِمْ وَمَا تُخْفِى صُدُورُهُمْ أَكْبَرُ ۚ قَدْ بَيَّنَّا لَكُمُ
ٱلْءَايَٰتِ ۖ إِن كُنتُمْ تَعْقِلُونَ ﴿١١٨﴾
هَٰٓأَنتُمْ أُو۟لَآءِ تُحِبُّونَهُمْ وَلَا يُحِبُّونَكُمْ وَتُؤْمِنُونَ بِٱلْكِتَٰبِ كُلِّهِۦ وَإِذَا لَقُوكُمْ قَالُوٓا۟ ءَامَنَّا
وَإِذَا خَلَوْا۟ عَضُّوا۟ عَلَيْكُمُ ٱلْأَنَامِلَ مِنَ ٱلْغَيْظِ ۚ قُلْ مُوتُوا۟ بِغَيْظِكُمْ ۗ إِنَّ ٱللَّهَ عَلِيمٌۢ بِذَاتِ
ٱلصُّدُورِ ﴿١١٩﴾
إِن تَمْسَسْكُمْ حَسَنَةٌ تَسُؤْهُمْ وَإِن تُصِبْكُمْ سَيِّئَةٌ يَفْرَحُوا۟ بِهَا ۖ وَإِن تَصْبِرُوا۟
وَتَتَّقُوا۟ لَا يَضُرُّكُمْ كَيْدُهُمْ شَيْـًٔا ۗ إِنَّ ٱللَّهَ بِمَا يَعْمَلُونَ مُحِيطٌ ﴿١٢٠﴾

O you who believe! Take not for intimate friends any outside your ranks. They will spare no effort to harm you. They would love to see you in distress. Rank hatred has already appeared from their mouths. What their hearts conceal is far worse. We have made clear to you the signs, if you would only use reason. (118)
Lo! You are the ones who love them, but they love you not, you believe in the Book, in the whole of it. When they meet you, they say, "We believe." But when they are alone, they bite their fingertips with rage at you. Say: "Perish in your rage; Allah knows well what is in the hearts (of people)." (119)
Whenever something good happens to you, it grieves them, while if some evil happens to you, they rejoice at it. But if you are patient and remain conscious of Allah, their cunning schemes will not in the least harm you; for Allah encompasses all that they do. (120)

Lā tattakhidhū biṭānatan (Take not into your intimacy)

Biṭānah

Biṭānah means the inner linings of a quilt or a coverlet. Thus *biṭānatu-r rajul* would mean members of one's family, intimate or special friends, confidants of one's secrets to whom one is open, or unreserved in conversation, and who know the inward state or circumstances of one's case or business[41].

41. *Lexicon*, p.221

Khabālā

The word *khabāl* means corruption and disorder. So the phrase *la ya'lūnakum khabālan* would mean they would spare no effort to cause confusion and disruption within your ranks.

'Anat

The word *'anat* means hard work, difficulty and trouble. *Wad-dū mā 'anittum*, that is, they wish you trouble and hardship so that you are enmeshed and bogged down in them.

The words *qad badati-l baghḍā'u min afwāhi-him* (rank hatred has already appeared from their mouths) refer to their provocations and anti-Islam utterances that clearly show that the People of the Book are ready to put up with anything except Islam and Muslims. In this regard, the Qur'ān refers to their saying that the polytheists are better than and preferable to the Muslims:

> *Have you not seen those who were given a portion of the Scripture that they believe in sorcery and false gods, and say about the unbelievers that they are better guided in the (right) way than the believers!* (Sūrah An-Nisā', 4:51)

In the phrase *hā antum ulā'i tuḥibbūnahum* (You are ones who love them), the second person pronoun – *antum* –is placed between *hā* and *ulā* where the particle *hā* signifies caution and is used for emphasis. Similar is the phrase *hā anā dhā* (here I am)!

The Qur'ān is the only perfect revealed Book

***Tu'minūna bil-kitābi kullihi* (you believe in the Book, in the whole of it)**

The relationship between the Qur'ān and the earlier scriptures is like the parts to the whole. The people of the Book were given only a portion of the Divine Scripture and the revelation of the whole was deferred, and was completed and bestowed upon the final Prophet. That is why we repeatedly read about the People of the Book words such as: "Just consider the case of those who have been given a portion of the Divine Scripture" (see verse 23 above). The complete Divine Scripture is the Qur'ān, just as the complete Divine religion is only Islam. Thus when a Muslim believes in the Qur'ān, he automatically believes in what was revealed before it; he believes in the whole of the Divine Scripture. All that was genuine and true in the previous scriptures is preserved in the Qur'ān.

Wa i<u>dh</u>ā <u>kh</u>alaw ..., that is, when they are alone with their own people. In its context, this is identical to verse 14 of Sūrah al-Baqarah that says, *wa i<u>dh</u>ā <u>kh</u>alaw ilā shayāṭīnihim qālū innā maʻakum* ... (when they are alone in the company of their devils – devilish allies, they say...) Both these verses are used in a similar context and their message is also identical.

Warning the Muslims to be vigilant of the People of the Book

These verses admonish the Muslims just as they are admonished in verse 28 above. Although couched in general terms, these verses are specifically addressed to those among the Muslims who were then too simple to fully grasp the scheming designs of the People of the Book. Alternatively, due to their weakness they were reluctant to break off their old ties with them, even though at this stage any links maintained by the People of the Book with Muslims were no longer inspired by any sincere consideration. They maintained their links with Muslims for using them to hatch conspiracies, for exploitation and in order to advance their selfish designs against them. That is why the Qur'ān categorically and most emphatically warns Muslims not to take those from outside as their close and intimate friends and protectors or share their secrets with them. They will spare no effort and miss no opportunity to cause Muslims damage and make them suffer hardships. They do not like the Muslims to succeed in their objectives. All they desire for them is troubles, worries and affliction. Their enmity was quite apparent from their utterances but what they conceal in their hearts against Muslims is far more sinister. This warning is concluded with the words that now that the Muslims are warned in clear terms against their enemies and their conspiracies, if they ignore this warning, they will do so at their own peril and with dire consequences.

Furthermore, appealing to the sense of self-respect of the Muslims, the Qur'ān draws their attention to the fact that while they were eager to befriend the People of the Book, the latter had no soft corner for them in their hearts. Indeed, they were hostile to them, although the Muslims believed in the Scripture in its entirety and believed in all the prophets of Allah. Yet the people of the Book refused to believe in the Qur'ān. When they met the Muslims, however, they proclaimed to be believers like them only to deceive them. And when they were alone with their own people, "they bite their fingertips with rage" at the Muslims. These enemies of Islam are told through the Prophet that they might perish in their own hate and rage against Islam but they will not be able to arrest the onward march of Islam.

With this parenthetical comment, the discourse turns again to the Muslims. They are told that their enemies are distressed and uncomfortable when any success comes their way but are overjoyed when they find Muslims in difficulties and afflicted with any misfortune. If, however, the Muslims stand firm and avoid the mistakes against which they are clearly warned, their enemies will not be able to do them any harm. Allah is fully aware of the conspiracies and machinations of their enemies. For further explanation of the last part of this verse, please also refer to verses 125 and 186 of the present sūrah.

It is worth remembering what Ibn Jarīr has noted while commenting on the verse *in taṣbirū wa tat-taqū* (...if you are patient and remain conscious of Allah). Ibn Jarīr says, the foremost commandment while encouraging *taqwā* here is enshrined in the words *lā tattakhidhū biṭānatan min dūnikum* (take not into your intimacy those outside your ranks). In other words, if you truly fear Allah, restrain yourselves from taking disbelievers as your intimate friends and sharing your secrets with them.

VERSES 121-129: THEMATIC CONTINUITY

This section extends to the end of the sūrah. It contains a detailed commentary on the battle of Uḥud and important lessons and issues. It also contains instructions on how to avoid similar mistakes and lapses. As explained in the introductory remarks to the sūrah, the setback suffered by the Muslims in the battle of Uḥud due to the injudicious action of a group among them, one way or another, affected or had an impact on all the groups involved in the controversy between Islam and the forces of *kufr*, of unbelief and rejection. The weaker Muslims felt dejected in the wake of this temporary setback while the hypocrites used it to plant doubts and suspicions in the minds of the sincere Muslims about Islam, the Prophet of Islam and the future prospects of the community. The Jews were also greatly encouraged by this military setback suffered by the Muslims. They resumed their hostile propaganda against Islam and plunged headlong into conspiracies against the Prophet, peace be upon him. Similarly, the old wounds of defeat suffered by the Quraysh at the battle of Badr that should have been somewhat healed were re-opened. They had renewed hopes in their hearts that Islam could yet be defeated.

There was clearly a need to remove various misunderstandings surrounding the battle of Uḥud. This commentary not only deals with these misunderstandings, but also points out the weaknesses and mistakes of the Muslims on this occasion, while admonishing them not to repeat them. This was necessary to purge the Muslim community of its weaknesses and to enable it to discharge its mission effectively as described in verse 110 above: "you are the best community, raised to guide humankind".

At this point in the discourse, the Muslims are promised that they would be victorious "if you are patient and remain conscious of Allah". Here, a most appropriate opportunity for a comprehensive commentary on the battle of Uḥud is created. The weaknesses and lapses of the Muslims, the need for patience and consciousness of Allah (*taqwā*) in their collective conduct are highlighted. These weaknesses and lapses caused this debacle. There was therefore the need for reformation and purification on both individual and community levels. In the light of these remarks, let us study the following verses.

Remember when you left your household (early) to position the faithful at their stations for battle. And Allah hears and knows all things. (121)

وَإِذْ غَدَوْتَ مِنْ أَهْلِكَ تُبَوِّئُ ٱلْمُؤْمِنِينَ مَقَٰعِدَ لِلْقِتَالِ ۗ وَٱللَّهُ سَمِيعٌ عَلِيمٌ ﴿١٢١﴾

Remember when two groups among you were inclined to lose heart, though Allah was their protector; and in Allah let the faithful put their trust. (122)

إِذْ هَمَّت طَّآئِفَتَانِ مِنكُمْ أَن تَفْشَلَا وَٱللَّهُ وَلِيُّهُمَا ۗ وَعَلَى ٱللَّهِ فَلْيَتَوَكَّلِ ٱلْمُؤْمِنُونَ ﴿١٢٢﴾

Allah had helped you at Badr, when you were a contemptible little force. So fear Allah, so that you may be truly grateful to Him. (123)

وَلَقَدْ نَصَرَكُمُ ٱللَّهُ بِبَدْرٍ وَأَنتُمْ أَذِلَّةٌ ۖ فَٱتَّقُوا۟ ٱللَّهَ لَعَلَّكُمْ تَشْكُرُونَ ﴿١٢٣﴾

Remember when you said to the faithful: "Is it not enough for you that Allah should help you with three thousand angels (specially) sent down?" (124)

إِذْ تَقُولُ لِلْمُؤْمِنِينَ أَلَن يَكْفِيَكُمْ أَن يُمِدَّكُمْ رَبُّكُم بِثَلَٰثَةِ ءَالَٰفٍ مِّنَ ٱلْمَلَٰٓئِكَةِ مُنزَلِينَ ﴿١٢٤﴾

Yes, if you remain firm, and act aright, even if the enemy should fall upon you all of a sudden, your Sustainer would help you with five thousand (specially) marked angels. (125)

بَلَىٰٓ ۚ إِن تَصْبِرُوا۟ وَتَتَّقُوا۟ وَيَأْتُوكُم مِّن فَوْرِهِمْ هَٰذَا يُمْدِدْكُمْ رَبُّكُم بِخَمْسَةِ ءَالَٰفٍ مِّنَ ٱلْمَلَٰٓئِكَةِ مُسَوِّمِينَ ﴿١٢٥﴾

وَمَا جَعَلَهُ ٱللَّهُ إِلَّا بُشْرَىٰ لَكُمْ وَلِتَطْمَئِنَّ قُلُوبُكُم بِهِۦ ۗ وَمَا ٱلنَّصْرُ إِلَّا مِنْ عِندِ ٱللَّهِ ٱلْعَزِيزِ ٱلْحَكِيمِ ﴿١٢٦﴾

Allah has only made it a message of hope for you, and an assurance to your hearts. All help comes from Allah alone, the Mighty, and the Wise. (126)

لِيَقْطَعَ طَرَفًا مِّنَ ٱلَّذِينَ كَفَرُوٓا۟ أَوْ يَكْبِتَهُمْ فَيَنقَلِبُوا۟ خَآئِبِينَ ﴿١٢٧﴾

And that He might cut off a portion of the Unbelievers or abase them so that they would withdraw frustrated. (127)

لَيْسَ لَكَ مِنَ ٱلْأَمْرِ شَىْءٌ أَوْ يَتُوبَ عَلَيْهِمْ أَوْ يُعَذِّبَهُمْ فَإِنَّهُمْ ظَٰلِمُونَ ﴿١٢٨﴾

It is not for you to decide, (but for Allah); He may turn to them in mercy, or punish them; for, surely they are wrongdoers. (128)

وَلِلَّهِ مَا فِى ٱلسَّمَٰوَٰتِ وَمَا فِى ٱلْأَرْضِ ۚ يَغْفِرُ لِمَن يَشَآءُ وَيُعَذِّبُ مَن يَشَآءُ ۚ وَٱللَّهُ غَفُورٌ رَّحِيمٌ ﴿١٢٩﴾

To Allah belongs all that is in the heavens and on earth. He forgives whom He pleases and punishes whom He pleases. Allah is most Forgiving, ever Merciful. (129)

WORD STUDY AND EXPLANATION

وَإِذْ غَدَوْتَ مِنْ أَهْلِكَ تُبَوِّئُ ٱلْمُؤْمِنِينَ مَقَٰعِدَ لِلْقِتَالِ ۗ وَٱللَّهُ سَمِيعٌ عَلِيمٌ ﴿١٢١﴾

Remember when you left your household (early) to station the faithful at their battle positions. And Allah hears and knows all things. (121)

Tubawwi'u-l mu'minīna

The verb *bawwa'a* (*yubawwi'u*) means to station, to post and to assign, while *maqā'id*, (singular, *maq'ad*) refers to places used for sitting, or places of ambush, and as indicated by its present context here, it means battle positions.

With this verse begins the commentary on the battle of Uḥud and its effects. As it had recently taken place and its memory was quite fresh in minds, a mere hint or a passing reference to it would have been enough for a contemporary audience. However, as this commentary deals with certain circumstances and effects that touched on conspiracies by some parties or were related to how people perceived and reacted to the attributes of Allah being the all-Hearing and all-Knowing, these are cited in the opening sentence. There was and is no room for any refuting or challenging the veracity of this account. It is by the One Who knows all and hears all. And whatever He has said is based on his flawless knowledge, hearing and seeing.

إِذْ هَمَّت طَّآئِفَتَانِ مِنكُمْ أَن تَفْشَلَا وَٱللَّهُ وَلِيُّهُمَا ۗ وَعَلَى ٱللَّهِ فَلْيَتَوَكَّلِ ٱلْمُؤْمِنُونَ ﴿١٢٢﴾
وَلَقَدْ نَصَرَكُمُ ٱللَّهُ بِبَدْرٍ وَأَنتُمْ أَذِلَّةٌ ۖ فَٱتَّقُوا۟ ٱللَّهَ لَعَلَّكُمْ تَشْكُرُونَ ﴿١٢٣﴾

Remember when two groups among you were inclined to lose heart, though Allah was their protector, and in Allah let the faithful put their trust. (122)
Allah had helped you at Badr, when you were a contemptible little force. So fear Allah, so that you may show your gratitude. (123)

Fashala

Fashala means to lose heart, to become weak-hearted. In war, the most important quality of a soldier is his morale and courage. Arms and weapons and other equipment are of secondary importance. That is why the Qur'ān begins this commentary by pointing out certain weaknesses of some groups.

Adhil-lah

Adhil-lah, (singular *dhalīl)*, means weak, helpless and an easy prey for others. It is an antonym of *'azīz* which means one who is dominant, mighty and exalted far above others. Moral degradation is the primary meaning of the word *adhillah* and is implied only by remote association. The word is also used in a good sense, as in the verse, "they are lowly or humble – *adhil-latin* – with the believers, and mighty – *a'izzatin* – against the rejecters" (Sūrah al-Mā'idah, 5:54). In other words, if the disbelievers wanted to exploit them for their nefarious designs, they would find them firm as a rock. At the same time, they regard the believers with tenderness and are ready to help and support them whenever feasible. In this verse, this word indicates the weakness of the believers in numbers and material terms but without any trace of moral weakness and any sense of humiliation.

A mischief of the hypocrites

The two groups referred to in the above verse, according to some commentators, are the Banū Salamah of Khazraj and the Banū Ḥārithah of the Aws tribe. On account of the hypocrites' machinations among them, they experienced cowardice and weakness for a time, but soon overcame these feelings. The hypocrites did not want to participate in this fight and the Prophet, peace be upon him, was well aware of this weakness in them. That is why, before going out to meet the Quraysh (in the battle of Uḥud), in order to assess the situation, he posed to the Muslims the question of whether they should fight the enemy from within Madīnah, or go out and confront them outside the city. All the true and sincere Muslims enthusiastically responded that they should go out of the city to meet them. The hypocrites, on the other hand, proposed fighting from within Madīnah and enumerated the alleged advantages of such a strategy. This gave the Prophet, peace be upon him, a clear picture of the morale of his army. The weakness of the hypocrites was quite apparent. So after listening to both the groups, he chose the course on which he had already decided – the one that his faithful and sincere followers had so enthusiastically expressed in their determination to fight the enemy outside the city.

With this conspiracy of the hypocrites thus coming to naught, for the time being they went along with the decision to fight the Quraysh outside the city. Later, using this as an excuse and saying that since their advice was ignored, their leader Ibn Ubayy returned to Madīnah with three hundred of his companions. Naturally this had a demoralising effect on some groups of the Muslims. To begin with, the total strength of Muslims was only one thousand men compared to three thousand men of the disbelievers' army. Of this one thousand, the flight of three hundred men at such a critical juncture was a serious blow and the weaker elements among the Muslim army were adversely affected.

Allah is the guardian of the believers

The Qur'ān draws attention to this weakness, saying that those who go out to fight in the cause of Allah, He Himself is their helper and patron, and they should have faith and trust in His help and support. When Allah and His help is with the believers, why should they worry and be unnecessarily concerned at the desertion of a group of hypocrites and cowards?

A reminder of Allah's help in the battle of Badr

After having made clear the implications of faith and trust in Allah, the Muslims are also reminded of the battle of Badr and how Allah had helped them and given them a resounding victory over their enemies despite their numerical and material weakness. Why should they lose heart now and despair of Allah's help and mercy? He is still their helper, patron and guardian as before.

Use of the word *taqwā* in its widest sense

In the sentence *fa-ttaqullāha laʻallakum tashkurūn* (so fear Allah, so that you may show your gratitude), the word *taqwā,* as pointed out in our comments on verse 120, is used in its widest sense. Here it means to have faith, to put trust in Allah as one's helper, patron and guardian, while refusing to be discouraged or act in a cowardly, fainthearted manner. To be truly grateful to Allah is not possible without this kind of *taqwā*. Those who are weak in their resolve and determination are defeated and humiliated by the Devil at every step and all the way. They will follow the path of falsehood instead of truth. Such people cannot fulfil their obligations to Allah as His true and grateful servants.

إِذْ تَقُولُ لِلْمُؤْمِنِينَ أَلَن يَكْفِيَكُمْ أَن يُمِدَّكُمْ رَبُّكُم بِثَلَٰثَةِ ءَالَٰفٍ مِّنَ ٱلْمَلَٰٓئِكَةِ
مُنزَلِينَ ﴿١٢٤﴾
بَلَىٰٓ ۚ إِن تَصْبِرُوا۟ وَتَتَّقُوا۟ وَيَأْتُوكُم مِّن فَوْرِهِمْ هَٰذَا يُمْدِدْكُمْ رَبُّكُم بِخَمْسَةِ ءَالَٰفٍ مِّنَ
ٱلْمَلَٰٓئِكَةِ مُسَوِّمِينَ ﴿١٢٥﴾

Remember when you said to the faithful: "Is it not enough for you that Allah should help you with three thousand angels (specially) sent down? (124)
"Yes, if you remain firm, and act aright, even if the enemy should fall upon you all of a sudden, your Sustainer would help you with five thousand (specially) marked angels. (125)

Musawwimīn

The word *musawwimīn* is derived from *sīma* and *sawma* meaning an emblem and a distinct mark. Thus the term *al-khaylu-l musawwamah* refers to the horses that bear distinct marks. For angels, it is used as a qualifying adjective stressing that Allah will send them especially for this purpose, wearing their distinct badges to participate in this battle.

Verses 121-129

This is a reference to the statement of the Prophet, peace be upon him, on the withdrawal of 'Abdullāh ibn Ubayy and his three hundred companions who, as mentioned in the next verse, caused some Muslims to feel somewhat disheartened. To encourage the Muslims, the Prophet, peace be upon him, told them they need not feel depressed on account of the withdrawal of three hundred weak and demoralised men, because Allah is sufficient for them as helper. And He will send down three thousand specially marked angels to help them.

The Divine words "*balā in taṣbirū wa tattaqū* (yes, if you remain firm, and act aright") are an affirmation from Allah of the Prophet's statement. The Prophet, peace be upon him, had assured the Muslims, trusting in Allah's promise for support. In place of three hundred men who had left them, Allah will send three thousand angels, and He promised another two thousand angels by His mercy and grace provided the Muslims remained firm, acted aright and faithfully abided by the commandments of Allah and His messenger. Allah fulfilled His promise of help and support to the Muslims in the battle of Uḥud. At the beginning of the battle, the Muslims thoroughly defeated the unbelievers and put many of them to the sword. But, a group of Muslims showed weakness and in clear violation of the orders of the Prophet, peace be upon him, left an important battle station, motivated by a desire to partake of the spoils of war. Thus, a battle that was clearly being won was lost because of weakness in *ṣabr*, patience and *taqwā*, God-consciousness. A clear victory was thus turned into a defeat. This is referred to in this sūrah in these words:

> *Allah did indeed fulfil His promise to you when you, with His permission, were about to annihilate your enemy, until you flinched and fell to disputing about the order, and disobeyed it after He brought you in sight (of the booty) that you covet. Among you are some who hanker after this world and some who desire the Hereafter. Then did He divert you from your foes in order to test you* (Sūrah Āli 'Imrān, 3:152).

وَمَا جَعَلَهُ ٱللَّهُ إِلَّا بُشْرَىٰ لَكُمْ وَلِتَطْمَئِنَّ قُلُوبُكُم بِهِۦ ۗ وَمَا ٱلنَّصْرُ إِلَّا مِنْ عِندِ ٱللَّهِ ٱلْعَزِيزِ
ٱلْحَكِيمِ ﴿١٢٦﴾
لِيَقْطَعَ طَرَفًا مِّنَ ٱلَّذِينَ كَفَرُوٓا۟ أَوْ يَكْبِتَهُمْ فَيَنقَلِبُوا۟ خَآئِبِينَ ﴿١٢٧﴾

Allah has made it but a message of hope for you, and an assurance to your hearts. All help comes from Allah alone, the Mighty, the Wise. (126)

And that He might cut off a portion of the Unbelievers or abase them so that they would withdraw, frustrated. (127)

The words "Allah has made it but a message of hope" refer to the promise of victory mentioned in the above verse. In other words, the special promise of help through angels on this occasion was given only as good news to you and to remove your dismay caused by the hostility of your enemies and the treacherous behaviour of the hypocrites. For, even if such a glad tiding was not revealed, the believers should always firmly believe that victory and success lies only in the hands of Allah. He is mighty and supreme as well wise, and as such none of His acts is without wisdom behind it.

The sentence "*li-yaqṭa-'a ṭarafan minalladhīna kafarū*...(that He might cut off a portion of the unbelievers ...") explains the purpose of specially encouraging the believers and the decision of Allah that the Quraysh would either be crushed in this battle or be beaten back with humiliation or at least, lose a portion of their strength.

لَيْسَ لَكَ مِنَ ٱلْأَمْرِ شَىْءٌ أَوْ يَتُوبَ عَلَيْهِمْ أَوْ يُعَذِّبَهُمْ فَإِنَّهُمْ ظَٰلِمُونَ ﴿١٢٨﴾
وَلِلَّهِ مَا فِى ٱلسَّمَٰوَٰتِ وَمَا فِى ٱلْأَرْضِ ۚ يَغْفِرُ لِمَن يَشَآءُ وَيُعَذِّبُ مَن يَشَآءُ ۚ وَٱللَّهُ غَفُورٌ
رَّحِيمٌ ﴿١٢٩﴾

It is not for you to decide, (but for Allah); He may turn to them in mercy, or punish them; for, surely they are wrongdoers. (128)
To Allah belongs all that is in the heavens and on earth. He forgives whom He pleases and punishes whom He pleases. Allah is Most Forgiving, Ever Merciful. (129)

A message of comfort to the Prophet, peace be upon him

This verse is addressed to the Prophet, peace be upon him. The attitude and behaviour of the hypocrites in this battle that left such an adverse effect on Muslims, was no less shocking to him. Allah has, in these words, consoled him that in this matter he neither had any power to intervene nor any responsibility for their behaviour and attitude. He had fully done his duty and if some of the groups still wronged their own selves, he need not worry about them. Leave their affair to Allah. If He wills, He will grant them an opportunity to repent and mend their ways, in which case He will forgive them. And if they are not eligible for His forgiveness, He will punish them. All power and authority in the heavens and earth rests with Him, to forgive or to punish whosoever

He wishes. The reference at the end to the two attributes of Allah being most Forgiving and ever Merciful indicates that He will punish only those who really and truly deserve to be punished.

Verses 130-143: thematic continuity

In this segment, the Muslims are encouraged to spend in the aforementioned jihād. The feelings of frustration and dismay among the Muslims caused by the defeat in the battle of Uḥud are also dealt with. In this regard, some aspects of the higher wisdom behind the recent events are explained to rekindle in hearts the zeal to spend and strive in Allah's cause. Although expressed in general terms, these verses as indicated by their context are clearly directed at those among Muslims who had shown some weakness in this battle or were badly affected by its outcome. This battle had thus brought to the surface many of the hitherto hidden weaknesses of many. It was most appropriate therefore that this moral and psychological garbage should be cleared once for all from within the Islamic community. Most of the subsequent discourse addresses this problem and is a part of the chapter on moral and spiritual purification.

The discourse on spending begins with a declaration of the prohibition of interest or usury because spending and sacrificing in a noble cause and consuming interest are poles apart; the two are irreconcilable and diametrically opposite to each other. When mentioning a concept or a practice, the Qur'ān also mentions its opposite along with it. Thus, in Sūrah al-Baqarah, *infāq* or spending in a noble cause is described side-by-side with the prohibition of usury or interest. The only difference between the two sūrahs is that while in al-Baqarah spending in the cause of Allah precedes the prohibition of usury, in the present sūrah, the prohibition of usury or interest precedes the commandment to spend. Both these styles have their special advantages. To understand the sequence of the text, however, it may be mentioned here that prohibiting interest before the commandment to spend is like admonishing someone not to tell lies prior to instructing him to speak the truth always. Please also refer to our comments contrasting usury and *infāq,* or spending, in Sūrah al-Baqarah[42].

Bearing these brief remarks in mind, let us now study the following verses:

42. Please refer to *Pondering over the Qur'ān*, vol 1, Sūrah al-Baqarah, verses 275-283 (Translator).

O you who believe! Devour not usury, doubled and multiplied, and fear Allah so that you may (really) prosper. (130)

يَـٰٓأَيُّهَا ٱلَّذِينَ ءَامَنُوا۟ لَا تَأْكُلُوا۟
ٱلرِّبَوٰٓا۟ أَضْعَـٰفًا مُّضَـٰعَفَةً ۖ وَٱتَّقُوا۟ ٱللَّهَ
لَعَلَّكُمْ تُفْلِحُونَ ﴿١٣٠﴾

And fear the fire, which is prepared for the unbelievers. (131)

وَٱتَّقُوا۟ ٱلنَّارَ ٱلَّتِىٓ أُعِدَّتْ لِلْكَـٰفِرِينَ ﴿١٣١﴾

And obey Allah and the Messenger that you may be shown mercy. (132)

وَأَطِيعُوا۟ ٱللَّهَ وَٱلرَّسُولَ لَعَلَّكُمْ
تُرْحَمُونَ ﴿١٣٢﴾

Vie with one another in the race for forgiveness from your Sustainer, and for the paradise whose extent is like that of the heavens and of the earth and that is prepared for the righteous. (133)

۞ وَسَارِعُوٓا۟ إِلَىٰ مَغْفِرَةٍ مِّن
رَّبِّكُمْ وَجَنَّةٍ عَرْضُهَا ٱلسَّمَـٰوَٰتُ
وَٱلْأَرْضُ أُعِدَّتْ لِلْمُتَّقِينَ ﴿١٣٣﴾

Those who spend (freely), whether in prosperity, or in adversity; who restrain anger, and pardon people, and Allah loves those who do good. (134)

ٱلَّذِينَ يُنفِقُونَ فِى ٱلسَّرَّآءِ وَٱلضَّرَّآءِ
وَٱلْكَـٰظِمِينَ ٱلْغَيْظَ وَٱلْعَافِينَ عَنِ
ٱلنَّاسِ ۗ وَٱللَّهُ يُحِبُّ ٱلْمُحْسِنِينَ ﴿١٣٤﴾

And those who, having done something to be ashamed of, or wronged their own souls, earnestly remember Allah and ask for forgiveness for their sins. And who can forgive sins except Allah? And they are never obstinate in persisting knowingly in (the wrong) they have done. (135)

وَٱلَّذِينَ إِذَا فَعَلُوا۟ فَـٰحِشَةً أَوْ
ظَلَمُوٓا۟ أَنفُسَهُمْ ذَكَرُوا۟ ٱللَّهَ فَٱسْتَغْفَرُوا۟
لِذُنُوبِهِمْ وَمَن يَغْفِرُ ٱلذُّنُوبَ إِلَّا
ٱللَّهُ وَلَمْ يُصِرُّوا۟ عَلَىٰ مَا فَعَلُوا۟ وَهُمْ
يَعْلَمُونَ ﴿١٣٥﴾

For such, the reward is forgiveness from their Sustainer, and gardens with rivers flowing underneath to abide therein forever. How excellent a reward for the workers (such as these)! (136)

أُو۟لَـٰٓئِكَ جَزَآؤُهُم مَّغْفِرَةٌ مِّن رَّبِّهِمْ
وَجَنَّـٰتٌ تَجْرِى مِن تَحْتِهَا ٱلْأَنْهَـٰرُ
خَـٰلِدِينَ فِيهَا ۚ وَنِعْمَ أَجْرُ ٱلْعَـٰمِلِينَ
﴿١٣٦﴾

Many are the examples (of people) who have passed away before you: travel through the earth, and see what was the end of those who rejected truth. (137)

قَدۡ خَلَتۡ مِن قَبۡلِكُمۡ سُنَنٞ فَسِيرُواْ فِي ٱلۡأَرۡضِ فَٱنظُرُواْ كَيۡفَ كَانَ عَٰقِبَةُ ٱلۡمُكَذِّبِينَ ١٣٧

This is a plain warning to people, a guidance and admonition to those who fear Allah! (138)

هَٰذَا بَيَانٞ لِّلنَّاسِ وَهُدٗى وَمَوۡعِظَةٞ لِّلۡمُتَّقِينَ ١٣٨

So lose not heart, nor feel distressed, for you shall gain mastery if you are true in faith. (139)

وَلَا تَهِنُواْ وَلَا تَحۡزَنُواْ وَأَنتُمُ ٱلۡأَعۡلَوۡنَ إِن كُنتُم مُّؤۡمِنِينَ ١٣٩

If a wound has touched you, do not lose heart, for indeed a similar wound has touched your enemy. Such days (of varying fortunes) We give to people by turns so that Allah may test you and know those who believe, and so that He may take to Himself from your ranks martyrs (witnesses to truth). And Allah loves not the wrongdoers. (140)

إِن يَمۡسَسۡكُمۡ قَرۡحٞ فَقَدۡ مَسَّ ٱلۡقَوۡمَ قَرۡحٞ مِّثۡلُهُۥۚ وَتِلۡكَ ٱلۡأَيَّامُ نُدَاوِلُهَا بَيۡنَ ٱلنَّاسِ وَلِيَعۡلَمَ ٱللَّهُ ٱلَّذِينَ ءَامَنُواْ وَيَتَّخِذَ مِنكُمۡ شُهَدَآءَۗ وَٱللَّهُ لَا يُحِبُّ ٱلظَّٰلِمِينَ ١٤٠

And so that Allah may purge those who are true in faith and wipe off the unbelievers. (141)

وَلِيُمَحِّصَ ٱللَّهُ ٱلَّذِينَ ءَامَنُواْ وَيَمۡحَقَ ٱلۡكَٰفِرِينَ ١٤١

Did you think that you would enter Paradise without Allah testing those of you who strove and fought hard (in His cause) and remained steadfast? (142)

أَمۡ حَسِبۡتُمۡ أَن تَدۡخُلُواْ ٱلۡجَنَّةَ وَلَمَّا يَعۡلَمِ ٱللَّهُ ٱلَّذِينَ جَٰهَدُواْ مِنكُمۡ وَيَعۡلَمَ ٱلصَّٰبِرِينَ ١٤٢

You did indeed wish for death before you met it. Now you have seen it with your own eyes. (143)

وَلَقَدۡ كُنتُمۡ تَمَنَّوۡنَ ٱلۡمَوۡتَ مِن قَبۡلِ أَن تَلۡقَوۡهُ فَقَدۡ رَأَيۡتُمُوهُ وَأَنتُمۡ تَنظُرُونَ ١٤٣

WORD STUDY AND EXPLANATION

يَـٰٓأَيُّهَا ٱلَّذِينَ ءَامَنُوا۟ لَا تَأْكُلُوا۟ ٱلرِّبَوٰٓا۟ أَضْعَـٰفًا مُّضَـٰعَفَةً ۖ وَٱتَّقُوا۟ ٱللَّهَ لَعَلَّكُمْ تُفْلِحُونَ ﴿١٣٠﴾
وَٱتَّقُوا۟ ٱلنَّارَ ٱلَّتِىٓ أُعِدَّتْ لِلْكَـٰفِرِينَ ﴿١٣١﴾
وَأَطِيعُوا۟ ٱللَّهَ وَٱلرَّسُولَ لَعَلَّكُمْ تُرْحَمُونَ ﴿١٣٢﴾

O you who believe! Devour not usury, doubled and multiplied fear Allah that you may (really) prosper. (130)
And fear the fire, which is prepared for the unbelievers. (131)
And obey Allah and the Messenger that you may be shown mercy. (132)

The significance of the rider clause *aḍ'āfan muḍā'afatan*

For the word *ribā* and some other questions concerning it, please refer to our comments on verses 275-283 in the *tafsīr* of Sūrah al-Baqarah[43]. The addition of the words *aḍ'afān muḍā'afatan* (doubled and multiplied) to the prohibition of usury (*lā ta'kulū ar-ribā*) here does not mean that in Islam only the usury involving compound interest is forbidden. Rather, these words are used only to portray the abhorrence of devouring it and its repugnance. A similar case in point is the verse 273 of Sūrah al-Baqarah where the Qur'ān speaks about some of the destitute but self-respecting people: "they beg not importunately from all and sundry" where the word "importunately" stresses the abhorrent nature of begging. Similarly, in verse 33 of Sūrah an-Nūr, the masters of slave girls are admonished: "force not your maids to prostitution when they desire chastity". The words "when they desire chastity" do not mean that they can be forced to prostitution if they are willing and ready to go along. The purpose in both cases is to depict the repugnant nature of the evil involved. The clause *aḍ'āfan mudā'afatan* (doubled and multiplied) performs a similar function in the verse under discussion. It emphasises the essentially cruel nature of consuming others' property unlawfully, by consuming usury.

Invitation to vie in spending rather than in devouring usury

The pre-eminence given to this clause in the present verse is noteworthy in terms of a subtle eloquence. As explained above, the subject under discussion here is spending in jihād in the cause of Allah. It is only as a preamble to it

43. *Pondering over the Qur'ān*, vol 1.

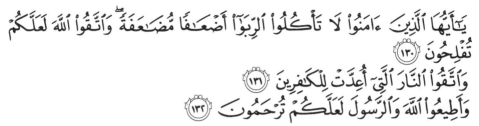

that the prohibition of usury is mentioned as a contrast to the spirit of genuine *infāq* or spending in the cause of Allah. Spending in the cause of Allah and consuming usury are diametrically opposed. Muslims are exhorted to vie with one another in spending in the cause of Allah, as this is the real arena where they should try to excel over others. The opening words "vie with one another in the race for forgiveness from your Sustainer, and for the Paradise ..." invite the believers to strive with their persons and wealth. These words imply that prior to extending to them the invitation to strive and spend in Allah's cause, they must turn their backs once and for all against the example of the Jewish moneylenders and capitalists who vied with one another in hoarding wealth by grabbing what belonged to others. Their example was generating among the Arabs similar purely materialistic trends. Those who are familiar with the Arabic language and its subtleties can very well appreciate that the usurious race depicted by the words *aḍʿāfam muḍāʿafatan* could not have been fully reinforced without these words. The Qur'ān exhorted the believers to strive for the Paradise "whose extent is like that of the heavens and of the earth" rather than waste their efforts in gathering, doubling and multiplying the worthless trinkets of material pleasures.

"And fear the fire, which is prepared for the unbelievers"

In the present context, this sentence clearly implies that those who do not desist from devouring usury after this warning, are the true unbelievers and for them awaits the fire of hell. By doubling and multiplying worldly riches, such people only provide fire for their life in the hereafter, and as such there is little wonder that this fire eagerly awaits receiving them.

۞ وَسَارِعُوٓاْ إِلَىٰ مَغۡفِرَةٖ مِّن رَّبِّكُمۡ وَجَنَّةٍ عَرۡضُهَا ٱلسَّمَٰوَٰتُ وَٱلۡأَرۡضُ
أُعِدَّتۡ لِلۡمُتَّقِينَ ١٣٣
ٱلَّذِينَ يُنفِقُونَ فِي ٱلسَّرَّآءِ وَٱلضَّرَّآءِ وَٱلۡكَٰظِمِينَ ٱلۡغَيۡظَ وَٱلۡعَافِينَ عَنِ ٱلنَّاسِۗ
وَٱللَّهُ يُحِبُّ ٱلۡمُحۡسِنِينَ ١٣٤

Vie with one another in the race for forgiveness from your Sustainer, and for the Paradise whose extent is like that of the heavens and of the earth that is prepared for the righteous. (133)
Those who spend (freely), whether in prosperity, or in adversity; who restrain anger, and pardon people, and Allah loves those who do good. (134)

A parable about the vastness of Paradise

Usurious transactions may bring tenfold, hundredfold or even a thousand-fold gain but it is transitory and limited to this worldly life only. In the hereafter, it will be used as fuel to roast those who engaged in usurious dealings. If, on the other hand, one were to spend in the cause of Allah it would earn him or her an immense reward including forgiveness from Allah and remaining forever in Paradise whose extent is far greater than all the heavens and earth put together. Why, then, should one waste efforts on such elusive gains and pleasures while, with a slight change in direction, one can have the joys and pleasures of a life eternal and a lasting abode in the life to come. This is referred to in Sūrah al-Ḥadīd:

> *Know that the life of this world is only a play and a pastime, an adornment and a cause for boasting among you, and rivalry in riches and children. This is as a rain whose vegetation delights the hearts of the tillers; then it withers and you see it turning yellow, and then it becomes dry and crumbles away. But in the hereafter there is a severe punishment, and forgiveness from Allah and (His) good pleasure; the life of this world is nothing but illusory enjoyment. Race towards (seeking) forgiveness from your Sustainer, and a Garden, the extent of which is as the extent of heaven and earth, prepared for those who believe in Allah and His Messengers. That is the grace of Allah, which He bestows on whom He pleases. And Allah is the Possessor of immense grace.* (Sūrah al-Ḥadīd, 57: 20-21)

This description of the extent of Paradise, however, is merely a parable through which only a vague idea can be conveyed about its true nature and pleasures. The words cannot fully capture its immense reality that is known to Allah alone. Humans may nonetheless purchase this eternal abode of bliss by spending in the cause of Allah.

"Those who spend (freely) ..."

In these words are described some of the essential conditions for an acceptable or genuine act of spending in Allah's cause. In the absence of these conditions, no spending can rank as *iḥsān* – a most noble act of virtue. We have discussed all these characteristics in Sūrah al-Baqarah, verses 262-265. The emphasis here on restraining anger and forgiving others is noteworthy as explained under 2:262-265[44].

44. Please refer to *Pondering over the Qur'ān*, vol 1, pp. 617-627 (Translator).

وَٱلَّذِينَ إِذَا فَعَلُواْ فَٰحِشَةً أَوۡ ظَلَمُوٓاْ أَنفُسَهُمۡ ذَكَرُواْ ٱللَّهَ فَٱسۡتَغۡفَرُواْ لِذُنُوبِهِمۡ
وَمَن يَغۡفِرُ ٱلذُّنُوبَ إِلَّا ٱللَّهُ وَلَمۡ يُصِرُّواْ عَلَىٰ مَا فَعَلُواْ وَهُمۡ يَعۡلَمُونَ ١٣٥
أُوْلَٰٓئِكَ جَزَآؤُهُم مَّغۡفِرَةٞ مِّن رَّبِّهِمۡ وَجَنَّٰتٞ تَجۡرِي مِن تَحۡتِهَا ٱلۡأَنۡهَٰرُ خَٰلِدِينَ
فِيهَا وَنِعۡمَ أَجۡرُ ٱلۡعَٰمِلِينَ ١٣٦

And those who, having done something to be ashamed of, or wronged their own souls, earnestly remember Allah and ask for forgiveness for their sins. And who can forgive sins except Allah? And they are never obstinate in persisting knowingly in (the wrong) they have done. (135)
For such, the reward is forgiveness from their Sustainer, and Gardens with rivers flowing underneath to abide therein forever. How excellent a reward for workers (such as these)! (136)

A hurdle in spending on others

In these verses, attention is focussed on a serious hurdle in the path of spending in the cause of Allah. As with usury that engrosses a person's whole attention, the unchecked desire to hoard ever more wealth is a serious barrier in the path of spending freely in Allah's cause. Indecency and immoral living also bar the door to spending for any good cause. People enamoured with such a luxurious lifestyle are so weakened morally by their subservience to their lusts and caprices that they are unable to pay attention to other matters besides the gratification of their own physical pleasures. That is why the Qur'ān while encouraging people to spend on others, at the same time forbids usury as well as other forms of indecency, debauchery and allied evils such as extravagance and wastage. For a fuller discussion of this aspect, please refer to our comments on verse 268 of Sūrah al-Baqarah[45]. It will be further discussed in comments on verses 26 and 27 of Sūrah Banī Israel.

Only those will truly be able to spend in Allah's cause, the Qur'ān says, who protect themselves from the evils of indecency and debauchery. And those who deliberately and stubbornly persist in sins, they will forever deprive themselves of all good and of Divine pleasure. If under the influence of emotions, a person commits a minor or a major sin, the remembrance of Allah should forthwith alert and prompt him to seek His forgiveness as a seeker of real success and prosperity. There is none other Allah who can forgive sins. So those who put all their hopes in the intercession of others

45. *Pondering over the Qur'ān*, vol 1, p. 629 (Translator).

with Allah, will be disappointed when they face chastisement for their misdeeds.

قَدْ خَلَتْ مِن قَبْلِكُمْ سُنَنٌ فَسِيرُوا۟ فِى ٱلْأَرْضِ فَٱنظُرُوا۟ كَيْفَ كَانَ عَٰقِبَةُ ٱلْمُكَذِّبِينَ ﴿١٣٧﴾
هَٰذَا بَيَانٌ لِّلنَّاسِ وَهُدًى وَمَوْعِظَةٌ لِّلْمُتَّقِينَ ﴿١٣٨﴾

Many were the examples (of people) that have passed away before you: travel through the earth, and see what was the end of those who rejected truth. (137) *This is a plain warning to people, a guidance and admonition to those who fear Allah!* (138)

The meaning of *sunan*

The word *sunan* (translated as 'examples') refers to the laws and the ways laid down by Allah for dealing with various groups and nations. A nation that obeys and abides by Allah's laws and commandments and follows His messengers is granted success and honour while the one that defies and violates His commandments and rejects His messengers is punished and ultimately destroyed. There are many manifestations of this Divine law on Allah's earth. In Arabia too, whose people were the first audience of the Qur'ān, there were many examples of this law in the form of ruins of ancient Arab peoples such as 'Ād, Thamūd, the people of Madyan and of Lot. It is these manifestations of Divine justice that are described here as the *sunan* or laws of Allah. The Qur'ān uses this word in this sense quite frequently. For instance, at one place we read: "*sunnatallāhi fi-lladhīna khalaw min qablu* (it was the practice (approved) by Allah amongst the people that have passed away") (Sūrah al-Aḥzāb, 33:38). At another place: "*fa hal yanẓurūna illā sunnata-l awwalīn* (are they but looking for the way the ancients were dealt with?") (Sūrah Fāṭir, 35:43).

These two verses, after the prohibition of usury and the exhortation to spend in the cause of Allah, are essentially a warning and stress the need to be vigilant. As mentioned above, although couched in general terms these verses are specially addressed to the weaker elements among Muslims who were still not fully committed to the cause or were plainly afflicted with hypocrisy. They are warned that they would face a fate similar to that of earlier people who rejected Allah's messengers. They can see their ruins all over their own land. But from this warning, only those will truly be able to benefit who fear Allah and are morally alive.

Verses 130-143

وَلَا تَهِنُوا وَلَا تَحْزَنُوا وَأَنتُمُ الْأَعْلَوْنَ إِن كُنتُم مُّؤْمِنِينَ ﴿١٣٩﴾

So lose not heart, nor feel distressed, for you shall gain mastery if you are true in faith. (139)

Wahn

Wahn means weakness, whether it concerns volition or action, or is of a physical or moral nature. In a ḥadīth, we read that once the Prophet, peace be upon him, said to his companions that a time will come when Muslims will be reduced to 'froth and scum that rises above flood waters'. They asked about the reason for it whereupon he told them that they would have *wahn* in their hearts. 'What is *wahn*?' they asked him, and he replied, 'It is the love of the worldly life and the dislike of death[46].' In the light of this ḥadīth, we can say that *wahn* is the weakness in resolve and morale and the abject cowardice that leads to an abject failure of volition and action. This in turn stems from the love of worldly life and the fear of death that bars one from striving in the cause of truth. In the present verse, the phrase *la tahinū* (lose not heart) also has precisely this meaning. In other words, the defeat in the battle of Uḥud should not demoralise you, break your spirit or disappoint you. The complete sentence would read: *la tahinū mimmā aṣābakum wa la taḥzanū 'alā mā fātakum,* (on account of this defeat that you experienced, do not be discouraged nor grieve over the loss that you suffered.)

إِن يَمْسَسْكُمْ قَرْحٌ فَقَدْ مَسَّ الْقَوْمَ قَرْحٌ مِّثْلُهُ ۚ وَتِلْكَ الْأَيَّامُ نُدَاوِلُهَا بَيْنَ النَّاسِ وَلِيَعْلَمَ اللَّهُ الَّذِينَ آمَنُوا وَيَتَّخِذَ مِنكُمْ شُهَدَاءَ ۗ وَاللَّهُ لَا يُحِبُّ الظَّالِمِينَ ﴿١٤٠﴾

If a wound has touched you, do not lose heart, for indeed a similar wound has touched the others (your enemy). Such days (of varying fortunes) We give to people by turns so that Allah may test you and know those that believe, and so that He may take to Himself from your ranks martyrs (witnesses to Truth). And Allah loves not the wrongdoers. (140)

Al-qawm

Al-qawm, literally a people, used in such a context, refers to a rival or the enemy. In this verse, it is a clear reference to the unbelievers of the Quraysh.

46. Please see Abū Dawūd

Al-ayyām

Al-ayyām, (plural of the word *yawm* or day) when used as here, refers to important historical days and events. Thus *ayyām al 'arab* means the Arab wars. The Qur'ān says *wa dhak-kirhum bi-ayyāmillāh* (and remind them of the famous events of history) that signify Divine mercy for some and punishment for others. In the present verse, our attention is drawn to the fact that all groups and nations experience such events of defeat and success in accordance with the Divine law and wisdom and the law laid down by Allah to test and sort out the good from the evil, the faithful and sincere from the false and the treacherous.

A conjunction in the absence of the connecting words

Wa li ya'lamallāhu alladhīna **(literally, so that Allah may know those)**

Before the conjunction the words *li-nabtliya kum* (so that Allah may test you) are omitted. Thus the complete sentence will read *li-nabtaliya kum wa li ya'lam allāhulladhīna āmanū*, "so that Allah may test you and know those that believe."

Aw yattakhidha minkum shuhadā' (or, so that He may take to Himself from your ranks martyrs (witnesses to Truth).

Shuhadā'

Those martyred in the cause of Allah are termed as *shuhadā'* or witnesses as they fulfil the collective obligation of the Muslim community of bearing witness to truth by sacrificing their lives for its cause. They rightly deserve the title of being the witnesses to truth and the word *shuhadā'* aptly describes their exalted role. This also shows that the early Muslims were infused with an intense desire for martyrdom and they vied with one another in seeking the exalted status of bearing witness to truth for which Allah provided them with special opportunities to satisfy their noble aspiration. This was part of the wisdom behind the setback that they suffered in the battle of Uḥud; it provided an opportunity for those among them who deserved to be exalted to the noble status of *shuhadā'* – witnesses to Truth, to achieve their hearts' desire.

وَلِيُمَحِّصَ ٱللَّهُ ٱلَّذِينَ ءَامَنُوا۟ وَيَمْحَقَ ٱلْكَٰفِرِينَ ﴿١٤١﴾

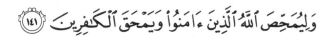

And so that Allah may purge those who are true in faith and wipe off the unbelievers. (141)

Wa li-yumaḥ-ḥis Allāhu alladhīna āmanū...

Tamḥīṣ

The word *mah-hasa* means to cleanse something of impurities and to remove from it all that is spurious and false. Thus *maḥ-ḥaṣa adh-dhahaba bi-n-nār* means He cleansed gold of all impurities with fire, thus making it pure.

The essential message

We would like to sum up the important points raised in the above verses as follows:

The setback in the battle of Uḥud caused dismay and frustration among some of the weaker Muslims. Many of them were assailed by doubts and misgivings. Were all the prophecies and glad tidings of victory promised to them false? Or were they mere words used to tighten control and hold on others? Or were they simply a clever ruse to exploit others for selfish ends? The hypocrites and the enemies found this a very opportune time to fan the flames of doubt so as to make the Muslims lose all hope of any future for Islam. The Qur'ān has, in these verses, countered this false propaganda admonishing the Muslims not to lose heart and spirit on account of this temporary setback, while assuring them that in the conflict between truth and falsehood they will always prevail and emerge victorious, provided they remain true and sincere believers.

The Qur'ān draws their attention to the fact that if they suffered a defeat or some loss – as they had recently at Uḥud – it is no reason to feel dejected and be disappointed. In this they are not alone; their enemies too had suffered a far greater loss in the battle and had suffered a most humiliating defeat in the battle of Badr. This cycle of victory and success is directed and controlled by the higher wisdom of Allah and takes effect only by His permission. It is wrong to draw from this the conclusion that the Divine law has undergone a drastic change and instead of the good and the virtuous Allah now loves, and has decided to side with, the evil and wicked people. The change in people's fortune is merely to test and try them and to help their capabilities flourish and develop. This is how the true and the false, the sincere and the hypocritical are distinguished and sorted out. And this is how those striving in the cause of truth and sacrificing their lives find an opportunity to prove their worth and achieve the noble status of being the witnesses to truth.

Tawḥīd means eradication of *kufr*

Furthermore, the believers are told that the victory achieved by the Quraysh in the battle of Uḥud does not mean that Allah now loves these cruel and unjust unbelievers. Rather, this is also a way how He destroys and finishes off the disbelievers. Thus Allah also wants to test and try the believers so as to separate them from unbelievers, to cleanse them and remove weaknesses and evils from them. This will free the believers from the hurdles blocking their path to progress and ensure the absolute destruction of the unbelievers. Falsehood in the world can survive only so long as it is to some extent supported by truth. Once this support is removed, falsehood cannot survive; it is bound to perish. Allah has created the world in truth and as such it is against its nature to support and nurture sheer falsehood. The wiping off of the unbelievers following the purgation of the Islamic society "*wa li-yumaḥ-ḥiṣ Allāhu alla<u>dh</u>īna āmanū,* And so that Allah may purge those that are true in faith and wipe off the unbelievers" refers to this Divine law. Whenever a Prophet and his companions emigrate from an unbelieving society, the chastisement that seizes the unbelievers in the wake of the emigration of the believers highlights this very wisdom. It is fully explained in Sūrah at-Tawbah.

أَمْ حَسِبْتُمْ أَن تَدْخُلُوا۟ ٱلْجَنَّةَ وَلَمَّا يَعْلَمِ ٱللَّهُ ٱلَّذِينَ جَٰهَدُوا۟ مِنكُمْ وَيَعْلَمَ ٱلصَّٰبِرِينَ ﴿١٤٢﴾

Did you think that you would enter Paradise without Allah testing those of you who strived and fought hard (in His Cause) and remained steadfast? (142)

The significance and various connotations of the word *'alima* used in the verse *wa lammā ya'lamillāhu-l la<u>dh</u>īna jāhadū minkum* (literally, and Allah has not yet distinguished those among you who strived and fought ..." has been discussed in our commentary on Sūrah al-Baqarah[47]. In its present context, *'alima* is used in the sense of distinguishing and separating.

47. Please refer to *Pondering over the Qur'ān*, vol 1, commentary on verses 60 and 143 of Sūrah al-Baqarah (Translator).

وَلَقَدْ كُنتُمْ تَمَنَّوْنَ ٱلْمَوْتَ مِن قَبْلِ أَن تَلْقَوْهُ فَقَدْ رَأَيْتُمُوهُ وَأَنتُمْ تَنظُرُونَ ﴿١٤٣﴾

You did indeed wish for death before you met it. Now you have seen it with your own eyes. (143)

The opposite of *jāhadū minkum,* (those who strived from among you), *al-ladhīna lam yujāhidū* (those who did not strive) is omitted as usual in the Arabic text. About the *fatḥah* on the last consonant in *ya'lama* in the sentence *wa ya'lama-ṣ ṣābirīna,* various authorities have offered various explanations but, in our view, this portion is conjoined to the above sentence *wa li-ya'lamallāhu al-ladhīna āmanū.* Since the discourse above turns to elucidating certain other aspects of the wisdom of the Divine law of test and trial, the subject of patience is therefore linked to jihād, while its final vowel – a *fatḥah* – automatically underlines the fact that *ṣābirīn,* those who remain steadfast, are also included among those distinguished and sorted out by Allah by putting them through a process of test and trial.

Hardships and trials in the path of truth are inevitable

Those who were disheartened by the defeat of Uḥud, are told that if they thought that the road to truth is free of hardships and trials and that only by verbally professing Islam they will win Paradise, they were utterly mistaken. No one will enter Paradise unless it is proven through test and trial that one is sincere and ready and eager to strive in the cause of Allah and, if necessary, is prepared to offer sacrifices for it. The defeat of Uḥud was just one such test. Before the battle, the Muslims showed great enthusiasm and fervour for jihād mostly through verbal professions and expressions of the desire to engage in jihād. As such, the true from the false among them had to be sorted and distinguished by putting them through a test where they faced death directly to test their resolve in the battlefield. This was just a criterion to separate the true from the false in the Muslims' ranks. Those weak in practice were far more profuse in their expressions of eagerness to fight in the cause of Allah in order to cover up their moral weakness. They are mentioned in Sūrah an-Nisā', verse 77 in these words:

> *Have you not turned your vision to those who were told to hold back their hands (from fighting) but establish regular prayer and give zakāh? When (at length) the order for fighting was issued to them, a section of them feared men as they should have feared Allah or even more, and*

they said: "Our Sustainer! Why have You prescribed fighting for us? If only You would grant us just a little more time!

Verses 144-148: thematic continuity

The following verses dispel a misunderstanding about Prophet Muḥammad, peace be upon him, and emphasise that he is the prophet of Allah and a mortal like all the other previous prophets and messengers of Allah. Like all human beings, he will also die one day or might be martyred in the cause of Allah. The religion of Allah – Islam – will nonetheless endure forever. Anyone who believes in Allah cannot and should not base his belief on the supposition that the Prophet is immortal and will live forever.

It was important to dispel this misunderstanding because otherwise the Prophet's death could leave the Muslims utterly shattered and demoralised. The hypocrites and other enemies would have found such a situation very conducive to create further trouble and mischief. That is why, as soon as some signs of this misunderstanding surfaced, the Qur'ān rectified the situation by dispelling it. It is reported that when the Muslims suffered a setback in the battle of Uḥud, it was rumoured that the Prophet, peace be upon him, had also been killed. This tragic news had a disastrous effect on the morale of many among the Muslims and they were plunged in despair. For them, all was lost now that the Prophet, peace be upon him, was no longer among them. There were some among them though who tried to save the situation by saying there was no use to life, after the demise of their beloved Prophet, peace be upon him. They should prefer to follow in his footsteps and strive on till they fall martyrs, fighting like him for the cause. This brought to the fore a serious weakness in the Muslims and its rectification by the Qur'ān was important to forestall any similar predicament in future.

The Qur'ān cites the example of earlier prophets and their faithful companions who similarly fought in the cause of Allah and suffered great difficulties and hardships in its path, but they never despaired or lost hope. The Muslims are encouraged to follow their noble example without being disheartened. They are assured that they are striving for a cause similar to that for which the earlier prophets and their companions strived. They should therefore steadfastly follow in the footsteps of their predecessors.

Verses 144-148

Muḥammad is no more than a Messenger: many were the Messengers who passed away before him. If he died or were slain, will you then turn back on your heels? If any did turn back on his heels, he will not do the least harm to Allah. And Allah will reward those who are grateful (to Him). (144)

وَمَا مُحَمَّدٌ إِلَّا رَسُولٌ قَدْ خَلَتْ مِن قَبْلِهِ
ٱلرُّسُلُ ۚ أَفَإِيْن مَّاتَ أَوْ قُتِلَ ٱنقَلَبْتُمْ
عَلَىٰٓ أَعْقَٰبِكُمْ ۚ وَمَن يَنقَلِبْ عَلَىٰ عَقِبَيْهِ
فَلَن يَضُرَّ ٱللَّهَ شَيْـًٔا ۗ وَسَيَجْزِى ٱللَّهُ
ٱلشَّٰكِرِينَ ﴿١٤٤﴾

No soul can die except by Allah's leave, according to a prescribed term. If any do desire a reward in this life, We shall give it to him; and if any do desire a reward in the hereafter, We shall give it to him. And swiftly shall We reward those who (serve Us with) gratitude. (145)

وَمَا كَانَ لِنَفْسٍ أَن تَمُوتَ إِلَّا
بِإِذْنِ ٱللَّهِ كِتَٰبًا مُّؤَجَّلًا ۗ وَمَن يُرِدْ
ثَوَابَ ٱلدُّنْيَا نُؤْتِهِۦ مِنْهَا وَمَن يُرِدْ
ثَوَابَ ٱلْءَاخِرَةِ نُؤْتِهِۦ مِنْهَا ۚ وَسَنَجْزِى
ٱلشَّٰكِرِينَ ﴿١٤٥﴾

Many prophets have fought (in Allah's way), and with them (fought) large bands of God-devoted men but they did not lose heart if they met with disaster in Allah's way, nor did they weaken (in will) nor give in. And Allah loves those who are firm and steadfast. (146)

وَكَأَيِّن مِّن نَّبِىٍّ قَٰتَلَ مَعَهُۥ رِبِّيُّونَ
كَثِيرٌ فَمَا وَهَنُوا۟ لِمَآ أَصَابَهُمْ فِى سَبِيلِ
ٱللَّهِ وَمَا ضَعُفُوا۟ وَمَا ٱسْتَكَانُوا۟ ۗ وَٱللَّهُ يُحِبُّ
ٱلصَّٰبِرِينَ ﴿١٤٦﴾

All that they said was: "Our Sustainer! Forgive us our sins and anything we may have done that transgressed our duty. Establish our feet firmly, and help us against the unbelievers." (147)

وَمَا كَانَ قَوْلَهُمْ إِلَّآ أَن قَالُوا۟ رَبَّنَا
ٱغْفِرْ لَنَا ذُنُوبَنَا وَإِسْرَافَنَا فِىٓ أَمْرِنَا
وَثَبِّتْ أَقْدَامَنَا وَٱنصُرْنَا عَلَى ٱلْقَوْمِ
ٱلْكَٰفِرِينَ ﴿١٤٧﴾

And Allah gave them a reward in this world, and the excellent reward of the hereafter. For Allah loves the good-doers. (148)

فَـَٔاتَىٰهُمُ ٱللَّهُ ثَوَابَ ٱلدُّنْيَا وَحُسْنَ ثَوَابِ
ٱلْءَاخِرَةِ ۗ وَٱللَّهُ يُحِبُّ ٱلْمُحْسِنِينَ ﴿١٤٨﴾

WORD STUDY AND EXPLANATION

وَمَا مُحَمَّدٌ إِلَّا رَسُولٌ قَدْ خَلَتْ مِن قَبْلِهِ ٱلرُّسُلُ ۚ أَفَإِي۟ن مَّاتَ أَوْ قُتِلَ ٱنقَلَبْتُمْ
عَلَىٰٓ أَعْقَـٰبِكُمْ ۚ وَمَن يَنقَلِبْ عَلَىٰ عَقِبَيْهِ فَلَن يَضُرَّ ٱللَّهَ شَيْـًٔا ۗ وَسَيَجْزِى ٱللَّهُ
ٱلشَّـٰكِرِينَ ﴿١٤٤﴾

Muḥammad is no more than a Messenger: many were the Messengers who passed away before him. If he died or were slain, will you then turn back on your heels? If any did turn back on his heels, he will not do the least harm to Allah. And Allah will reward those who are grateful (to Him). (144)

'Aqib or *'aqab* (plural *a'qāb*) means heel and *inqalaba 'ala 'aqibay-hi* means to turn back on one's heels or retreat. Here it refers to abandoning Islamic faith and reverting to a state of ignorance or unbelief.

In other words, Muḥammad, peace be upon him, is one of the many other Messengers of Allah that have gone before him. And like other Messengers, he too can experience trials and hardships; and just as they died, he also has to experience death. Being a Messenger of Allah does not mean that he is immortal and that he will never die or that he cannot be killed or encounter any defeat or hardship. Therefore, if anyone had embraced Islam under this erroneous impression and is now assailed by doubts after the defeat at Uḥud and is inclined to revert to unbelief, he will do no harm to Allah, but will ruin himself both in this life and in the one to come. Those who, even after witnessing Islam, fail to distinguish between it and the ignorance of unbelief, Allah has no use for them. Let them go the way they would like to go. Only those who have been blessed with Islam and are grateful to their Sovereign Sustainer truly deserve Allah's blessings and favours. They cannot even for a moment entertain the idea of returning to *jāhiliyyah* (the days of ignorance) from which Islam had rescued them.

وَمَا كَانَ لِنَفْسٍ أَن تَمُوتَ إِلَّا بِإِذْنِ ٱللَّهِ كِتَـٰبًا مُّؤَجَّلًا ۗ وَمَن يُرِدْ ثَوَابَ ٱلدُّنْيَا
نُؤْتِهِۦ مِنْهَا وَمَن يُرِدْ ثَوَابَ ٱلْـَٔاخِرَةِ نُؤْتِهِۦ مِنْهَا ۚ وَسَنَجْزِى ٱلشَّـٰكِرِينَ ﴿١٤٥﴾

No soul can die except by Allah's leave according to a prescribed term. If any do desire a reward in this life, We shall give it to him; and if any do desire a reward in the hereafter, We shall give it to him. And swiftly shall We reward those who (serve Us with) gratitude. (145)

In construction, the phrase *kitāban mu'aj-jalan* (a prescribed term) is similar to the phrase *wa'd Allāh* (4:122, 10:4) or *ṣun'a Allāh al-ladhī atqana kulla shay'in* (the handiwork of Allah Who has ordered everything to perfection) (27:88).

Two specific weaknesses of the hypocrites

In this verse, two weaknesses of the weaker elements in the Muslim community and the hypocrites are pointed out. One, they do not believe that the time of death of every person is fixed and that no one will die before the completion of the prescribed term of life, and that once this term is over, no one will be able to avert death even for a single instant. Therefore, a person's first concern should be to faithfully, firmly and resolutely discharge his obligations towards Allah rather than fleeing from them. The time and manner of every person's death is already fixed and cannot be altered.

The second weakness of the hypocrites was their erroneous belief that whatever they gained or achieved in life was solely due to their own planning and efforts. And they did not want to risk these achievements by being overly concerned with the betterment of their life in the hereafter. This is because they feared that this could make them lose all their material achievements. This was, however, a totally false and erroneous belief. Allah grants those who worship this world whatever He has decreed for them but they have no share in the reward of the life in the hereafter. As against this, Allah blesses the seekers of the life hereafter with their reward in the life hereafter besides granting them their share of this worldly life as He has decreed for them. Therefore, the correct attitude for a wise person is that he should focus on the life hereafter and be content with whatever Allah grants him of his portion in this world, rather than throw away the eternal blessings of the life in the hereafter and spend all his efforts in vain pursuit of the fleeting pleasures of this transitory life.

And swiftly shall We reward those who are grateful (to Him)

This means that those who are truly and sincerely grateful for the great blessing in the form of the final and complete guidance from their Sovereign Sustainer, shall be fully rewarded for their gratitude and response to the message of truth. As for those who, even after receiving light and guidance, seek darkness and persist in error, they will be doomed to wander in the dark recesses of error

وَكَأَيِّن مِّن نَّبِيٍّ قَٰتَلَ مَعَهُۥ رِبِّيُّونَ كَثِيرٞ فَمَا وَهَنُواْ لِمَآ أَصَابَهُمۡ فِي سَبِيلِ ٱللَّهِ وَمَا
ضَعُفُواْ وَمَا ٱسۡتَكَانُواْۗ وَٱللَّهُ يُحِبُّ ٱلصَّٰبِرِينَ ١٤٦
وَمَا كَانَ قَوۡلَهُمۡ إِلَّآ أَن قَالُواْ رَبَّنَا ٱغۡفِرۡ لَنَا ذُنُوبَنَا وَإِسۡرَافَنَا فِيٓ أَمۡرِنَا وَثَبِّتۡ أَقۡدَامَنَا
وَٱنصُرۡنَا عَلَى ٱلۡقَوۡمِ ٱلۡكَٰفِرِينَ ١٤٧
فَـَٔاتَىٰهُمُ ٱللَّهُ ثَوَابَ ٱلدُّنۡيَا وَحُسۡنَ ثَوَابِ ٱلۡأٓخِرَةِۗ وَٱللَّهُ يُحِبُّ ٱلۡمُحۡسِنِينَ ١٤٨

Many prophets have fought (in Allah's way), and with them (fought) large bands of men devoted to Allah but they did not lose heart if they met with disaster in Allah's way, nor did they weaken (in will) nor give in. And Allah loves those who are firm and steadfast. (146)
All that they said was: "Our Sustainer! Forgive us our sins and anything we may have done that transgressed our duty: establish our feet firmly, and help us against the unbelievers." (147)
And Allah gave them a reward in this world, and the excellent reward of the hereafter. For Allah loves the good-doers. (148)

Wahn

For this word, please refer to our comments on verse 139 above.

Wahn, ḍaʿf and *istikāna*

These three terms carry a shared sense of weakness but with subtle difference in nuance. *Wahn* is the cowardice resulting from fear of death and love of worldly life, while the collapse and weakening of volition and action consequent upon this *wahn* is called *ḍaʿf*. The abject surrender to the enemy as a result of *ḍaʿf* is known as *istikāna* (submission or yielding).

A tradition of the Prophets and their companions

Many a time in history, the verse says, when Allah's prophets strived in the cause of Allah they were accompanied by righteous servants of Allah in this struggle. They faced hardships and setbacks but never as a result of these did they lose heart, or despaired, or abjectly surrendered to their enemy. They stood fast and persevered in the path of truth and Allah blessed them, for such are the people that He likes and is pleased with.

This is a reference to the battles that earlier prophets such as Mūsā, Dāwūd, Sulaymān and others, peace be upon them all, had to fight in the cause of Allah. A battle of prophet Samuel, one that is similar to the battle of Badr, has already been mentioned in Sūrah al-Baqarah[48]. The purpose of alluding to these previous encounters between the believers and the disbelievers is to admonish and encourage the Muslims who felt rather downhearted after the setback in the battle of Uḥud. There is nothing strange, they are told, for a prophet and his companions to fight nor is there anything unusual for them to face trouble and hardships in this path. This is an essential part of the example of the prophets and a logical consequence of the Divine law of trial and test that Allah has laid down for His servants. Let no one be under the illusion that the prophet and his companions succeed in their struggle for truth without suffering any hurt or going through a strenuous process of test, an essential condition for their success in this path. Allah loves only those who are steadfast in His cause and never waver in their commitment. How can the true and steadfast be distinguished and marked out from the false and the insincere opportunists and hypocrites without subjecting them to this process of test and trial?

All that they said was: "Our Sustainer! Forgive us our sins ..."

This underlines the fact that whenever the earlier prophets and their companions faced hardships and trials, they did not indulge in the kind of loose talk and excuses that the weaker Muslims and the hypocrites were occupied with, in creating various doubts in minds against the Prophet of Islam, peace be upon him. Instead of attributing the hardships to the Prophet, the earlier believers considered them a result of their own weakness and excesses. They prayed for forgiveness to Allah for their lapses and Allah blessed them with power, government and authority, with a most excellent reward reserved for them in the life to come. They are the ones who have attained to the highest status of *iḥsān* in the sight of Allah – the good-doers with whom He is really and truly pleased.

Verses 149-155: thematic continuity

In the following verses also, the commentary on the weaknesses of the Muslims that came to the fore in the battle of Uḥud continues. The Qur'ān examines these weaknesses one by one and brings out their inner core while teaching Muslims how to overcome and get rid of them. Various beneficial effects of this trial concerning training and purgation of the Muslim society achieved through this process are also outlined.

48. See *Pondering over the Qur'ān*, vol 1, Sūrah al-Baqarah, commentary on verses 246-252.

يَٰٓأَيُّهَا ٱلَّذِينَ ءَامَنُوٓاْ إِن تُطِيعُواْ
ٱلَّذِينَ كَفَرُواْ يَرُدُّوكُمۡ عَلَىٰٓ
أَعۡقَٰبِكُمۡ فَتَنقَلِبُواْ خَٰسِرِينَ ١٤٩

O you who believe! If you obey the unbelievers, they will drive you back on your heels, and you will turn back to your own loss. (149)

بَلِ ٱللَّهُ مَوۡلَىٰكُمۡۖ وَهُوَ خَيۡرُ
ٱلنَّٰصِرِينَ ١٥٠

Indeed, Allah is your protector, and He is the best of helpers. (150)

سَنُلۡقِي فِي قُلُوبِ ٱلَّذِينَ كَفَرُواْ
ٱلرُّعۡبَ بِمَآ أَشۡرَكُواْ بِٱللَّهِ مَا لَمۡ
يُنَزِّلۡ بِهِۦ سُلۡطَٰنٗاۖ وَمَأۡوَىٰهُمُ
ٱلنَّارُۖ وَبِئۡسَ مَثۡوَى ٱلظَّٰلِمِينَ
١٥١

Soon shall We cast terror into the hearts of the unbelievers, for they joined partners with Allah, for which He had sent no authority. Their abode will be the hellfire. And evil is the home of those who wrong their own selves! (151)

وَلَقَدۡ صَدَقَكُمُ ٱللَّهُ وَعۡدَهُۥٓ
إِذۡ تَحُسُّونَهُم بِإِذۡنِهِۦۖ حَتَّىٰٓ إِذَا
فَشِلۡتُمۡ وَتَنَٰزَعۡتُمۡ فِي ٱلۡأَمۡرِ
وَعَصَيۡتُم مِّنۢ بَعۡدِ مَآ أَرَىٰكُم
مَّا تُحِبُّونَۚ مِنكُم مَّن
يُرِيدُ ٱلدُّنۡيَا وَمِنكُم مَّن يُرِيدُ
ٱلۡأٓخِرَةَۚ ثُمَّ صَرَفَكُمۡ عَنۡهُمۡ
لِيَبۡتَلِيَكُمۡۖ وَلَقَدۡ عَفَا عَنكُمۡۗ
وَٱللَّهُ ذُو فَضۡلٍ عَلَى ٱلۡمُؤۡمِنِينَ ١٥٢

Allah did indeed fulfil His promise to you when, with His permission, you were about to annihilate your enemy, until you flinched and fell to disputing about the order, and disobeyed the Prophet after Allah brought you in sight of what you covet. Among you were some that hankered after this world and some that desired the hereafter. Then Allah did divert you from your foes in order to test you but He forgave you: for Allah is full of grace to those who believe. (152)

۞ إِذۡ تُصۡعِدُونَ وَلَا تَلۡوُۥنَ
عَلَىٰٓ أَحَدٖ وَٱلرَّسُولُ يَدۡعُوكُمۡ
فِيٓ أُخۡرَىٰكُمۡ فَأَثَٰبَكُمۡ غَمَّۢا
بِغَمّٖ لِّكَيۡلَا تَحۡزَنُواْ عَلَىٰ مَا
فَاتَكُمۡ وَلَا مَآ أَصَٰبَكُمۡۗ
وَٱللَّهُ خَبِيرُۢ بِمَا تَعۡمَلُونَ ١٥٣

Remember, when you were fleeing, without even casting a side-glance at any one, and Allah's Messenger in your rear was calling you back. There did Allah give you one distress after another, to teach you not to lose heart or to grieve for the loss suffered or the ill that had befallen you, for Allah is well aware of all that you do. (153)

ثُمَّ أَنزَلَ عَلَيۡكُم مِّنۢ بَعۡدِ ٱلۡغَمِّ أَمَنَةٗ
نُّعَاسٗا يَغۡشَىٰ طَآئِفَةٗ مِّنكُمۡۖ
وَطَآئِفَةٞ قَدۡ أَهَمَّتۡهُمۡ أَنفُسُهُمۡ
يَظُنُّونَ بِٱللَّهِ غَيۡرَ ٱلۡحَقِّ ظَنَّ ٱلۡجَٰهِلِيَّةِۖ
يَقُولُونَ هَل لَّنَا مِنَ ٱلۡأَمۡرِ مِن
شَيۡءٖۗ قُلۡ إِنَّ ٱلۡأَمۡرَ كُلَّهُۥ لِلَّهِۗ يُخۡفُونَ فِيٓ
أَنفُسِهِم مَّا لَا يُبۡدُونَ لَكَۖ يَقُولُونَ لَوۡ
كَانَ لَنَا مِنَ ٱلۡأَمۡرِ شَيۡءٞ مَّا قُتِلۡنَا هَٰهُنَاۗ
قُل لَّوۡ كُنتُمۡ فِي بُيُوتِكُمۡ لَبَرَزَ ٱلَّذِينَ
كُتِبَ عَلَيۡهِمُ ٱلۡقَتۡلُ إِلَىٰ مَضَاجِعِهِمۡۖ
وَلِيَبۡتَلِيَ ٱللَّهُ مَا فِي صُدُورِكُمۡ
وَلِيُمَحِّصَ مَا فِي قُلُوبِكُمۡۚ وَٱللَّهُ عَلِيمُۢ
بِذَاتِ ٱلصُّدُورِ ١٥٤

After (the excitement) of the distress, He sent down calm slumber, overcoming a group among you, while another group was worried about their own lives. They were moved by unfounded doubts about Allah like those of the days of ignorance. They said: "Do we have a say in these matters?" Say: "Indeed, this affair is wholly Allah's." They hide in their minds what they dare not reveal to you. They say (to themselves): "If we had had any say in this matter, we should not have been killed here." Say: "Even if you had remained in your homes, those for whom death was decreed would certainly have gone forth to the place of their death;" but (all this happened so that) Allah might test what is in your breasts and purge what is in your hearts. For Allah knows well the secrets of your hearts. (154)

إِنَّ ٱلَّذِينَ تَوَلَّوۡاْ مِنكُمۡ يَوۡمَ ٱلۡتَقَى
ٱلۡجَمۡعَانِ إِنَّمَا ٱسۡتَزَلَّهُمُ ٱلشَّيۡطَٰنُ
بِبَعۡضِ مَا كَسَبُواْۖ وَلَقَدۡ عَفَا ٱللَّهُ عَنۡهُمۡۗ
إِنَّ ٱللَّهَ غَفُورٌ حَلِيمٞ ١٥٥

Those of you who turned back on the day the two hosts met – it was Satan who caused them to slip, because of some (evil) they had done. But Allah Has forgiven them, for surely Allah is Oft-Forgiving, Most Forbearing. (155)

WORD STUDY AND EXPLANATION

يَٰٓأَيُّهَا ٱلَّذِينَ ءَامَنُوٓاْ إِن تُطِيعُواْ ٱلَّذِينَ كَفَرُواْ يَرُدُّوكُمۡ عَلَىٰٓ
أَعۡقَٰبِكُمۡ فَتَنقَلِبُواْ خَٰسِرِينَ ١٤٩
بَلِ ٱللَّهُ مَوۡلَىٰكُمۡۖ وَهُوَ خَيۡرُ ٱلنَّٰصِرِينَ ١٥٠

O you who believe! If you obey the unbelievers, they will drive you back on your heels, and you will turn back to your own loss. (149)
Nay, Allah is your protector, and He is the best of helpers. (150)

Anti-Islam propaganda of the disbelievers and hypocrites

In the wake of the Muslim defeat at Uḥud, the unbelievers and the Jews thought perhaps the time had come when they could wipe off all traces of humiliation suffered by them at the battle of Badr. Through a propaganda campaign, they tried to persuade the Muslims that their idea that Muḥammad was a Messenger of Allah and that he enjoyed the help and support of the angels was not true. For, they argued, if it were true, why would Muslims suffer this setback at Uḥud? The Muslims were victorious in the battle of Badr and now it was the other party who had the upper hand, because success or defeat in battle depended on strategy and resources. It was wrong to attribute such things to Divine support and help from angels and it was simplistic to think that only they deserved heavenly help.

Response to the anti-Islam propaganda

This propaganda of the unbelievers did have some impact on the weaker elements among the Muslims. Through their machinations and whispering campaign, the hypocrites lent their support to this anti-Islam propaganda. That is why the Muslims were warned that if they succumbed to these machinations of the unbelievers, they would take them back into the darkness of ignorance and error from which Islam had rescued them. All their successes and achievements would be turned into distress and deprivation. The unbelievers were not their well-wishers and friends nor could they be their guardians and supporters to help them in their difficulties. As Muslims, their true helper and guardian is Allah alone, so they should call upon Him alone for help and guidance. He is the best helper. In verse 118 above, the same warning is stressed: "O you who believe! Take not into your intimacy those outside your ranks."

سَنُلْقِى فِى قُلُوبِ ٱلَّذِينَ كَفَرُوا۟ ٱلرُّعْبَ بِمَآ أَشْرَكُوا۟ بِٱللَّهِ مَا لَمْ يُنَزِّلْ
بِهِۦ سُلْطَـٰنًا وَمَأْوَىٰهُمُ ٱلنَّارُ وَبِئْسَ مَثْوَى ٱلظَّـٰلِمِينَ ﴿١٥١﴾

Soon shall We cast terror into the hearts of the unbelievers, because they joined partners with Allah, for which He had sent no authority: their abode will be the hellfire. And evil is the home of those who wrong their own selves! (151)

Verses 149-155

Polytheism has no firm basis

The existing aggressive attitude of the unbelievers towards Muslims is a passing phase and will not last long as it has no solid basis. Very soon Allah will cast terror into their hearts and break down their morale. This is so because they have set up as rivals to Allah for which there is no evidence in nature and reason, in the physical universe, or in the revealed scriptures. Such superstitious beliefs cannot for long ignore the truths about life nor provide any enduring support. Secondly, their attachment to so many gods and goddesses is bound to confuse their hearts and minds and divide them into mutually conflicting groups, robbing them of the single-mindedness that lies at the heart of high resolve and courage. The word *ẓālimīn* – those who wrong their own selves – refer to the polytheists. *Shirk*, attributing partners to Allah, is described in the Qur'ān as the greatest wrong or injustice. First and foremost, it is a great wrong and an act of injustice against one's own self jeopardising a person's entire future welfare. Allah has given the human being excellence over all the rest of His creation and it is this self-realisation on the part of each human being that holds the secret to his authority and nobility. When a human being adores and worships some creature that is far inferior to him and takes this creature quite unjustly as his sustainer and master, he utterly degrades himself. He thus throws away not only his God-given exalted position as a human being, but falls far below to the lowest of the low; a falcon reduced to a weak and wretched gnat.

وَلَقَدْ صَدَقَكُمُ ٱللَّهُ وَعْدَهُۥٓ إِذْ تَحُسُّونَهُم بِإِذْنِهِۦ ۖ حَتَّىٰٓ إِذَا
فَشِلْتُمْ وَتَنَٰزَعْتُمْ فِى ٱلْأَمْرِ وَعَصَيْتُم مِّنۢ بَعْدِ مَآ أَرَىٰكُم مَّا تُحِبُّونَ ۚ
مِنكُم مَّن يُرِيدُ ٱلدُّنْيَا وَمِنكُم مَّن يُرِيدُ ٱلْءَاخِرَةَ ۚ ثُمَّ صَرَفَكُمْ
عَنْهُمْ لِيَبْتَلِيَكُمْ ۖ وَلَقَدْ عَفَا عَنكُمْ ۗ وَٱللَّهُ ذُو فَضْلٍ عَلَى ٱلْمُؤْمِنِينَ ﴿١٥٢﴾

Allah did indeed fulfil His promise to you when you, with His permission, were about to annihilate your enemy, until you flinched and fell to disputing about the order, and disobeyed the Prophet after Allah had brought you in sight of what you covet. Among you were some that hankered after this world and some that desired the hereafter. Then Allah did divert you from your foes in order to test you, but He forgave you: for Allah is full of grace to those who believe. (152)

Ḥassa and *yaḥussu* means to kill the enemy, exterminating and wiping them out. The rider *bi-idhnihi* (with His permission) shows that this result was made possible not merely because of the Muslim stratagem and strength but was above all a manifestation of Allah's will and wisdom.

Fashala means to lag, to slacken or to show weakness.

Tanāza' fi-l amr is an idiomatic phrase on the pattern of *tanāza' fi-l ḥadīth* that means people offering varying opinions on a certain matter. In the present context, it means that they diverged in interpreting the commandment of the Prophet.

Mā tuḥibbūn

And the words *mā tuḥibbūn* (what you covet) refer to the desire for victory in battle. At other places the Qur'ān explicitly states: "And another (favour) which you do love – help from Allah and a speedy victory" (Sūrah aṣ-Ṣaff, 61.13).

The real cause of the setback at Uḥud

This is in refuting the false anti-Islam propaganda of the unbelievers and the hypocrites who said the Muslims were simply deluded into thinking that Allah and His angels help and support them, for, it that were true, why were they not helped in the battle of Uḥud? As pointed out in verse 149 above, some weaker Muslims were affected by this poisonous propaganda. To counter this, the Qur'ān tells them that as far as Allah's promise of help and support is concerned, it was also fulfilled in the battle of Uḥud. In the beginning, the Muslims freely despatched the unbelievers and they had to withdraw. Victory was clearly in sight. But, before breaking down the enemy and forcing them to surrender, the Muslims slackened their effort. The troops that had been stationed by the Prophet, peace be upon him, to guard the hilltop passage way in their rear were instructed by the Prophet in explicit terms not to leave it. They were told to hold on to their position under all circumstances. But, they differed among themselves in interpreting the purpose behind the commandment of the Prophet, peace be upon him. Most of them, thinking that victory was near at hand, abandoned their positions and contrary to the explicit commandment of the Prophet, peace be upon him, joined others in gathering the spoils of war. Some among them wanted this world while others desired the life hereafter. Allah does not like the presence among the believers' ranks of the people who would ignore the commandment of Allah's Prophet in their eagerness to gain material riches.

In His wisdom therefore, Allah decided to put you through a trial so that those who desired this world should be separated from your ranks.

He therefore turned your attention away from the unbelievers and, as a consequence, your victory was turned into defeat.

Divine help is conditional

The promised help for Muslims is not unconditional. It could never be assumed that no matter how they behave or conduct themselves, they would still be victorious. This help is subject to the Muslims not being slack in fulfilling their obligations, and avoiding disagreement in respect of obeying the commandments of Allah and His messenger. This help will come provided they do not love worldly goods and pleasures over and above their life in the hereafter.

Since Allah is most forgiving and compassionate, He does not punish the Muslims even if they are found lacking in this respect or have some of these weaknesses in them. In such a case, He puts them through various tests and trials to cleanse them of their weaknesses so that they can qualify for and enjoy Allah's most bounteous help and support. This is clearly manifested in His dealing with them. This in itself is a yet another form of Allah's forgiveness and grace in dealing with them, as pointed out at the end of the verse which says: "Allah is full of grace to those who believe."

With respect to the battle of Uḥud, we may note here that almost all the historians and biographers are agreed that the initial attack of the Muslims was highly successful. They had almost overrun their enemy when a detachment of theirs stationed to guard the hilltop passage in their rear with clear instructions from the Prophet, peace be upon him, not to leave their places under any conditions, abandoned their posts and joined in collecting war booty. Only a few of them were left behind. The enemy took advantage of this situation and attacked the Muslims with such ferocity from the rear that the Muslim army was totally confounded. The verse refers to this incident.

۞ إِذْ تُصْعِدُونَ وَلَا تَلْوُۥنَ عَلَىٰٓ أَحَدٍ وَٱلرَّسُولُ يَدْعُوكُمْ فِىٓ
أُخْرَىٰكُمْ فَأَثَٰبَكُمْ غَمًّۢا بِغَمٍّ لِّكَيْلَا تَحْزَنُوا۟ عَلَىٰ مَا فَاتَكُمْ وَلَا
مَآ أَصَٰبَكُمْ ۗ وَٱللَّهُ خَبِيرٌۢ بِمَا تَعْمَلُونَ ﴿١٥٣﴾

Remember, when you were fleeing, without even casting a side-glance at any one, and Allah's Messenger in your rear was calling you back. There did Allah give you one distress after another, to teach you not to lose heart or to grieve for the loss suffered or the ill that had befallen you, for Allah is well aware of all that you do. (153)

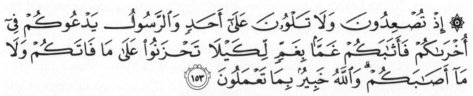

Aṣʻada

The word *iṣʻada* means to go up a higher side. A derivative from it is the proverb *iṣʻada fi-l ʻadw* meaning to exert oneself vigorously in running and to flee haphazardly in any direction.

G͟hammam bi g͟hammin

In the phrase *g͟hammam bi g͟hammin*, the particle *bi* is suggestive of *talabbus* or a state of confusion with the addition of distress upon distress[49]. Thus, the pain of defeat that they suffered was compounded by yet another grief. In our opinion, this refers to the grief that the Muslims suffered as a result of a rumour spread by the unbelievers that the Prophet, peace be upon him, was martyred in the battle. This rumour is mentioned in history and books of *sīrah* and this verse also hints at it. It refers to the way the Muslims fled from the battlefield in great confusion with the Prophet, peace be upon him, all this while calling out to them. "O Allah's servants, come to me. Come to me." The *g͟hamm* or grief is prefixed by the particle *fa* that is used in Arabic for consequence, and clearly indicates that this grief was related to the person of the Prophet, as a warning to the Muslims for their failure to respect and comply fully with his explicit instruction.

Sequence of this verse

In order to understand the proper sequence of this verse, we need to recast another glance over the previous verse, verse 152, that states "*t͟humma ṣarafakum ʻanhum li-yabtaliyakum* (then Allah did divert you from your foes in order to test you)". In other words, because of their disobedience and lapses, Allah made them taste defeat in order to test them. Furthermore, the verse makes it clear that instead of punishing them for their disobedience, Allah chose to put them through a test so as to forgive them and to bestow His bounty and grace upon them. Following this, the words "*id͟h tuṣʻidāna* (remember, when you were fleeing) to "*fa at͟hābakum g͟hammam bi g͟hammin* ...(there did Allah give you one distress after another") gives the nature and detail of this trial. And the words "*li kay la tahzanū ʻālā mā fātakum wa la mā aṣābakum* (to teach you not to lose heart or to grieve for the loss suffered or the ill that had befallen you)" underline the lesson that the believers could learn and benefit from in the light of this experience, provided they faithfully and sincerely follow the teachings of Islam and persevere in its cause.

49. See *Lexicon*, under *il-tabasa* (Translator).

The purpose of trial (*ibtilā'*)

We may note here that the tests and trials from Allah are not a form of punishment for humans. Every trial is in fact a manifestation of Divine grace and mercy. Punishment is the fate of the unbelievers, whereas the believers are put to test and tried. Punishment is meant to destroy and wipe off the unbelievers, while tests and trials are aimed at cleansing the believers of their mental and moral weaknesses or ills. One is death and the other signifies life. According to the Divine law, so long as Allah wills to give respite to a people, He does not send against them the punishment that is reserved for hardened criminals and rebels. Instead, they are put through various tests and trials in order to cleanse them of their various moral weaknesses and ills. He destroys a people only when they are utterly corrupt and devoid of all signs of moral and spiritual life.

Ameliorating aspects of the battle of Uḥud

But, was there something in the trial of Uḥud that saved the Muslims from grief? For an answer to this, we need to bear in mind that this was not the kind of grief due to a failure, loss of an opportunity or experiencing some other loss that is quite natural and quite hurtful. Rather, it refers to the despair and loss of morale that destroys courage and determination. In verse 139 above – *la tahinū wa lā taḥzanū* – the Muslims are warned against this kind of grief. At that time, there were numerous causes and factors that could induce and cause despair and demoralisation and they needed to be addressed properly to rectify the situation. Thus, for example, some among the Muslims thought that a prophet and his companions must always succeed in whatever they undertake and vanquish their enemy. As such, any defeat suffered by the prophet and his companions was in their eyes tantamount to making all their claims to be the bearers of the truth doubtful. Similarly, there were others among them who presumed that since they were Muslims and had responded to the call of the Prophet, they should be immune to any adverse consequences of their mistakes. Still others placed all their trust and confidence in their own opinion and strategy and failed to realise that human efforts and schemes were not the only decisive factor in these matters but only Divine planning and scheme was the real power that guided and controlled all things. There were yet others who still had in their minds some pre-Islamic misconceptions of the Days of ignorance.

The following verses contain references and hints to all these diverse groups. Obviously, with all these misconceptions and wishful thinking prevalent among them, the Muslims could hardly cope successfully with all the diverse challenges that confronted them at every turn. It was a special manifestation of Allah's mercy and grace that, through the trial of Uḥud, He cleansed the Muslims of much of their wishful thinking and spurious notions that could cause havoc to their trust and morale at some critical juncture. Some of the verses dealing with this subject are given above and others are given in the following pages. In particular, we would like to quote here a verse from Sūrah al-Ḥadīd that elucidates a most important aspect in this regard:

> *No misfortune can happen on earth or in your souls but We have recorded in a book before We bring it into existence. That is indeed very easy for Allah: In order that you may not despair over matters that pass you by, nor exult over favours bestowed upon you. For Allah does not love any vainglorious boaster.* (Sūrah al-Ḥadīd, 57:22)

ثُمَّ أَنزَلَ عَلَيْكُم مِّنۢ بَعْدِ ٱلْغَمِّ أَمَنَةً نُّعَاسًا يَغْشَىٰ طَآئِفَةً مِّنكُمْ ۖ وَطَآئِفَةٌ قَدْ
أَهَمَّتْهُمْ أَنفُسُهُمْ يَظُنُّونَ بِٱللَّهِ غَيْرَ ٱلْحَقِّ ظَنَّ ٱلْجَٰهِلِيَّةِ ۖ يَقُولُونَ هَل لَّنَا مِنَ
ٱلْأَمْرِ مِن شَىْءٍ ۗ قُلْ إِنَّ ٱلْأَمْرَ كُلَّهُۥ لِلَّهِ ۗ يُخْفُونَ فِىٓ أَنفُسِهِم مَّا لَا يُبْدُونَ لَكَ ۖ يَقُولُونَ
لَوْ كَانَ لَنَا مِنَ ٱلْأَمْرِ شَىْءٌ مَّا قُتِلْنَا هَٰهُنَا ۗ قُل لَّوْ كُنتُمْ فِى بُيُوتِكُمْ لَبَرَزَ ٱلَّذِينَ كُتِبَ
عَلَيْهِمُ ٱلْقَتْلُ إِلَىٰ مَضَاجِعِهِمْ ۖ وَلِيَبْتَلِىَ ٱللَّهُ مَا فِى صُدُورِكُمْ وَلِيُمَحِّصَ مَا فِى
قُلُوبِكُمْ ۗ وَٱللَّهُ عَلِيمٌۢ بِذَاتِ ٱلصُّدُورِ ﴿١٥٤﴾

After (the sorrow) of distress, He sent down calm, slumber, overcoming a group among you, while another group was worried about their own lives. They were moved by unfounded doubts about Allah like those of the days of ignorance. They said: "Do we have a say in these matters?" Say: "Indeed, this affair is wholly Allah's." They hide in their minds what they dare not reveal to you. They say (to themselves): "If we had had any say in this matter, we should not have been killed here." Say: "Even if you had remained in your homes, those for whom death was decreed would certainly have gone forth to the place of their death"; but (all this happened so that) that Allah might test what is in your breasts and purge what is in your hearts. For Allah knows well the secrets of your hearts. (154)

Amanah, nu'ās and importance of sleep in the battlefield

Amanah means rest, peace and tranquillity, while *nu'ās* means a nap and sleep and is used here in apposition to *amanah,* elucidating the nature of *amanah* or tranquillity. Sleep is a source of peace and comfort and also a sign of one's peace of mind and mental concentration. A person whose mind is distracted with worries finds it hard to go to sleep. Such a person cannot do anything with confidence and determination. Therefore for an army to get an opportunity during war to rest and to utilise it effectively is crucial. One of the tactics used against the enemy to demoralise it, is not to allow it to refresh its forces by having an opportunity to rest and have sleep. But it is only by the grace and mercy from Allah that an army can have such an opportunity. It also depends to a large extent on the psychological state and emotional condition of the sleeper. One of the special blessings on Muslims in the battle of Badr, as enumerated in Sūrah al-Anfāl, was that they had a sound sleep the night before the battle and were fully ready and alert the next day. In the present verse, we are told that a group among the Muslims enjoyed peaceful sleep while another group continued to be worried about their lives, even though the enemy had withdrawn and they faced no real danger. Scared and frightful, they thought the enemy was poised to attack them.

Ẓan-na-l jāhiliyyah

The words *yag͟hshā ṭā'ifatan* [50] highlights *ḥāl*, circumstance or condition; while *ẓanna-l jāhiliyyah* explains the nature of *g͟hayra-l ḥaqq* as used in the sentence *yaẓunnūna bi-llāhi g͟hayra-l ḥaqqi ẓanna-l jāhiliyyah.* The purpose is to show the disgusting nature of their views. They claimed to be Muslims yet their concept of Allah, His attributes and His dealings with people and life were no better than those of the dark period of *jāhiliyyah*, the pre-Islamic days of ignorance. One example and a manifestation of their beliefs of the pre-Islamic days of ignorance, is given in the words *yaqūlūna law kāna lanā ...* (they say: "If we had had any say in this matter, we should not have been killed here").

An ellipsis

The conjunctive to *wa li-yabtaliya Allāhu* (so that Allah might test what is ...) is omitted, in places such as these. Not only is the conjunctive omitted but often the thing whose cause is thus described is also left out. An example of this is the verses 22-23 of Sūrah al-Ḥadīd quoted above. Similarly, looking at the present verse, by removing the ellipsis, in its context the verse would read: "Even if you had followed your own opinion, you would not have been able to avert your decreed death and you would have been killed at precisely the

50. "A group was moved by unfounded doubts about Allah like those days of ignorance."

places where Allah had so decreed. But Allah has accomplished this through His Messenger to make it a source of grief for you and to bring out in the open your hidden weaknesses."

Commentary on the battle of Uḥud

This verse is also a part of the commentary on the effects and consequences of the defeat in the battle of Uḥud. As the above survey shows, Allah's promise of victory to His messenger and the believers was indeed true. The weaknesses within the Muslim community, however, had to be removed and rectified.

After the defeat at Uḥud, the Qur'ān says, a group of Muslims did indeed remain steadfast in their faith without being assailed by doubts or raising complaints against Allah and the Messenger. They firmly held on and did not lose heart. And whatever distress they suffered, they attributed it to their own shortcomings. They were fully content and pleased with the judgement of Allah. They were the people, who instead of panicking and losing heart, reposed their trust in Allah and slept peacefully in the night. This was a clear and strong sign of their firm conviction and faith.

There was also, however, another group among the Muslims who was continually worried about their own lives. They were assailed by suspicions about Allah and His promises, unworthy of those laying claim to *īmān* and *Islām;* they were rather closer to those of the pre-Islamic days of ignorance. They thought that Allah's messenger, being self-opinionated, took arbitrary decisions and did not give due regard to their views. They said that if their opinion was accepted and the Muslims had, as they suggested, fought the enemy from within the city of Madīnah, they would not have faced the sad consequences that followed and they would not have been killed nor suffered such humiliation.

Repudiating their assertion, the Qur'ān tells them that the matters of life and death were not dependent upon their efforts but are governed by Divine decree. Even if they had stayed in their homes, those who were destined to die would have nevertheless died at precisely the places appointed for their death. As the Muslims had certain weaknesses, so Allah desired to put them through a situation that would bring these weaknesses into the open, so that He may test their intentions and free them of their weaknesses. Allah is well acquainted with the diseases of hearts and He also knows how to cure them.

إِنَّ ٱلَّذِينَ تَوَلَّوْا۟ مِنكُمْ يَوْمَ ٱلْتَقَى ٱلْجَمْعَانِ إِنَّمَا ٱسْتَزَلَّهُمُ ٱلشَّيْطَٰنُ بِبَعْضِ مَا
كَسَبُوا۟ وَلَقَدْ عَفَا ٱللَّهُ عَنْهُمْ إِنَّ ٱللَّهَ غَفُورٌ حَلِيمٌ ﴿١٥٥﴾

Verses 149-155

Those of you who turned back on the day the two hosts met – it was Satan who caused them to slip, because of some (evil) they had done. But Allah has forgiven them, for surely Allah is Oft-Forgiving, Most Forbearing. (155)

In verse 122 above, we have read how some weaker Muslims were dismayed by the machinations of the hypocrites especially by the discouraging attitude of their leader, 'Abdullāh ibn Ubayy. Some of these people soon realised their mistake and recovered from its effects, but others slipped and were trapped. Though forgiven by Allah, these people later on realised the error of their behaviour. It was due to some of their previous mistakes, the Qur'ān says, that the Satan caused them to go astray on this occasion.

One sin leads to another, and Satan can misguide only those in whose hearts sin is firmly rooted. It is important therefore that whenever one commits a sin, one should not allow it to take roots in one's heart. Rather, one should try to wipe off its effects, through *istighfār*, seeking forgiveness of Allah and sincere repentance – *tawbatun naṣūḥan.* Otherwise, it is this kind of people who prove to be a burden and a trial for the community of believers. As shown above, the trial that the Muslims encountered at Uḥud was obviously the result of similar weaknesses in some of the weaker Muslims. These weaknesses almost turned victory into a setback and a defeat.

VERSES 156-189: THEMATIC CONTINUITY

The commentary on the situation created by the battle of Uḥud and related issues continues in the following verses.

يَٰٓأَيُّهَا ٱلَّذِينَ ءَامَنُواْ لَا تَكُونُواْ كَٱلَّذِينَ
كَفَرُواْ وَقَالُواْ لِإِخۡوَٰنِهِمۡ إِذَا ضَرَبُواْ فِي
ٱلۡأَرۡضِ أَوۡ كَانُواْ غُزّٗى لَّوۡ كَانُواْ عِندَنَا
مَا مَاتُواْ وَمَا قُتِلُواْ لِيَجۡعَلَ ٱللَّهُ ذَٰلِكَ
حَسۡرَةٗ فِي قُلُوبِهِمۡۗ وَٱللَّهُ يُحۡيِۦ وَيُمِيتُۗ
وَٱللَّهُ بِمَا تَعۡمَلُونَ بَصِيرٞ ١٥٦

O you who believe! Be not like those who have disbelieved, who say about their brethren (who die) when they are travelling through the earth or while engaged in jihād: "If they had stayed with us, they would not have died, or been killed," for Allah may make it a source of bitter regret in their hearts. It is Allah alone who gives life and death, and Allah sees what you do. (156)

And if indeed you are killed, or die, in Allah's cause, surely Allah's forgiveness and mercy are far better than what they hoard. (157)

وَلَئِن قُتِلْتُمْ فِي سَبِيلِ ٱللَّهِ أَوْ مُتُّمْ
لَمَغْفِرَةٌ مِّنَ ٱللَّهِ وَرَحْمَةٌ خَيْرٌ مِّمَّا
يَجْمَعُونَ ١٥٧

And if you die, or are killed, it is surely to Allah that you shall be gathered together. (158)

وَلَئِن مُّتُّمْ أَوْ قُتِلْتُمْ لَإِلَى ٱللَّهِ تُحْشَرُونَ
١٥٨

It is part of the mercy of Allah that you are gentle with them. Were you severe or harsh-hearted, they would surely have dispersed from around you. So bear with them, and ask for (Allah's) forgiveness for them; and consult them in matters of public concern. Then, when you have taken a decision, put your trust in Allah. Verily, Allah loves those who put their trust (in Him). (159)

فَبِمَا رَحْمَةٍ مِّنَ ٱللَّهِ لِنتَ لَهُمْ ۖ وَلَوْ كُنتَ
فَظًّا غَلِيظَ ٱلْقَلْبِ لَٱنفَضُّوا۟ مِنْ حَوْلِكَ ۖ
فَٱعْفُ عَنْهُمْ وَٱسْتَغْفِرْ لَهُمْ وَشَاوِرْهُمْ
فِي ٱلْأَمْرِ ۖ فَإِذَا عَزَمْتَ فَتَوَكَّلْ عَلَى ٱللَّهِ ۚ إِنَّ
ٱللَّهَ يُحِبُّ ٱلْمُتَوَكِّلِينَ ١٥٩

If Allah helps you, none shall prevail against you; but if He forsakes you, who is there, after that, that can help you? In Allah alone, then, let the believers put their trust. (160)

إِن يَنصُرْكُمُ ٱللَّهُ فَلَا غَالِبَ لَكُمْ ۖ وَإِن
يَخْذُلْكُمْ فَمَن ذَا ٱلَّذِى يَنصُرُكُم مِّنۢ
بَعْدِهِۦ ۗ وَعَلَى ٱللَّهِ فَلْيَتَوَكَّلِ ٱلْمُؤْمِنُونَ ١٦٠

No prophet could (ever) be false to his trust. If any person is so false, he shall, on the Day of Judgment, restore what he misappropriated; then shall every soul receive its due in full, whatever it earned, and none shall be dealt with unjustly. (161)

وَمَا كَانَ لِنَبِىٍّ أَن يَغُلَّ ۚ وَمَن يَغْلُلْ
يَأْتِ بِمَا غَلَّ يَوْمَ ٱلْقِيَٰمَةِ ۚ ثُمَّ تُوَفَّىٰ
كُلُّ نَفْسٍ مَّا كَسَبَتْ وَهُمْ لَا
يُظْلَمُونَ ١٦١

Is the one who follows the good pleasure of Allah like the one who incurs the wrath of Allah, and whose abode is in Hell? What an evil destination! (162).

أَفَمَنِ ٱتَّبَعَ رِضْوَٰنَ ٱللَّهِ كَمَنۢ بَآءَ
بِسَخَطٍ مِّنَ ٱللَّهِ وَمَأْوَىٰهُ جَهَنَّمُ ۚ وَبِئْسَ
ٱلْمَصِيرُ ١٦٢

هُمْ دَرَجَٰتٌ عِندَ ٱللَّهِۗ وَٱللَّهُ بَصِيرُۢ بِمَا
يَعْمَلُونَ ﴿١٦٣﴾

They are of different ranks in the sight of Allah, and Allah sees all that they do. (163)

لَقَدْ مَنَّ ٱللَّهُ عَلَى ٱلْمُؤْمِنِينَ إِذْ بَعَثَ
فِيهِمْ رَسُولًا مِّنْ أَنفُسِهِمْ يَتْلُواْ عَلَيْهِمْ
ءَايَٰتِهِۦ وَيُزَكِّيهِمْ وَيُعَلِّمُهُمُ
ٱلْكِتَٰبَ وَٱلْحِكْمَةَ وَإِن كَانُواْ
مِن قَبْلُ لَفِى ضَلَٰلٍ مُّبِينٍ ﴿١٦٤﴾

Allah did confer a great favour on the believers when He raised up a messenger in their midst, who recites to them His verses, and purifies them, and teaches them the Scripture and wisdom, while, before that, they were surely in manifest error. (164)

أَوَلَمَّآ أَصَٰبَتْكُم مُّصِيبَةٌ قَدْ أَصَبْتُم
مِّثْلَيْهَا قُلْتُمْ أَنَّىٰ هَٰذَاۖ قُلْ هُوَ مِنْ عِندِ
أَنفُسِكُمْۗ إِنَّ ٱللَّهَ عَلَىٰ كُلِّ شَىْءٍ قَدِيرٌ
﴿١٦٥﴾

What! When a single misfortune befell you, although you had inflicted twice as much on (your enemies), you said, "How has this come about?" Say (to them): "It is from yourselves. For Allah has power over all things." (165)

وَمَآ أَصَٰبَكُمْ يَوْمَ ٱلْتَقَى ٱلْجَمْعَانِ فَبِإِذْنِ
ٱللَّهِ وَلِيَعْلَمَ ٱلْمُؤْمِنِينَ ﴿١٦٦﴾

What you suffered on the day the two armies met, was by the command of Allah, so that He might mark out the believers. (166)

وَلِيَعْلَمَ ٱلَّذِينَ نَافَقُواْۚ وَقِيلَ لَهُمْ تَعَالَوْاْ
قَٰتِلُواْ فِى سَبِيلِ ٱللَّهِ أَوِ ٱدْفَعُواْۖ قَالُواْ
لَوْ نَعْلَمُ قِتَالًا لَّٱتَّبَعْنَٰكُمْۗ هُمْ
لِلْكُفْرِ يَوْمَئِذٍ أَقْرَبُ مِنْهُمْ لِلْإِيمَٰنِۚ
يَقُولُونَ بِأَفْوَٰهِهِم مَّا لَيْسَ فِى قُلُوبِهِمْۗ
وَٱللَّهُ أَعْلَمُ بِمَا يَكْتُمُونَ ﴿١٦٧﴾

And mark out the hypocrites also, who when told: "Come, fight in the way of Allah, or (at least) drive (the foe from your city)," they said: "Had we known that it would come to a fight, we would certainly have followed you." They were that day nearer to unbelief than to faith, saying with their lips what was not in their hearts, but Allah has full knowledge of all they conceal. (167)

(They are) the ones who say (of their brothers), while they themselves remained behind: "If only they had listened to us they would not have been killed." Say: "Avert death from your own selves, if you speak the truth." (168)

ٱلَّذِينَ قَالُواْ لِإِخۡوَٰنِهِمۡ وَقَعَدُواْ
لَوۡ أَطَاعُونَا مَا قُتِلُواْۗ قُلۡ فَٱدۡرَءُواْ
عَنۡ أَنفُسِكُمُ ٱلۡمَوۡتَ إِن كُنتُمۡ
صَٰدِقِينَ ١٦٨

Think not of those who are killed in Allah's way as dead. Nay, they live, finding their sustenance in the presence of their Sustainer. (169)

وَلَا تَحۡسَبَنَّ ٱلَّذِينَ قُتِلُواْ فِي سَبِيلِ ٱللَّهِ
أَمۡوَٰتَۢاۚ بَلۡ أَحۡيَآءٌ عِندَ رَبِّهِمۡ يُرۡزَقُونَ
١٦٩

They rejoice at the favour Allah has bestowed on them, and are happy for those left behind who have not yet joined them, that they will have no fear nor will they have (cause to) grieve. (170)

فَرِحِينَ بِمَآ ءَاتَىٰهُمُ ٱللَّهُ مِن فَضۡلِهِۦ
وَيَسۡتَبۡشِرُونَ بِٱلَّذِينَ لَمۡ يَلۡحَقُواْ بِهِم
مِّنۡ خَلۡفِهِمۡ أَلَّا خَوۡفٌ عَلَيۡهِمۡ وَلَا هُمۡ
يَحۡزَنُونَ ١٧٠

They rejoice in the grace and the bounty from Allah, and that Allah will not let the reward of the believers be lost. (171)

۞ يَسۡتَبۡشِرُونَ بِنِعۡمَةٖ مِّنَ ٱللَّهِ وَفَضۡلٖ
وَأَنَّ ٱللَّهَ لَا يُضِيعُ أَجۡرَ ٱلۡمُؤۡمِنِينَ ١٧١

Of those who answered the call of Allah and the Messenger, even after injury had afflicted them – for those who do good and refrain from evil, there is a great reward for them. (172)

ٱلَّذِينَ ٱسۡتَجَابُواْ لِلَّهِ وَٱلرَّسُولِ مِنۢ
بَعۡدِ مَآ أَصَابَهُمُ ٱلۡقَرۡحُۚ لِلَّذِينَ أَحۡسَنُواْ
مِنۡهُمۡ وَٱتَّقَوۡاْ أَجۡرٌ عَظِيمٌ ١٧٢

Those to whom people said: "A great army is gathering against you, so be afraid of them", but it (only) increased their faith. And they said: "For us Allah is sufficient, and an excellent guardian is He." (173)

ٱلَّذِينَ قَالَ لَهُمُ ٱلنَّاسُ إِنَّ ٱلنَّاسَ قَدۡ
جَمَعُواْ لَكُمۡ فَٱخۡشَوۡهُمۡ فَزَادَهُمۡ إِيمَٰنٗا
وَقَالُواْ حَسۡبُنَا ٱللَّهُ وَنِعۡمَ ٱلۡوَكِيلُ
١٧٣

And they returned with grace and bounty from Allah, while no harm touched them. They had been striving after Allah's good pleasure and Allah is the Possessor of tremendous bounties. (174)

فَانقَلَبُوا۟ بِنِعْمَةٍ مِّنَ ٱللَّهِ وَفَضْلٍ لَّمْ
يَمْسَسْهُمْ سُوٓءٌ وَٱتَّبَعُوا۟ رِضْوَٰنَ ٱللَّهِ ۗ
وَٱللَّهُ ذُو فَضْلٍ عَظِيمٍ ﴿١٧٤﴾

It is only Satan that suggests to you the fear of his allies. Do not be afraid of them, but fear Me, if you are (true) believers. (175)

إِنَّمَا ذَٰلِكُمُ ٱلشَّيْطَٰنُ يُخَوِّفُ أَوْلِيَآءَهُۥ فَلَا
تَخَافُوهُمْ وَخَافُونِ إِن كُنتُم مُّؤْمِنِينَ ﴿١٧٥﴾

Let not those grieve you who rush headlong into unbelief: surely they cannot harm Allah in any way. Allah desires to assign no portion to them in the hereafter; for them awaits a painful punishment. (176)

وَلَا يَحْزُنكَ ٱلَّذِينَ يُسَٰرِعُونَ فِى ٱلْكُفْرِ ۚ
إِنَّهُمْ لَن يَضُرُّوا۟ ٱللَّهَ شَيْـًٔا ۗ يُرِيدُ ٱللَّهُ أَلَّا
يَجْعَلَ لَهُمْ حَظًّا فِى ٱلْءَاخِرَةِ ۖ وَلَهُمْ عَذَابٌ
عَظِيمٌ ﴿١٧٦﴾

Those who bartered away faith for unbelief, not the least harm will they do to Allah, but they will have a grievous punishment. (177)

إِنَّ ٱلَّذِينَ ٱشْتَرَوُا۟ ٱلْكُفْرَ بِٱلْإِيمَٰنِ لَن
يَضُرُّوا۟ ٱللَّهَ شَيْـًٔا وَلَهُمْ عَذَابٌ أَلِيمٌ
﴿١٧٧﴾

Let not the unbelievers think that Our respite given to them is good for them. We grant them respite that they may increase in their evildoing, and they will have a shameful punishment. (178)

وَلَا يَحْسَبَنَّ ٱلَّذِينَ كَفَرُوٓا۟ أَنَّمَا نُمْلِى لَهُمْ
خَيْرٌ لِّأَنفُسِهِمْ ۚ إِنَّمَا نُمْلِى لَهُمْ لِيَزْدَادُوٓا۟
إِثْمًا ۚ وَلَهُمْ عَذَابٌ مُّهِينٌ ﴿١٧٨﴾

Allah will not leave the believers in the state in which you are now, until He sets apart the bad from the good, nor will He disclose to you the secrets of the unseen. But He chooses whomsoever He pleases of His messengers. So believe in Allah and His messengers; if you believe and act righteously, you will have a great reward. (179)

مَّا كَانَ ٱللَّهُ لِيَذَرَ ٱلْمُؤْمِنِينَ عَلَىٰ مَآ
أَنتُمْ عَلَيْهِ حَتَّىٰ يَمِيزَ ٱلْخَبِيثَ مِنَ ٱلطَّيِّبِ ۗ
وَمَا كَانَ ٱللَّهُ لِيُطْلِعَكُمْ عَلَى ٱلْغَيْبِ وَلَٰكِنَّ
ٱللَّهَ يَجْتَبِى مِن رُّسُلِهِۦ مَن يَشَآءُ ۖ فَـَٔامِنُوا۟ بِٱللَّهِ
وَرُسُلِهِۦ ۚ وَإِن تُؤْمِنُوا۟ وَتَتَّقُوا۟ فَلَكُمْ أَجْرٌ
عَظِيمٌ ﴿١٧٩﴾

وَلَا يَحۡسَبَنَّ ٱلَّذِينَ يَبۡخَلُونَ بِمَآ ءَاتَىٰهُمُ
ٱللَّهُ مِن فَضۡلِهِۦ هُوَ خَيۡرٗا لَّهُمۖ بَلۡ هُوَ
شَرّٞ لَّهُمۡۖ سَيُطَوَّقُونَ مَا بَخِلُواْ بِهِۦ
يَوۡمَ ٱلۡقِيَٰمَةِۗ وَلِلَّهِ مِيرَٰثُ ٱلسَّمَٰوَٰتِ
وَٱلۡأَرۡضِۗ وَٱللَّهُ بِمَا تَعۡمَلُونَ خَبِيرٞ ١٨٠

And let not those who covetously withhold the gifts which Allah has given them of His grace and think that it is good for them: indeed, it is bad for them. That to which they so covetously cling will, on the day of judgement, be hung about their necks. To Allah belongs the heritage of the heavens and the earth. And Allah is well acquainted with all that you do. (180)

لَّقَدۡ سَمِعَ ٱللَّهُ قَوۡلَ ٱلَّذِينَ قَالُوٓاْ إِنَّ
ٱللَّهَ فَقِيرٞ وَنَحۡنُ أَغۡنِيَآءُۘ سَنَكۡتُبُ مَا
قَالُواْ وَقَتۡلَهُمُ ٱلۡأَنۢبِيَآءَ بِغَيۡرِ حَقّٖ
وَنَقُولُ ذُوقُواْ عَذَابَ ٱلۡحَرِيقِ ١٨١

Allah has indeed heard the saying of those who said: "Behold, Allah is poor while we are rich!" We shall certainly record what they have said as well as their killing of the prophets in defiance of all right, and We shall say to them: "Taste (now) the punishment of the burning fire! (181)

ذَٰلِكَ بِمَا قَدَّمَتۡ أَيۡدِيكُمۡ وَأَنَّ ٱللَّهَ
لَيۡسَ بِظَلَّامٖ لِّلۡعَبِيدِ ١٨٢

"This is because of the (unrighteous deeds) which your hands have sent on before you, for Allah is not in the least unjust to His servants." (182)

ٱلَّذِينَ قَالُوٓاْ إِنَّ ٱللَّهَ عَهِدَ إِلَيۡنَآ
أَلَّا نُؤۡمِنَ لِرَسُولٍ حَتَّىٰ يَأۡتِيَنَا بِقُرۡبَانٖ
تَأۡكُلُهُ ٱلنَّارُۗ قُلۡ قَدۡ جَآءَكُمۡ رُسُلٞ
مِّن قَبۡلِي بِٱلۡبَيِّنَٰتِ وَبِٱلَّذِي قُلۡتُمۡ فَلِمَ
قَتَلۡتُمُوهُمۡ إِن كُنتُمۡ صَٰدِقِينَ ١٨٣

They (also) said: "Allah has made a contract with us not to believe in any messenger unless he show us a sacrifice consumed by fire (from heaven)." Say: "There came to you messengers before me, with clear signs and even with what you ask for. Why then did you kill them, if you speak the truth?" (183)

فَإِن كَذَّبُوكَ فَقَدۡ كُذِّبَ رُسُلٞ
مِّن قَبۡلِكَ جَآءُو بِٱلۡبَيِّنَٰتِ وَٱلزُّبُرِ
وَٱلۡكِتَٰبِ ٱلۡمُنِيرِ ١٨٤

Then, if they reject you, so were rejected messengers before you, who came with clear signs, scriptures, and the book of enlightenment. (184)

Every human being shall taste death. And only on the Day of Judgment shall you be requited in full recompense. Only he who is saved from the fire and admitted to the Garden will have attained the object (of life): For the life of this world is but an illusory enjoyment. (185)

كُلُّ نَفْسٍ ذَآئِقَةُ ٱلْمَوْتِ ۗ وَإِنَّمَا
تُوَفَّوْنَ أُجُورَكُمْ يَوْمَ ٱلْقِيَٰمَةِ ۖ
فَمَن زُحْزِحَ عَنِ ٱلنَّارِ وَأُدْخِلَ
ٱلْجَنَّةَ فَقَدْ فَازَ ۗ وَمَا ٱلْحَيَوٰةُ ٱلدُّنْيَآ
إِلَّا مَتَٰعُ ٱلْغُرُورِ ﴿١٨٥﴾

You shall certainly be tried and tested in your possessions and in your persons. And you shall certainly hear much that will grieve you from those who received the Scripture before you and from those who worship many gods, but if you persevere and restrain yourselves by remaining conscious of God, that indeed is the most resolute course. (186)

۞ لَتُبْلَوُنَّ فِىٓ أَمْوَٰلِكُمْ
وَأَنفُسِكُمْ وَلَتَسْمَعُنَّ مِنَ
ٱلَّذِينَ أُوتُوا۟ ٱلْكِتَٰبَ مِن قَبْلِكُمْ
وَمِنَ ٱلَّذِينَ أَشْرَكُوٓا۟ أَذًى
كَثِيرًا ۚ وَإِن تَصْبِرُوا۟ وَتَتَّقُوا۟ فَإِنَّ
ذَٰلِكَ مِنْ عَزْمِ ٱلْأُمُورِ ﴿١٨٦﴾

And remember when Allah accepted a solemn pledge from those who were given the Scripture, saying: "Make it known to humankind, and not conceal it." But they tossed it away behind their backs and bartered it away for a paltry price. And how evil was their bargain! (187)

وَإِذْ أَخَذَ ٱللَّهُ مِيثَٰقَ ٱلَّذِينَ أُوتُوا۟
ٱلْكِتَٰبَ لَتُبَيِّنُنَّهُۥ لِلنَّاسِ وَلَا تَكْتُمُونَهُۥ
فَنَبَذُوهُ وَرَآءَ ظُهُورِهِمْ وَٱشْتَرَوْا۟ بِهِۦ
ثَمَنًا قَلِيلًا ۖ فَبِئْسَ مَا يَشْتَرُونَ ﴿١٨٧﴾

Think not that those who exult in what they have brought about, and love to be praised for what they have not done, that they have escaped the punishment. They will have a painful chastisement. (188)

لَا تَحْسَبَنَّ ٱلَّذِينَ يَفْرَحُونَ بِمَآ أَتَوا۟
وَّيُحِبُّونَ أَن يُحْمَدُوا۟ بِمَا لَمْ يَفْعَلُوا۟ فَلَا
تَحْسَبَنَّهُم بِمَفَازَةٍ مِّنَ ٱلْعَذَابِ ۖ وَلَهُمْ
عَذَابٌ أَلِيمٌ ﴿١٨٨﴾

To Allah belongs the dominion of the heavens and the earth. And Allah has power over all things. (189)

وَلِلَّهِ مُلْكُ ٱلسَّمَٰوَٰتِ وَٱلْأَرْضِ ۗ وَٱللَّهُ
عَلَىٰ كُلِّ شَىْءٍ قَدِيرٌ ﴿١٨٩﴾

WORD STUDY AND EXPLANATION

يَٰٓأَيُّهَا ٱلَّذِينَ ءَامَنُوا۟ لَا تَكُونُوا۟ كَٱلَّذِينَ كَفَرُوا۟ وَقَالُوا۟ لِإِخْوَٰنِهِمْ إِذَا ضَرَبُوا۟ فِى ٱلْأَرْضِ
أَوْ كَانُوا۟ غُزًّى لَّوْ كَانُوا۟ عِندَنَا مَا مَاتُوا۟ وَمَا قُتِلُوا۟ لِيَجْعَلَ ٱللَّهُ ذَٰلِكَ حَسْرَةً فِى قُلُوبِهِمْ
وَٱللَّهُ يُحْىِۦ وَيُمِيتُ وَٱللَّهُ بِمَا تَعْمَلُونَ بَصِيرٌ ﴿١٥٦﴾
وَلَئِن قُتِلْتُمْ فِى سَبِيلِ ٱللَّهِ أَوْ مُتُّمْ لَمَغْفِرَةٌ مِّنَ ٱللَّهِ وَرَحْمَةٌ خَيْرٌ مِّمَّا يَجْمَعُونَ ﴿١٥٧﴾
وَلَئِن مُّتُّمْ أَوْ قُتِلْتُمْ لَإِلَى ٱللَّهِ تُحْشَرُونَ ﴿١٥٨﴾

O you who believe! Be not like those who have disbelieved and who say about their brethren (who die) when they are travelling through the earth or are engaged in jihād: "If they had stayed with us, they would not have died, or been killed," so that Allah may make it a source of bitter regret in their hearts. It is Allah alone who gives life and death, and Allah sees what you do. (156)
And if you are killed, or die, in Allah's cause, surely Allah's forgiveness and mercy are far better than what they hoard. (157)
And if you die, or are killed, it is surely to Allah that you shall be gathered together. (158)

Use of the preposition *li*

The preposition *li,* meaning *of* or *about* in the verse *wa qālū li-ikhwānihim* is used in a sense similar to the verse *wa qāla-l ladhīna kafarū li-llaladhīna āmanū law kāna khayran mā sabaqūnā ilayhi* (The unbelievers say of those who believe: "If (this new message) were a good thing, (such people) would not have gone to it first, before us!" (Sūrah al-Aḥqāf, 46:11). The word *ikhwān* refers to kinsmen and relatives. *Ghuzzan* is the plural of *ghāzī,* meaning a fighter or a campaigner.

The clause before *li-yajʿala-llāhu* (*that Allah may make it*) is omitted. If expanded, the clause would read that the reason why this wrong notion is so entrenched in their minds is because Allah wants to punish them because of their hypocrisy by making their erroneous belief a source of continuous grief and distress for them. Many examples of such cases of ellipsis (*ḥadhaf*) have been mentioned above.

Admonition to Muslims

This is also an admonition to the Muslims, warning them against following in the footsteps of the unbelievers and the hypocrites, while informing them that the real reason for the cowardice on the part of the hypocrites is their misconception that death and life are subject to their own schemes and efforts. When any of their close associates is killed during a journey or war, they sorrowfully proclaim that had he been with them or listened to them, he would not have suffered death in this manner. This is precisely what they said about those killed in the battle of Uḥud, even though life and death rests with Allah alone: He gives life or death to whomever He wills. Whatever manner, time or place He has prescribed for a person's death, it will take its course as prescribed and no amount of precautions will be of any avail. Even if one were to live behind fortified walls of castles, death will definitely seek him out. People who think they can escape death by their devices cannot avoid the encounter with it. Their cunning schemes cannot help them. These only betray their cowardice, and an abiding anguish will pursue them all through life. The believers should guard against this dangerous temptation. Life and death rest in the hands of Allah alone and He is well aware of whatever humans do in this life.

As a further encouragement, the believers are told that if they were martyred in the cause of Allah or met their death, there was nothing to worry about, because the forgiveness and the reward they are destined to receive is far better than all the transitory pleasures of this life that its votaries are so engrossed with.

This verse does not, however, encourage recklessness. Rather, it draws attention to the futility of trying to save one's life by abandoning one's obligations. The only correct behaviour is to do whatever one's duty might entail, faithfully and with fortitude, while firmly believing that death is inevitable and will come at its appointed time. At the same time, one needs to bear in mind that to lay down one's life in the performance of one's duty is far more valuable and important than all that earthly life offers and all its treasures. This subject is further elaborated below in verses 167-171.

The verse ends by emphasising that whoever dies inevitably returns to Allah. Why should a true believer then be scared of meeting his Creator and Sovereign Sustainer? This is precisely the real significance and purpose of sacrifice in the cause of Allah.

فَبِمَا رَحْمَةٍ مِّنَ ٱللَّهِ لِنتَ لَهُمْ ۖ وَلَوْ كُنتَ فَظًّا غَلِيظَ ٱلْقَلْبِ لَٱنفَضُّوا۟ مِنْ حَوْلِكَ ۖ فَٱعْفُ
عَنْهُمْ وَٱسْتَغْفِرْ لَهُمْ وَشَاوِرْهُمْ فِى ٱلْأَمْرِ ۖ فَإِذَا عَزَمْتَ فَتَوَكَّلْ عَلَى ٱللَّهِ ۚ إِنَّ ٱللَّهَ يُحِبُّ
ٱلْمُتَوَكِّلِينَ ﴿١٥٩﴾

إِن يَنصُرْكُمُ ٱللَّهُ فَلَا غَالِبَ لَكُمْ ۖ وَإِن يَخْذُلْكُمْ فَمَن ذَا ٱلَّذِى يَنصُرُكُم مِّنۢ بَعْدِهِۦ ۗ
وَعَلَى ٱللَّهِ فَلْيَتَوَكَّلِ ٱلْمُؤْمِنُونَ ﴿١٦٠﴾

It is part of the mercy of Allah that you are gentle with them. Were you severe or harsh-hearted, they would surely have dispersed from around you. So bear with them, and ask for (Allah's) forgiveness for them; and consult them in matters of public concern. Then, when you have taken a decision, put your trust in Allah. Verily, Allah loves those who put their trust (in Him). (159)
If Allah helps you, none shall prevail against you; but if He forsakes you, who is there, after that, that can help you? In Allah alone, then, let the believers put their trust. (160)

The construction *fa bimā raḥmatin* (it is part of the mercy) is similar to the construction *fa bimā naqḍihim mīthāqahum*[51] (as result of violation of their covenant). In general the grammarians take the particle *mā* in *fabi-mā* as a mark of emphasis. In our opinion, sometimes the particle *mā* is also used simply to create harmony in the sentence.

The word *faẓẓ* means crude, impolite and harsh, while *ghalīẓ-al qalb* means hard-hearted or stern.

Endorsement of the Prophet's attitude towards the hypocrites

This verse represents an aside following the harsh words used for the hypocrites. This could naturally harden the attitude of the Prophet, peace be upon him, and his sincere companions toward these hypocrites. At that stage, this was obviously not desirable in the sight of Allah. The attitude and conduct of the hypocrites was extremely objectionable and they misused and misinterpreted the leniency of the Prophet, peace be upon him. Essentially, however, they were sick people and therefore Allah wanted to grant them some respite so that if they had any good in them they would realise what was right and rectify their behaviour. The lenient attitude and kind treatment with which they were hitherto treated by the Prophet was for this very reason approved by Allah. However, while clarifying the wisdom behind this lenient attitude, it is made clear that these hypocrites did not value their spiritual health and the possibility of reform and indeed were far from being inclined to take any bitter medicine.

It is purely a blessing of Allah that He made His Messenger so kind and compassionate trying to reform them in an equally kind and compassionate

51. See Sūrah an-Nisā' 4:155 and Sūrah al-Mā'idah 5:13 (Translator).

manner. Had he been harsh with them they would, like wild animals, have scattered from around him. They were not the people who appreciate truth or their own moral and spiritual health and purification. They were afflicted with numerous ills and deficient in so many ways, but the Prophet, peace be upon him, is admonished to treat them kindly and gently, overlooking their moral flaws and lack of appreciation and pray to Allah for their forgiveness.

It may be noted here that later on when a group of the hypocrites disappointed the Prophet, peace be upon him, and it became clear that they were not amenable to any reformation, the Prophet and the Muslims were explicitly commanded to change their attitude toward them. Rather than treat them gently as before – a gentleness that they persistently misused, they were to adopt a stern attitude toward them to bring them to their senses and persuade them to follow the right path. A more detailed discussion on this issue will be found in the commentary on verses 73 and 123 of the present sūrah and verse 9 of Sūrah at-Taḥrīm.

It is also noteworthy that while advising the Prophet to forgive and to pray for them, he is also commanded to *shāwir hum fi-l amr* – consult them in public concern. There is a special reason for this commandment at this place and we would like to explain it briefly here.

In matters of religion the Prophet, peace be upon him, did not depend on any advice from others. All his utterances, actions and functions were guided by Divine revelation. In political and administrative matters, however, he always consulted with his companions, thus setting an important precedent by his personal example for mutual consultation. Shūrā or consultation has, therefore, always been a fundamental feature of the political system of Islam.

Following this principle of mutual consultation, the Prophet, peace be upon him, also consulted with his companions concerning the battle of Uḥud, whether they should fight against the enemy from within the city or march forth and confront the enemy outside the city. The purpose of this consultation, as pointed out above, was to mark out clearly the weak elements within their ranks. And that is precisely what happened. The weak and the hypocrites among them insisted that the fighting should be done from within the city, from behind the fortifications. They thought they would, by this show of fervour, be able to conceal their weakness and hypocrisy. The sincere and true believers, however, thought differently and proposed to confront the enemy outside the city. This was a sound advice and was also the opinion of the Prophet himself. Acting on this advice, he decided to face the enemy outside the city[52]. When the hypocrites failed to get their way they were furious and gave vent to their anger in various ways. A group of them separated from the main body of the Muslims, on the pretext that their advice was not appreciated. Another group, who reluctantly went along to the battle, found an opportunity to spread frustration among the Muslims after their setback in the battle. They said the Muslims had suffered defeat because their advice was turned down, and that if they had listened to them and followed their advice, they would not have suffered the defeat. They wanted to cause mischief and spread dissatisfaction among the Muslims but as pointed out earlier, prudence at this stage called for forgiveness and generous treatment. No restrictions were imposed upon them and as before they continued to enjoy all their civil and social rights notwithstanding their mistakes and misbehaviour. Thus we find that the above verse advises the Prophet, peace be upon him, not only to overlook their mistakes and ask for their forgiveness but to consult them, as before, in matters of common interest even though their weakness and rancour was by now quite obvious.

Correct attitude concerning the question of majority and minority

The rider clause *fa i<u>dh</u>ā 'azamta fa-tawakkal 'ala-llāh* (then, when you have taken a decision put your trust in Allah) following the commandment *wa*

---

52. A report that has found place in the books of history and *sīrah* that the Prophet, peace be upon him, was also of the view that they should fight the enemy from within the city, but some zealous companions forced him to confront the enemy outside the city. This is, however, a baseless report. When the Prophet, peace be upon him, consulted the companions on this subject, he did not disclose his own personal opinion so that the people would be able to express their opinions freely. He also wanted to gauge the morale of his companions. 'Abdullāh ibn Ubayy and his comrades insisted on fighting the enemy from within the city while the sincere, devoted companions proposed to confront the enemy outside in the battlefield.

Having thus assessed the morale of both the groups, the Prophet went to his apartment and came out clad in battle dress, clearly signalling that they would be going out to confront the enemy. His devoted companions surmised that perhaps the Prophet, peace be upon him, had taken this stance under pressure from them. Therefore, they offered apologies and sought to withdraw their proposal. At this, the Prophet, peace be upon him, said that no prophet takes off his armour after having put it on. In other words, after the decision is made, it cannot be changed.

When the hypocrites found that their scheme had failed, 'Abdullāh Ibn Ubayy along with his three hundred supporters separated from the Muslim army. It may be mentioned here that the Prophet, peace be upon him, invariably used some wise means or method to gauge the morale of the army. At the time of the Battle of Badr also, he had used such a course and the speech of the chief of the Anṣār on that occasion is an eloquent testimony to this.

Verses 156-189

shāwir-hum fi-l amr (and consult them in affairs (of moment), also suggests that the purpose of consultation in administrative and political matters is to lend strength to the rulers and to reinforce confidence in their decisions. Consultation is necessary, but after the consultation, a ruler may carry out whatever decision he is satisfied with and place his trust in Allah. It makes no difference whether majority or minority votes support the decision of the ruler. A majority *per se* is not a proof of the soundness of an opinion or its rectitude nor does a minority signify deficiency and a proof that it is always wrong. However, there is greater chance that a majority opinion would be more sound and correct. Therefore, if it is taken as conclusive in settling disputes and conflicts it is safer and comparatively more expedient, especially in the present times when desires and caprice play such a prominent part in people's lives. There are few who would use their power and authority within the confines of the law and not overstep the bounds.

Noteworthy points

The above two verses draw our attention to the following important points:

1. The advisable course for the common people as well as for the people in power and politicians is of leniency and forgiveness. This would generate mutual goodwill and trust among people and lend coherence and strength to the collective system. Harshness and severity is not conducive to collective welfare and well-being. Rather, it is one of its maladies and represents a condition of sickness. For health the basic requirement is healthy food, but sometimes medicine is needed to restore health. Similarly, in social life the basic requisite is leniency, while at times firmness and severity may be necessary due to some need or emergency.
2. Mutual consultation in social life is a reflection of the goodwill, trust and confidence that ought to exist between government and the governed. This eliminates tyranny and harshness and paves the way to mutual co-operation that is the real basis of collective strength and solidarity.
3. There is no justification for any blind trust, a life of passivity or idleness on the part of individuals, nor can these be justified in social life that is based on determination and action.
4. Real strength and power comes from trust in Allah. Material means and equipment are only of secondary importance.
5. Reposing our trust in Allah is the necessary consequence of our *īmān* or faith. Any claim to believe in Allah while refusing to put one's trust in Him only shows the hollowness of such a claim.

وَمَا كَانَ لِنَبِيٍّ أَن يَغُلَّ وَمَن يَغْلُلْ يَأْتِ بِمَا غَلَّ يَوْمَ ٱلْقِيَٰمَةِ ثُمَّ تُوَفَّىٰ كُلُّ نَفْسٍ مَّا كَسَبَتْ وَهُمْ لَا يُظْلَمُونَ ﴿١٦١﴾

أَفَمَنِ ٱتَّبَعَ رِضْوَٰنَ ٱللَّهِ كَمَنۢ بَآءَ بِسَخَطٍ مِّنَ ٱللَّهِ وَمَأْوَىٰهُ جَهَنَّمُ وَبِئْسَ ٱلْمَصِيرُ ﴿١٦٢﴾

هُمْ دَرَجَٰتٌ عِندَ ٱللَّهِ وَٱللَّهُ بَصِيرٌۢ بِمَا يَعْمَلُونَ ﴿١٦٣﴾

No prophet could (ever) deceive or be false to his trust. If any person is so false, he shall, on the Day of Judgment, restore what he misappropriated. Then shall every soul receive its due in full, whatever it has earned, and none shall be dealt with unjustly. (161)
Is the one who follows the good pleasure of Allah like the one that incurs the wrath of Allah, and whose abode is in Hell? What an evil destination! (162).
They are of different ranks in the sight of Allah, and Allah sees all that they do. (163)

The verb *ghalla, yaghullu* means to be dishonest, treacherous and disloyal. Its noun *ghill* meaning rancour or hatred is the antonym of the word *naṣaḥa (naṣīḥah)* that means goodwill and friendliness. The lexicologist, Zajjāj, as mentioned by the author of *Lisān al-'Arab*, explains the sentence *mā kāna li-nabīyin an yaghulla* as meaning *mā kāna li-nabīyin an yakhūna ummatahu* (a prophet can never be false or treacherous to his community). The word *ghill* has been used in the Qur'ān at several places in the sense of enmity, rancour, and jealousy. For instance, we read: *wa lā taj'al fī qulūbinā ghillan lil-ladhīna āmanū* ("and leave not, in our hearts, rancour (or sense of injury) against those who have believed." (Sūrah al-Ḥashr, 59:10). As such, there is no reason for restricting its meaning merely to financial dishonesty.

An allegation of the hypocrites

This verse answers the allegations of the hypocrites against the Prophet, peace be upon him, after the defeat in the battle of Uḥud. In order to cause frustration among the Muslims, they alleged that the Prophet, peace be upon him, had misused their trust in him and that he had exposed their lives and properties to unnecessary risk for personal ambition. They also said that they had advised the Prophet to fight against the enemy from within the walls of the city but he ignored their advice as he held their lives in very low estimation. Moreover, he had led them out of the city to a completely inappropriate place and caused the loss of so many lives. This was, they alleged, a clear act of ill will to the people, treachery and dishonesty.

There are references to this allegation in the above verses, and it is further elucidated in the verses below. The Qur'ān repudiates this allegation declaring it to be a wrong and completely baseless accusation. No prophet is ever dishonest or disloyal to his community. Whatever he does, and whatever course he follows is always in search of the pleasure of Allah in accordance with the commandments revealed to him. A prophet is well aware that all cases of dishonesty and disloyalty will be presented before Allah and will be fully requited. Those who sincerely seek God's pleasure and those who incur His wrath are not similar and cannot be treated alike. The two groups will have separate and different ranks and abodes depending on their deeds. Allah watches the deeds of all people.

The wording of the Qur'ān as well as its textual coherence supports the above interpretation of this verse. Some interpreters, as is clear from the *tafsīr* of Ibn Jarīr, have also preferred this interpretation. We need not, therefore, give credence to the tradition reported in some *tafsīr* books that this verse was revealed in refutation of the accusation of the hypocrites who had blamed the Prophet, peace be upon him, for a sheet of cloth found missing from the war spoils. This report is baseless because, firstly, it is reportedly related to the battle of Badr. The Muslims had suffered a setback in the battle of Uḥud and there was no war booty involved in that battle. In the present context, it is the battle of Uḥud that is under discussion, so why would it refer to a past event that had happened during the battle of Badr quite a long time ago without any prior reference or context? The hypocrites were not that foolish to blame the Prophet for something that no one could believe and thus make them a laughing stock. Not only the hypocrites but even the staunchest enemies of the Prophet, peace be upon, among the Quraysh ever dared accuse him of any minor or major financial dishonesty. In the Days of Ignorance as well as in Islam, he was universally known, as *al-Amīn,* the honest one, and his friends as well as his enemies were equally impressed by his honesty. Some foolish people, who spoke against him concerning financial matters, never implied any dishonesty on his part; the nature of a complaint was about his giving more to some than to others. On all such occasions, his accusers were deeply remorseful when the real situation was explained to them, as for instance, what happened after the liberation of Makkah and the battle of Ḥunayn. Therefore, it is incomprehensible that the hypocrites would accuse him of dishonesty about a trivial thing like a piece of cloth. They could, however, understandably plant doubts in the minds of the weaker Muslims through launching a whispering campaign that Muḥammad, peace be upon him, was, God forbid, not truly a well-wisher of his community and was ready to sacrifice them at the altar of his personal ambition. The defeat of Uḥud had given them an opportunity for such poisonous propaganda and they used it as far as they could, especially because they were opposed to fighting the enemy outside the city and because their opinion had not found acceptance by the Prophet, peace be upon him, and his faithful companions.

لَقَدْ مَنَّ ٱللَّهُ عَلَى ٱلْمُؤْمِنِينَ إِذْ بَعَثَ فِيهِمْ رَسُولًا مِّنْ أَنفُسِهِمْ يَتْلُوا۟ عَلَيْهِمْ ءَايَٰتِهِۦ
وَيُزَكِّيهِمْ وَيُعَلِّمُهُمُ ٱلْكِتَٰبَ وَٱلْحِكْمَةَ وَإِن كَانُوا۟ مِن قَبْلُ لَفِى ضَلَٰلٍ
مُّبِينٍ ١٦٤

Allah did confer a great favour on the believers when He raised up a messenger from among themselves, who recites to them His verses, and purifies them, and teaches them the book and wisdom, while, before that, they were surely in manifest error. (164)

Blessings of the Prophet, peace be upon him

This verse is also found in Sūrah al-Baqarah with some difference in wording[53]. All its important parts have already been explained there. Viewed in the context of coherence, we find that this verse presents positively what is described negatively in the above verse that absolves the Prophet, peace be upon, from the false accusation of ill-will and disloyalty to his community. And now, in the present verse, the great favour of Allah to all people of the world, especially the Arabs among them, is mentioned by raising him as the final prophet for their guidance. This great favour is stated in three different perspectives.

Firstly, Allah raised a messenger from among them so that any lack of familiarity with the language, difference of race, unfamiliarity with their trends and inclinations, or ignorance of their present and past conditions would not constitute any cause for any prejudice, mistrust or suspicion. They could thus easily put their trust in him as a part of their own family. His voice and call they will recognise and they could thus respond to his message that so perfectly resonates with their genuine feelings. The words of the verse "from among themselves" underline this clearly.

Secondly, regarding the purpose and the mission of the Prophet, he recites to them the messages of Allah, purifies their thinking, morals, and practice from error; and he teaches them the Scripture and the wisdom. So they

53. Cf. The Qur'ān, 2:129 and 2:151.

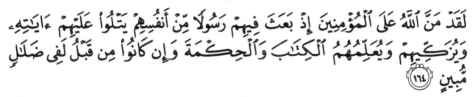

should just consider, who else could be their greatest well-wisher other than the Prophet, peace be upon him? His advent, mission and efforts have indeed brought about such a glorious change in their society and improvement in all aspects of their lives, individual and social, material and spiritual.

Thirdly, it was a special favour to them as they were, more than anyone else, in great need of this Divine message. The Arabs were an unlettered people with no knowledge about prophets or Divine law or Sharī'ah. They had been steeped in the darkness of unbelief and ignorance. By raising the Prophet from among them, Allah rescued them and brought them out of darkness into the light and showed them the straight path. All this is clearly implied by the words *wa in kānū min qablu la-fi ḍalālin mubīn* (while, before that, they were surely in manifest error)." The particle *in* used in the sentence is known as a lighter (*mukhaffafah*) *in* and carries the sense of *inna* (surely or verily) for emphasis as indicated by the *la* in *la-fi ḍalālin mubīn* (they were surely in manifest error).

أَوَلَمَّآ أَصَٰبَتۡكُم مُّصِيبَةٞ قَدۡ أَصَبۡتُم مِّثۡلَيۡهَا قُلۡتُمۡ أَنَّىٰ هَٰذَاۖ قُلۡ هُوَ مِنۡ عِندِ أَنفُسِكُمۡۗ
إِنَّ ٱللَّهَ عَلَىٰ كُلِّ شَيۡءٖ قَدِيرٞ ١٦٥

What! When a single misfortune befell you, although you had inflicted twice as much on (your enemies), you said, " How has this come about?" Say (to them): "It is from yourselves: For Allah has power over all things." (165)

The Arabic letter *alif* with a *fat-ḥah* is an interrogative letter while the letter *waw* is a conjunctive. In Arabic the interrogatory letter is always placed at the beginning of a sentence, as for instance in the verse *afa bihādha-l ḥadīthi antum mud-hinūn* (would you then look down with disdain upon a message like this? (Sūrah al-Wāqi'ah, 56:81). The interrogatory sentence is expressive of surprise while the conjunctive *wāw* (and) shows that this was also part of the objections that have been answered above.

A misconception and its correction

As mentioned above, some people wrongly believed that a messenger of Allah and his companions are immune from all hardships and difficulties. Also, they believed that when he undertakes any venture, angels would accompany him to help and support him and if he and his companions have to fight, they would always be victorious. Those who had such a notion about the messengers and prophets of Allah, were naturally greatly shaken in their belief by the setback suffered by the Muslims at Uḥud. If Islam were indeed the true religion and Muḥammad, peace be upon him, was the messenger of Allah, why then did he suffer a defeat? The hypocrites tried to exploit this psychological condition of the weaker elements. They presented this defeat as an argument to denigrate the Prophet and his status in the community. The Qur'ān has tackled this misunderstanding at some length in this and the following verses, while explaining the wisdom behind the trials and tribulations that the believers inevitably have to go through.

Firstly, they are told that it is not they alone who have suffered such a setback that should thus plunge them in such suspicion and despair. Their enemies too had suffered a two-fold loss at their hands. In the battle of Badr, they had killed seventy leaders of the enemy while taking another seventy as prisoners. Even in the battle of Uḥud, the Muslims were dominant and some of the enemy were killed and others wounded by them. However, due to their own mistake, they had later suffered defeat. Allah has full control over victory and defeat, but His power is always subject to His wisdom.

Secondly, it is stressed that the Muslims were themselves responsible for their defeat as has been explained above in verse 152: "Allah did indeed fulfil His promise to you when you with His permission were about to annihilate your enemy, until you flinched and fell to disputing about the order, and disobeyed the Prophet after Allah brought you in sight of what you covet. Among you were some who were infatuated with worldly pleasures and others who desired the hereafter. So Allah did divert you from your foes in order to test you but He forgave you, for Allah is full of grace to those who believe."

وَمَآ أَصَٰبَكُمۡ يَوۡمَ ٱلۡتَقَى ٱلۡجَمۡعَانِ فَبِإِذۡنِ ٱللَّهِ وَلِيَعۡلَمَ ٱلۡمُؤۡمِنِينَ ١٦٦
وَلِيَعۡلَمَ ٱلَّذِينَ نَافَقُواْۚ وَقِيلَ لَهُمۡ تَعَالَوۡاْ قَٰتِلُواْ فِي سَبِيلِ ٱللَّهِ أَوِ ٱدۡفَعُواْۖ قَالُواْ لَوۡ نَعۡلَمُ
قِتَالٗا لَّٱتَّبَعۡنَٰكُمۡۗ هُمۡ لِلۡكُفۡرِ يَوۡمَئِذٍ أَقۡرَبُ مِنۡهُمۡ لِلۡإِيمَٰنِۚ يَقُولُونَ
بِأَفۡوَٰهِهِم مَّا لَيۡسَ فِي قُلُوبِهِمۡۚ وَٱللَّهُ أَعۡلَمُ بِمَا يَكۡتُمُونَ ١٦٧
ٱلَّذِينَ قَالُواْ لِإِخۡوَٰنِهِمۡ وَقَعَدُواْ لَوۡ أَطَاعُونَا مَا قُتِلُواْۗ قُلۡ فَٱدۡرَءُواْ عَنۡ أَنفُسِكُمُ
ٱلۡمَوۡتَ إِن كُنتُمۡ صَٰدِقِينَ ١٦٨

What you suffered on the day the two armies met, was by the command of Allah, so that He might mark out the believers, (166)
And mark out the hypocrites also, who when told: "Come, fight in the way of Allah, or (at least) drive (the foe from your city)," they said: "Had we known

that it would come to a fight, we would certainly have followed you." They were that day nearer to unbelief than to faith, saying with their lips what was not in their hearts, but Allah has full knowledge of all they conceal. (167)
(They are) the ones who say (of their brothers), while they themselves remained behind: "If only they had listened to us, they would not have been killed." Say: "Avert death from your own selves, if you speak the truth." (168)

These verses explain the wisdom behind the trial that the Muslims faced. It was by the commandment of Allah and its purpose was to separate the true believers from the hypocrites, so that everyone would know who, in their community, were trustworthy and dependable and those who were not. This trial was necessary for the purgation of the Muslim community. If the true and sincere Muslims and the hypocrites were left unsorted as before, the rot could affect and ultimately destroy the entire community.

Wa qīla lahum ta'ālaw (These were told: "Come ...) refers to a group of the hypocrites who were called upon to join and participate in jihād on this occasion, reminding them of the reward for their efforts, whether they were victorious or the enemy backed down, the purpose of defending the community would be achieved. But they did not respond to this call for jihād and instead tried to cover their hypocrisy and cowardice by insisting that they did not believe there would be any fight between the Muslims and their enemies. Moreover, they made out that if they believed there would be fighting, they would surely have gone forth to fight. The Qur'ān comments that they were nearer to unbelief (*kufr*) than belief (*īmān*) while they offered these false excuses to cover their weakness, hypocrisy and cowardice. They uttered with their mouths what was not in their hearts for Allah knew what they concealed in their hearts.

The Qur'ān says that they sat back in their homes, and while some of their friends and relatives joined the jihād and were killed, they said that had these people listened to them and remained at their homes like them they would not have been killed. They thus betrayed their motive, the fear of death, for not joining the jihād. That was the real reason why they so desperately tried to avoid joining the jihād. What really held them back was their cowardice and hypocrisy. They falsely excused themselves saying that they did not see any possibility of war. At the end, the Qur'ān asks them that if they were so versed in matters of life and death, they should first of all try to save themselves from their own doom.

وَلَا تَحْسَبَنَّ ٱلَّذِينَ قُتِلُوا۟ فِى سَبِيلِ ٱللَّهِ أَمْوَٰتًۢا ۚ بَلْ أَحْيَآءٌ عِندَ رَبِّهِمْ يُرْزَقُونَ ﴿١٦٩﴾
فَرِحِينَ بِمَآ ءَاتَىٰهُمُ ٱللَّهُ مِن فَضْلِهِۦ وَيَسْتَبْشِرُونَ بِٱلَّذِينَ لَمْ يَلْحَقُوا۟ بِهِم مِّنْ خَلْفِهِمْ
أَلَّا خَوْفٌ عَلَيْهِمْ وَلَا هُمْ يَحْزَنُونَ ﴿١٧٠﴾
۞ يَسْتَبْشِرُونَ بِنِعْمَةٍ مِّنَ ٱللَّهِ وَفَضْلٍ وَأَنَّ ٱللَّهَ لَا يُضِيعُ أَجْرَ ٱلْمُؤْمِنِينَ ﴿١٧١﴾

Think not of those who are killed in Allah's way as dead. Nay, they live, finding their sustenance in the presence of their Sovereign Sustainer; (169)
They rejoice at the favour Allah has bestowed on them, and are happy for those left behind, who have not yet joined them that they will have no fear nor will they have (cause to) grieve. (170)
They rejoice in the grace and the bounty from Allah, and that Allah wastes not the reward of the believers. (171)

Warning the hypocrites

This admonition is directed at the hypocrites to warn them not to regard those who die striving in the cause of Allah as dead. In fact these hypocrites, rather than the martyrs, are dead. The martyrs are alive and are enjoying the blessings of their Sustainer in His presence. These hypocrites, due to their ignorance, mourn their passing away and pity them for being killed while saying that had they followed their advice they would still be alive. However, they are gravely mistaken for the martyrs are happy, enjoying the special blessings of their Sovereign Sustainer without any fear or grief. While the hypocrites express grief over their death, the martyrs continuously receive glad news about their children who follow in their footsteps, eagerly waiting to join them and enjoy a similar status and blessings, without any fear of the future or any grief about their past.

Special position of martyrs' believing descendants

The Qur'ān has, at several places, mentioned that the offspring of the sincere believers and members of their families, who, like them, lived and died as true believers, will also be joined with them in Paradise. They will be raised to similarly exalted status though some of them, on the basis of their own deeds, did not qualify for a similar high position. This is the special blessing of Allah upon the martyrs and the truthful. All their believing children will be brought together with them to perfect their ultimate sense of happiness. For this, the ranks of the predecessors will not be lowered. Instead, the ranks of their descendants will be raised to bring them together. We shall further discuss this issue in our comments on Sūrah at-Ṭur[54].

By reflecting on these verses, we can realise how eloquently the Qur'ān has removed the evil effects of the whispering campaign of the hypocrites to demoralise the Muslims in general and the families and the children of the martyrs in particular.

ٱلَّذِينَ ٱسْتَجَابُوا۟ لِلَّهِ وَٱلرَّسُولِ مِنۢ بَعْدِ مَآ أَصَابَهُمُ ٱلْقَرْحُ ۚ لِلَّذِينَ أَحْسَنُوا۟ مِنْهُمْ
وَٱتَّقَوْا۟ أَجْرٌ عَظِيمٌ ﴿١٧٢﴾
ٱلَّذِينَ قَالَ لَهُمُ ٱلنَّاسُ إِنَّ ٱلنَّاسَ قَدْ جَمَعُوا۟ لَكُمْ فَٱخْشَوْهُمْ فَزَادَهُمْ إِيمَٰنًا وَقَالُوا۟
حَسْبُنَا ٱللَّهُ وَنِعْمَ ٱلْوَكِيلُ ﴿١٧٣﴾
فَٱنقَلَبُوا۟ بِنِعْمَةٍ مِّنَ ٱللَّهِ وَفَضْلٍ لَّمْ يَمْسَسْهُمْ سُوٓءٌ وَٱتَّبَعُوا۟ رِضْوَٰنَ ٱللَّهِ ۗ وَٱللَّهُ ذُو فَضْلٍ
عَظِيمٍ ﴿١٧٤﴾
إِنَّمَا ذَٰلِكُمُ ٱلشَّيْطَٰنُ يُخَوِّفُ أَوْلِيَآءَهُۥ فَلَا تَخَافُوهُمْ وَخَافُونِ إِن كُنتُم مُّؤْمِنِينَ ﴿١٧٥﴾

Of those who answered the call of Allah and the Messenger, even after injury had afflicted them – for those who do good and refrain from evil, there is a great reward for them. (172)
Those to whom people said: "A great army is gathering against you, so be afraid of them", but it (only) increased their faith. And they said: "For us Allah is sufficient, and an excellent guardian is He." (173)
And they returned with grace and bounty from Allah, while no harm touched them. They followed Allah's good pleasure and Allah is the Possessor of bounties unlimited. (174)
It is only the Satan that suggests to you the fear of his allies. Do not be afraid of them, but fear Me, if you are (true) believers. (175)

High morale of the sincere believers after the setback at Uḥud

The words "of those (*al-ladhīna*)" refer to the true believers mentioned above making the verse mirror the prevalent situation at the time. Thus, a principle stated in the previous verse (172) finds a definitive context here. In other words, this great reward is reserved only for those sincere believers of high resolve and faith who were neither disheartened nor discouraged by the setback at Uḥud and who immediately thereafter enthusiastically responded

54. Cf. The Qur'ān, 52:21 and 13:22-23 (Translator).

to the call of Allah and His Messenger for a fresh venture in pursuit of the retreating enemy.

Books of history and *sīrah* say that in the wake of the Muslim defeat in the battle of Uḥud, the Makkan army decided to beat a hasty retreat and left the field. On the their way back at al-Rawḥā', Abū Sufyān and his commanders realised that they had made a serious mistake by beating such a hasty retreat. They could have finished off the tiny state of Madīnah. With this in mind, they tried to reorganise their forces. To harass the Muslims, they used the services of the hypocrites who spread the rumour that the Quraysh were preparing to launch a fresh attack against Madīnah with fresh arms and men. On hearing this news, the Prophet, peace be upon him, ordered the Muslims to get ready to pursue the Quraysh army. This Muslim army consisted entirely of those who had previously participated in the battle against the disbelievers. This was a precautionary measure, most probably to keep this fighting force free of any hypocrites. The Prophet, peace be upon him, pursued the Quraysh up to Hamrā' al-Asad, some eight miles from Madīnah. When Abū Sufyān found out that the morale of the Muslims was still high and unbeaten, he abandoned his scheme and hastened to Makkah. And the Muslims returned to Madīnah, successfully achieving their purpose.

In the words, *lil-l ladhīna aḥsanū min-hum wa ttaqaw* (for those who do good and refrain from evil), the term *"aḥsanū"* is used in the sense of doing one's best to meet one's obligations of loyalty and obedience toward Allah and His messenger, while the term *taqwā* here means keeping clear of all traces of hypocrisy. This is an extremely high rank and the status of those striving for it depends on their sincerity and their practical deeds and performance.

Alladhīna qāla lahumu-nnāsu...(those to whom people said...) These words describe the reaction of the above-mentioned believers, highly determined and sincere – the people of *iḥsān.* When the hypocrites told them that the Quraysh were about to launch another attack with fresh forces and arms, they did not panic and instead this news only reinforced their belief and strengthened their resolve. The more water is drawn out of a well with copious resource, the more water gushes out. And a bonfire consumes wet wood and burns all the more furiously. Similar is the case of the people of strong faith and high resolve. Instead of weakening or slowing them down, the obstructions and hardships that they face steel their determination in the pursuit of their goal. Every trial or difficulty gives them a fresh impetus to bring to the fore their hidden capabilities and every trial opens for them a new door to fresh achievements. "The more stressed my feelings are, the more easily they flow," says a great Urdu poet.

Verses 156-189

Wa qālū ḥasbunā-llāh wa niʿma-l wakīl **(And they said: "For us Allah is sufficient, and an excellent guardian is He)"**

This is the practical manifestation of the increase in the believers' faith referred to above in the words: "it (only) increased their faith". The real source of all moral power and spiritual strength of the believers is their faith: "For us, Allah is sufficient." A believer firmly believes that all powers and control rests with Allah alone, without His sharing them with anyone. So why should a servant, in doing a duty prescribed for him by Allah Himself, be frightened by any other power? The best power that a servant can entrust his affairs to is Allah. Why should one who thus entrusts his affairs to his best Guardian, Allah, panic or be assailed by feelings of fear and anxiety?

"It is only the Satan that suggests to you the fear of his allies"

In other words, all feelings of fear and panic in the believers are planted by the Satan to demoralise them and frighten them with fear of his allies. "Do not fear them but fear Me alone, if you are true believers", the Qur'ān reminds the believers. The words "Satan and his allies" here, clearly refer to the Quraysh and their confederates. They have no real power nor can they pose any real threat to the Muslims. The hypocrites tried to weaken and demoralise the believers by these imaginary dangers, to make them abandon their obligations to Allah and His cause.

وَلَا يَحْزُنكَ ٱلَّذِينَ يُسَٰرِعُونَ فِى ٱلْكُفْرِ ۚ إِنَّهُمْ لَن يَضُرُّوا۟ ٱللَّهَ شَيْـًٔا ۗ يُرِيدُ ٱللَّهُ أَلَّا يَجْعَلَ
لَهُمْ حَظًّا فِى ٱلْءَاخِرَةِ ۖ وَلَهُمْ عَذَابٌ عَظِيمٌ ﴿١٧٦﴾
إِنَّ ٱلَّذِينَ ٱشْتَرَوُا۟ ٱلْكُفْرَ بِٱلْإِيمَٰنِ لَن يَضُرُّوا۟ ٱللَّهَ شَيْـًٔا وَلَهُمْ عَذَابٌ أَلِيمٌ ﴿١٧٧﴾
وَلَا يَحْسَبَنَّ ٱلَّذِينَ كَفَرُوٓا۟ أَنَّمَا نُمْلِى لَهُمْ خَيْرٌ لِّأَنفُسِهِمْ ۚ إِنَّمَا نُمْلِى لَهُمْ لِيَزْدَادُوٓا۟ إِثْمًا ۚ
وَلَهُمْ عَذَابٌ مُّهِينٌ ﴿١٧٨﴾
مَّا كَانَ ٱللَّهُ لِيَذَرَ ٱلْمُؤْمِنِينَ عَلَىٰ مَآ أَنتُمْ عَلَيْهِ حَتَّىٰ يَمِيزَ ٱلْخَبِيثَ مِنَ ٱلطَّيِّبِ ۗ وَمَا كَانَ
ٱللَّهُ لِيُطْلِعَكُمْ عَلَى ٱلْغَيْبِ وَلَٰكِنَّ ٱللَّهَ يَجْتَبِى مِن رُّسُلِهِۦ مَن يَشَآءُ ۖ فَـَٔامِنُوا۟ بِٱللَّهِ وَرُسُلِهِۦ ۚ وَإِن
تُؤْمِنُوا۟ وَتَتَّقُوا۟ فَلَكُمْ أَجْرٌ عَظِيمٌ ﴿١٧٩﴾

Let not those grieve you who rush headlong into unbelief: surely they cannot harm Allah in any way. Allah desires to assign no portion for them in the hereafter; and for them awaits a severe punishment. (176)

Those who bartered away faith for unbelief, not the least harm will they do to Allah; there is in store for them a painful punishment. (177)
Let not the unbelievers think that our respite given to them is good for them. We grant them respite that they may increase in their evildoing, and they will have a shameful punishment. (178)
Allah will not leave the believers in the state in which you are now, until He sets apart the bad from the good. Nor will He disclose to you the secrets of the unseen. But He chooses whomsoever He pleases of His messengers. So believe in Allah and His messengers; if you believe and act righteously, you will have a great reward. (179)

An aside addressed to the Prophet, peace be upon him

These verses are addressed to the Prophet, peace be upon him, and the Muslims and represent a digression in the discourse. From the preceding verses and as mentioned in the introduction to the sūrah, there were some among the ranks of the believers who were in fact mere hypocrites.

After the setback of Uḥud suffered by the Muslims, some of these hypocrites openly reverted to their previous state of *kufr* while others began to pave the way back for their reversion. They laboured under the false illusion that they could defeat the new religion – Islam – with the support and help of its arch enemies, the Quraysh. All their efforts were from now onwards directed against Islam and the Muslims, while offering every possible help and support to the unbelievers and their cause. Commenting on this situation, the Qur'ān tells the Muslims that they need not be overly worried about the machinations of the hypocrites and their allies. They cannot in the least frustrate Allah and His cause. Allah wishes that those who prefer unbelief to belief should have no portion in the life hereafter, so He allows them a free rein to condemn themselves by their own actions. A painful chastisement is in store for such people in the life hereafter. They are given respite despite their hostility. What they regard as their success is in fact meant to prove the argument against them so that when their measure of sins is filled, they would be destroyed. A humiliating chastisement awaits them, both in this life and in the one to come.

The higher wisdom behind the event of Uḥud

"Allah will not leave the believers in the state in which you are now": This refers to the wisdom behind the trial of the Muslims at the battle of Uḥud. The Muslim community, the verse says, had so far been comprised of various elements, a mixed lot, with the raw and immature, the good and bad, and sincere believers side by side with the hypocrites. This situation could not continue as it was clearly against Divine wisdom. The community raised for the guidance of humankind could not continue to be a hotchpotch of diverse elements. So Allah willed to separate the true and the sincere believers from the false claimants to belief, to provide the faithful believers an opportunity to flourish and develop their latent capabilities in order to serve the cause of Allah.

Giving the knowledge of the unseen to all Muslims so that they would recognise true believers from the hypocrites in their ranks, is against the Divine law; the knowledge of the unseen is not for everyone to enjoy. Such knowledge of the unseen is granted by Allah only to some of His chosen messengers, giving them whatever knowledge of the unseen He chooses to give them. Another way of sorting out the true and the false within the Muslim community was through a process of test and trial that was fully in accord with the law that Allah has laid down for this purpose. The battle of Uḥud itself was one such test that the Muslim community was put through and, at the end of it, the two groups stood out clearly distinct from each other.

"So believe in Allah and His messengers"

This is an admonition to the Muslims to remember the essential lesson of this trial and the blessings that accrued from this trial while exhorting them to do their best to fulfil their obligations of *īmān* (faith) and *taqwā* (God-consciousness). Thus after this moral and spiritual purgation, the evil of hypocrisy would never raise its head among them. The verb 'believe' is used here in its fullest sense, with a promise of a great reward at the end.

وَلَا يَحْسَبَنَّ ٱلَّذِينَ يَبْخَلُونَ بِمَآ ءَاتَىٰهُمُ ٱللَّهُ مِن فَضْلِهِۦ هُوَ خَيْرًا لَّهُم ۖ بَلْ هُوَ شَرٌّ
لَّهُمْ ۖ سَيُطَوَّقُونَ مَا بَخِلُوا۟ بِهِۦ يَوْمَ ٱلْقِيَٰمَةِ ۗ وَلِلَّهِ مِيرَٰثُ ٱلسَّمَٰوَٰتِ وَٱلْأَرْضِ ۗ وَٱللَّهُ بِمَا
تَعْمَلُونَ خَبِيرٌ ١٨٠
لَّقَدْ سَمِعَ ٱللَّهُ قَوْلَ ٱلَّذِينَ قَالُوٓا۟ إِنَّ ٱللَّهَ فَقِيرٌ وَنَحْنُ أَغْنِيَآءُ ۘ سَنَكْتُبُ مَا قَالُوا۟
وَقَتْلَهُمُ ٱلْأَنۢبِيَآءَ بِغَيْرِ حَقٍّ وَنَقُولُ ذُوقُوا۟ عَذَابَ ٱلْحَرِيقِ ١٨١
ذَٰلِكَ بِمَا قَدَّمَتْ أَيْدِيكُمْ وَأَنَّ ٱللَّهَ لَيْسَ بِظَلَّٰمٍ لِّلْعَبِيدِ ١٨٢

And let not those who covetously withhold the gifts which Allah has given them of His grace that it is good for them: nay, it is bad for them. That to which they so covetously cling will, on the day of judgement, be hung about their necks. To Allah belongs the heritage of the heavens and the earth; and Allah is well acquainted with all that you do. (180)

Allah has indeed heard the saying of those who said: "Behold, Allah is poor while we are rich!" We shall certainly record their word and the killing of the prophets in defiance of right, and We shall say to them: "Taste (now) the punishment of the burning fire! (181)

"This is because of the (unrighteous deeds) which your hands sent on before you, for Allah is not in the least unjust to His servants." (182)

Weakness of the hypocrites in spending in Allah's cause

Hypocrites are unwilling to make any sacrifice whether in terms of their persons or their wealth. The Muslims are warned here to guard against this moral weakness. Those who are reluctant to spend in the cause of Allah out of what He has granted them; not as a privilege owed to them but purely out of His bounty, they should not think that they are doing something very beneficial for their future life. The wealth that they hoard by neglecting their obligations and keeping back what they owe to Allah will be put around their necks as shackles. And the ornaments and necklaces of gold that are paraded as trophies of pride and beauty will on that day prove to be so many instruments of their humiliation and punishment.

The verse goes on to say that the heavens and the earth and whatever is in them all belong to Allah alone and will ultimately return to Him. Whatever human beings are given in this life is to test them. And He is fully aware of how we have been using or misusing the gifts given to us by Him. All human beings will be called to account and be judged in the light of His faultless, all-comprehensive knowledge. He will reward or punish them depending on their performance in their earthly life.

Allah has indeed heard the saying of those who said: "Behold, Allah is poor while we are rich!"

Hypocrites mock Allah's appeal to spend

This is an admonition and a warning to the hypocrites for the way they mocked, in their private meetings, the Qur'ānic call to spend in Allah's cause. Thus when the Qur'ān called upon Muslims to give a goodly loan to Allah, they mocked this call by saying 'Allah has become poor while we are richer, so we are being asked to loan to Him.' Most of these hypocrites were originally from the Jews and they mocked Allah and the call to spend in His cause, as their predecessors are reported in the Qur'ān: "The Jews say: "God's hand is tied up."[56]

A subtle point of eloquence

The Qur'ānic response ("We shall certainly record their word") to their mockery is extremely significant as it is expressive of great wrath and displeasure towards these people. And even more significant and suggestive is the fact that this statement is made along with "(their act) of slaying the prophets in defiance of right." In other words, this derogatory statement will be recorded along with their other crimes, including their killing Allah's prophets without any justification, a crime that the Jews had been guilty of in their history many a time. Aligning the Jews and the hypocrites together concerning their blasphemous assertion, and using a similar pronoun for the two groups go to show two things. One, with the utterance of this monstrosity, these hypocrites morally and spiritually had reverted and re-joined the community that they pretended to leave while joining the fold of Islam. Two, this mockery of the hypocrites as well as the Jewish utterance (mentioned above) are equally reprehensible crimes and will not go unpunished. They will be surely called to account: "Taste (now) the penalty of the scorching fire!" – a penalty that will bc a consequence of their misdeeds, as "Allah is not in the least unjust to His servants".

ٱلَّذِينَ قَالُوٓاْ إِنَّ ٱللَّهَ عَهِدَ إِلَيۡنَآ أَلَّا نُؤۡمِنَ لِرَسُولٍ حَتَّىٰ يَأۡتِيَنَا بِقُرۡبَانٖ
تَأۡكُلُهُ ٱلنَّارُۗ قُلۡ قَدۡ جَآءَكُمۡ رُسُلٞ مِّن قَبۡلِي بِٱلۡبَيِّنَٰتِ وَبِٱلَّذِي قُلۡتُمۡ فَلِمَ
قَتَلۡتُمُوهُمۡ إِن كُنتُمۡ صَٰدِقِينَ ١٨٣
فَإِن كَذَّبُوكَ فَقَدۡ كُذِّبَ رُسُلٞ مِّن قَبۡلِكَ جَآءُو بِٱلۡبَيِّنَٰتِ وَٱلزُّبُرِ وَٱلۡكِتَٰبِ
ٱلۡمُنِيرِ ١٨٤
كُلُّ نَفۡسٖ ذَآئِقَةُ ٱلۡمَوۡتِۗ وَإِنَّمَا تُوَفَّوۡنَ أُجُورَكُمۡ يَوۡمَ ٱلۡقِيَٰمَةِۖ فَمَن زُحۡزِحَ
عَنِ ٱلنَّارِ وَأُدۡخِلَ ٱلۡجَنَّةَ فَقَدۡ فَازَۗ وَمَا ٱلۡحَيَوٰةُ ٱلدُّنۡيَآ إِلَّا مَتَٰعُ ٱلۡغُرُورِ ١٨٥
۞ لَتُبۡلَوُنَّ فِيٓ أَمۡوَٰلِكُمۡ وَأَنفُسِكُمۡ وَلَتَسۡمَعُنَّ مِنَ ٱلَّذِينَ أُوتُواْ
ٱلۡكِتَٰبَ مِن قَبۡلِكُمۡ وَمِنَ ٱلَّذِينَ أَشۡرَكُوٓاْ أَذٗى كَثِيرٗاۚ وَإِن تَصۡبِرُواْ
وَتَتَّقُواْ فَإِنَّ ذَٰلِكَ مِنۡ عَزۡمِ ٱلۡأُمُورِ ١٨٦

They (also) said: "Allah has made a contract with us not to believe in any messenger unless He showed us a sacrifice consumed by fire (from heaven)."

Say: "There came to you messengers before me, with clear signs and even with what you ask for. Why then did you kill them, if you speak the truth?" (183)
Then if they reject you, so were rejected messengers before you, who came with clear signs, scriptures, and the book of enlightenment. (184)
Every soul shall taste of death. And only on the Day of Judgment shall you be requited in full. Only he who is saved from the fire and admitted to the Garden will have attained the object (of life). For the life of this world is but an illusory enjoyment. (185)
You shall certainly be tried and tested in your possessions and in your persons; and you shall certainly hear much that will grieve you, from those who received the Scripture before you and from those who worship many gods. But if you persevere, and restrain yourselves, that indeed is the most resolute course. (186)

As the discourse moves from hypocrites to the Jews, yet another mischief of theirs is mentioned and refuted. The Prophet, peace be upon him, and the Muslims are at the same time comforted with the words that they will have to hear many more hurtful things from the People of the Book and the polytheists to test their patience and steadfastness

A Jewish shenanigan

The Jewish machinations referred here was the subterfuge that they employed to silence the Muslims telling them that God had commanded them not to affirm the claim of any would-be prophet unless he brought them a sacrifice that was consumed by a fire from heaven to show Divine acceptance. They said this purely out of mischief. The Torah does mention this miracle in the case of some prophets. For instance, in 1 Kings 18:37-38 the prophet Elijah, and in 2 Chronicles 7:1, Prophet Solomon is mentioned as having brought such a sacrifice. But nowhere in the Torah is it mentioned as a necessary condition for anyone being a true prophet or that without such a miracle no prophet is even worth serious consideration. As regards the prophecies about the final Prophet in their scriptures, no such conditions are mentioned. They came up with this excuse as a ruse for rejecting the Prophet out of sheer mischief. The Qur'ān takes into account their peculiar mind-set and instructs the Prophet to tell them that many prophets and messengers came to them before him with clear signs and with the miracle that they demanded of him. Why then did they kill these prophets? Does this not show that they are not sincere in their assertions? Even if this miracle is shown, they may still not believe, and even after witnessing it they may still obstinately persist in their rejection and come up with a fresh excuse for not responding to the call to believe.

Verses 156-189

The Prophet, peace be upon him, is further comforted and told not to worry if they persist in rejecting his call, as it was not due to any failing on his part, or because he had not brought them a miracle as demanded by them. The real reason for their refusal is their unwillingness to believe. Other prophets who preceded him were also denied and their people rejected their message although they performed miracles, and brought with them illuminating scriptures.

Bayyināt, zubur and *kitāb munīr*

Three expressions used here are *bayyināt*, *zubur* and *kitāb munīr*. *Bayyināt* means clear and perspicuous and is used as an adjective to define verses (*āyāt*). On its own, when used in the Qur'ān, the word *ayāt* is used in two senses: clear and conclusive argument or in the sense of palpable miracles.

Zubur is the plural of *zabūr* and it means a piece, fragment and a scripture. The use of *Zabūr* for the Psalms of David is well known. Here it refers to the books of various prophets that are included in the Torah.

The term *kitāb munīr* refers to the Torah, the only scripture before the revelation of the Qur'ān that can be so described.

The verse *kullu nafsin dhā'iqatu-l mawt* ("every soul shall have a taste of death") carries a message of comfort as well as a warning. It is a warning to the hypocrites and the enemies of Islam, and a message of hope and comfort for the believers. All people, believers as well as their enemies, will confront death and then return to Allah. Everyone will on the day of judgement receive his or her full reward or punishment. Those who are successful that day and enter Paradise will be the really successful ones. Compared to Paradise, the life of this world and its glitter is no more than an illusion and a mirage. The losers are those who deprive themselves of everlasting blessings in the life hereafter by pursuing the transitory glitter of this world.

"You shall certainly be tried and tested in your possessions and in your persons"

Perseverance, fortitude and *taqwā*

In these words, the Muslims are admonished to persevere in the path of *taqwā* or piety and show fortitude in the face of hardships and difficulties. They are warned that they would encounter bitter hostility and suffer losses, in terms of life as well as in property, at the hands of the People of the Book and the polytheists, to try and test their patience, self-restraint and *taqwā*. So if they, despite all these obstacles and difficulties, stand firm and fully observe and respect the Divine limits, they would have achieved the position that is the special characteristic of Allah's eminent prophets of inflexible resolve and of their devoted followers, which indeed is the key to success in this path.

وَإِذْ أَخَذَ ٱللَّهُ مِيثَٰقَ ٱلَّذِينَ أُوتُوا۟ ٱلْكِتَٰبَ لَتُبَيِّنُنَّهُۥ لِلنَّاسِ وَلَا تَكْتُمُونَهُۥ فَنَبَذُوهُ
وَرَآءَ ظُهُورِهِمْ وَٱشْتَرَوْا۟ بِهِۦ ثَمَنًا قَلِيلًا ۖ فَبِئْسَ مَا يَشْتَرُونَ ١٨٧
لَا تَحْسَبَنَّ ٱلَّذِينَ يَفْرَحُونَ بِمَآ أَتَوا۟ وَّيُحِبُّونَ أَن يُحْمَدُوا۟ بِمَا لَمْ يَفْعَلُوا۟ فَلَا تَحْسَبَنَّهُم
بِمَفَازَةٍ مِّنَ ٱلْعَذَابِ ۖ وَلَهُمْ عَذَابٌ أَلِيمٌ ١٨٨
وَلِلَّهِ مُلْكُ ٱلسَّمَٰوَٰتِ وَٱلْأَرْضِ ۗ وَٱللَّهُ عَلَىٰ كُلِّ شَىْءٍ قَدِيرٌ ١٨٩

And remember when Allah accepted a solemn pledge from those who were given the Book, saying: "Make it known to humankind, and do not conceal it," but they tossed it away behind their backs and bartered it away for a paltry price: and how evil was their bargain! (187)
Think not that those who exult in what they have brought about, and love to be praised for what they have not done, that they have escaped the punishment. They will have a painful chastisement. (188)
To Allah belongs the dominion of the heavens and the earth; and Allah has power over all things. (189)

Commandment to declare and explain the truth openly

This is the final warning given to the People of the Book in this sūrah. They were very active in their opposition to Islam, the message of truth, citing their presumed covenants with Allah. At the same time they forgot about their real covenant with Him that they would make known the teachings of Allah's scripture to all people and not conceal them. They have ignored this covenant for the paltry gain of worldly benefits. This covenant has been mentioned in both the Torah and the Injīl (Gospels) at several places in various styles and manners. In the interests of brevity, we will cite here only two. In the Torah we read:

> Therefore shall ye lay up these my words in your heart and in your soul, and bind them for a sign upon your hand, that they may be as frontlets between your eyes. And ye shall teach them your children, speaking of them when thou sittest in thine house, and when thou walkest by the way, when thou liest down, and when thou risest up. And thou shalt write them upon the doorposts of thine house, and upon thy gates: (Deuteronomy 11:18-21)

Just consider the extent to which the scripture and teachings they had been admonished to spread and explain were so completely forgotten and had distorted beyond recognition.

Similarly, in the Injīl too this admonition is found in extremely moving forms and styles and contains the following precept worth inscribing in gold letters:

> What I tell you in darkness, that speak ye in light: and what ye hear in the ear, that preach ye upon the housetops. (Matthew 10:27)

In short, the Qur'ān says, they failed to be true to their covenant with their Sovereign Sustainer and openly and shamelessly bartered away Divine law and teachings for paltry worldly benefits. At the same time, they are well pleased and proud of their performance. On top of that, they expect to be praised for something that they never did. Such people, the verse says, are not immune from Divine chastisement. They will be punished in this world while a painful punishment awaits them in the life to come.

Mafāzah

The word *mafāzah* means a place of refuge or a sanctuary.

"They love to be praised for what they have not done" refers to their failure in meeting their responsibility towards the book of Allah. They failed to disseminate its teachings openly, explain and elucidate them and to implement them in accordance with the covenant taken from them. They are guilty of gross violation of their covenant and, worse still, they distorted the Divine teachings to gain some worldly profit. Nevertheless, they still desire to be regarded as the bearers of the scripture and a people especially chosen by Allah. They consider that they alone deserve all blessings and bounties of Allah both in this world and in the life hereafter. The Qur'ān has described this wishful thinking of the People of the Scripture as *amānī* (false hopes and desires) in Sūrah al-Baqarah, verse 78[55].

"To Allah belongs the dominion of the heavens and the earth; and Allah has power over all things"

This is the reinforcement of the warning in the previous verse. All powers rest with Allah alone and no one can interfere with His decision. Those who are openly in revolt against Him are always within His grasp; He has power over all things.

55. Cf. The Qur'ān, 2:111: "And they say: 'None shall enter Paradise unless he is a Jew or a Christian.' Those are their (vain) desires. Say 'Produce your proof if you are truthful'."

VERSES 190-200: THEMATIC CONTINUITY

The conclusion of the sūrah

This segment constitutes the conclusion of the sūrah and bears a remarkable similarity to the conclusion of Sūrah al-Baqarah. The supplication in this part especially is a true reflection of the supplication with which Sūrah al-Baqarah ends.

This conclusion opens by drawing attention to a universal truth that as far as the signs of Allah are concerned, they abound in every part and corner of the heavens and the earth. As such, to believe in the message of the Prophet does not require the sign of any burnt offering consumed by a heavenly fire. For this, people need instead to open their ears to listen to Him and open their eyes to see the signs of Allah everywhere around them, while using their reason to reflect upon the purpose and wisdom behind the creation of the heavens and the earth.

The people who are upright and morally and spiritually alive remember Allah while sitting, standing and lying down during their waking hours. They ponder over the creation of the heavens and the earth and are convinced that there is a higher and nobler purpose behind their creation; they are not created merely for fun. They realise, therefore, that there must be a day of reckoning when people are judged and then rewarded or punished, depending on their performance in earthly life. They eagerly seek to guard against wasting this opportunity and supplicate to Allah against failure to live up to the nobler goal and consequent chastisement in the hereafter.

Such people do not look for, or wait for miracles to happen. When these morally and spiritually alive people hear the Prophet inviting them to Allah, they find deep resonance with it in their hearts and they eagerly respond to his call. For them, the message as well as the personal example of the Prophet, peace be upon him, turns out to be the most potent miracle transforming them completely.

Such were the people who enthusiastically responded to the call of Islam. They were ready to stand up and offer whatever sacrifices were needed in this path. Allah gives them glad tidings of acceptance of their efforts along with a great reward.

As to the opponents of truth who were trying their best to frustrate the call of Islam, no one should be deluded by their worldly success and achievements. Like everyone else, they are also given some respite in this life to test and try them, as determined by a higher wisdom behind this respite. Soon, however, this respite will come to an end and they will find that the ultimate success is for the faithful and obedient servants of Allah only.

Of the People of the Book those who, unlike others, had steadily and consistently followed the path of truth were consequently blessed in that they responded and believed in the final Prophet of Allah. They will have their full reward for their perseverance and for abiding by the truth.

The segment closes with a brief but comprehensive admonition to the Muslims to do their best to meet the responsibilities they are charged with by Allah as the final community of the faithful. In the light of these brief remarks, let us now study these verses closely:

In the creation of the heavens and the earth, and the alternation of night and day, there are indeed many signs for people of understanding, (190)

إِنَّ فِي خَلْقِ ٱلسَّمَٰوَٰتِ وَٱلْأَرْضِ
وَٱخْتِلَٰفِ ٱلَّيْلِ وَٱلنَّهَارِ لَءَايَٰتٍ لِّأُو۟لِى
ٱلْأَلْبَٰبِ ﴿١٩٠﴾

People who remember Allah, standing, sitting, and lying on their sides, and reflect on the creation of the heavens and the earth (impelling them to supplicate): "Our Sustainer! You have not created (all) this for nothing! You are far exalted to do anything in vain. So save us from the punishment of the fire. (191)

ٱلَّذِينَ يَذْكُرُونَ ٱللَّهَ قِيَٰمًا وَقُعُودًا
وَعَلَىٰ جُنُوبِهِمْ وَيَتَفَكَّرُونَ فِى خَلْقِ
ٱلسَّمَٰوَٰتِ وَٱلْأَرْضِ رَبَّنَا مَا خَلَقْتَ هَٰذَا
بَٰطِلًا سُبْحَٰنَكَ فَقِنَا عَذَابَ ٱلنَّارِ ﴿١٩١﴾

"Our Sustainer! Those You (condemn) to enter the Fire, You surely cover them with shame, and never will wrongdoers find any helpers! (192)

رَبَّنَآ إِنَّكَ مَن تُدْخِلِ ٱلنَّارَ فَقَدْ
أَخْزَيْتَهُۥ ۖ وَمَا لِلظَّٰلِمِينَ مِنْ أَنصَارٍ ﴿١٩٢﴾

"Our Sustainer! We have heard the call of one calling (us) to faith, 'Believe in your Sustainer,' and we have believed. Our Sustainer! Forgive us our sins, remove from us our ills, and gather us (at death) with the virtuous! (193)

رَّبَّنَآ إِنَّنَا سَمِعْنَا مُنَادِيًا يُنَادِى
لِلْإِيمَٰنِ أَنْ ءَامِنُوا۟ بِرَبِّكُمْ فَـَٔامَنَّا ۚ
رَبَّنَا فَٱغْفِرْ لَنَا ذُنُوبَنَا وَكَفِّرْ عَنَّا
سَيِّـَٔاتِنَا وَتَوَفَّنَا مَعَ ٱلْأَبْرَارِ ﴿١٩٣﴾

رَبَّنَا وَءَاتِنَا مَا وَعَدتَّنَا عَلَىٰ رُسُلِكَ وَلَا
تُخْزِنَا يَوْمَ ٱلْقِيَٰمَةِ ۗ إِنَّكَ لَا تُخْلِفُ ٱلْمِيعَادَ
١٩٤

"Our Sustainer! Grant us what You have promised us through Your messengers, and do not disgrace us on the Day of Judgment. Surely, You never fail to fulfil Your promise." (194)

فَٱسْتَجَابَ لَهُمْ رَبُّهُمْ أَنِّى لَآ أُضِيعُ
عَمَلَ عَٰمِلٍ مِّنكُم مِّن ذَكَرٍ أَوْ أُنثَىٰ ۖ
بَعْضُكُم مِّنۢ بَعْضٍ ۖ فَٱلَّذِينَ هَاجَرُوا۟
وَأُخْرِجُوا۟ مِن دِيَٰرِهِمْ وَأُوذُوا۟ فِى
سَبِيلِى وَقَٰتَلُوا۟ وَقُتِلُوا۟ لَأُكَفِّرَنَّ
عَنْهُمْ سَيِّـَٔاتِهِمْ وَلَأُدْخِلَنَّهُمْ جَنَّٰتٍ
تَجْرِى مِن تَحْتِهَا ٱلْأَنْهَٰرُ ثَوَابًا مِّنْ
عِندِ ٱللَّهِ ۗ وَٱللَّهُ عِندَهُۥ حُسْنُ ٱلثَّوَابِ
١٩٥

And their Sustainer has accepted of them, and answered them: "Never will I allow to be lost the work of any of you, male or female. You are members, one of another. Those who have left their homes, or been driven out of them, or suffered harm in My cause, or fought or been slain, verily, I will blot out from them their iniquities, and admit them into gardens with rivers flowing beneath. A reward from the presence of Allah, and from His presence is the best of rewards." (195)

لَا يَغُرَّنَّكَ تَقَلُّبُ ٱلَّذِينَ كَفَرُوا۟ فِى
ٱلْبِلَٰدِ ١٩٦

Let not the strutting about of the unbelievers through the land deceive you. (196)

مَتَٰعٌ قَلِيلٌ ثُمَّ مَأْوَىٰهُمْ جَهَنَّمُ ۚ
وَبِئْسَ ٱلْمِهَادُ ١٩٧

It is but a brief enjoyment, then their abode is Hell, and how evil a resting-place! (197)

لَٰكِنِ ٱلَّذِينَ ٱتَّقَوْا۟ رَبَّهُمْ لَهُمْ جَنَّٰتٌ
تَجْرِى مِن تَحْتِهَا ٱلْأَنْهَٰرُ خَٰلِدِينَ فِيهَا
نُزُلًا مِّنْ عِندِ ٱللَّهِ ۗ وَمَا عِندَ ٱللَّهِ خَيْرٌ
لِّلْأَبْرَارِ ١٩٨

On the other hand, for those who fear their Sovereign Sustainer, shall be Gardens, with rivers flowing beneath. There they will dwell (forever) – a gift from the presence of Allah. And that which is with Allah is best for the righteous. (198)

And there are, certainly, among the People of the Book, those who believe in Allah, in the revelation to you, and in the revelation to them, bowing in humility to Allah. They do not sell Allah's signs for a paltry price. For them is a reward with their Sustainer, and Allah is swift at reckoning. (199)

وَإِنَّ مِنْ أَهْلِ ٱلْكِتَٰبِ لَمَن يُؤْمِنُ
بِٱللَّهِ وَمَآ أُنزِلَ إِلَيْكُمْ وَمَآ أُنزِلَ إِلَيْهِمْ
خَٰشِعِينَ لِلَّهِ لَا يَشْتَرُونَ بِـَٔايَٰتِ ٱللَّهِ
ثَمَنًا قَلِيلًا ۗ أُو۟لَٰٓئِكَ لَهُمْ أَجْرُهُمْ
عِندَ رَبِّهِمْ ۗ إِنَّ ٱللَّهَ سَرِيعُ
ٱلْحِسَابِ ١٩٩

O you who believe! Persevere in patience and constancy; vie in such perseverance; strengthen each other; and fear Allah so that you may prosper. (200)

يَٰٓأَيُّهَا ٱلَّذِينَ ءَامَنُوا۟ ٱصْبِرُوا۟
وَصَابِرُوا۟ وَرَابِطُوا۟ وَٱتَّقُوا۟ ٱللَّهَ لَعَلَّكُمْ
تُفْلِحُونَ ٢٠٠

WORD STUDY AND EXPLANATION

إِنَّ فِى خَلْقِ ٱلسَّمَٰوَٰتِ وَٱلْأَرْضِ وَٱخْتِلَٰفِ ٱلَّيْلِ وَٱلنَّهَارِ لَءَايَٰتٍ لِّأُو۟لِى ٱلْأَلْبَٰبِ
١٩٠
ٱلَّذِينَ يَذْكُرُونَ ٱللَّهَ قِيَٰمًا وَقُعُودًا وَعَلَىٰ جُنُوبِهِمْ وَيَتَفَكَّرُونَ فِى خَلْقِ ٱلسَّمَٰوَٰتِ
وَٱلْأَرْضِ رَبَّنَا مَا خَلَقْتَ هَٰذَا بَٰطِلًا سُبْحَٰنَكَ فَقِنَا عَذَابَ ٱلنَّارِ ١٩١
رَبَّنَآ إِنَّكَ مَن تُدْخِلِ ٱلنَّارَ فَقَدْ أَخْزَيْتَهُۥ ۖ وَمَا لِلظَّٰلِمِينَ مِنْ أَنصَارٍ ١٩٢

In the creation of the heavens and the earth, and the alternation of night and day, there are indeed many signs for people of understanding, (190)
People who remember Allah, standing, sitting, and lying on their sides, and reflect on the creation of the heavens and the earth (impelling them to supplicate): "Our Sustainer! You have not created (all) this for nothing! You are far exalted to do anything in vain. So save us from the punishment of the fire. (191)
"Our Sustainer! Those You (condemn) to enter the Fire, You surely cover them with shame, and never will wrongdoers find any helpers! (192)

The vision of the insightful people

As against the blind opponents of truth who were solely driven by their lusts and desires in their opposition with the false excuses detailed above, these verses speak of the wise and insightful people, honest and upright, who welcome the truth that finds resonance with their nature and common sense. They are deeply conscious of Allah and always remember Him whatever the conditions and circumstances. They reflect on the creation of the heavens and the earth and realise that this vast and immense universe is definitely created for a higher purpose. The life on earth will not end with physical death, for there must be a day of judgement and recompense when the good and the evil should be rewarded or punished for their actions, to manifest the Divine wisdom behind the creation, life and the universe.

These verses merely make a passing reference to the signs in the creation of the heavens and the earth and the alternation of night and day. At other places in the Qur'ān, however, these signs are described in great detail, further elucidating diverse aspects of these signs in the physical universe. These signs manifest not only the awesome power of the Creator but also the great wisdom that lies behind the creation, and the infinite compassion and mercy that comprehends everything. These signs show in the creation great diversity as well as a marvellous harmony within its various and diverse parts, clearly suggesting that far from being an accident or a chance happening this universe is the creation of an all-powerful, all wise, most compassionate, an all forgiving, all-hearing and all-knowing Creator. As such, it cannot continue infinitely, or come to a sudden end, without differentiating and sorting out the good from the evil. For, in such a case, it would mean that it has no creator or controller that it came into existence by chance and once it is created it will continue to exist forever. Or that even if it has a creator, and a God, He is, God forbid, essentially a capricious God Who has made some people poor, others rich, some oppressors and others the oppressed, to watch their misery and enjoy Himself. Clearly, both these suppositions are at variance with the power and the wisdom witnessed in His creation. It is utterly against the majesty of such an all-knowing and all-wise God to do anything purposeless.

By contemplating the universe and the signs of power and wisdom apparent everywhere in it, one is not only led to believe in the presence of God, but also in a day of reckoning. Deeply moved by the thought of it, a person is impelled to supplicate for protection against the impending punishment and humiliation in store for those who regard this world merely as a sport and an enjoyment with no higher purpose or goal.

This is the more obvious and simple message of the above verses. Upon further consideration, we learn a few more basic and quite significant facts that are just as valuable.

Verses 190-200

Noteworthy points

(1) In the sight of the Qur'ān, the truly wise people are those who reflect over the creation and come to believe in God, its Creator, and are moved to prepare for their life hereafter. The people who fail to realise this basic truth are not really wise people, even if they measure and explore the heavens and the earth, the moon, the galaxies, stars and planets. They are not, according to the Qur'ān, the truly wise people, for how could they observe and examine even minuscule particles but miss out the most significant and obvious truth: that this universe has a creator and a God who watches over it and a day of reckoning that is inevitable.

(2) As far as the existence of God is concerned, it does not need much thinking or contemplation to arrive at this truth. His existence is a self-evident fact, or rather the most evident of all the basic truths of life and the universe. Each and every part of this universe proclaims His existence and our own nature bears testimony to it. Human reason, if it is sound, can see Him just as healthy eyes can see the sun. To reach God and to find Him, one only has to think of Him and remember Him. The question of the life hereafter is, however, somewhat different and calls for serious thought and reflection.

(3) As to the remembrance of Allah, it is required at all times and conditions, sitting, standing, morning or evening, in hardship as well as in ease, without any specific limits. Just as breathing is necessary for our physical life, so the remembrance of Allah is necessary for our spiritual health and welfare. From these verses, it is quite clear that the most eminent characteristic of wise people is their remembrance of Allah; they are never heedless or oblivious to it.

(4) Just as the remembrance of Allah is necessary, so also is contemplation; the two go together. In the absence of contemplation, remembrance is often reduced to a verbal exercise and can hardly help in gaining deeper insight into the higher wisdom. An essential characteristic of the remembrance of the wise is that it is accompanied with contemplation. In their case, the two go hand in hand. Pondering and reflecting, they gradually and steadily grow in wisdom and insight, as it is through contemplation alone that they attain the certainty of belief in the life hereafter.

(5) Through their reflection over creation, the people of understanding realise that it is not created in vain or merely for sport and amusement, but has a higher purpose and wisdom behind it. They also realise that there must inevitably be a day of reckoning when the purpose of its creation is fully achieved through the fullest manifestation of perfect justice. Through this, they also realise that the real humiliation will, on that day, be the

lot of those who place all their hopes on notions of false intercession and intercessors. These unfortunate people will have no helpers or supporters to intervene on their behalf with Allah[56].

رَّبَّنَآ إِنَّنَا سَمِعۡنَا مُنَادِيٗا يُنَادِي لِلۡإِيمَٰنِ أَنۡ ءَامِنُواْ بِرَبِّكُمۡ فَـَٔامَنَّاۚ رَبَّنَا فَٱغۡفِرۡ لَنَا
ذُنُوبَنَا وَكَفِّرۡ عَنَّا سَيِّـَٔاتِنَا وَتَوَفَّنَا مَعَ ٱلۡأَبۡرَارِ ١٩٣
رَبَّنَا وَءَاتِنَا مَا وَعَدتَّنَا عَلَىٰ رُسُلِكَ وَلَا تُخۡزِنَا يَوۡمَ ٱلۡقِيَٰمَةِۗ إِنَّكَ لَا تُخۡلِفُ ٱلۡمِيعَادَ ١٩٤
فَٱسۡتَجَابَ لَهُمۡ رَبُّهُمۡ أَنِّي لَآ أُضِيعُ عَمَلَ عَٰمِلٖ مِّنكُم مِّن ذَكَرٍ أَوۡ أُنثَىٰۖ بَعۡضُكُم مِّنۢ
بَعۡضٖۖ فَٱلَّذِينَ هَاجَرُواْ وَأُخۡرِجُواْ مِن دِيَٰرِهِمۡ وَأُوذُواْ فِي سَبِيلِي وَقَٰتَلُواْ وَقُتِلُواْ
لَأُكَفِّرَنَّ عَنۡهُمۡ سَيِّـَٔاتِهِمۡ وَلَأُدۡخِلَنَّهُمۡ جَنَّٰتٖ تَجۡرِي مِن تَحۡتِهَا ٱلۡأَنۡهَٰرُ ثَوَابٗا
مِّنۡ عِندِ ٱللَّهِۚ وَٱللَّهُ عِندَهُۥ حُسۡنُ ٱلثَّوَابِ ١٩٥

"Our Sustainer! We have heard the call of one calling (us) to faith, 'Believe in your Sustainer,' and we have believed. Our Sustainer! Forgive us our sins, remove from us our ills, and gather us (at death) with the virtuous! (193)
"Our Sustainer! Grant us what You have promised us through Your messengers, and do not disgrace us on the Day of Judgment. Surely, You never fail to fulfil Your promise." (194)
And their Sustainer has accepted of them, and answered them: "Never will I allow to be lost the work of any of you, whether male or female. You are members, one of another. Those who have left their homes, or have been driven out of them, or suffered harm in My cause, or fought or been slain, verily, I will blot out from them their iniquities, and admit them into gardens with rivers flowing beneath. (This is a) reward from the presence of Allah, and from His presence is the best of rewards." (195)

The response of the truly wise people to the Islamic call

In these verses is portrayed the attitude of the wise people mentioned above concerning the message of Allah and His messenger. They do not engage in futile quibbling, nor do they ask for miracles. They are moved by the message of Allah's Messenger; to them his message is the cry of their own, the two being in perfect resonance with each other. The messenger calls them to believe in Allah Whose presence they find evident in the very depths of their own being. For them, therefore, the countenance of the Messenger is a sufficient miracle.

56. If the validity of false intercession on the day of judgement is admitted, it turns the world into a meaningless play, as in the case of a flat refusal to believe in the life hereafter.

So when they hear his call, they do not turn away but enthusiastically respond and supplicate to their Creator to forgive their sins, wipe off their lapses, and include them among His truly faithful servants.

A subtle allusion to the People of the Book

The words, "to make us die with the truly pious" are expressive of their desire to be included among the truly faithful servants of Allah. That is, when they die they should be in the company of those truthful servants who, till the last moments of their life on earth, remained faithful to their covenant with their Sustainer. As discussed at another place, the core meaning of the term *birr*[57] is fidelity, fulfilment of promises and covenants, and discharging one's duties and obligations. In this, there is also a subtle allusion to the People of the Book from whom a covenant was taken to support and respond to the final Messenger, but who contrary to their covenant, were at the time exerting all their efforts and energies in opposing him and his message. It is worth bearing in mind that it is the People of the Book who form the backdrop of the discourse here.

A supplication that meets immediate acceptance

Fa-stajāba lahum rabbuhum (And their Sustainer has accepted of them) is a glad tiding of the acceptance of their supplication and this is described in the most eloquent words. This is, as it were, the moment the supplicants are forthwith met with the gracious acceptance from their Sustainer. This is when the supplications are offered with sincerity, at the most appropriate time and place, and when they receive instantaneous Divine acceptance.

Eloquent significance of the supplication

It is also worth noting here that the support of the wise people for the truth is not mentioned in the form of a claim to believe and support but is rather couched in the form of a supplication. This shows they were fully aware of their onerous responsibilities that go with the declaration, "We have believed" and that they are fully conscious of the hardships of the path. So, instead of proclaiming their *īmān* with pride, they submit to their Sustainer with modesty and extreme humility, saying in fact that just as He granted them the power to say "we have believed", so they hope He would also forgive all their past and future lapses and help them shoulder their responsibilities and successfully face the hardships of the path.

57. Please see comments on verses 44 and 177 of Sūrah al-Baqarah, *Pondering over the Qur'ān*, vol. 1.

"Never will I allow to be lost the work of any of you, whether male or female"

Encouragement to the weak and oppressed

This is an encouragement to the believers who were experiencing severe torture and persecution for actively responding to the Islamic message during its most critical phase. The torture and persecution, however, could not make the believers abandon their faith and revert to their previous state of unbelief.

The Muslim community was passing through a phase of *hijrah* and jihād. The enormous hardships that the believers encountered are referred to in the verse: "those who have left their homes, or been driven out of them, or suffered harm in My cause, or fought or been slain". They are the ones who supported the cause of truth, risking whatever they possessed for the love of Allah. These early Muslims included the free as well as slaves, and men and women who suffered horrendous forms of torture and persecution, so reprehensible in fact, that just reading about them makes one's hair stand on end. The enemies of Islam specially targeted weak Muslims, women and the slaves. It was indeed the miracle of Islam that all these hardships and persecution failed to make even a single Muslim renounce his or her belief. The poor and weak ones among them proved to be far more firm and resolute during this trial.

The special message of consolation and encouragement given in the above verse for the oppressed Muslims has a special significance. Allah promises them: "Never will I allow to be lost the work of any of you." They served the cause of His *dīn*, Islam, and they all, men and women, will receive their full recompense. The addition of the words "whether a male or a female", confirms that Allah's promise of reward includes all men and all women striving and suffering for the Divine cause, and striving side by side. How great an encouragement it must have been for these oppressed men and women, and how important the light of hope that it enkindled in the hearts of these oppressed women who were subjected to the worst forms of persecution simply because of embracing Islam.

"You are members, one of another"

Men and women are equal and possess similar rights

These words explain why in the sight of Allah the deeds of both men and women have equal importance. They are both from the same species – human beings – and are children of the same parents, Adam and Eve. They both possess physical bodies made of flesh and bones. In these words, the Qur'ān repudiates all false notions and religious concepts that taught that, compared to man; woman was a lower creature. As we hope to discuss this issue in the next sūrah, here we would confine ourselves to this brief hint.

Action and the reaction

"*Thawābun min 'indi Allāh* (a reward from the presence of Allah)"

The word *thāba, yathūbu, thawban* originally means to return and to come back and one of its derivatives is *thawāb* that signifies the fruit or the result of one's work or efforts, good or bad depending on the nature and quality of one's action. However, it is mostly used in a good sense, as something good gained in consequence of a good deed. By describing the enduring rewards and gifts to be granted by Allah to His servants for their small and insignificant deeds as *thawāb,* our Sustainer Most Gracious has immensely enhanced the importance of human deeds. Otherwise, there is hardly any comparison between the abiding reward in the hereafter and trifling human deeds in this worldly life, just as it is impossible to compare a miniscule speck of dust to the mighty Himalayas. It is this wide gap between the deeds of humans and their enduring reward from Allah that the words "from the presence of Allah, and from His presence is the best of rewards" seek so beautifully to bridge. It is like saying in fact that though this is a reward for your efforts and works, it is from Allah Who has infinite treasures of the best of rewards. He is Most Generous and He blesses whomsoever He wishes with whatever and howsoever He wills.

لَا يَغُرَّنَّكَ تَقَلُّبُ ٱلَّذِينَ كَفَرُوا۟ فِى ٱلْبِلَٰدِ ﴿١٩٦﴾
مَتَٰعٌ قَلِيلٌ ثُمَّ مَأْوَىٰهُمْ جَهَنَّمُ ۚ وَبِئْسَ ٱلْمِهَادُ ﴿١٩٧﴾
لَٰكِنِ ٱلَّذِينَ ٱتَّقَوْا۟ رَبَّهُمْ لَهُمْ جَنَّٰتٌ تَجْرِى مِن تَحْتِهَا ٱلْأَنْهَٰرُ خَٰلِدِينَ فِيهَا نُزُلًا
مِّنْ عِندِ ٱللَّهِ ۗ وَمَا عِندَ ٱللَّهِ خَيْرٌ لِّلْأَبْرَارِ ﴿١٩٨﴾

Let not the strutting about of the unbelievers through the land deceive you. (196)
It is but a brief enjoyment, then their abode is Hell, and how evil a resting-place! (197)
On the other hand, for those who fear their Sustainer, are gardens with rivers flowing beneath. There they will dwell (forever), a gift from the presence of Allah. And that which is with Allah is best for the righteous. (198)

***Lā-yaghurran naka...*(Let not the strutting about of the unbelievers through the land deceive you)**

These words are directed at the Muslims in general, although the singular is used while addressing a group that, as explained at another place, shows that each and every member of the group is addressed individually.

Taqallub means coming and going, moving about freely. Depending on its context, the word may also carry a sense of arrogance, exultation and strutting about proudly. It clearly refers to the dominance and control that the unbelievers at the time enjoyed over the affairs of the land while the Muslims were oppressed and weak.

Nuzūl is the food, the first thing offered to a guest on his arrival. *Matā'un qalīl* is the *khabar* (predicate) while its *mubtada'* (or subject) is omitted in order to focus the attention on the predicate.

Encouragement of Muslims

This further reinforces the message of comfort and encouragement for the weak and oppressed Muslims. Addressing the Muslims, especially the oppressed Muslims, the Qur'ān tells them that they should not be deceived by the present transient dominance of the unbelievers. It is short-lived and then they will abide in hell and that is a most evil place. They are assured that true and enduring success and prosperity is reserved only for those who embrace the life of piety and remain steadfast in its pursuit. First and foremost, their Sustainer Most Gracious will grant them Paradise as a special gift from Him, while there are much more and far better gifts that He has for His obedient servants.

وَإِنَّ مِنۡ أَهۡلِ ٱلۡكِتَٰبِ لَمَن يُؤۡمِنُ بِٱللَّهِ وَمَآ أُنزِلَ إِلَيۡكُمۡ وَمَآ أُنزِلَ إِلَيۡهِمۡ
خَٰشِعِينَ لِلَّهِ لَا يَشۡتَرُونَ بِـَٔايَٰتِ ٱللَّهِ ثَمَنٗا قَلِيلًاۚ أُوْلَٰٓئِكَ لَهُمۡ أَجۡرُهُمۡ
عِندَ رَبِّهِمۡۗ إِنَّ ٱللَّهَ سَرِيعُ ٱلۡحِسَابِ ١٩٩
يَٰٓأَيُّهَا ٱلَّذِينَ ءَامَنُواْ ٱصۡبِرُواْ وَصَابِرُواْ وَرَابِطُواْ وَٱتَّقُواْ ٱللَّهَ لَعَلَّكُمۡ تُفۡلِحُونَ
٢٠٠

And there are, certainly, among the People of the Book, those who believe in Allah, in the revelation to you, and in the revelation to them, bowing in humility to Allah. They do not sell Allah's signs for a paltry price. For them is a reward with their Sustainer, and Allah is indeed swift at reckoning. (199)
O you who believe! Persevere in patience and constancy. Vie in such perseverance and strengthen one other. And fear Allah that you may prosper. (200)

Verses 190-200

Appreciating the good people among them

As in the above verses and in the sūrah as a whole, the People of the Book have been severely criticised for their conduct and attitude. Now, as the sūrah closes, the sincere ones among them, who faithfully followed the teachings of their scriptures and later embraced Islam, are praised for their efforts and sacrifices. In this, there is an extremely subtle suggestion that the good they had in their ranks have by now been separated and absorbed in the community of Islam; and that whoever is left behind is nothing more than buttermilk with its cream removed. All such people will find their special reward waiting for them with their Sustainer. They are also assured that their promised reward will be given to them without any delay, even before their sweat has dried. This is precisely the message the words *innallāha sarī'u-l ḥisāb* (Allah is swift at reckoning) carry when used, as here, in a context of hope and comfort. Allah is very quick in settling an account!

O you who believe! Persevere in patience and constancy. Vie in such perseverance. Strengthen one another. And fear Allah so that you may prosper. (200)

This, last verse of the sūrah, sums up all the basic instructions that the Muslims needed to discharge their obligations with respect to the Islamic Sharī'ah and meeting the challenges and difficult conditions in which they found themselves. These instructions concern four matters that were to be adopted and strictly adhered to.

Patience or *ṣabr*

Firstly, they are advised about *ṣabr*[58] or patience. This has been discussed at length in our *tafsīr* of Sūrah al-Baqarah. The real essence of *ṣabr* is firm adherence to truth in the face of all difficulties and resistance, whether these emanate from within, or are extraneous and originate from without. In the absence of this moral quality of patience, and without strengthening it, no one can truly do full justice to truth and discharge his or her responsibility toward it.

Muṣābirah

Secondly, the Muslims are admonished about *muṣābirah,* meaning to persevere and be steadfast in truth in the struggle against adversaries trying

58. Refer to commentary on verses 45 and 175 of Sūrah al-Baqarah, *Pondering over the Qur'ān,* vol. 1.

to outdo them in these qualities. This was especially advised on this occasion because the armed confrontation between the Muslims and their enemies had by this time already begun. And clearly in this conflict, the party destined to win the final victory was bound to be the one that excelled the other in steadfastness and perseverance. Victory in the battlefield really depends not on numbers and arms but on the moral character and conduct of a people.

Murābiṭāh

Thirdly, the virtue *murābiṭāh* is admonished. It is a word derived from *ribāṭ al khayl* that, in its primary sense, means keeping the warhorses ready to defend and to secure borders. In modern times, tanks and jets and other weaponry have replaced the warhorses so with a change in conditions the sense of the word will also change. After patience – *muṣābirah* – the mention of *murābiṭāh* is in fact an admonition to make material preparations along with moral and spiritual preparation through *muṣābirah,* patience.

Taqwā

Fourthly, *taqwā* is enjoined. This means to safeguard sincerely and actively all laws and commandments prescribed by Allah, bearing in mind the terrible consequences of violating them. The word *taqwā* has also been discussed at length in the beginning of the *tafsīr* of Sūrah al-Baqarah.

In short, the Muslims are admonished to abide by the above four instructions to achieve true success and prosperity in this life and in the one to come.

With these last lines, Allah most graciously has enabled this humblest servant of His to complete the *tafsīr* of sūrah Āli 'Imrān. I seek His forgiveness for any lapses and mistakes and beseech Him to open our hearts to whatever is sound and correct therein.

Wa ākhiru da'wānā ani-l ḥamdu lillāhi rabbi-l 'ālamīn. Our last supplication is that all thanks and praise belongs to Allah, the Sovereign Sustainer of the universe.

Amin Ahsan Islahi,
Thursday 23 Rabī'al-Thānī 1386
11 August 1966 C.E.

Verses 190-200

INDEX

A
a lam tara, 60
'a 'aslamtum, 53
'abd, 101
'Abdullāh ibn 'Abbās, 164
'Abdullāh ibn Ubayy, 188, 220, 231
Abrahamic, 121, 122, 153-155; law, 153
Abū Sufyān, 241
'Ād, 197
Adam, 5, 27, 74, 75, 77, 93, 112, 144, 259; and Eve, 25; breathing of Allah into Adam, 22; earliest prophet, 5
aḍ-ḍāllin, 26
adhā, 173
adhillah, 185
aḥad, 129
aḥādīth (sing. *ḥadīth*), 12, 53, 54
ahl al-kitāb, 110
ahl as-sunnah, 28
aḥsanū, 241
'Ā'ishah, 28
a'izzatin, 185
ajma'īn, 147
al-Amīn; *see* Muḥammad
al-ayyām (sing. *yawm*), 199
al-Farrā', 28
'Alī, 28
Alif Lām Mīm, 1, 9, 10
Alif Lām Rā, 19
al-'ilm, 48, 51, 151, 113
'alima, 201
al-Kisā'ī, 28
al-kitāb, 51
al-qawm, 198
amān, 56
amanah, 217, 218
amānī, 250
'anat, 180
anṣār (sing. *nāṣir*), 102, 231
Anṣārūllāh, 104
'aqab (pl. *a'qāb*), 205; *see also a'qāb*
aqlām (sing. *qlam*), 88
ar-rāsikhūna fi-l 'ilm, 28
aṣ'ada, 215
awliyā', 69
Aws (tribe), 186
ayāh mutashābihāh, 25
āyāt (sing. *āyāh*), 248; *muḥkamāt*, 20; *mutashābihāt*, 22
āyatin, 99
āyatu-l kursī, 10
aymān, 134
azwāj muṭahharah, 39

B
Bacca, 136; *see also* Bakkah
Badr, 2-4, 25, 31-36, 182, 183, 185, 187, 200, 207, 211, 218, 231, 234, 237
Bakkah, 150, 155; *see also* Makkah
Ba'l, 155
Ba'lbak, 155
Banī Ismā'īl; *see* Ismā'īl
Banū Ḥārithah, 186
Banū Salamah, 186
bawwa'a, 184
Bayyināt, 248
biṭānah, 179
burhān, 24

C
Christ, 94, 95
Christian(s), 2, 4, 5, 11, 12, 26, 27, 32, 33, 43, 51, 53, 54, 57, 58, 73, 74, 79, 85, 88-90, 99, 101, 104, 110, 112-115, 117, 119, 121-123, 127, 133, 136, 138, 142, 143, 148, 149, 158, 165, 167, 173; scholars, 127
Criterion, 9, 12, 13

D
ḍa'f, 207
Daḥḥāk, 164
David, 33, 94, 98, 156, 248; *see also* Dāwūd
da'wah, 166
Dāwūd, 207; *see also* David
Deuteronomy, 112, 249
dīn, 1, 40, 51, 56, 70, 73, 259

E
Elijah, 100, 247
Eve; *see* Adam

F
Farāhī, Ustādh, 28, 56, 109, 128, 146, 155
fashala, 185, 213
fatāwā, 130
faẓẓ, 229
fi-sabilīllāh, 34
fi-sabīliṭ-ṭāghūt, 34
fisq, 172

G
Genesis, 112, 136
ghamm, 215
ghill, 233
Goliath; *see* Jālūt
Gospel(s), 9, 12, 13, 55, 83-85, 88, 91, 94-102, 107, 112, 113, 115, 116, 118-120, 142, 249; *see also* Injīl
Greek scholastics, 27